NATO

AND THE

DEFENSE

OF THE

WEST

by

Prince Hubertus (zu) Löwenstein

and

Volkmar von Zühlsdorff

Translated by Edward Fitzgerald

FREDERICK A. PRAEGER, *Publisher*

New York

BOOKS THAT MATTER

Published in the United States of America in 1962
by Frederick A. Praeger, Inc., Publisher
64 University Place, New York 3, N.Y.

Library of Congress Catalog Card Number: 62-20189

Printed in the United States of America

Foreword

THE NORTH ATLANTIC TREATY ORGANIZATION

NATO was founded by the free nations of the world when they came to realize that, after the subjugation of the East European countries, the Prague *coup d'état,* and the Berlin Blockade, the tide of Soviet imperialism could be stemmed only by a united effort.

The Federal Republic of Germany joined on May 9, 1955, six years after attempts to establish a European defense community had failed.

The participation of the United States has to be noted with grateful satisfaction. America's powerful might and its great moral strength have given support to the Western world's urge for freedom. This important fact is not the foregone conclusion it is so often assumed to be.

The presence of U.S. forces in Europe underlines America's unequivocal warning that in case of conflict it would consider itself directly involved. Paul-Henry Spaak—at that time General-Secretary of NATO—made this point in his address at Bonn University on April 23, 1958, when he said: "My generation has lived through two wars. We are convinced that these two world wars would not have broken out if it had been known in 1914 and 1939 that the U.S.A. would enter the war full force within the first few days. Today, the presence of U.S. forces at the Western border of the free world makes it clear to everyone that if Europe were attacked, America would immediately enter the war with all its armed forces. I, personally, am convinced that this is a decisive factor in the preservation of peace."

The equal status of the Federal Republic in NATO gives our new state the necessary external security without which internal political stability is not possible. Fifty million Germans can thus live in freedom.

The enemies of NATO in the Federal Republic claim that it obstructs the reunification of Germany. This can easily be refuted: Although it was not possible until now to secure freedom for the seventeen million Germans oppressed in the Soviet Zone, NATO has certainly prevented further Soviet expansion and has safeguarded the freedom of the Federal Republic without which reunification in freedom would be impossible.

But NATO can accomplish its task of keeping the peace and can maintain its decisive influence only if we do everything in our power to strengthen the alliance and fulfill the duties we have assumed. The defensive bastions of atlantic freedom form an unbroken line from the North Cape to Turkey. There must not be any weak link on the territory of the Federal Republic. This would obviously invite penetration and would only serve to increase the danger of war instead of diminishing it.

Beyond this, we must speed up the development of this military alliance into a political community in which the consciousness of our common heritage is kept alive. An auspicious beginning has been made. We have also made great progress in economic cooperation and in aiding the underdeveloped countries. Thus NATO makes its contribution to keeping the free world free and to fuse its members into an increasingly cohesive political and economic community.

Contents

CHARTS

NATO
AND THE
DEFENSE
OF THE
WEST

1

The Right to Self-Defense

OPENING QUOTE

This book is concerned with freedom, and with the North Atlantic Treaty Organization (NATO), an alliance of fifteen nations that defends not only the independence of its own members, but indirectly that of the so-called neutrals. Over and above this, it keeps alive the hope of freedom in all those countries which have already fallen victim to Communism—including even the hope of the Russian people themselves, since freedom, like peace, is indivisible.

What is called NATO today has existed under various names and in different forms, throughout Western history: the Hellenic symmachy against the despotic kings of Persia in the fifth century B.C.; the all-embracing peace of the Roman Empire; the joint efforts to ward off the Huns, the Avars, the Magyars, the Mongols, and the Saracens; the struggles during the Middle Ages, up to the liberation of Vienna in 1683; and, in our own day, the combined Allied breaking of the Soviet blockade of Berlin in 1948–49. Thus NATO may be a sober defensive alliance, born of the need of the moment; but it is also the core of a more profound historical reality: the shared destiny of the West which, in essence and mission, forms a single civilization.

What the West defended, both in the days of antiquity and in the Christian era, was always one thing: freedom. Not merely national or political independence—other peoples as well have fought for that—but freedom as an ethical value. Perhaps the idea of freedom was imperfectly articulated in early Western thought, but throughout the centuries it has broadened steadily—from the daring Greek conception that all citizens are free, and that there must be no slaves amongst the Greeks (which even then struck the East as sacrilege), to the gradually unfolding revelation of the Christian creed that man is free because he is a man—regardless of country, race, or class, as children of the same Father.

It is hardly necessary to point out that this special mission of the Western world does not amount to a monopoly of civilization. The Persian Empire attained a high level of civilization; the Arab world transmitted Greek philosophy to the West; and in myriad ways the East nourished Europe. Nevertheless, the victories of the West over Darius and Xerxes, over Attila, over Abdarrahman, over Soliman I, and over Kara Mustafa preserved man's freedom. Any defeat would have been fatal. The civilization of some of the aggressors can no more mitigate this judgment than it can be a consolation for the Hungarians, Poles, and other satellites that the Russians once produced a Dostoevski and a Tolstoy.

Augustine said that a people is an ordered multiplicity of beings, endowed with reason and held together by their common love for that which is dear to them. The West is held together by its love of liberty. This is the very law of its life and its abiding historical mission, to which no nation of the West can be untrue—as happened in Germany under the tyranny of Hitler—without courting disaster. This is also the basis of NATO, which is an alliance of the free and a covenant for peace. On this basis, the members of NATO are moving toward a closer union, a confederation, a commonwealth.

To be a member of NATO therefore means more than enjoyment of protection through a military alliance; it also signifies membership in the great spiritual community of free nations on both sides of the Atlantic. Only because freedom is its law of life has NATO gained the strength to defend the peace against Communism. This is not mere wishful thinking—the first decade of its existence has proved that NATO can fulfill its task. For years, the Russians had extended their empire westward, seemingly without let or hindrance; but since the North Atlantic Treaty was signed in Washington on April 4, 1949, they have not been able to penetrate one further step into Europe.

Thus NATO is not a pallid document, of interest only to lawyers, generals, and professional politicians; it is a live and active organization that extends from the Aleutians to the Caucasus, from the North Pole to the Tropic of Cancer.

The territory of the nations brought together in NATO comprises approximately 8 million square miles, with a population of

450 million people. Kingdoms and republics, parliamentary and Presidential states, and a great variety of races, peoples, and nations have joined hands within its boundaries. The size of NATO members ranges from Luxemburg to Canada; the population, from the 163,000 people in Iceland to the 180 million in the United States. But the smallest and the biggest—as it should be in such an organization—have the same voice and the same vote in the North Atlantic Council, the highest body of the Alliance. The nations joined together freely, and not one is held to the union by force.

How very different from the Warsaw Pact! The fate of Hungary in 1956 has shown what happens to a people within the orbit of Communism if it dares to aspire to freedom. Hardly four days after the Hungarian Prime Minister, Imre Nagy, had proclaimed the neutrality of his country, Soviet tanks were rumbling through the streets of Budapest. The same thing happened on June 17, 1953, in the Soviet Zone in Germany, and in 1959 in Tibet. Force governs in the Soviet Union, in Red China, and in the satellites. Individuals and peoples are oppressed by the secret police—be it the KGB, the AVO, the SSD; by the apparatus of the Communist Party; by concentration camps, by "class justice," by terror; and, in the last resort, by the overwhelming strength of the Red Army. The Warsaw Pact is not at all a voluntary contract. The Soviet Union drew the satellite countries into its orbit by a combination of force, treachery, and deceit—about 400,000 square miles, inhabited by 92 million people —and wherever the Communist Party carries out the orders of Moscow, the will of the people becomes of no consequence.

In addition, during the Second World War, the Soviet Union directly annexed about 184,000 square miles of territory inhabited by 23 million people. This urge to conquest is not a policy that could ever change, tactical intervals aside, because it is a function of the system itself. A regime that knows no freedom at home cannot bring peace and freedom abroad. Oppression is just as much its law of life as liberty is that of NATO.

The paradox of the situation is that the Soviet regime, which threatens everyone and is itself threatened by no one, loudly proclaims its "need for security." Its leaders do not seriously believe in the likelihood of any attack from outside; they feel threatened only because freedom still exists somewhere in the world, and freedom always has been attractive to people deprived of their rights. The Soviet need for security is no more than the wish to protect itself against freedom outside its borders. The men in the Kremlin would feel wholly secure only if they could subjugate the world to their totalitarian regime.

The immediate task of NATO is thus quite clear: it must ensure that the Soviet Union keeps the peace. This presupposes political determination and sufficient military power to curb the Russians' aggressive urges. The Soviet Union must be convinced that its own collapse would be the inevitable concomitant of aggression.

If Russia is denied war, this might, in the long run, liberate internal forces that, through the iron dialectic of Marxism, would turn against the sterile dialecticians of force. The revolt in the Soviet Zone of Germany in June, 1953, the revolts in the penal camps of Vorkuta in the Arctic Circle, in Yugoslavia, and in Poland; the Hungarian people's fight for freedom, waged by its working class and youth; and even the rising in Tibet in 1959—all are symptoms of the potential for revolt. So far they always have been suppressed by military force, but this does not mean that they have been destroyed. They will continue to operate, sometimes openly and sometimes underground, as long as their cause remains: the Communist suppression of human freedom.

In this situation, the West cannot be passive. NATO will never launch a military attack, but it must be constantly on the offensive, spiritually and politically. The aim of freedom is not only to maintain itself where it rules, but also to extend its benefits to those deprived of it. In this respect, there can be no recognition of a status quo, no boundary line between men who have a right to freedom and men to whom it can be denied. Such recognition would be highly immoral, and throw doubt on the commitment of the West.

This is no mere question of tactics. The more firmly the West retains the initiative, the smaller will be the margin left for Soviet propaganda, and the weaker its effect. A moral offensive also may help to reduce the danger of war, because it will compel the Soviets to defend themselves on this level.

While preparing this book, the authors had many opportunities to see NATO in action: in Great Britain, France, and Germany; in the Benelux countries and Scandinavia; in Italy, Greece, Turkey, Iceland, and the United States; in the Mediterranean, the Baltic, and the Atlantic. We have described some of our direct impressions in short, personal sketches, in the hope that these may bring to life the far-reaching, colorful, complex reality that today is NATO.

The thirty-ton jet bomber A3D-2 landed on the angled flight deck of the U.S. aircraft carrier *Forrestal* with a shock so heavy that it caused the powerful steel hull to shudder. Its engines were still howling at full pitch so that, if the landing proved unsuccessful, it could climb into the air again. For a moment it looked as though its high speed—125 miles an hour—would carry it over the end of the short landing deck into the sea, but the hook lowered by the pilot caught in one of the six steel hawsers stretched across the deck; for a split second, the *Sky Warrior* reared into the air, and then came obediently to a halt.

While the bomber was quickly rolled away, the arresting gear was drawn back into place and the flight deck made ready for the next landing. In quick succession, the planes of the reconnaissance squadrons came in, after a turn of duty in the air, which had taken them in all directions around the U.S. Sixth Fleet in the Mediterranean. Forward, the next group of planes were already being hurled into the air by the rumbling catapults, which sent a jet of silver steam hissing along the length of the flight deck at every launching.

Just routine exercises? Of course; but at the same time, grim necessity, because it is the job of this fighting unit—an aircraft carrier, surrounded by a circle of destroyers and jet fighters—to be prepared at any moment to ward off an attack. She is always on the move and rarely keeps to a straight course—even at each launching and landing she turns her bows into the wind—so that the Soviet rocket bases in southern Russia and the Crimea could not aim their missiles accurately, even if they could fix her position by radar.

The U.S. Sixth Fleet is a powerful force. It consists of 50 ships, 200 planes, and 25,000 men. Two aircraft carriers—the *Forrestal* and a sister ship—two or three cruisers, and twenty destroyers form the actual fighting units. It also has an amphibious landing force of 1,800 fully equipped marines, and a supply fleet of tankers and other vessels which carry reserve stores of all kinds. Land-based reconnaissance planes cooperate with the fleet and take part in anti-submarine exercises.

Most modern equipment has been added to the usual radar and sonar devices on board the ships themselves. Special radar planes, called "flying saucers" by the crew because of their peculiar shape, are able to detect approaching enemy planes from a very great distance. And as a new weapon against submarines, unmanned heli-copters directed by remote control can be sent out to drop depth charges on the target long before it reaches striking range.

"In the event of a surprise attack by the Russians, we would be one of their first targets," declared the Commander of the Fleet, Vice-Admiral David McDonald on board his flagship, the heavy cruiser *Springfield*. McDonald is thoroughly familiar with the Euro-pean theater. Before taking over the Sixth Fleet just prior to our visit there in July, 1960, he had for a long time been assigned to U.S. Headquarters of Naval Forces Eastern Atlantic and Mediterranean.

There are 100 planes on board the *Forrestal*, and the same num-ber on board her sister aircraft carrier. They include supersonic jet bombers, ready to take to the air at a moment's notice and carry their nuclear loads to strategic targets in South Russia and the Ukraine within a matter of hours. Even Moscow would not be out of their reach. This, and not naval warfare, is the main significance and task of the U.S. Sixth Fleet. It is, in one sense, part of the strategic air force on the Mediterranean front, a powerful, floating airfield, almost immune to the long-distance rockets of the enemy, and at the same time independent of the political disturbances to which land bases are exposed.

Helicopters maintain contact between ships. During exercises they are always in the air, ready to help in case of accidents. But they can land only on the decks of the aircraft carriers and the cruisers; the deck of the destroyer *Mitcher*, which we visited, was too small. The helicopter which brought us there hovered a few feet above the deck, travelling at the same speed and along the same course as the destroyer, while we were lowered in a sling.

The telephone number of the Head Post Office on board the *Forrestal* is 799. Any of the thousands of stations on board connect one with any part of the free world; and daily an enormous number of letters arrive and are dispatched. Contact between the crew and their families and friends is never broken. Seven shops on board the carrier provide anything, from toothbrushes to handsome jewelry. The *Forrestal* produces its own fresh water—if necessary, about 200,000 gallons a day. Nearly 200 miles of pipes and over 250 miles of electric wiring run through the ship's interior, which is a self-contained community.

"We can stay at sea almost indefinitely," Rear-Admiral Forsyth Massey, Commander of Carrier Division 4, told us. "We have enough fuel, supplies, and munitions on board, and additional stores can be taken on at sea. The United States is our base, and the Atlantic Ocean is our lifeline."

This independence has made the U.S. Sixth Fleet a powerful weapon which has done a great deal to dampen any Soviet inclination toward aggressive warfare. In case of war, it is essential that the nuclear bombers respond instantly to an alert. "Once we have got them into the air, we have justified our existence," said the Admiral. What would happen to the fleet itself is a question of secondary importance both for him and for his men. He and his crew, down to the youngest sailor, know that the danger would be great if the Soviets were to send many submarines and planes armed with nuclear weapons. But they recognize and accept this fact calmly, in the line of duty. "We are expendable," they say without pathos or bitterness, and are convinced that the contribution of their fleet to the preservation of peace is worth any sacrifice. It is this conviction which binds them together in a spirit of unshakable solidarity.

However, the Soviet Union might find it difficult to assemble the forces for such a concentrated attack, without thereby leaving itself exposed elsewhere; and it cannot hope to launch a blow against the U.S. Sixth Fleet alone; such an attack would mean general war.

At the Macedonian Maneuvers

A tent is camouflaged by dusty branches somewhere in the mountains of Macedonia, where the September sun blazes down on a parched countryside. On the desk of our host, the Commander of the Greek Ninth Division, Major-General Pantelis Zaroukliotes, lie a cross and a Bible, alongside piles of maps and papers. An ikon of the Madonna hangs above the camp-bed. The autumn maneuvers of the Greek Army on the Bulgarian frontier, known as "Alexander the Great," are approaching their climax.

A plane from the *Forrestal* brought us to Greece. It carried us across the Corinthian isthmus over Actium and Lepanto—historic names of two historic naval battles which had saved the West from Eastern despotism, one under Augustus in 31 B.C., the other under Don Juan d'Austria in 1571. Then, below us in the evening sun, the Acropolis, eternal symbol of beauty and devotion to the gods, unthinkable without freedom. To our right lay Marathon, where in 490 B.C. the power of the self-confident Persians was challenged for the first time. To the left lay Salamis, in 480 B.C. the scene of a decisive naval victory under the joint leadership of Eurybiades, the Lacedemonian, and the Athenian Themistocles. "Here, by our victory over the Persian, Median, and Punic fleet, we brought salvation to the sacred land of Hellas," reads a contemporary epitaph. For the first time, Athens and Sparta were united in a Hellenic Symmachy— *Nia Symmachia dia ten Eirenen*, an alliance for peace. That same name is once again borne proudly in Greece—by NATO.

Time and again, the Greeks have had to defend liberty against the assault of despotic powers. The Athenians, Herodotus tells us, were prepared to join the symmachy under the leadership of their rivals, the Spartans, because Persian tyranny appeared intolerable. Darius, however, thought that the struggle of the Ionian Greeks in Asia Minor, which Athens supported, was a blasphemous offense: he took his bow and shot an arrow high above the clouds, into the sky, and called upon the gods to grant that he punish the Athenians for their sacrilege.

Herodotus tells us that an army of over a million men, including 80,000 horsemen, and a fleet of 1,200 ships, was mobilized by the great Persian king. Perhaps he exaggerated, but there is no doubt that the Persian forces were enormously superior to those of little Greece. Nevertheless, freedom triumphed, by verdict of the gods.

After the Second World War, the Greeks were the first people to defend their freedom against the Eastern despotism. The cost was great—400,000 men, women, and children, out of a total population of only 8 million. The day before the Communists had to evacuate Athens, they slaughtered 8,000 men and carried off many children, some of whom have not returned to their homes to this day.

Major-General Zaroukliotes fought in that civil war against the Communists, and was held prisoner for eight difficult months. He knows what is at stake in the world-wide struggle. In a few short words, with the help of a map, he explained the job of the Ninth Division to us. In Athens, we had discussed the general plan of the maneuvers with the Chief of the Greek General Staff, General Konstantinos Dovas; Headquarters in Aminthion had instructed us further: The enemy is assumed to attack from Bulgaria, to have air superiority, and to employ tactical atomic weapons. His target is Kozani, the gateway to the south. The task of the Greek Army is to hold the mountain chain between Edessa and Katerini, and to throw the enemy across the river Axios. Simultaneously, the enemy has invaded Yugoslavia, which is resisting.

"The Ninth Division forms the left wing of the Greek forces," explained Major-General Zaroukliotes. "The Twenty-seventh Regiment is in the north, the Thirty-second Regiment in the south, and the First Regiment is stationed at Aminthion as a reserve." This is the classic triangular battle order which has come down practically unchanged from the days of antiquity.

"One company maintains contact with the Yugoslav forces on our left wing, and the Tenth Greek Division stands to our right. Our support consists of some units from Army Corps A—tanks, an anti-tank company, an armored group staff, a reconnaissance company, and an anti-aircraft unit. Our artillery is equipped with Honest John rockets, sent for the maneuvers by the U.S. Southern Europe Task Force (SETAF) stationed in Northern Italy."

The main purpose of the Ninth Division is to defend the Edessa Valley along a twenty-mile front. This is a long stretch for one division, but mountainous terrain facilitates the task of defense. The enemy had established four bridgeheads this side of the Axios, but Greek sapper companies had already mined the roads, and reinforcements had been put in to hold up the enemy advance until the main line of defense could be completed.

We had met the troops during the night, on our way from Salonika, as they moved in long columns towards the front line, silently, without lights, the vehicles camouflaged with foliage. Now, as we inspected the positions with the Major-General in a jeep, we saw them again. We visited the artillery first; then we went forward to inspect the mortar companies, and finally the front-line troops in their foxholes. They had dug themselves in so deeply to protect themselves against atomic attack, and camouflaged their positions in the hillside scrub so carefully, that we did not see them until we had come very close. Even the 15.5 cm. guns of B Battery of the Hundred-fifty-first Artillery Regiment, positioned in the valley, were hardly visible from any distance.

"A fine bit of work," said Lieutenant-Colonel von Köckritz, the German military attaché, "particularly when you remember that these men are reservists just called up for the maneuvers." All the men came from the immediate neighborhood, some from Pella, the birthplace of Alexander the Great. They were artisans, merchants, doctors —but mostly peasants and farm hands with tanned faces, some of them bearded; mostly young recruits, with a sprinkling of older men who had gathered experience in many years of actual fighting against the Communists. They were disciplined and efficient troops—still clean and tidy after many days in the field, content with their frugal rations and a swig or two of the tart, resin-flavored local wine—ready for action at a moment's notice. On the roads they had motor vehicles, and in the mountains donkeys and mules so sure-footed that they could get through where even jeeps and caterpillar tractors were useless. These soldiers were worked hard. During the last days of the maneuvers, they had to attack while live bullets whistled over their heads, to drive the enemy back according to plan.

One of the frontiers of the free world lies here, and thus a line of defense for Great Britain, Germany, the United States—for all NATO countries. It is a frontier which must be strengthened. Greek mobilization has reached its maximum level; the country now needs more modern equipment, heavy weapons, and greater firepower. To achieve this, the Greeks need help; any further increase in their military budget would be at the expense of living standards, and play straight into the hands of the Communists. George Themelis, the acting Minister for National Defense, had explained this to us. We had stood in his study, looking at a map of Macedonia and Thrace—one of the critical areas on NATO's southern front, because the terrain lies open for a broad Soviet attack which could separate the fighting forces of the two allies, Greece and Turkey. "We are ready," declared the Minister, "we shall not be taken by surprise." And he added quietly: "We shall hold the front."

JET BOMBERS REFUEL IN THE AIR

"Come in, Westover! Come in, Westover!" A clear and urgent voice sounded over the short-wave radio in the control room of the Westover Air Force Base, Massachusetts. It was an alert from Headquarters Strategic Air Command in Omaha. The room came alive instantly. The radio operator reported back, and as he quickly noted down the code words—"Romeo, Whiskey, Charlie, November . . ." —an officer sitting beside him deciphered the message. Our host, Colonel O. F. Lassiter, Commander of the Ninety-ninth Bomber Wing, had turned to go after the first few words. Before he had reached the door, the decoding officer called out, not without pride, "Decoding completed. Seventeen seconds."

Outside, we could hear the sirens, and on the way to the airfield we met pilots and crews in their special cars with bright-red flashing lights. They converged upon the field from all directions—from their living quarters, the club, the barber, the PX. When a team is "on call" (a period of seventy-two hours), the men stay together, their special cars close by, their flight papers and strategic target maps at hand.

As we pulled up to let them pass—for they have absolute priority, even over the Commander himself—we could see the first crews with their flight helmets, parachutes strapped to their backs, racing to their planes. The ground personnel were at their stations. Soon the plane doors closed and the jet engines started up with a roar. First the tankers, then the bombers rolled majestically to take off along runways bordered by blue lights. Among the machines were the four-engined jet tankers KC-135, the Strato-tankers KC-97, a number of piston-engined planes, the six-engined jet bombers B-47, and the eight-engined B-52s. By the time our car arrived, the exercise was over. It had been a "Cocoa" alarm, a routine exercise. But the men never know beforehand, so that each test alert carries genuine urgency. It would be just like this, here and on all the air bases of the Western world, if one day Soviet squadrons should break through the world-wide radar warning chain. It is a good thing that the Soviets know this too. . . .

"Eight minutes for the bombers until the engines started up," said Major-General Hunter Harris, Commander of the Eighth Air Force, "and seven for the tankers." An excellent performance, but he was not entirely satisfied. Since enemy jet bombers fly at supersonic speeds, the warning period is measured out in hours, and in the case of rockets it is a matter of minutes. Thus the ceaseless effort to save precious seconds has become a matter of life and death. Strategic Air Command (SAC) tries to get the last plane of that third of its fleet which is always on the alert into the air within fifteen minutes, ready to repulse the enemy and deliver the counter-blow.

"By the way," said the General, "at ten minutes past twelve some of our jet tankers are taking off. Would you like to go up with them?"

A few hours later, equipped with flight helmets, parachutes, and oxygen masks, we were sitting in one of the largest of the new tankers, the four-engined KC-135, flying at 38,000 feet and at over 600 miles an hour, on our way to a rendezvous point somewhere between heaven and earth, where we were to refuel a jet bomber carrying nuclear weapons.

The pilots, Captain Wyman T. Smalley and Wayne A. Thurn, and their men, made a crew which inspired absolute confidence.

When we joined them, they had already been at work for four hours, checking over every detail before they took their plane into the air.

At 1410 hours, the bomber reported its presence over Fort Wayne, Indiana; the pilot took us down to about thirty thousand feet—still at the height of Mount Everest—and throttled back a little. Very soon the bomber appeared on the horizon. Lying on our bellies and looking through a rear window in the floor of the tanker, we could see the great Stratofortress B-52, a beautiful machine, even larger than our tanker, and capable of almost supersonic speeds.

Arrogantly, like a mighty fish, the bomber drew near. The sergeant lying beside us was watching its every movement and directing it by radio and light signals: "Higher! A little to the right! No, that's too far! A little to the left! A couple of feet lower! Come in now!" Slowly the sergeant lowered the telescopic steel piping, called the boom, and directed it toward the silver nose of the bomber. The first time he failed, and drew it back so hard it barely missed the cockpit, but at the second attempt he succeeded. For a moment or two the groping boom wavered around the fuel hole, then it connected. The oil fuel was now pumped into the bomber under tremendous pressure, at the rate of 1,000 gallons a minute. With one supplementary refueling like this, the Stratofortress is capable of flying half-way around the earth.

The two huge machines hang together precariously, and the pilots need utmost sensitivity to harmonize their movements. On one occasion they veered apart, and contact was automatically broken. But immediately the boom was recoupled, and the refueling continued. Finally the tanks were filled, but for practice, the coupling and uncoupling maneuvers were repeated half a dozen times. The aim is to attain a precision which will permit refueling in any weather, in darkness, if need be, and while observing radio silence (as would be necessary in an emergency), until it becomes a matter of routine for whole squadrons at a time. Today, SAC alone refuels one plane in the air every three and a half minutes, over land, over mountains, and over the sea.

Other sections of the U.S. Air Force, such as Tactical Air Command (TAC), SAC's smaller but no less efficient brother, have extended their range of operations and increased their striking power by this air refueling system. A tanker plane of TAC, the KB-50J, a development of the Hiroshima bomber, can even refuel three planes at a time. When we took part in such an operation from the TAC Headquarters in Langley, Virginia, the three planes simultaneously refueled in the air were two supersonic F-101 Voodoos and a B-66 jet bomber. This time, we were able to watch the operation in comfort from two large, convex observation windows. Hoses about fifty feet long reached out from the wings and the tail of our tanker, splaying out at the nozzles like shuttlecocks. The Voodoos, with their fuel pipes jutting out like cobra heads, had to fly directly on to the mark—no easy task for a supersonic plane which can just about keep itself in the air at this lowest speed of two hundred and fifty miles an hour. There were anxious moments; we held our breath, for example, when a young pilot overflew the fluttering shuttlecock and came perilously near to the wings of our tanker.

The importance of air refueling was demonstrated in the Lebanon crisis in July, 1958. TAC units at Myrtle Beach, South Carolina, were alerted. The order to take off came without warning, but the planes were in the air quickly. The first refueling took place over the Bahamas, the second over the Azores, and the third over the South of France. They enabled the force to fly non-stop and land in Turkey within eighteen hours and two minutes of the first alert. This performance was sufficiently impressive to act as a swift warning to the Soviets, who thereupon did not send a single soldier to Baghdad.

During 1958, SAC refueled 180,000 planes in the air. Nonetheless, even experienced crews will heave a sigh of relief when they hear the words "Mission completed, break contact." On our trip, the pilot of the Stratofortress below us raised his hand in thanks and farewell and turned away, while we continued on our own course, almost to the foot of the Rocky Mountains.

With a smile, Captain Smalley turned to us. "We're serving lunch now," he said. "What would you gentlemen like, roast beef or chicken?"

We were flying eastwards, and the sun began to dip rapidly toward the horizon. Previously, the speed of our jet tanker had made it appear to stand still. By the time we approached the Atlantic coast, we had flown almost 4,000 miles; the weight of the heavy parachutes on our backs, somewhat uncomfortable after this long flight, lightened suddenly when the captain lowered the nose of the plane and we descended rapidly from 44,000 feet to 10,000 feet. In Westover, a snow storm reduced visibility to zero; but with the help of radar and directional radio, known as Ground Controlled Approach (GCA), we were talked down. A calm and confident voice sounded from the control tower: "Course correct. Another five miles to the runway.

Descent correct. Another two miles. You're slightly to the right of the runway. Course correct. Another mile. Everything OK. A quarter of a mile more. Course correct. You're right in the center of the runway now. Descent absolutely correct. Ready now! Set her down!" At that moment, the red landing cross and the long, lateral rows of lights emerged through the snow flurry. The great tanker landed on the snow-covered runway, with perfect accuracy, at 150 miles an hour.

2

Pax Atlantica

At the underground headquarters of SAC Offutt Air Base, near Omaha, Nebraska, in the central control room, three red telephones stand on a raised platform. From here, the entire strategic air power of the United States—distributed over almost seventy bases throughout the world—can be alerted simultaneously, should the Soviets ever launch a large-scale surprise attack on the West.

The duty officer walks to the telephone, lifts the receiver, and pushes a red button. Instantly, the bulbs are lighting up on the clustered console before him, not one is missing. All the bases have reported, and are standing by to receive orders. "This is a maintenance test," says the officer in a clear voice into the phone. "Respond." At once the lights on the console are starting to go out, by twos and threes, until the last one has blinked off. Only a few seconds have passed since he took up the receiver. This apparatus is the latest model. The oldest one, to the left, would take ninety seconds to make contact; the one in between, twenty seconds.

The headquarters of SAC, in the heart of the United States, is an impressive organization. One can feel the tremendous power which is directed from here and could be exercised against any aggressor, should it ever become necessary. We had watched a test alert at the headquarters of the Ninety-ninth Bomber Wing in Westover, Massachusetts, and knew what it would be like in case of attack —at strategic air bases throughout the world, from the Pacific to the Arctic; in the West Indies, in Morocco, Turkey, and Canada; in

17

Greenland, Great Britain, Spain, and the United States itself: 3,000 bombers and tankers, with 250,000 men, would go into action. In addition, there would be the British Bomber Command and the tactical air forces of almost all NATO states, as well as the intercontinental ballistic missiles—the Atlas, the Titan, the Snark—and the intermediate-range Thors, Jupiters, and Minutemen.

SAC is the sharpest sword in the armory of peace. Although it is a United States force, it is organized for world-wide defense; its tremendous deterrent power protects Europe, and in the event of a Soviet attack, it would be NATO's strongest weapon. SAC and NATO coordinate their defense plans; a special liaison office in Paris, known as "SAC Zebra," keeps permanent contact with SHAPE, NATO's headquarters in Europe. General Thomas S. Power, the Commander of SAC, was appointed in August, 1960, as chief of the newly established Joint Strategic Target Planning Staff in the Pentagon, to coordinate retaliation planning against selected targets in Soviet and Soviet-controlled territory.

"All nations must accept that the defense of freedom is their own task," said General Power. "Only then shall we be effective in our task, the defense of peace." He speaks with the quiet confidence of a man who bases his acceptance of great responsibilities on firm moral and religious convictions. Like most of his fellow officers, he knows that more is at stake than strategy and politics in the struggle against Communism. His own serenity has communicated itself to his staff, to his headquarters, and to the whole strategic air force. One never hears a loud or arrogant word. The great power held by these men has not turned them into "militarists"; they have remained "civilian" gentlemen.

General Power is of Irish extraction, born in New York in 1905, and married to an Englishwoman. He joined the Air Force as a young man, and obtained such a thorough education in its technical and tactical schools that, although he has no academic degree, he took over the Research and Development Department of the Air Force in 1954 and rapidly turned it into a major command. Although he is fifty-six years old, he still pilots every kind of plane including jets. He neither smokes nor drinks, and keeps himself fit with judo. He took up the sport after the war, passed severe tests with seven Japanese masters, and is now entitled to the coveted Black Belt. He insists on the same training for his officers; on occasion, he will take a plane into the air, hand the controls over to the co-pilot, and invite his companions to a practice bout at 30,000 feet.

The development of the strategic air arm, begun under General Curtis E. LeMay, has been continued by General Power, who was LeMay's second-in-command before he became his successor. Like LeMay, he makes a point of attending personally to details—he appears unexpectedly at air bases all over the world, unnoticed by press and public, intent only on his job.

"Peace is our profession." These words of General Power are the watchword of SAC. Strength is necessary, and preparedness, and the widest possible dispersal of bases. Only in combination do these three factors create a deterrent, for then, no matter how thoroughly the enemy might prepare an attack, he will know that the West would still have sufficient nuclear bombers on the runways and in the air to seek out strategic targets and inflict devastation. The crews are excellently trained, not only for flight at great heights, but also for low altitude flights; they could, if necessary, evade the enemy's radar warning system by flying below it.

But what if, nonetheless, the Soviet Union should attack? What if, like many an earlier despotism, it should fall victim to its own propaganda, count on the disunity of the West and on the chaos caused by a nuclear attack? Who can know the minds of totalitarian rulers committed to revolutionary goals?

General Power considered these questions seriously. "The Soviet Union knows that the West will never attack first," he said. "Therefore they would have the advantage of the first blow. But that would not ruin us, provided we remain alert, and our counter-offensive could be counted on to devastate the enemy's war potential, both nuclear and conventional."

General Power and his staff would direct the operations of the strategic air force from this extensive headquarters—which looks like the bridge of a battleship—thousands of miles from the front. Intricately mounted maps of every conceivable theater of war, twenty feet high and eight feet wide, rapidly would give a clear picture of any contingency. Not only the red telephones, but short-wave radio as well, can provide instant connection with any base, or with any airborne plane in the world. All information relevant to the United States and Canada that comes into the North American Air Defense Command (NORAD) is immediately available to SAC by television.

"Would you like to know what flying weather is like in Tokyo, Capetown, or Berlin, or between Moscow and Smolensk?" inquired Captain Edwin Derryberry, who showed us around. The information was available at once. Numerous electronic brains instantly can supply information about present strength and supplies anywhere in the world; the situation after an attack; the forces necessary, both in strength and in kind, to meet any given situation; evasion possibilities; and even—if provided with sufficient data—possible Soviet plans.

SAC headquarters are fifty feet underground. They are bomb- and radiation-proof, except perhaps against a direct hit by an H-bomb. During an alert, the thick steel doors close automatically, and the whole underground complex is independent of the outside world. It has its own water supply, its own power station, its own radiation-proof ventilation, dormitories, supplies for thirty days, and, of course, full radio, radar, telephone, and television facilities. Of course, there are alternate headquarters, and not only underground. Since 1961, SAC maintains airborne command posts, big KC-135 jets outfitted with such marvels of effective communication facilities in the smallest space that even an all-out global war could be directed from the air.

The Western armies in Europe, and the tactical fleets and air forces, represent the shield of freedom, ready to intercept enemy attack; the strategic air forces are the sharp sword which will pierce the aggressor's armor and destroy his war potential in his own country. This graphic simile was first used by General Norstad, and NATO now refers to its basic defense concept in terms of the "shield and the sword."

The sword, that is to say the nuclear and long-range weapons, is wielded by the nuclear powers of NATO, primarily the United States, because only the latter is technically and economically in a position to build and develop an adequate number of such weapons. Great Britain contributes, although to a lesser degree, while the efforts of France, which in 1960 joined the "Atomic Club," are still in the development stage. In terms of organization, the sword consists of the U.S. Strategic Air Command, the U.S. Sixth Fleet, the British Bomber Command, and the ring of rocket bases. Its destructive power is enormous. It could deliver an immediate counter-blow at an aggressor, strike him everywhere at once, and destroy his offensive potential, in particular his nuclear weapons. Since the Soviet Union is well aware of this, the main objective of the sword is already achieved—to convince the Kremlin that aggression could not possibly pay, and thus to preserve the peace.

The shield, on the other hand, is held primarily by NATO's European members, including Turkey, whose territories it defends.

The United States provides the Seventh Army in Germany, SETAF in Italy, and the Tactical Air Forces.

The shield also defends the advanced bases of the sword forces: the radar stations, the navigational posts, the rocket bases, and the airfields, with their communications and supply apparatus. It has a further task as well: should the enemy launch a limited attack, the shield forces would bring it to a halt. This would create an interval of time which should give the men in the Kremlin the opportunity to realize that they could not hope to overrun Europe without being put to the sword. They could stop their advance and enter into negotiations. If they were to reject this opportunity and insist, like Hitler, on continuing aggression, it would be wholly clear that they had chosen war.

The hopes of the world rest on the power of this shield and this sword, because power is the only deterrent which the Soviet leaders respect.

THE ATLANTIC—LIFELINE OF THE FREE WORLD

In the event of war in Europe, NATO would need a daily minimum of 250,000 tons of supplies. Otherwise, the people of Europe could not be fed, and the Supreme Allied Commander Europe (SACEUR) would not be able to supply his vast front, his armies, his tactical air forces, and the ships in the North Sea, the Baltic, and the Mediterranean. However, he knows that in the event of a Soviet attack, the United States would ship adequate supplies for both military and civilian demands—if the Supreme Allied Commander for the Atlantic (SACLANT) is able to keep the NATO supply lines open.

We were in Norfolk, Virginia, at the headquarters of Admiral Jerauld C. Wright, at that time the Supreme Allied Commander Atlantic.* Admiral Wright, who had been chiefly responsible for organization of NATO's Atlantic Command, is one of the world's leading strategists for combined air, sea, and land operations; as

* In 1960, Admiral Wright resigned his command. His successor, Admiral Robert L. Dennison, served on the staff of the Supreme Commander of the Pacific Fleet during World War II, later was Chief of Staff to the Commander of the Amphibious Force with the Pacific Fleet. He then was Commander-in-Chief of the Naval Forces in the Eastern Atlantic and the Mediterranean (CINCELM), now known as U.S. Naval Forces Europe.

adviser to two Presidents, he has contributed greatly to the development of modern American sea power.

"Many people are under the impression that sea power and navies are out-dated," said Admiral Wright, "a sort of romantic foil to atomic reality. But nothing could be further from the truth." He turned to a map which shows the earth from the perspective of the North Pole. We could see the Soviet empire, embracing half the world in a great semi-circle, capable of aggression from the Bering Straits to the Elbe. "The only way to defend Europe, the Atlantic, and North America, is to defend them jointly," said Admiral Wright. He pointed to the North Atlantic between Norway and Iceland: "This is where they would try to break through with their submarines, in order to drive a wedge between Europe and America. If they were to succeed, it would sever NATO's jugular vein. After that, they could deal with each continent one by one."

Admiral Wright's Deputy, the British Vice-Admiral Wilfrid John W. Woods,* added: "The Soviets would have between 500 and 600 submarines." At the beginning of the Second World War, he explained, Hitler had fifty-seven; they could not compare with modern submarines in armament and range, yet in the first few months of the war they sank over a million tons of merchant shipping. Later on, they were held in check by the introduction of radar and sonar, but toward the end of the war, the Allied convoy losses again rose threateningly.

It was not difficult to realize that so many Soviet submarines, armed with atomic torpedoes and rockets, would represent a deadly threat to the merchant fleets of the Atlantic community. Moreover, those submarines could provide mobile bases for atomic rockets, some of which can be discharged from beneath the surface and could attack strategic land objectives in Europe and America.

This lends enormous importance to the defense of the sea narrows at the entrances to the Baltic and the Black Seas. They are relatively easy to close; and submarines in these land-locked seas would be less dangerous, more easily sought out, and destroyed.

Apart from submarines, the Red Navy consists of 37 cruisers, 230 destroyers and frigates, and 2,000 smaller vessels, supported by about 4,000 naval planes. These forces are grouped in four separate fleets, with bases in the Pacific, the Baltic, the Black Sea, and at Murmansk. The Soviet fleet in the Pacific is held in check by a ring

---

* In April, 1960, Vice-Admiral Wilfrid John W. Woods was succeeded by Rear-Admiral Charles L. G. Evans of the British Royal Navy.

of strategic bases from the Philippines, over Japan and Formosa to Hawaii, and by the U.S. Seventh Fleet, which defends NATO's rear, the western seaboard of the United States.

The main problem for SACLANT is the Soviet fleet at Murmansk; SACEUR is primarily responsible for dealing with the Soviet Baltic and Black Sea fleets. But if those forces should manage to break through the Belt and the Skagerrak in the north, and the Dardanelles and then Gibraltar in the south. . . . Admiral Wright obviously had that in mind when he said, "To support SACEUR is one of our main tasks."

In addition, there is the defense of the NATO left flank, the rapid discovery and destruction of Soviet submarine packs, and the defense of the coasts of North America and Europe against rocket-firing submarines.

In view of these tasks, it is quite clear that, even today, sea power and navies are something more than a decorative piece of romanticism.

"Our striking force is never still," declared Admiral Wright's Chief of Staff. "Like the Sixth Fleet, it is on the move day and night, and for the same reason—in order not to offer Soviet long-range missiles a good target."

United States aircraft carriers carry bombers equipped with nuclear weapons, and in the event of a Soviet attack they, together with SAC, would immediately launch a nuclear counter-offensive against the harbors, bases, and airfields of the aggressor.

From the window of the Admiral's room at headquarters, we could see SACLANT's ships lying at anchor along the quays of the great harbor and the broad river—cruisers, destroyers, speedboats, minesweepers, submarines, tankers, supply ships, and auxiliary vessels of all kinds, as required by the manifold needs of a modern fleet. Yet what we saw was only a small part of the tremendous concentration of power at SACLANT's command; just those ships which had put in for repairs or overhaul, or which were here for special missions. The main fleet was out at sea. Admiral Wright was getting ready to fly on a tour of inspection of the U.S. Second Fleet, which was holding maneuvers in the Caribbean.

The Second Fleet is a part of the Atlantic naval forces of the United States. As they say in the Navy, the Commander of SACLANT has two hats. He is not only a NATO officer and Supreme Commander of the Allied Forces in the Atlantic; he is at the same time the Supreme Commander of the U.S. Atlantic Fleet. In this capacity, he commands 200 ships of all kinds: aircraft carriers, cruisers, destroyers; over 1,000 naval planes; and a quarter of a million men. His sphere of command extends from one pole to the other, and even in peacetime he exercises full and direct command over all these forces.

The U.S. Atlantic Fleet remains under the Admiral's command when he puts on his NATO hat. In addition, SACLANT commands the naval forces of Britain, Canada, France, Portugal, Norway, Denmark, and Holland, as well as the naval base at Keflavik in Iceland.

"In 1952, there were eight different national fleets here in the North Atlantic," said Admiral Wright. "Today, for all practical purposes, they have become one single fleet, which is stronger and has greater striking power than the sum of the eight."

The famous British Home Fleet, for many generations the most powerful in the world, is also under SACLANT, whose sphere of operations extends from the American and Canadian coasts to those of Europe and Africa, taking in the Azores, the Faroes, the Bahamas, Iceland, and Greenland—an area of well over a million square miles. During the ten or twelve naval exercises which are held every year, and conducted very realistically with submarines and planes, SACLANT exercises the direct and supreme command over this NATO force, just as he would in the event of war. Between maneuvers, each nation remains responsible for its own ships, while SACLANT's task is to draw up strategic plans, to urge the national authorities (through the Standing Group, NATO's "general staff,") to maintain a high level of preparedness, and to set up a cadre organization which could exercise direct supreme command over the united NATO fleets in the event of war.

SACLANT has not only fleets at his command, but also landing forces, and naval air units equipped with the most modern planes, including the vertical take-off Convair XFY-1, which does not need a special flight deck, and the night fighter FD-3 Skylight, which is armed with air-to-air rockets of the Sparrow type.

The West's submarine defense has advanced considerably since the first U.S. atomic submarine, the *Nautilus*, was launched in 1954. This vessel, with its atomic battery, already has gone several times around the world, more than half the time under water. Her batteries have an enormous capacity—they could produce enough current for a town of 20,000 inhabitants, and the first set lasted for 62,562 miles. These power resources enabled the *Nautilus* on her voyage from Pearl Harbor to Portugal and England to sail under the ice mass of the

Arctic Ocean, and to open up a new sea route to Siberia and East Asia via the North Pole. Of immediate strategic importance, this route may, in the future, benefit world trade.

Since atomic submarines do not need to surface to recharge their batteries, they can stay submerged almost indefinitely. In 1958, the *Seawolf* set a record for submerged endurance—sixty days.

A new era in naval warfare has been started by these nuclear-propelled submarines, of which the United States Navy had 23 operating and 38 under construction in 1961. Six of these (and 23 more of those being built) are equipped to carry and fire sixteen Polaris missiles each, armed with nuclear warheads and having a range of about 1,500 miles—a valuable addition to the power of the deterrent. The new atomic fleet will also make it easier for SACLANT to thwart Soviet plans to separate Europe and America in the event of war. Thus the Atlantic will remain a powerful ally of Europe, bringing her the men, the arms, and the supplies without which she could never hope to withstand a Soviet attack.

THE RADAR WATCH IN ICELAND

A subdued hum of machinery filled the darkened control room of Radar Station Rockville, near the big United States air base at Keflavik, in Iceland. The staff on duty watched the instrument panels carefully. One whole wall was covered by a large glass map, which showed the flight space at a glance. Behind it was the shadowy silhouette of an orderly, armed with a sponge and black chalk, ready to record the newest information.

"Nothing special," reported Captain G. E. Kentosh to the officer who accompanied us. On the radar screen before him, the circling green indicator was sketching the silhouette of the nearby mountains and the broad surface of the sea. The indicator rotates ceaselessly, day and night, while the duty teams work in shifts throughout the twenty-four hours. "There's a C-118. She's just taken off in the direction of Prestwick." He pointed to another light spot on the screen, which was moving away from us. "This is a C-54 on a routine mission." And again: "That's a Boeing 707 of Pan-American Air Lines." He was about to say something else, but stopped abruptly. To the left, almost on the periphery, a new spot, hardly visible at first, had appeared. In quiet but urgent tones he now began to speak into his microphone: "Approach from northwest. Longitude 27.12. Latitude 64.57. Course 123 degrees. Speed 180 knots. Plane not reported here."

The radio operator's attempts to make contact with the unidentified object were unsuccessful. Was it a civilian plane which had strayed off course? Was it an enemy reconnaissance craft? Or was it . . . ? Whatever it was, a strange plane which failed to identify itself when requested to do so had to be taken seriously; that is the whole object of this world-wide guard. Any moment might conceivably be the decisive one, and the danger would be incomparably greater if we were ever to be caught off-guard.

The alert was given. Four minutes later an F-89D jet fighter was in the air. We watched it on the radar screen as it made its way toward the interloper. Within ten minutes, the two points had met. Then came the report over the loudspeaker: the stranger was a civilian passenger plane, making for Keflavik for an emergency landing because its radio was out of order.

Life is hard on these bases in Iceland. Rockville is only one of the four radar stations there. The northernmost is near the Arctic Circle and can be reached only by air or sea. During the winter months, storms of such violence rage there that—as happened once while we were in Iceland—fully loaded trucks are simply blown over the cliffs into the sea. High concrete walls are necessary to protect the men on their way between their quarters and the control rooms.

Keflavik, about thirty-five miles southwest of Reykyavik, was built on a barren expanse of lava desert. It dates back to 1940, when the British (and, a year later, the Americans) came to Iceland. There are hangars and workshops, a runway of two miles, long enough for the most modern jet planes, training grounds, radar and radio towers, a meteorological station, living quarters for the men, a church, a hotel, cinemas, and numerous administrative buildings. A tour of inspection takes several hours. During the Second World War, 60,000 men were stationed here, practically as many as the total population of Reykyavik. There are still 5,000 men at the base, all Americans; most of them are Air Force personnel, but there are a few hundred Marines, and a few civilians. When we visited it, the base was under the command of Major-General Henry G. Thorne, Jr., an American and an officer of NATO. Like the Icelanders themselves, he was a dedicated fisherman, and in the summer months, when trout and salmon are plentiful, he used to go angling with his boon companion, the Icelander Methusalem Methusalasson, whose family has owned the same little farm there since the year 1532.

A squadron of jet fighters is always standing by to deal with any warning from the radar station. But danger does not threaten only from the air: should the Soviet fleet—and in particular its submarines—ever attempt to sail out from Murmansk in a bid to break through into the Atlantic and cut the lifeline between the United States and Europe, Iceland would lie on its route.

"Without Iceland," Admiral Wright had said to us when we visited him at Norfolk, Virginia, "it would hardly be possible to guarantee United States supplies for a European front." And therefore this small northern nation, with no army of its own and a police force of only 250 men, is vital to the greater community of NATO—just as the Icelanders themselves can hardly hope to retain their freedom without NATO help.

The men who live on this barren island, where volcanoes, hot geysers, and vast glaciers exist side by side, are a tough and independent people with a will of their own. Iceland is a country of wild, almost primeval beauty, where masses of flowers bloom, all crowded together in the span of a very short summer. Then the long winter night descends, often lit up by an aurora borealis which outshines the stars. The Icelanders are not only a highly gifted and vigorous people, and daring seamen (they discovered America five hundred years before Columbus did); they are also a people of great literary ability. The world has reason to cherish their Eddas and their ancient sagas. Down to this day, the Icelanders are among the most highly educated peoples in Europe, and their democratic parliament, the Althing, can look back on a thousand years of uninterrupted history.

Astonishing, in this land of determined individualists, is the existence of a strong Communist party, the Workers' League. It has a great deal of money at its disposal, and runs a well-edited newspaper, the *Tjodviljinn* or "People's Will." It claims to be patriotic, but like Communist parties everywhere in the Western world, it does its best to exacerbate every political and economic problem. Ninety-seven per cent of Iceland's exports still consist of fish. When, in 1952, the Icelandic government unilaterally extended its territorial waters from three to four miles, and Great Britain retaliated by boycotting Icelandic fish, the Soviet Union offered to take a fixed quota, and ever since then it has bought one-third of the entire catch for the countries behind the Iron Curtain. The Soviets exploit this situation to their political advantage; their aim is to get Iceland out of NATO. They might even have succeeded (notice to end the agreement that leases Keflavik base to NATO had actually been given) when the fate of the Hungarian people demonstrated to the Icelanders just what the Russians mean by freedom.

That the Icelanders have managed to make a living for themselves for thousands of years from their barren little island is really a victory of mind over matter, since less than half of Iceland is at all habitable, and only a part of this is really arable. However, with what they could wrest from this barren soil, and what they could take from the sea, the Icelanders did manage, although it was a frugal, Spartan existence, both socially and economically. With the arrival of the British and then of the Americans during the Second World War, the modern age dawned for Iceland almost overnight. But to give this new era a sound economic basis by industrialization, modernization, and a strong export trade, is a task beyond the strength of this small country.

There are already a number of factories processing frozen meat, fish, and dairy products, and making textiles, electrical equipment, cement, and other industrial commodities. But the great water power resources of the country are almost untapped. Capital is urgently needed for this purpose, and adequate markets must be found in the West for the export trade.

It is an obligation implicit in the whole spirit of the North Atlantic community that its members should join together to help this small ally solve her problems.

3

The Defense of Europe

WITH THE *Diavoli Rossi* IN NORTHERN ITALY

In close formation, their wing tips almost touching, the jet planes of the Italian Sixth Fighter-Bomber Brigade raced over the wide expanse of the airfield at Ghedi, near Lake Garda. They were flying so low that they almost skimmed the radio masts of the control tower, while the exhaust from their engines all but bowled us over.

"A trifle low," commented General Bianchi, drily, but by that time the six F-84-F Thunderstreaks were already far away, and climbing at a steep angle into the sky. These *Diavoli Rossi*, or Red Devils, carried out the exercise with astounding precision—the close triangular formation did not slip for one moment.

General Luigi Bianchi is the NATO Commander of the Fifth Allied Tactical Air Force (Fifth ATAF), whose headquarters are in Vicenza. His job is to defend Italy in the air, from the Alps to the Gothic Line along the Appenines ridges. Seven Italian wings, the Fifty-sixth Tactical Air Force (Fifty-sixth TAF), and two United States squadrons are under his command, equipped with F-84-F Thunderstreaks, F-86-K Sabre jets, and F-100 Super-Sabres.

The various wings are ready for action at a moment's notice—as we were able to see for ourselves, when, at the General's suggestion, we fired a starting pistol. It was only a matter of minutes before the engines were roaring and the six machines took off in rapid succession.

Within a few seconds they had disappeared from sight, but they returned time and again to perform breath-taking maneuvers over

29

our heads. From a delta formation they changed to a hexagonal, then to an open U formation, followed by an X, then an arrow, and finally they raced off in line. They looped in perfect circles, and ended in victory rolls which left white trails in the blue sky, like gigantic mathematical symbols. Again and again they were dead on, or at least very close to, the small target circles—no matter whether they attacked from a few feet off the ground or from a height so great that they were almost invisible. The climax of the demonstration was a mock attack on an aircraft carrier, or some land-based concentration of firepower. Five planes roared down toward their target in a tight X formation, then zoomed up again over it, weaving outwards and upwards like ribbons in the breeze; then descended from five different directions, to meet again above the target and release their bombs almost simultaneously; the sixth plane had been left to release a further stick of bombs while climbing almost vertically. It was a concentrated attack, which the defenders of any enemy target would have found extremely difficult to deal with because it came from so many different directions.

Once again the squadron took off and climbed into the sky almost vertically. Their exhaust fumes left silver lines in the sky which opened out sixfold, like the feathers of a coat of arms, and remained there for a long time, picked out against the dark blue sky of Lombardy.

The *Diavoli Rossi,* one of the seven Italian squadrons of the Fifth ATAF, are the pride of the Italian Air Force. By their extraordinary aerobatics they have won themselves the reputation of being Italy's "National Air Team." But these aerobatics, impressive as they are at air displays, are not an end in themselves; they are a necessary part of the NATO shield forces which defend Europe. Their tactical tasks in Northern Italy are particularly difficult. If an attack were ever launched from this direction, the enemy would seek to break into the plains by way of one of the classic passes through the mountains, through the Ljubljana Gate from Yugoslavia, or, after violating Austrian neutrality, through Klagenfurt and Carinthia, or through the Kanal Valley to Friuli. In mountain valleys, any flying is precarious; but with fast jet planes, such flights demand a high degree of accuracy, if they are not to end in disaster.

The Italian Air Force also has top-quality, Italian-designed and Italian-built planes. For example, the light jet bomber G-91, produced by the Fiat Works according to the specifications of SHAPE, came out best in a series of detailed tests arranged by AFCENT at

Fontainebleau and by the NATO Advisory Group for Air Research and Development at Paris. This G-91 is the first plane developed to NATO specifications. It is a relatively simple, inexpensive, and very tough plane, which is equally suitable for air combat, ground support, or reconnaissance. It is powered by a Bristol Orpheus turbo-jet engine, which gives it a high speed. If necessary, it can operate independently of airfields; its landing speed of only eighty miles an hour allows it to land on any flat surface. SACEUR has therefore adopted this G-91 model as the standard NATO light fighter-bomber, close-support, and reconnaissance plane. An international force of French, German, Italian, Greek, and Turkish pilots is now being trained in Central Europe, together with the necessary ground personnel, and the United States government has agreed to provide its European allies with fifty supplementary planes of this type.

As a NATO Commander, General Bianchi is subordinate to AFSOUTH in Naples, while as an Italian Commander he is subordinate to the Chief of the Italian General Staff, who has his headquarters in Rome. There are strategic reasons for the concentration of the main defense forces in Northern Italy. "You get into a boot from the top," once said the Byzantine General Narses, and that still holds true today. The main threat to Italy, and thus to the NATO southern front, still comes from the northeast. Therefore the crack divisions of the Italian Army, which is once again 400,000 strong, are stationed in the Po Valley, where they will have the nuclear support of the highly mobile U.S. Southern Europe Task Force (SETAF), which consists of 6,200 men equipped with Honest John rockets and Corporal guided missiles. On the other hand, the Italian Navy faces southeast; it is part of the Allied Naval Forces in the Mediterranean, with their headquarters in Malta.

The Italian Supreme Command and NATO headquarters for Southern Europe agree in their judgment of the situation. As in Greece, the mountainous terrain of Northern Italy favors the defense. There is a limit to the number of divisions the Soviet Union could deploy against Italy, and it would be difficult to keep them supplied over Alpine passes subject to constant attack. Before making the attempt at all, the Russians would first have to violate the neutrality of Yugoslavia or Austria, or both; but this would probably not prove a moral embarrassment. Once determined to unleash a world war, they would hardly bother about Austria's neutrality, even though they themselves have guaranteed it. What attitude Yugoslavia would take is still an open question.

"In all probability Tito would postpone his decision to the last moment," said General Luigi Mancinelli, the former Italian Chief of Staff, in Rome. "And what he then decides will, no doubt, be greatly influenced by what he thinks about the attacker's chances of success. This means that we shall always have to keep strong forces in the north."

CHANNEL COMMAND

"There are always 3,000 ships within the purview of Channel Command," Admiral Sir Guy Grantham told us in his Plymouth headquarters. "From that alone you can see how important our job is." As the predecessor of Vice-Admiral Sir Alexander Bingley, he was in charge of Channel Command, which includes the waters between England and France, and a narrow strip of the Atlantic. Sir Guy was decorated for his services, first in the Norway campaign and afterwards in the Mediterranean, but all he will consent to say about it in the biography provided in *Who's Who* is a statement of classic brevity: "On active service from 1939 to 1945." He was Commander of the British Mediterranean Fleet with headquarters at Malta, and Commander of the NATO naval forces there, before he was transferred to Plymouth. Today he is back in Malta again—as Governor.

During the Second World War, he had personal experience of the difficulties involved in carrying supplies through narrow waters, under attack from enemy submarines and land-based planes.

"Channel Command is a nerve center. The greater part of United States supplies for Europe, and also for SACEUR, would come through the Channel. It is here that we should have to decide into which harbors—British, French, Belgian, Dutch, German, or others—to divert convoys, in order that the supplies reach their destinations as quickly and safely as possible."

Channel Command has no strategic tasks, and it therefore has no task force comparable with the Atlantic Fleet or the U.S. Sixth Fleet in the Mediterranean. "Some people think we hardly matter, because we're so small," Sir Guy said with a smile, "but all the main seaways come together here; and however close our contact with Norfolk, Virginia, SACLANT is a long way off; one must know the water around this island intimately—where the rocks and sandbanks are, and where submarines can operate and where they can't." In other words, Channel Command is the great shunting station which directs troops and supplies into harbor, once they have been safely brought across the Atlantic under the protection of SACLANT.

"We are not concerned with the comings and goings of warships; we are responsible for civilian ships, and work with the civilian administrations." England has shown her competence in coordinating a motley collection of soldiers, experts, laymen, and enthusiastic amateurs. "Think of Dunkirk," said the Admiral. "After the Anglo-French defeat, we managed to get back not only because our ships' commanders showed initiative, but because innumerable civilians, seafaring men, fishermen, yachtsmen, and so on, did, too. You couldn't have organized that from Norfolk, Virginia."

The underground headquarters of Channel Command, deep under the steep ridge of hills behind Portsmouth, reminded us of SAC in Nebraska. In the control room, one can survey the British coasts. The position of every ship is marked, and every ship can be given direct instructions. The headquarters of Channel Command are bomb-proof, radiation-proof, and independent of the outside world.

But although headquarters are important, Channel Command is prepared to continue its work without a central leadership. "During our recent maneuvers, we acted on the assumption that our headquarters here had been put out of action," said Sir Guy. The lower command posts, and the captain of every single ship, must know the master plan and be able to carry on independently in an emergency.

Too much organization can be a source of weakness in a nuclear war, and Sir Guy sees the situation realistically. "Channel Command is committed, above all, to the prevention of war. But if the Soviets attack, victory will go to the side which can get the most out of what a nuclear attack leaves still standing."

The primary task of Channel Command is to take over the convoys from America as they arrive in European waters. SACLANT has then done his job, and thereafter it is up to Channel Command to protect them and bring them safely into port. For this purpose, it has a fleet of destroyers, minesweepers, and anti-submarine corvettes, supported by Royal Air Force Coastal Command, which has its headquarters in Northwood near London. In accordance with the British system, which has no parallel in the United States or in any European country, a double command operates here: The Navy and the Air Force cooperate as equals, and neither has superiority over the other. Even in Great Britain, there are people who would like to see Coastal Command in the navy-blue uniform of the British Navy and not in the light-blue uniform of the Air Force, but so far, tradition has proved stronger.

Of course the question immediately arises: Might not this double command lead to difficulties, if only for reasons of prestige? Commander P. D. Hoare, then attached to Plymouth Headquarters Staff, did not think so. "It might occasionally in peacetime," he admitted, "but certainly not in war. At such times no one stands on his dignity. We all sit on our fannies 150 feet underground and work together."

The Commander of the Naval Air Arm attached to Channel Command, Air Marshal Sir Bryan V. Reynolds, is at the same time the Commander of the air units in the eastern Atlantic, that is to say, in the adjacent section of the Atlantic under SACLANT. Thanks to this, a very large air space has a unified command.

Channel Command is not an exclusively British affair: it controls the supplies of France, Belgium, and Holland, as well as those of Great Britain, and those countries play an active role. "Fortunately we don't have any political problems here," said Sir Guy with satisfaction. All such problems are settled in the Channel Committee, which is composed of the Naval Commanders of the four nations concerned.

It is further evidence of the joint fate of the European people that the original fortifications of Plymouth were built by French prisoners during the Napoleonic Wars. At the same time, British prisoners of war were building defensive works for their French captors on the other side of the Channel. In 1942, the underground headquarters in Southwick was built by Canadian engineers, in expectation of a German attack. Today these nations are friends and allies within the North Atlantic community.

THE GERMAN *Bundeswehr* ON MANEUVERS

With the deep roar of engines throttled back, the squadron of eighteen transport planes, U.S. C-47s and double-tailed French Noratlas, went down to 1,200 feet above the theater of operations on the Heuberg in southern Swabia. Suddenly, almost simultaneously, the trapdoors opened; the parachute troops jumped, one after the other, until 400 men were sailing to the ground, followed by parachutes carrying their arms and ammunition. It all happened so quickly that the first plane, relieved of its burden, had turned away before the first man had reached the ground. The white parachutes swung in the air against a dark-blue September sky like white froth on a tossing sea.

The ground wind was sharp and gusty, and some of the men were dragged, but they soon got control of their parachutes. The men belong to the Nineteenth Battalion of the First German Airborne Division from Kempten. They are well trained—one hears only an occasional quiet command, as when a dropped pack is not quickly recovered; then the men are taking cover in a nearby wood, sending out scouts, laying a landing cross for the second wave. Smoke signals show them the direction of the wind and where they must land. Two jeeps, two trailers, 81 mm. and 120 mm. mortars, and a large container with first-aid materials sail down rapidly. Within a few minutes, the battalion is on the move towards the valley of the Schmei near Kaiseringen, where two bridges have already been seized by commandos flown in by helicopters.

The men know their orders. They must hold the armored columns of the enemy until reinforcements can be moved up. This time it is only an exercise, part of the autumn maneuvers of the German *Bundeswehr*, the armed forces of the German Federal Republic. Nonetheless, they take the job seriously—as seriously as the officers from the Soviet military mission in Frankfurt, who are silently attentive observers. The Russians are not in uniform and drive a gray Volkswagen; the soldiers cannot recognize them, yet each man behaves as if he knew that it rests on his devotion—and NATO's determination—to ensure that performance of duty today will prevent a grim tomorrow.

Eighty thousand men and 15,000 army vehicles took part in the maneuvers. There was no cohesive front, but individual exercises along the entire eastern frontier of the German Federal Republic, from Schleswig-Holstein to Austria, and in inland locations. They were maneuvers of the German armed forces, but many other NATO countries were involved, not merely as guests and observers, but also as participants. One hundred and eight Italian parachutists from the parachute training school in Pisa, members of the famous *Folgore* division, whose intrepidity and chivalry at El Alamein won the respect of their British foes, dropped near Fallingbostel in Lower Saxony to seize bridges behind the enemy lines. Dutch F-84 jet fighters gave the Fifth Armored Division ground support in its exercises near Bergen-Hohne. Near Amberg, where the Fourth

Grenadier Division was offering obstinate resistance to an armored breakthrough, U.S. F-100 Super-Sabers, their engines screaming, joined the battle, and a U.S. landing force was dropped, with admirable precision, behind the defense line.

At night, a bridge was thrown across the Naab near Schwandorf. The experts had said it could not be done without searchlights; but lights would have called down low-level air attacks and given away both position and plans; so the sappers of the *Bundeswehr* painted their construction materials with luminous paint and worked in darkness. Amphibious U.S. tanks assisted them. It was an eerie sight: girders and supports seemed to be moving of their own accord, and joining themselves together in obedience to some magic command. Within a few hours, a fifty-ton bridge was completed, and, still under cover of darkness, the waiting troops crossed to the other side.

The Second Grenadier Division from Giessen crossed the Rhine near Weissenthurm, opposite Neuwied. Sappers built a seventy-ton bridge across the Rhine at a point where it is more than 300 yards wide. This was the exact spot where, in 55 B.C., Caesar threw his first bridge across the Rhine, although, to quote the fourth book of his *Commentaries*, "on account of the breadth and depth of the river and the speed of the current, the difficulties were very great."

Men dug themselves in on the ridges at Teisendorf in Upper Bavaria, and not merely for protection against conventional arms. In the absence of shelters, the earth offers the best protection against radiation, blast, and the heat of atomic explosions. "In these days of nuclear weapons," General Adolf Heusinger, then Inspector-General of the *Bundeswehr*, told them, "the spade is as important as it was in World War I. The defense relies on the man who has dug himself in and fights on." Again and again, the CO glanced at the Geiger counter to check the radiation level, because the enemy was assumed to have used atomic shells. Each man was equipped with an ABC mask to protect himself against atomic, biological, and chemical air pollution.

The enemy, the Red Army, has violated Austrian neutrality, invaded near Salzburg, and is advancing toward Munich. Battle group B-8 of the First Mountain Division is blocking his advance. The obstinate resistance of the frontier defense force has given the Division time to take up its present positions. Such is the realistic maneuver situation. The muzzles of the machine guns, the new FN automatic rifles of Belgian manufacture, and behind them the barrels of the 10.5 cm. battery and of the light and heavy mortars, are directed into the valley. The Company Commanders and observers scan the opposite slopes through their field glasses. They are in touch with each other by radio.

Then the attack begins. A barrage of enemy artillery is suggested by the judges through the explosion of smoke bombs. A little later, Red infantry breaks out from the opposite woods and fans out into the open, supported by tanks and a squadron of jet fighters.

The advancing line is well spread out, in accordance with the requirements of atomic warfare. It meets with fierce fire from the ridges, but nonetheless, the defenders (the Third Company of the Twenty-seventh Infantry Battalion) are driven back. Not because the master plan calls for retreat—broad play is left to the tactical skill of the leaders and the competence of the troops—but because, despite a favorable defensive position, the enemy forces are too strong.

The judge announces that the artillery observation post has been destroyed by a direct hit, so that the mortars are now firing blindly. Before long, the Red attackers are in possession of the ridges formerly held by the Third Company. But only for one hour—then reinforcements launch a counter-offensive which finally throws the enemy back to his starting positions.

"On September 25, after a short period of political tension, strong Red forces drawn up along the Lower Elbe advanced under cover of darkness into the territory of the Federal Republic in a southwesterly direction, in order to establish a bridgehead over the Aller, near Essel. The NATO defense forces stationed near Hannover move forward to attack the enemy forces as they march towards the Elbe." This was the hypothetical situation for the concluding exercise of the autumn *Bundeswehr* maneuvers. Within its framework, the Blue Grenadier Brigade 50, under Brigadier-General Ulrich de Maizière, met the Red Armored Brigade 60, under Colonel Hans-Georg Lueder, between Fallingbostel and Winsen. Supervision of the maneuvers lay in the hands of Brigadier-General Müller-Hille-brand, the Commander of the First Armored Division, stationed in Hannover, to which both the units taking part in the exercise belong.

The Red infantry is equipped with atomic weapons, and supported by strong armored groups which, given Soviet military thinking, would be the case in reality. Their aim is to launch a mass attack against the weakest part of the defensive front, and, if possible, break through to the Rhine, thus driving a wedge between the northern and southern NATO forces.

Enemy tanks advance, echelonned in depth. A green light rocket goes up, then another, leaving long, comet-like tails behind them: "Advance the field of fire!" So the defenders have been driven back. Then a red rocket goes up to indicate an important target, perhaps the firing platforms of the defense.

Supported by a heavy barrage, the attackers advance in clouds of smoke and dust, reaching the marshy ground along the river Hohne, which they wished to cross. But there are not many places suitable for crossings, and the defense holds. It is making good use of the new anti-tank weapons, and in particular of the guided rockets SS-10. These rockets are attached to a wire from the firing to the moment of impact. The anti-tank men guide them throughout to their targets.

But then a tactical atomic shell falls among the defenders, and the way is free for the Red tanks to break through. Like enormous turtles, the steel giants tip themselves into the water and then clamber up the shallow bank on the other side, rolling forward to the higher ground of the Kallenberg and the Hamberg. A second atomic shell, twice as large as the first, tears a big gap in the defense reserves. "Twenty per cent loss," decides the umpire.

Thanks to superior tank forces and the use of atomic artillery, the enemy breakthrough has been successful. But it was only a local tactical success; Red now comes up against Blue's defense in depth, which also employs nuclear weapons to wipe out the attackers. In the umpire's final summing up, he decided that the breakthrough of the enemy armored column towards the Aller River had been prevented by the NATO forces, and that a counter-offensive had thrown him back.

The *Bundeswehr* is still in the formative period; but these maneuvers proved that it has made some progress. The good performance of the troops was acknowledged by all the NATO observers, including the then Commander-in-Chief of the Allied Forces in Central Europe (CINCENT), General Jean Etienne Valluy. The exercises tested the organization of the reorganized Divisions, and demonstrated the striking power of the new armored and anti-tank units with their new weapons.

"I am a NATO soldier." That was a phrase one heard often, not only from the officers, but also, with obvious pride, from the young recruits. It is like a regeneration of forces from earlier centuries, before nationalism split up the original unity of the West. In our own day, this idea of community is coming alive again—not in romantic retrospect, but in the sober conceptions of the twentieth century.

The new army also has a new style—discipline, to be sure, but little heel-clicking. In part this is a heritage from the old German youth movement, a comradeship in the relations between superior and subordinate. Even *The Times* (London) described it as "a community of many thinking individuals." This is the source of its strength; today, it is the only sound basis of an effective defense. Even the older officers have come to realize that freedom and discipline are not mutually exclusive, but that discipline is all the stronger when it stems from inner freedom.

It was in this atmosphere that the Federal Chancellor, Dr. Konrad Adenauer, met members of the young army. The men spoke to him confidently and freely. They could feel that he was concerned with them, and with their efforts to give their best. He had been driven around everywhere in an army jeep, and had taken a bird's-eye view of the whole terrain from a helicopter. He inspected everything with keen interest, from the new anti-tank weapons to the rations distributed among the troops. After nine hours, he was still fresh and vigorous.

"Gentlemen," he said in his final address to the troops, "not only do I thank you warmly, I also want to congratulate you; what you have shown me today has made a deep impression on me. For our part we shall see to it that you receive everything necessary for the equipment of a modern army."

4

When the West Disarmed

The foregoing descriptions illustrate the defensive strength of the fifteen allied nations—on land, at sea, and in the air. Little of it was in existence a decade ago. When the North Atlantic Alliance came into being on April 4, 1949, it had to forge its own weapons. The people, tired of war, had hoped for a future of peace and co-operation—a "peoples' peace" had been the slogan of the West. The Atlantic Charter of August 14, 1941, declared: "After the final destruction of the Nazi tyranny, they hope to see established a peace which will afford to all nations the means of dwelling in safety within their own boundaries, and which will afford assurance that all the men in all the lands may live out their lives in freedom from fear and want."

Even the Soviet Union affixed its signature on January 1, 1942. And when the fifteen allies came together in San Francisco on June 26, 1945, and signed the Charter of the United Nations, the nations of the world believed that at last a world league for peace had been founded, strong enough to settle all future disputes.

At the end of the war in Europe, the Western powers immediately withdrew their troops and air fleets; and as soon as Japan was defeated, they demobilized their men and disbanded their armies. On May 8, 1945, the United States had over 3 million men in Europe; one year later, there were only 391,000; in the same period, Great Britain's European army had dwindled from far over a million to 488,000. Of Canada's 299,000 men, not one remained in Europe; they all went back to their homes. The economies of the democratic countries rapidly converted to civilian production. In sum, the

40

European nations turned their efforts to the difficult tasks of post-war reconstruction.

But before long, it became clear that the peace had not been secured. The Soviet Union was unwilling to have the advance of the world revolution, and of the Red Army, held up by treaty obligations. Before 1933, the Soviet Union had not hesitated to lend surreptitious aid to Hitler, because through him—as Dmitri Manuilsky, the Comintern expert for German questions, declared at the meeting of the Executive Committee of the Communist International in Moscow on December 15, 1941—it hoped to destroy German democracy. "The chief enemy is not Hitler; the chief enemy is the system of Severing, Brüning, and Hindenburg," he said; "in the present stage of the development of the German Revolution, Hitler is undoubtedly our ally."

The men of the Kremlin also share responsibility for the outbreak of the Second World War. The cynical Ribbentrop-Molotov pact of August 23, 1939, concluded while negotiations were still proceeding between the Soviet Union and Great Britain and France for the defense of Poland, freed Hitler from his last restraints by removing his fear of a two-front war. The Soviet government was well aware that this must lead to world war, because on March 31 of that year, Great Britain had guaranteed the integrity of Poland's territory. Nevertheless, in a secret protocol supplementing his treaty with Hitler, Stalin agreed to carve up Poland, and a little later both invaded it—Hitler on September 1, Stalin on September 17, 1939.

This evil game ended profitably for the Kremlin, though it imposed enormous sacrifices on the Russian people. Communist Russia conquered wide tracts of territory and many peoples. But even this did not satisfy Stalin's appetite. He was determined to bring in the whole harvest—first Germany, then the rest of free Europe; and after that, the whole world.

"The Charter of the United Nations was founded on two assumptions," said Lord Ismay, the first Secretary-General of NATO, in his report for 1954. "First, that the five powers holding permanent seats in the Security Council—China, France, the United Kingdom, the United States, and the Soviet Union—would be able to reach lasting agreement on major matters. Secondly, that apart from Russia's known claims on Japan, none of these powers sought any territorial aggrandizement. Unfortunately, neither of these assumptions proved correct."

Thus the Soviet Union maintained its armies—over 4 million

men—at war strength and in complete readiness. The Soviet armament industry, greatly strengthened during the war by U.S. loans
totalling eleven billion dollars, and after the war by the dismantling
of German factories and by the forced labor of kidnapped German
scientists, technicians, and skilled workmen, continued to work at
high pressure. The Kremlin used this power to subjugate nations,
and thus to extend the frontiers of the Soviet empire far to the west.

Even during the war, there had been no lack of warning voices.
One was that of John Foster Dulles, who later became the U.S. Secretary of State. No one who knew anything at all about Communism
could be in the least surprised that the occupation of a country by
Soviet troops was fundamentally different from an occupation by
troops of the Western powers. No military occupation is ever agreeable; it always means infringement of personal liberty and interference with private property. But military occupation by the
Western powers did not fundamentally interfere with a country and
its people, or destroy their way of life. The Red Army, however, as
an instrument of world revolution, deliberately encroaches on the
political, economic, and social life of the countries it occupies, in
order to bring about fundamental structural changes. It gives the
Communist minority dictatorial power, it destroys the religious,
moral, and legal traditions of the people, and distorts the fundamental ideas of humanity, to force the vanquished into the harsh
mold of Soviet thought and behavior.

That anyone in the West could have harbored the hope that as
allies in war, the men in the Kremlin would change their ways and
their aims, can be explained only by the great desire for peace among
the democratic nations and their governments. Stalin deliberately
encouraged such wishful thinking by various measures, such as the
dissolution of the Communist International on June 10, 1943, greater
liberty for the Orthodox Church (whose spokesmen supported the
"national war"), and "democratic" terminology in public speeches.
But in all important actions, Stalin remained true to the aims of
world revolution and Soviet imperialism.

The world was given a preview of things to come when on
April 26, 1943, the Soviet Union broke off diplomatic relations with
the democratic Polish government-in-exile. The mass graves of 4,000
murdered Polish officers had been found near Katyn, and the Polish
Premier, Igor Sikorski, asked the International Red Cross to conduct
an inquiry. Stalin used this as a pretext; the real reason for breaking
off relations was to clear the way for a Polish Communist govern-

ment, dependent on Moscow. On August 2, 1943, such a government was formed: despite the protest of the Western powers, the Soviet government recognized the "Lublin Committee" as the provisional government of Poland and established diplomatic relations with it. It was the first step to the transformation of Poland into a Soviet satellite state.

At the Yalta Conference in February, 1945, Stalin promised to allow free and democratic elections in Poland, but he cynically broke his word. Even at that time, the democratic government-in-exile had to appeal to the Western powers, because the Russians were forcibly resettling and even deporting the Polish population. The appeal for help was in vain, and since then the Polish people have never been able to shake off the Soviet three-prong grip of the KGB, the Communist Party, and the Red Army. The Communist government even agreed to the annexation of a great part of Poland—the whole of Eastern Poland, consisting of more than 70,000 square miles—by the Soviet Union. The Soviet extension of Polish territory to the west at the expense of Germany—something which the Polish government-in-exile had long refused to accept—was no compensation, because it shackled Poland still more closely to the Soviet Union.

Other nations suffered a similar fate at Soviet hands; but it seems particularly tragic that Poland should once again be dismembered and deprived of its liberty, because it was in defense of Poland, and to guarantee her territory, that the Western powers had gone to war in 1939.

On the basis of the secret supplement to the Ribbentrop-Molotov pact in 1939, the Soviet Union swallowed up the Baltic states of Estonia, Latvia, and Lithuania as early as 1940, and by mass deportations and executions turned the military occupation into a Communist system. Carelia, an area of 17,500 square miles with a population of 500,000, which was first wrenched from Finland at the time of the Soviet attack in 1940, became a Soviet territory. The northern part of East Prussia, about 5,000 square miles with a remaining population of 350,000, was also seized. In June, 1945, Czechoslovakia was deprived of Ruthenia, an area of about 4,000 square miles with a population of 725,000, which provided the Soviet Union with a common frontier with Hungary. In the same way, Rumania lost Bessarabia and Northern Bukovina—about 19,000 square miles inhabited by 3.5 million people. Thus the Soviet Union exploited the Second World War to make territorial gains amounting to approximately 124,000 square miles, an area about the size of

Germany after the Versailles Treaty, and inhabited by over 23 million people.

"Only one power emerged from the war with additional territory," said Paul-Henri Spaak, the Belgian Premier and Foreign Minister, and until January, 1961, the Secretary-General of NATO, speaking in 1948 before the General Assembly of the United Nations, "and that power is the Soviet Union." He put it politely, but in fact it was a revolting spectacle: the Soviet Union, already ruling over a vast area, grasping the territory of its small neighbors—particularly since the annexations were followed by brutal "purges," repression, deportations to Siberia, and murder.

These annexations are only a small part of the total land and population conquered by the Soviet Union after World War II. Within a single year, Albania, Bulgaria, Rumania, Poland, and Hungary became Soviet satellites. The Red Army, overwhelmingly superior to the forces of those smaller countries, adorned with the prestige of victory over the strongest military power in Europe (and consistently concealing the great contribution of the United States), rarely had to shoot. Its presence was all that was required to give the local Communist politicians the upper hand, and finally total power—no matter how little support they could muster among the people. They alone had armed support and were allowed for months to murder left and right. Any potential opponent was eliminated. In Bulgaria, for example, 15,000 political prisoners, including 1,500 well-known politicians, were murdered. The local Communist parties seized the key positions in the trade unions, the police forces, and the army. At first—merely to stage a democratic farce for the benefit of the Western powers—one or two other parties were allowed to indulge in some innocuous activity; but they soon lost all power.

The spectacular "liquidation" of the most prominent leaders of the opposition was usually kept for the final stage of the proceedings; it was the culminating act of violence by which the Russians made known to the people and to the world that the conquest was now complete. On September 23, 1947, Nicolas Petkoff was hanged in Bulgaria. On October 29, 1947, Dr. Julius Maniu, the leader of the Rumanian Peasants' Party, was sentenced to life imprisonment. In November, 1947, Stanislav Mikolaitshik managed to save his life by fleeing from Poland. One wave of terrorism followed the other; "fascists," "agents of capitalism," and "enemies of the people"—in other words, opponents of the reigning Communist clique—were systematically purged.

All these satellites in Central and Eastern Europe are tied to the Soviet Union and to each other by what are called treaties of mutual assistance. The first of these countries was Czechoslovakia, which President Eduard Benes handed over through such a treaty as early as December 12, 1943. Benes surely hoped that with this voluntary gesture of surrender he had bought future freedom for his country, but he was mistaken. All he managed to gain was that Czechoslovakia, of which Moscow felt sure, was saved up to be the final victim of open Communist seizure. Yugoslavia accepted such a treaty on April 11, Poland on April 21, 1945; Rumania on February 4, Hungary on February 18, and Bulgaria on March 18, 1948.

In all, twenty-three mutual assistance pacts were concluded; after Yugoslavia freed herself in 1949, sixteen remained. In reality they were not voluntary contracts, but—despite occasional Soviet concessions—one-sided instruments through which the Kremlin consolidated its control. There was, of course, no real need for such treaties; the power which assured compliance was in the hands of the all-pervasive organization of the Communist Party, backed up by fear of the KGB, and the constant threat of the Red Army.

By the same means the Russians turned their part of occupied Germany into a Communist satellite. They thereby thought to make up for what they had failed to do in 1918 and 1919, when no Red Army was on German soil to suppress the resistance of the working class against Communism. Now the Soviet Army brought the future rulers of East Germany along in its baggage: Wilhelm Pieck, the first "President of the German Democratic Republic"; Walter Ulbricht, the "Premier"; and many other orthodox Communists, trained in Moscow, hoisted into power and kept in power by the Red Army against the will of the German population.

At the same time, the Russians sought to obtain influence in the Western zones. They were greatly assisted by German Communists, who presented themselves to the United States, British, and French occupation authorities as "the only real anti-fascists," and were successful in obtaining important appointments, even in the licensed press. Severe pressure was put on the German Social Democratic Party to persuade it to unite with the Communist Party, as it had been forced to do in East Germany. In West Germany, this attempt was foiled, thanks largely to the firm attitude taken by the Chairman of the Social Democratic Party, the late Kurt Schumacher.

In July, 1946, Molotov, then Soviet Foreign Minister, demanded a share in the control of the Ruhr district, the industrial heart of

West Germany. That, however, was going too far—the Soviets clearly wanted to use their own zone as a lever to obtain rule of Germany and ultimately of all Europe.

The picture would be incomplete if it were confined to Europe. In the Near East, immediately after the war, the Russians tried—with the assistance of the troops they had stationed there—to detach the province of Azerbaijan from Persia. A Communist puppet government had been already appointed, but the Soviet Union had to give way to the determined pressure of both Great Britain and the United States, and abandon its plans, at least for the time being. In the Far East, the vast Chinese Republic fell into the hands of Communism. Leaders trained in Moscow, such as Mao Tse-tung and Chou En-lai, were able to arm and equip their troops with supplies taken by the Red Army from the Japanese in Manchuria when—in violation of a non-aggression pact between the Soviet Union and Japan—the Soviets entered the final stage of the war against a beaten Japan. Thanks to this vast supply of arms, the Chinese Communists were able to defeat the forces of Chiang Kai-shek. Their zone of occupation in North Korea was turned into a "people's democracy" down to the thirty-eighth parallel; and on October 30, 1948, the Soviet Union established diplomatic relations with the puppet government there, thus laying the basis for the Korean War of 1950—an attempt to "reunite" the country by Communist-trained North Koreans with Chinese Communist assistance. The various insurrections in Indo-China, Vietnam, Laos, and Cambodia, also were all initiated or supported by the Communists.

The ruthless advance of the Red Army, and with it those other armies of secret police, political commissars, and party officials, into an ever-growing arc of countries around the Soviet Union, almost had to create the impression that the men in the Kremlin were determined to carry on the war, now against their former allies. It was an attitude of uncompromising hostility which the Western powers had not provoked. On the contrary, as Lord Ismay observed in his report, "The Western powers, remembering the splendid fighting qualities of the Red Army and the sufferings of the Soviet people at the hands of the Nazi invaders, went to the very limit of conciliation in their efforts to reach an accommodation with the Soviet government, and to make the United Nations into an effective instrument for the preservation of world peace." But the Soviet Union either rejected or systematically foiled all their efforts.

In Greece, during the war, as in so many other countries, the

Russians had strengthened the native Communists by exploiting the fight against National Socialism. At first the Communist "Liberation Front" (EAM) and the partisan groups of "The Greek Army of Liberation" (ELAS) cooperated with the anti-Communist Hellenic Democratic National Army (EDES) against the Italian and German occupation troops. But after November 2, 1944, when the German Army evacuated Greece, the country was torn by guerrilla struggles. The Greek government-in-exile returned to Athens from London, but it could establish its authority only where British troops could come to its assistance. When ELAS threatened to occupy Athens itself, clashes took place between the Communists and British units. An armistice and other agreements were concluded with the rebels, but in fact the authority of the Greek government under the leadership of Archbishop Damaskinos remained limited to the cities.

However, it is misleading to talk of a "civil war." What was actually taking place was another attempt to bring a country under Soviet control by insurrection, armed force, and invasion. The attempt reached its peak on December 24, 1947, when the Communist General Markos set up a Soviet counter-government in Macedonia. Regrettable as they were, the events in Greece did much to open the eyes of the world to the existence of a systematic Soviet conspiracy, and to provoke the adoption of counter-measures.

In 1947, the Security Council of the United Nations appointed a commission to investigate Communist irruptions in Greece. This commission placed full responsibility for the disorders on Albania and Bulgaria. But when, on the basis of this report, the Security Council sought to adopt measures to protect Greece and restore order, it found itself thwarted by the Soviet Union. Its use of the veto condemned the United Nations to impotence against the will of the overwhelming majority of its members.

This was only one case among many. Together they undermined confidence that the U.N. would be able to protect its members' liberties. If the very power which threatened world peace was in a position to paralyze the U.N., the free peoples of the world would have to develop their own defense against the Soviet Union.

In the case of Greece, the United States came to its aid. On March 12, 1947, in a message to Congress, President Harry S. Truman propounded what was to become known as the Truman Doctrine. He declared that the United States must assist all nations who were themselves prepared to fight for their freedom. Congress acted

at once. It voted 400 million dollars for assistance to Greece—and
to Turkey, which was under Soviet pressure to cede certain territory
and bases at the entrance to the Black Sea. That was the beginning
of generous assistance programs launched by the United States to
help the free world to overcome the economic, social, and military
weaknesses left by the Second World War and its aftermath.

At the same time, it was imperative that Europe unite for defense
against a common danger. Already in March, 1946, in a speech at
Fulton, Missouri, Winston Churchill proposed such a union; at that
time, however, the Western world was not yet ready. Illusions about
the peaceable intentions of the Soviet Union had not yet been completely dissipated. Nevertheless, the idea had been born; it was taken
up again in September, 1947, by the Canadian Foreign Minister St.
Laurent, and then by Ernest Bevin, in the House of Commons.

Any doubt as to the urgent necessity for an alliance of free nations was dispelled by the brutal coup d'état in Prague on February
22, 1948, which wrested power from President Eduard Benes, cost
the Czech Foreign Minister, Jan Masaryk, his life, and brought the
last state behind the Iron Curtain. On March 17, 1948—two days
after Jan Masaryk's death—Great Britain, France, Belgium, Holland,
and Luxemburg signed the agreement for mutual defense known as
the Brussels Treaty Organization.

The Brussels Treaty went far beyond the provisions of its predecessor, the Dunkirk Agreement, signed on March 4, 1947, which was
a bilateral pact between Great Britain and France directed—at least
according to its formal text—against only one potential aggressor:
Germany. The next step toward European unity would have been a
loose network of such bilateral treaties. That was Bevin's plan, but
it was not considered adequate by the Benelux countries (Holland,
Belgium, and Luxemburg) and the United States, whose assistance
Europe needed.

The Pan-American agreement for mutual support, signed on
September 2, 1947, and known as the Rio Treaty, provided a better
model. It was an agreement by all the nations of the American continent to take collective action against any attack from outside, no
matter whence it might come. Now five Western European countries
—Great Britain, France, Belgium, Holland, and Luxemburg—agreed
that if any one of them should be "the object of an armed attack
in Europe," the others should provide "all the military aid and other
assistance in their power" to the victim of aggression. Article 4 of
this pact stressed that such action would be taken "in accordance

with the provisions of Article 51 of the Charter of the United Nations."

The reference to the United Nations Charter was deliberate: the U.N. was created after the Second World War as an instrument for international peace; had it been able to realize the goals of its charter—to maintain peace, or, if necessary, to restore peace by appropriate joint action—there would have been no call for regional arrangements such as the Brussels Treaty. But because the Soviet Union, which had been responsible, directly or indirectly, for almost all the attacks, disturbances, and unlawful actions, was itself a member of the Security Council, the latter often was impotent. By its misuse of the veto (so far the Soviet Union has used it on no fewer than a hundred occasions) the Soviet government usually succeeded in preventing the U.N. from exercising its police function. To put it bluntly, it was as though the organized underworld in a city had managed to secure a decisive voice in its police department.

Thus, since the U.N. could not defend them, the Western nations had to create their own defensive alliances. But they wanted to articulate all agreements within the framework of the U.N., and to this end used Article 51 of the Charter: "Nothing in the present Charter shall impair the inherent right of individual or collective self-defense, if an armed attack occurs against a member of the organization, until the Security Council has taken the measures necessary to maintain international peace and security."

The right of veto came into the Security Council at the obstinate insistence of Stalin. It expresses not only the general principle that none of the great powers may be outvoted, but moreover, on September 13, 1944, at the Dumbarton Oaks Conference, Stalin declared, through the Soviet Ambassador, Andrei Gromyko, that each member of the Security Council should be allowed to vote even when it is a party to the matter in dispute. In other words the Soviet Union wanted the unlimited veto in the Security Council to be able to thwart any U.N. action which would assist future victims of Soviet aggression.

It was such a shameless admission of Soviet postwar plans that the Western delegates were aghast and dismayed. President Roosevelt did his utmost to dissuade Stalin. But Stalin cared little that his demand violated the established principle, that no one can be a judge in his own cause, and that it threw international law back to its status ante-dating the old League of Nations. Precisely this was Stalin's intent. When the Soviet Union attacked Finland in

1939, the League of Nations could not save the gallant Finnish people, but on December 14, 1939, it expelled the Soviet Union from the League. Stalin was determined to avoid repetition of such blows to Soviet prestige. He therefore insisted on his demand, and curtly rejected Roosevelt's personal intercession.

The Brussels Treaty also made reference to Germany. In the event of "a renewal by Germany of a policy of aggression," the signatories agreed to give each other all possible assistance. However, Germany was not singled out, as it had been in the Dunkirk Agreement. In the Brussels Treaty, the Western European powers joined together against any aggressive action or armed attack in Europe. Where such an attack might come from was already quite clear— and equally clear that the threat no longer emanated from a defeated, disarmed, and partitioned Germany. In fact, since a number of the signatory powers to the Brussels Pact were also occupation powers, Germany became part of the territory under pact protection. If Germany was still mentioned as a possible aggressor, it was with a cautious side-glance at the likely aggressor, the Soviet Union—one could not, after all, be certain that Stalin, pleased with his successful subjugation of Czechoslovakia, might not make the Brussels Treaty an excuse for a sudden drive towards the Atlantic and the Mediterranean.

The Russians were keeping 4 million men under arms; in Rumania, Bulgaria, and Hungary, in open defiance of the peace treaties of 1947, they were setting up Red satellite armies. And in the Soviet-occupied zone of Germany, the build-up of a para-military police force began as early as 1945. Against the enormous power of the Soviet bloc, the West was weak, its forces poorly equipped and coordinated. Little more than America's atom bomb stood between the Soviet Armies and Western Europe's freedom.

5

From the Prague
Defenestration to NATO

It had become obvious that Europe, impoverished by the war, demoralized, and shaken to its foundations, would fall easy victim to Bolshevism unless help were forthcoming from America. Only the U.S. atom bomb held the Red Army in check. But the atom bomb could not stem the persistent attack on the broad "second front," where the Communists hoped to conquer not by weapons but by misery—by the hunger, unemployment, and impoverishment which were driving millions in France and Italy into the arms of Communism.

The atom bomb could not revive the economy or mend the web of society. This required different measures. Above all, it was necessary to restore the courage and self-confidence of the peoples of Europe; and to this cause, the United States contributed generously, with a greater faith in the future of the old continent than that of some of the peoples of Europe themselves.

Such a policy was also in the interest of the United States. In the jet age, the Atlantic and Pacific Oceans had lost their roles as protective barriers; and the second front of Soviet aggression, international in character and penetrating all frontiers by economic and propagandistic subversion, left little room for isolationism of the old school. Prosperity and a high standard of living were not likely to prove adequate protection for the United States if the free countries of the other half of the world fell victim to Bolshevism.

As the atom bomb protected the West militarily in those precarious days, so the Marshall Plan brought the Soviet offensive on the second front to a halt. This plan, which was announced on June 5, 1947—hardly three months after the signing of the Dunkirk agreement—by the U.S. Secretary of State, George C. Marshall, in a speech at Harvard University, was of almost unparalleled generosity. And every bit as important as the material help it afforded to Europe was the spirit in which it was given. The people of Europe were in rags, but the United States did not offer them alms as though they were beggars. Instead, it approached them as equal partners, in sober terms but in a spirit of brotherhood and with that respect for human dignity which is democracy's heritage from Christianity, and can be found even in its most secular forms. While Moscow seeks to exploit the humiliation of human beings in order to turn them into "proletarians" and these into obedient Communists, the Marshall Plan was the expression of a fundamentally different attitude, a belief in the value of the human soul created in freedom.

The policy of the Marshall Plan was in accordance with the spirit of the American people. The original plans—conceived in the Kremlin, as we now know—to destroy Germany's industry and to turn her into an "agricultural country," were firmly rejected by such men as Cordell Hull and Henry L. Stimson, and when they became publicly known they were equally firmly rejected by the great majority of the American people. It was quickly recognized that to pauperize Germany, to proletarianize her, and, in the inevitable upshot, sovietize her, would drag other nations into the abyss, too. As early as 1947 the former President of the United States, Herbert Hoover, declared in a report that to keep Germany in chains would mean keeping Europe in rags. The Marshall Plan put an end to such dangers; the policy of bringing Germany back into the Western world was begun.

The Brussels Treaty was an earnest demonstration of Europe's will to live. Under the pressure of a common fate, her peoples moved closer together, and they gradually began to approach that inner unity which had already been a hope in the days of Stresemann, Briand, and Sir Austin Chamberlain, and which had now become the urgent need of the moment. This also proved that Europe was prepared and anxious to help herself—in other words, that it would not be a waste of time and energy for the United States to assist her.

Thus, although the defense of Europe was the hard core of the

Brussels Treaty, its significance went far beyond that. The preamble made a solemn profession of faith in the "fundamental human rights, in the dignity and worth of the human person." It was meant seriously, as affirmation of a concept which has existed throughout our long history, ever since there has been a defense of the West.

Of course, it requires some courage to express such ideas publicly, because in our day we have heard so many high-sounding words that sometimes it might seem as if the values behind them had lost their meaning. Whoever denies this runs the danger of being told that he is not a realist, and of being asked what, after all, we have to set against the monolithic system behind the Iron Curtain.

The truth is that we have everything to set against Bolshevism; everything that amounts to human dignity and a self-responsible existence under the divine law; and this is precisely what the preamble to the Brussels Treaty tries to express. Whoever thinks he is not committed to these values will not be persuaded by words. All that is left for him is to seek the direct experience of its opposite: the harsh encounter with reality behind the Iron Curtain, with a regime that denies and brutally violates the God-given rights of man.

The five signatory powers of the Brussels Treaty were appealing to the common heritage of Western Europe when they agreed to act together "to fortify and preserve the principles of democracy, personal freedom, and political liberty, the constitutional traditions and the rule of law." But they went even further; they decided to strengthen the economic, social, and cultural ties by which they were already united, to raise the living standards of their peoples, and to coordinate their efforts "to create a firm basis for European economic recovery." Other states, "inspired by the same ideals and animated by the like determination," were to be invited to join the pact. In other words, the preamble to the Brussels Treaty set out the idea of European unity, and thereby it became the basis for the Western European Union. At the same time, it declared its belief in human liberty, which unites Europe and the United States; and thus it became the precursor of the North Atlantic Alliance.

On the very day that the Brussels Treaty was signed—March 17, 1948—the President of the United States, Harry S. Truman, once again stressed the solidarity of his country with Europe. "I am sure," he told Congress, "that the determination of the free countries of Europe to protect themselves will be matched by an equal determination on our part to help them." Without the support of the United States, the defense of Europe would surely be in vain.

But what Europe needed and hoped for was more than a promise on the part of the United States to come to its aid after a Soviet attack. At that time, the Soviet armies would still have been able to break through to the Atlantic coast in a quick drive. And once they had done so, the reconquest of Europe—after all the devastation, the deportations, and the wholesale murders of a Soviet occupation—would be, as the French Premier Henri Queuille put it, "the liberation of a corpse." Some way had to be found to exert the might of the United States before the catastrophe.

And that was not a speculation about the future. The Soviet threat was an immediate one; it hung over Europe and demanded prompt decisions. The men in the Kremlin were taking the first steps to attack Berlin, the outpost not only of West Germany, but of Western Europe and the entire free world. On March 31, 1948, two weeks after the signing of the Brussels Treaty, Stalin flung down his challenge and began the blockade of Berlin. At first it was the "little blockade," directed not against the general population of the city but solely against the Western allies. But this was clearly only the preliminary to an action which might easily lead to war. Great Britain and France were just as much attacked as the United States. They were threatened by a common enemy, and joint action was the only answer.

Although the full blockade did not start until later—on June 24, 1948—the basic decision was taken in the first few days: to hold Berlin at all costs. The Western powers decided not to retreat on the Berlin issue, even if the Soviets used military force. It was not an easy decision to make, and the radio- and teleconferences between the military governors in Berlin and their governments in London, Paris, and Washington went on ceaselessly. Once again the world seemed on the verge of war. But a word of General Lucius D. Clay clarified the situation. He declared that weakness on our part would cost important prestige, and that if war were desired by the Soviet government it would not be averted by weakness. The air lift then became an impressive demonstration to the Soviets of both the power and the determination of the Western allies.

The pressure of these dramatic events accelerated the progress of the Western countries towards a closer community. Radical measures were required for this—in America, nothing less than a break with the deeply rooted tradition of "no entangling alliances," a tradition as old as the United States itself. On April 11, 1948, Secretary of State George C. Marshall and Under-Secretary Robert M. Lovett approached the leaders of the two parties in the Senate. A few days later, on April 17, the supreme organ of the Brussels Treaty Organization, the Consultative Council of the Foreign Ministers of the five signatory countries, met in Brussels and appointed a standing Military Committee. On April 28, the Canadian Premier, Louis S. St. Laurent, rose in the Canadian Parliament to propose the formation of a single, all-embracing Atlantic defense system which would incorporate the provisions of the Brussels Treaty. A week later the British Foreign Secretary, Ernest Bevin, welcomed the suggestion in the House of Commons.

On April 30, the five Defense Ministers and the Chiefs of their General Staffs met in London to decide how much of the required arms and equipment they could supply from their own production, and how much they would have to ask the United States to contribute. From the following July on, United States and Canadian experts were present as observers at the meetings of the Defense Committee of the Brussels Treaty Organization. Stalin's attack on Berlin had brought the Western powers still more closely together. On July 6, the ambassadors of the signatory powers of the Brussels Treaty and the Canadian Ambassador met at the State Department in Washington for discussions. These discussions lasted until September 9, and led ultimately to the North Atlantic Treaty. In September, while the Berlin blockade was still at its height, the five Brussels Treaty powers decided to form a unified defense force to be known as UNIFORCE. The Commanders-in-Chief of the allied armies, navies, and air forces came together in a standing committee under the chairmanship of Field Marshal Viscount Montgomery, and appointed Commanders-in-Chief for the combined allied forces: the French General de Lattre de Tassigny for the land forces, the British Air Marshal Sir James Robb for the air forces, and the French Vice-Admiral Jaujard for the navies. The first headquarters of this UNIFORCE was in Fontainebleau near Paris, and today it is the headquarters of the Commander-in-Chief of the NATO Forces in Central Europe.

In these important six months, the decisive connecting links between Europe and the United States were rapidly established, and the community of the Atlantic peoples, which subsequently gave birth to NATO, became ever closer.

The decision to involve itself in an alliance on the other side of the Atlantic was a much more revolutionary step for the United States than for Europe. The countries of Europe had long been used to strengthening their influence by dominion or alliances overseas, but the American people had always fought shy of involvements, and had, indeed, been especially proud to stand on their own. Since the revolution of 1776 and the War of Independence, the policy of non-involvement had been a strict principle of America's foreign policy. George Washington had laid it down in his farewell address delivered on September 19, 1796: "Why forgo the advantages of so peculiar a situation? Why quit our own to stand upon foreign ground? Why, by interweaving our destiny with that of any part of Europe, entangle our peace and prosperity in the toils of European ambition, rivalship, interest, humor or caprice?"

For 150 years, the United States scrupulously adhered to this principle of non-involvement; and then, towards the end of the First World War, it intervened and actually took part in the fighting, but —and the United States set great store by the distinction—as an "associated," and not as an "allied," power.

Subsequently, the Senate refused to ratify a guarantee for the French borders, given by President Woodrow Wilson together with Great Britain on June 28, 1919. It also rejected the Versailles Treaty, and even the Charter of the League of Nations. When Hitler came on the scene, made a pact with Japan and Moscow and conquered France, the United States felt itself threatened at home for the first time since 1812. This time America became an "ally," not merely an "associated power," and it also joined the new league of nations, the United Nations. But a military alliance in peacetime? That was a different matter. Would the Senate ever agree to bind the United States in this way?

It is the historical service of the leader of the Republican opposition in the Senate, Arthur H. Vandenberg, once a convinced isolationist, that he gave the proposal his approval. It was he, in fact, who introduced the motion empowering the President of the United States to conclude regional defense pacts within the framework of the United Nations. On June 11, 1948, this motion was carried in the U.S. Senate by a vote of sixty-four to four, and is known as the Vandenberg Resolution.

The disappointment and indignation at the outrageous behavior of the Soviet Union were so great that for the first time in history the Senate agreed to limit its jealously guarded right to accept or reject international treaties, and gave the President a free hand to do what he considered necessary. He was empowered to take the United States into a system of collective security which would be effective without, and if necessary against, the Soviets. At the same time the United States was to take preventive action to preserve the peace of the world by leaving no prospective aggressor in any doubt as to its determination to exercise its right of self-defense, either alone or in conjunction with other powers in accordance with Article 51 of the Charter of the United Nations, should its security be prejudiced by aggression.

The ideas of this Senate resolution reappeared on September 9, 1948, in the recommendations of the diplomats meeting in Washington. The proposals met with approval, and at the end of October, the Consultative Committee of the Brussels Treaty Organization announced that "complete agreement in principle" existed concerning the formation of a "North Atlantic Defense Pact." The drafting of the text of the new pact began in Washington on December 10.

This time, too, a representative of the Canadian government took part. Encouraged by the determined attitude of Great Britain, the Canadian Foreign Minister publicly declared on June 10 that in the view of his government, the best way to ensure peace was for the free peoples of the world to build up and maintain overwhelming power under the leadership of Great Britain, the United States, and France against any enemy or possible combination of enemies. And on October 13, the Ottawa government announced its readiness to take part in the proposed alliance. Thus Great Britain's initiative in the matter of the Atlantic Pact also strengthened the Commonwealth ties.

The fact that the two countries of the North American continent had joined forces with the signatories of the Brussels Treaty lent the developing alliance such a compelling force that a number of other states felt drawn to it. They became persuaded that membership in an alliance of free nations would preserve them from the fate of the satellite countries far more certainly than any precarious neutrality which must depend on the whim of Moscow. The governments of Norway, Denmark, Portugal, and Italy were invited to join the new alliance, and they all accepted. The participation of Italy as a Mediterranean power was strongly recommended by France, which also persuaded the other members of the Alliance that, as part of the French mother country, the three Algerian Departments should be included in the area covered by the agreements.

Even in this preparatory period preceding the conclusion of the North Atlantic Treaty, the Soviets did their utmost to disrupt the unity of the Western nations, and they launched a wave of propaganda in which threats alternated with promises and enticements of all kinds. The various national Communist parties were mobilized; for example, on February 22, 1949, the General Secretary of the French Communist Party, Maurice Thorez, publicly stated that in the event of a war with Moscow, French Communists would not fight against the Soviet Union. Four days later, his colleague, the Italian Communist Party leader Palmiro Togliatti, went even further and declared that in such a case it would be the duty of all Italians to fight not for their own country but for the Red Army. This of course was open incitement to high treason. At the same time, mass strikes were instigated, and in the Po Valley over a million agricultural laborers walked out.

This was an all-out offensive ordered by the Kremlin. The Berlin blockade was continuing; the Soviets were still trying to subdue the people of free Berlin by cutting off their supplies, though it was becoming clear that they would fail, thanks to the air lift and the determination and sacrifices of the Berliners themselves. All the more furiously did Moscow rail against the defensive alliance the Western nations were jointly building in order to stem the Red flood, not only in Berlin but everywhere in Europe.

The antics of Thorez and Togliatti were backed up by thinly veiled threats of war, and Moscow announced that in 1949 the Soviet Union would spend twenty per cent more on armaments than in the previous year. On January 29, 1949, the Soviet Foreign Ministry published a note whose tone of violent abuse and wild accusations would in former times undoubtedly have led to a rupture of diplomatic relations, perhaps even war.

The Soviet White Book warned the countries of the Western European Union against proceeding any further along "the path of resistance to the Peoples' Democracies and the Soviet Union," and in unctuous phrases, which would have sounded comic if they had not been so sinister, it sought to establish the blasphemous claim that resistance to the Bolshevist regime was, so to speak, sinful, a punishable crime against the higher morality. In place of the Gospel this regime puts the "good tidings" of Marxism, and on the throne of the Lord of history it sets the leading functionary of the Central Committee of the Communist Party as the representative of the world proletariat.

This form of atheism which denies God but at the same time seeks to overthrow Him and replace Him by dialectical materialism is not dry theory buried in philosophical tomes. It is a program of action which affects everyday politics. The establishment of Communism all over the world is presented as the true meaning of history. Once this is accepted, every murder and every brutal attack on other people becomes an "act of liberation," while every defense against Bolshevism is "aggression." In this topsy-turvy world of make-believe, the Soviet White Book declares that the North Atlantic Treaty—which is exclusively defensive if ever a treaty was—was formed "to realize a policy of aggression, a policy intended to unleash a new war."

The strongest Soviet pressure was applied, with a mixture of intimidation and enticement, to Norway. Already during negotiations about a possible Scandinavian defensive alliance, Norway had insisted that such an alliance must cooperate closely with the Western powers. She was unable to get this demand accepted, because majority opinion in Sweden was committed to the policy of neutrality, which had proved advantageous to the country during two world wars.

On February 5, 1949, the Norwegian Premier Halvard Lange flew to Washington to take part in the negotiations for establishing the North Atlantic Treaty. A few hours before his plane left, the Soviet Ambassador presented him with a note from the Kremlin calling on Norway to conclude a pact of non-aggression with the Soviet Union. The Norwegian Premier refused to do so. That act required a great deal of courage, because the threat implicit in the Soviet proposal was a very real one for a small country which has, like Norway, a joint frontier—if only a short one—with the Soviet Union. On March 3, Norway decided to join the North Atlantic Alliance. Denmark followed suit on March 11. Norway joined with the one proviso that, so long as her territory was not attacked or threatened by attack, no foreign troops should be stationed on her soil.

In the same way, Portugal made it a condition of her membership that in times of peace the Azores would remain free of foreign troops, and that her close cooperation with Spain would remain unaffected by her membership in the North Atlantic Alliance.

On March 15, 1949, the signatories to the Brussels Treaty and the governments of the United States and Canada formally invited Denmark, Iceland, Italy, Norway, and Portugal to join the North Atlantic Treaty Organization. Three days later, before it was signed, its text was made public. On March 31, a last attempt was made to torpedo the treaty. In a memorandum which was handed to each one of the proposed signatories separately, the Soviet government alleged that the treaty would be a violation of the United Nations Charter and of the decisions of the Council of Foreign Ministers. The twelve powers concerned made a joint reply in a note which was handed over two days later. The note was short and to the point. In twenty-one lines it simply stated that the text of the North Atlantic Treaty was itself the best rebuttal of the Soviet charges, because it showed beyond all shadow of doubt that the proposed alliance was not directed against any nation or group of nations but exclusively against the possibility of an armed attack by an aggressor.

On April 4, 1949, the Foreign Ministers of the twelve original treaty powers met in Washington and formally signed the North Atlantic Treaty. Within five months, all the parliaments concerned had ratified it. It was during this period that Jacob Malik, the Soviet delegate to the Security Council, got in touch with United States delegate Philip C. Jessup, with a view to opening negotiations for ending the Berlin blockade. These negotiations led to a four-power agreement on May 5 in New York. Thus, within a few weeks after it came into existence, NATO already contributed to the abandonment by the Soviets of their Berlin blockade, which was an attack on the life of the city and of the free world as a whole. The blockade ended on May 12, 1949.

6

An Alliance for Peace

The North Atlantic Treaty is one of the briefest and clearest of international documents. Its aim, as set down by its signatories in the preamble, is "to safeguard the freedom, common heritage and civilization of their peoples, founded on the principles of democracy, individual liberty, and the rule of law." The deed is short, consisting of a preamble and fourteen articles. It is also clear: it sets down its objectives, and for this it needs no codicils, no explanatory correspondence, no subsequent interpretations, overt or covert. To date the Treaty has been supplemented on two occasions—not because it had to be changed, but in order to accept three further signatories: Greece and Turkey by the protocol of October 22, 1951, and the German Federal Republic by the protocol of October 23, 1954, which came into force on May 5, 1955.

Article 5 is the hard core of the Treaty. This is the declaration that an armed attack on any one of the allies will be regarded as an attack against them all, and that they would then, individually and in concert, do everything necessary to assist the attacked party and to restore the security of the North Atlantic Treaty area—if need be by armed force.

For the members of NATO this means, as Arthur H. Vandenberg pointed out in the U.S. Senate on July 6, 1949, that they can rely absolutely on their allies. And for the Soviet Union it was a clear and unambiguous warning that in the future there was to be no opportunity of defeating and subjugating the free nations of the world one at a time. With this, the advance of the Red Army and of the Bolshevist system in Europe was brought to a stop. If the democratic countries, including the United States, had been under such clear and definite obligations in 1939, then, in the words of Paul-Henri Spaak, "the Second World War would probably not have broken out." The two totalitarian rulers, Hitler and Stalin, would hardly have dared to march into Poland if that country had been protected by an alliance as strong as NATO.

At the same time, Article 5 makes it quite clear that the alliance is a purely defensive one. In its origin, its character, and its wording, the North Atlantic Treaty is very clearly an instrument of defense. Like Bismarck's careful system of the Triple Alliance, the Re-insurance Treaty, and the Mediterranean Ententes, it limits the *casus foederis*, the event when the allies must act, only to the case of armed aggression against one of the partners to the treaty. Should one of those partners himself commit the aggression, then he would stand alone, and no fellow member of the alliance would be under any obligation to assist him. This is no mere theory: despite her membership in the Triple Alliance, Italy remained neutral in 1914 (later she even took up arms against her allies) because Germany, although not alone responsible for the First World War, had formally been first to declare war on France. In the same way, NATO did not support the intervention of Britain and France in Egypt in 1956, even though Moscow certainly had a hand in the game and even posed an ultimatum, threatening the use of nuclear rockets. On the contrary, the United States not only did not support Britain and France, but sided against their action, because, although Egypt had broken solemn agreements and cut the lifeline of the British Empire, she had not taken up arms first.

We have already pointed out that for the United States to enter even a defensive alliance in time of peace represented a radical change in foreign policy. As General Nathan S. Twining, then chairman of the Joint Chiefs of Staff, said to us during a discussion in the Pentagon, "The old idea of Fortress America, strongest behind her ocean barrier, is dead and buried. The Soviets must be made to realize with absolute clarity that any attack on a member of NATO means war, and that we should strike back." Then he added, "And that includes Berlin."

For some European countries as well, which in the past were always rather hesitant about declaring what their attitude would be in the event of a conflict, the North Atlantic Treaty means a new line. The decision of the fifteen allies to stand one for all and all for one, as laid down in Article 5, forms the basis of the "deterrent" which plays such a decisive role today in all planning for the prevention of war. Determination alone, of course, is not enough; it will "deter" only when a powerful armed force stands behind it. And that is the basic significance of Article 3. The allies, who disarmed unilaterally after the war, have now, in view of Soviet aggressions, undertaken to rebuild their defense—not only each country for itself, but all together, jointly, by means of mutual assistance.

When the North Atlantic Treaty first came into being, what the various governments understood by "mutual assistance" did not go very far. It meant that each country should make its own preparation militarily and economically, to the best of its ability and in accordance with its size, resources, position, and economic structure. But to what extent each country was to assist its allies in the task of rearmament, by industrial production, transport, labor power, armaments, or troops, was left to its own discretion. The growing strength of each, by increasing the total power of NATO, was to benefit all.

In a speech delivered before the Foreign Affairs Committee of the U.S. Senate on April 27, 1949, Secretary of State Dean Acheson indicated the limitations of Article 3 of the Treaty, which, he said, "does not bind the United States to the proposed military assistance program, nor indeed to any program. It does bind the United States to the principle of self-help and mutual aid. Within this principle each party to the pact must exercise its own honest judgment as to what it can and should do to develop and maintain its own capacity to resist, and to help others."

In practice, however, the United States went ahead at once and set its allies a good example. It interpreted the idea of assistance very liberally indeed. NATO allies, who had formally requested military and financial assistance on the very day of the signing of the treaty, were provided with no less than a billion dollars to meet their needs in the year 1950 alone, and a generous aid program was signed by President Truman and approved by Congress on October 6, 1949—which was, incidentally, only two weeks after the first Soviet atomic explosion had become known. Up to the year 1959, U.S. help for its NATO allies amounted to twenty billion dollars.

It soon became evident that, in order to strengthen and develop the power and resources of the allies and of NATO as a whole, some form of joint planning was necessary, including a unified command, a common form of training, and, as far as possible, the standardization of equipment. Once again the Soviet Union, thanks to its aggressive policy, and above all the war in Korea, accelerated this development in the free world, indirectly and unwillingly, to be sure —"dialectically," to use Marxist terminology—but nevertheless effectively. Under the pressure of the Soviet menace, the sovereign states of the Western alliance were beginning in 1950 to entrust their troops to international commanders and integrated staffs. Ironically, this was not a dialectic which, in the spirit of the Marxist conception of history, furthered the spread of Communism. On the contrary, it strengthened the bulwark of freedom. Hardly ever in world history has an alliance in peacetime led to such a closely knit military association.

Thus Soviet policy helped the Western powers to recognize a political necessity, a necessity which derives from the change in our historical situation. We no longer live in the era of what might be called cabinet wars. Alliances can no longer be planned and concluded by governments alone; if they are to have any reality, they must be approved by public opinion and reach into the economic, social, and cultural, as well as the military, spheres. In sum, they must be alliances of peoples and not merely of governments. The fact that NATO is well on the way to becoming such an alliance gives it a historical advantage and a moral superiority over all other kinds of entente, alliance, or security pacts.

Every military alliance, even if it is exclusively defensive, must take the possibility of war into account. NATO was formed in the first place because there was a grave danger of war. Here too, however, the Treaty is formulated with caution. The obligation to support an ally is not automatic, since each of the allies is entitled to decide for itself whether, in fact, armed aggression has been committed, and, if it has, what measures are necessary. This is a formula which was adopted out of consideration for the U.S. Constitution, according to which—except in the case of a direct attack on its territory or armed forces—Congress declares war, and not the President.

In practice, however, this apparent restriction has limited significance; clearly, so long as any NATO state can be in any doubt as to whether its existence is at stake, the critical event, aggression by a big power, has not yet taken place. As far as the United States is concerned, a Soviet violation of NATO territory would almost everywhere be an attack on American troops. And because the forces of NATO are under a joint command and closely integrated, immediate collective defense has become practically a certainty.

In a certain sense the fact that each member of the NATO alliance has a right to decide its intervention for itself even makes for greater effectiveness. For example, once the *casus foederis* arises, none of the allies is compelled to wait for a joint decision before taking action—as was the case with the League of Nations, which thereby was completely paralyzed at the time of the Sino-Japanese conflict in 1932.

Article 6 of the Treaty defines the area which is defended by the North Atlantic Alliance. When Greece and Turkey joined the Treaty powers, this article was supplemented by the London protocol of October 22, 1951. According to the new version, the *casus foederis* will operate in the event of an armed attack:

"1. on the territory of any of the parties in Europe or North America, on the Algerian Departments of France, on the territory of Turkey, or on the islands under the jurisdiction of any of the parties in the North Atlantic area north of the Tropic of Cancer;

"2. on the forces, vessels, or aircraft of any of the parties, when in or over these territories or any other area in Europe in which occupation forces of any of the parties were stationed on the date when the Treaty entered into force, or the Mediterranean, or the North Atlantic area north of the Tropic of Cancer."

This security guarantee covered the German Federal Republic even before it joined the North Atlantic Treaty powers—if only indirectly, because an attack on the territory of the German Federal Republic would have been an attack on the Allied occupation forces and thus on the United States, Great Britain, and France. Today, Article 6 provides that the same applies to Berlin so long as the Western powers maintain garrisons there.

With regard to the organs and the administration of the Alliance, the Treaty wisely confines itself to a general provision: the establishment of a council on which each of them shall be represented, which council shall be so organized as to be able to meet promptly at any time. It is left to the council itself to create whatever organs it may require. Only one other body was ordered to be set up by the Treaty itself, namely, a Defense Committee, which must consist of the defense ministers of the allied powers. This body worked out a strategic plan for "the joint defense of the North Atlantic area." Later, in 1951, it was merged with the permanent committee of the North Atlantic Council.

Thus the whole extensive structure of NATO as it exists today has arisen from the decisions of the North Atlantic Council. The fact that the Treaty itself left such a wide margin has not hampered developments. On the contrary, in this way it was possible to create just the organs which the given situation and its tasks required, and to give them all necessary powers; and then, if the situation made it necessary or desirable, to reorganize or dissolve them. In this way, too, the structure of NATO has been saved from any bureaucratic rigidity, and it has been able to develop according to the living forces which have themselves arisen within the framework of the alliance.

Article 10 of the Treaty lays it down clearly: NATO is not an exclusive organization, it can be extended if required. Of course, any such extension would make sense only if it would strengthen the alliance. Therefore the treaty limits the circle of those states which may be invited to join it to Europe, because apart from the United States, Canada, and Turkey, the only powers in a position to make any effective contribution to the defense against Bolshevism are the European powers. The members of the alliance were of the opinion that this, their most urgent task, would be complicated rather than simplified by the admission of non-European nations. And not even every European country would be welcome, because a member can be a source of strength to the alliance only if it is prepared and able to further the principles of NATO both at home and abroad, to extend the limits of freedom and to work for the preservation of peace. Thus it would, for example, be an absurd idea to take the Soviet Union or one of the "peoples' democracies" into NATO, because it would immediately disrupt the spirit from which the strength of the alliance derives; and instead of the agreement of free peoples we should have a situation like that in the Security Council of the United Nations, with a Soviet veto operating. NATO would be paralyzed and finally destroyed. This calculation was at the back of the Soviet note of March 31, 1954, in which the Soviet Foreign Minister, Molotov, made the ingenuous suggestion that the Soviet Union might be prepared to join the North Atlantic Alliance.

Although the defense provided by NATO is restricted to a clearly defined geographical area, the principles which have to be defended are not restricted to any particular territory, but represent a moral position.

So far three countries—Greece, Turkey, and the German Federal Republic—have been admitted to NATO as new members under Article 10. Sweden was also invited to join, but her government preferred to continue the policy of neutrality. In 1949, when she was pressed by Norway and Denmark—two Scandinavian countries whose confidence in the effectiveness of neutrality had been shattered during the Second World War—she refused to be persuaded. It is only fair to say that the balance was probably tipped by her consideration for another Scandinavian neighbor a little farther to the east. The Swedes believed that if they joined NATO, Moscow might begin to step up the pressure on Finland so that in the end that gallant little country would be unable to hold out.

Switzerland has a very long tradition of neutrality, and she is not likely to break with it now in order to join NATO. But the Swiss are arming themselves vigorously against the Soviet threat, and they leave no one in doubt that their sympathies lie with the North Atlantic Treaty powers. All Swiss political parties (except, of course, the small Communist Party) are agreed that the Swiss Army, which was always one of the most efficient in the world, must be equipped with the best in modern arms, because without that any defense against an aggressor equipped with atomic weapons would be hopeless from the start. The majority of the Swiss Social-Democratic Party is also definitely in favor of nuclear arms for the Swiss Army.

At its foundation in 1921, the Irish Free State adopted a policy of rigid neutrality, and the subsequent establishment of the Republic of Eire did nothing to change this policy. However, Eire is now a member of the United Nations and of various Western organizations, and is beyond all question attached to the Western world.

The Austrian situation is somewhat different. The treaty of May 15, 1955, neutralizes the country, and she is thereby barred from joining NATO. The Soviet Union saw to this with a view, among other things, to cutting off direct connections between Germany and Italy, not only overland, but also by air. This was part of the price which had to be paid for the withdrawal of the Russian occupation forces. But the Austrian people, though they carefully maintain their formal neutrality, also leave no doubt that their sympathies are with the free world, and they are well aware that NATO indirectly defends Austria's freedom and independence.

Apart from such tiny states as Liechtenstein, Monaco, San Marino, and Andorra, the only country in Europe this side of the Iron Curtain which remains a possible new ally for NATO is Spain. However, although Spain is of considerable strategic importance for the defense of the West, the Spanish government has not been invited to join. Article 10, which provides for the admission of new members, also provides that any such decision shall be by unanimous agreement; and it is unlikely that Spain will be invited to join as long as General Franco remains head of the Spanish state, because the Scandinavian members, most of which have Social-Democratic governments, are opposed to his admission. Indirectly, however, Spain is already part of the NATO defense system. By an agreement signed on September 26, 1953, the Spanish government leased bases on Spanish territory to the United States, and in return it received arms, supplies, and financial support, amounting by 1959 to 255 million dollars. The sixteenth U.S. Air Force, which is part of the U.S. Strategic Air Command, has its headquarters in Torrejon, with further bases in Moron, Saragossa, Seville, and Madrid.

In addition, on August 16, 1960, a new independent state arose in NATO's strategic area, namely, the Republic of Cyprus. On July 6, 1960, the governments of Great Britain, Greece, and Turkey, and the representatives of the Greek and Turkish ethnic groups on the island, signed the Treaty of Nicosia, thus settling a once bitter conflict in true NATO spirit. Under the terms of that treaty, Great Britain is to retain bases on the island, and there is a possibility that the new republic will apply for membership in NATO.

The most urgent task of NATO was to organize an effective defense against the military power of the Soviet Union; but all the allies were well aware that their ultimate task would go much further. "Peace," wrote Lord Ismay, the first Secretary-General of NATO, in his 1954 report on the first years of NATO activity, "is not merely the absence of war; its maintenance requires continuous cooperation by governments in the economic, social, and cultural field, as well as in the military." In other words, what NATO ought to envisage is "the development of a North Atlantic community which is more deeply rooted than in the mere necessity for a common defense against aggression. But this means no less than a permanent union of the free Atlantic peoples to serve their greater unity, and to protect and further those things which they have in common as free democracies."

This is the formula which was drawn up on behalf of NATO by the Foreign Ministers of Italy, Canada, and Norway—Professor Gaetano Martino, Lester B. Pearson, and Halvard Lange (sometimes referred to as the Three Wise Men)—and adopted on December 13, 1956, by the North Atlantic Council at its meeting in Paris. It is a fundamental document which also embraces the non-military tasks of NATO as they were outlined in Article 2: economic cooperation among the allies; the maintenance and development of cultural, scientific, and educational relations among them; and political agreement. This aspect of NATO, like its military defense activities, has assumed considerable dimensions, and will be discussed further at a later point.

The North Atlantic Treaty was expressly fitted into the broader framework of the United Nations; and in the very first article of the treaty the signatories reiterate their acceptance of the aims and principles of the U.N. In Article 1, they accept its rules for peace; and in Article 5, they even undertake to stop the struggle against armed aggression as soon as the Security Council of the U.N. shall have taken the necessary steps to re-establish peace.

There is no doubt that the ideas which led to the formation of the United Nations are in the best Western tradition, a development of Dante's universal kingdom of peace, of Hugo de Grotius' conception of international law, of Henry IV of France's Grand Design, of Immanuel Kant's World Republic, and, in our own century, of the League of Nations. Unfortunately, in practice it is possible for the Soviet Union and its satellites to cripple the work of the United Nations. Given the veto provisions, it is not easy to see how the Security Council could take on any effective measures against Soviet aggression—unless by some fortunate chance the Soviet delegates were absent (as they were from the session which dealt with the Communist invasion of South Korea).

This is the reason why the countries of the free world had to take additional measures in their own defense. Should NATO ever find it necessary to repulse armed Soviet aggression, it would, fortunately, not have to obtain prior permission from the Security Council, as required by Article 53 of the Charter of the United Nations. NATO bases its self-defense expressly on Article 51, and this means on natural law.

The concluding articles of the North Atlantic Treaty make provision for the ratification, depositing, and duration of the treaty.

Thus this historic document, brief and sober, contains little more than is normally necessary for the official registration of any ordinary association: aims and objects, organs, membership, and provision for dissolution. One can say that the North Atlantic Treaty is a product of Anglo-Saxon juridic thought. It remained for the reality which brought the treaty into being to clothe its dry bones with living flesh.

7

The Growth of the
Atlantic Community

The fate of NATO took a decisive turn on June 25, 1950, when the North Korean Army, using Soviet equipment and Soviet tanks of the T-34 type, as well as squadrons of planes, invaded the territory of the South Korean Republic, and, advancing rapidly, occupied the South Korean capital of Seoul.

This blatant act of aggression took the free world by surprise. Only one year after the Berlin blockade, illusions about the peaceful intentions of the Soviet Union again had become so strong that, despite numerous warnings by General Douglas MacArthur, the United States forces in Japan had only seventeen obsolescent light tanks of the M-24 type available, and five of these were unserviceable. The heavy U.S. tanks of the Pershing and Sherman types, the only ones powerful enough to stand up to the Russian T-34s, had been put into mothballs after the war, and had to be put through the workshops of the Eighth U.S. Army before they could be used. And only ninety-two of them were available.

It was therefore all the more remarkable that the counter-move was made so quickly and vigorously. On the very day of the attack, the Security Council of the U.N.—at the motion of the U.S. delegation—ordered the North Korean government to cease hostilities. When this order was ignored, the U.N. immediately imposed economic and military sanctions and called on all its members to rally to the rescue of the Republic of South Korea. On June 27, President

Truman ordered the naval and air forces of the United States into action against the invaders. Ultimately, military contingents from fifteen nations, under the command of General MacArthur, took part in the war of defense, while thirty-eight member countries supported South Korea with arms and economic aid.

The Soviets seemed as much taken by surprise at this determined resistance as the free world had been by their aggression. The fact that the Security Council was able to take such rapid action was owing entirely to the chance absence of the Soviet delegation from the session. Perhaps the Soviet government could not imagine that the Security Council would be so depraved as to answer the glorious advance of the revolution with anything but paper protests. When the Kremlin recognized its mistake, it indulged in an outburst of "moral" indignation, because in its view the attack on South Korea was not aggression at all, but "maintenance of the status quo."

Status quo, Mr. Khrushchev explained to the American journalist Walter Lippmann, is not, as most people think, the maintenance of a fixed state of affairs, but the permanent Communist revolution expanding the power of the Soviets. To oppose this process would be an attempt to upset the status quo. The West therefore should recognize the boundaries of the Soviet empire not merely as they exist today but, far beyond that, in their potential extension—which means, according to the Marxist-Leninist doctrine, throughout the world. If revolutionary Communism is the only worthwhile order; if it alone has the historical mission to rule the world; then, logically, all resistance to it is illegitimate, even immoral. And Communism, as Khrushchev told Adlai Stevenson in Moscow in the summer of 1958, "utilizes every national awakening and every instance of social unrest, and thus spreads from country to country." Khrushchev also asserted that his interpretation of the status quo, if it were generally accepted, would result in an improvement of international relations. The peoples of the free world, however, regard this interpretation as an attempt to justify unlimited Soviet expansion.

It was in these circumstances that the threat of a "European Korea" first took shape, and the NATO powers realized that they had no time to lose. The danger was direct and imminent, and if peace was to be preserved, the Soviet Union had to be shown that NATO would be prepared to act at once in any such eventuality. The Soviet government maintained an "advance guard" of 22 divisions, supported by 6,000 planes, along the Iron Curtain, backed by the whole power of the Red Army, against which the Atlantic Treaty powers could muster at best 14 divisions and perhaps 1,000 planes. And even these troops—like the U.S. forces in Japan at the outbreak of the Korean war—were intended as occupation rather than battle troops. They were trained differently, they were variously equipped, and they were without a unified command. In the event of war, a unified command would have had to be created in haste.

Even the deployment of the occupation forces in Germany and Austria served administrative purposes rather than defense. For example, the only British armored division on the continent was stationed well to the west of its main base, and the infantry divisions even farther west—an excellent position for repelling aggression from France, but not from the east. Furthermore, these British troops were supplied from Hamburg—an hour's journey by car from the Russian garrisons. And the U.S. Army supply lines farther south were not much more favorably placed; they ran parallel to the Iron Curtain. Field Marshal Viscount Montgomery, the chairman of the Joint General Staff of the Western European Union, summed up the situation in a report submitted to the governments of the Brussels signatory powers on June 15, 1950, ten days before the outbreak of the Korean war. What he said was brief and to the point: "As things stand today, and in the foreseeable future, there would be scenes of appalling and indescribable confusion in Western Europe if we were ever attacked by the Russians."

The fact that the Western powers were able to afford such a careless policy without meeting with military disaster, was owing solely to the existence of the nuclear deterrent in United States hands —at that time Soviet atomic weapons were not yet operative. However, the Soviets, who are realists despite their love for dialectical distortions of the truth, realized from the Korean example that the free world was determined to defend its freedom. Thus Truman's courageous decision saved more than Korea—it may well have saved Europe. Korea gave NATO a great impetus, and with that campaign, it entered a new phase.

During the first period of its existence, from the opening session of the North Atlantic Council in Paris on September 17, 1949, until the outbreak of the Korean war, the allies had taken some basic measures to build up the NATO organization. The Council had constituted itself and decided that ordinarily it would be composed of the Foreign Ministers of the signatory powers, and that it would hold a regular meeting once a year. Arrangements were made for extraordinary sessions to be called at special request, in the event of a crisis or actual aggression. It was also decided that the chairman-ship of the Council should be taken in rotation and alphabetical order by the signatory powers. The first to occupy the chair was the U.S. Secretary of State, Dean Acheson.

A Defense Committee was set up, as provided for in Article 9, to draw up a unified plan of defense for NATO as a whole. Five Regional Planning Groups were also formed, and a Military Com-mittee consisting of the Chiefs of Staff of the member countries or their representatives. The executive body of this committee is the Standing Group, which consists of one representative each of Great Britain, France, and the United States. The second session of the Council in Washington on November 18, 1949, added a Defense Financial and Economic Board, and a Military Production and Supply Board.

Clearly, these numerous committees could no longer be effect-ively guided or controlled by the North Atlantic Council during its few meetings; a permanent organ had become necessary. This was created in May, 1950, as the Council of Deputies of the Foreign Ministers, which became a sort of standing conference of ambassa-dors in London.

The most urgent task pending was to work out a general plan for North Atlantic defense. The over-all strategic objectives had to be agreed upon, and the necessary means determined. This was no easy task, but the newly formed Standing Group did the job in less than thirty days, so that in December, 1949, hardly three months after the first steps had been taken, the NATO Council in Paris unanimously adopted the proposals placed before it. As an American officer pointed out to us, this was a remarkable performance, con-sidering that the Pentagon had taken two years to solve the same problem for the United States.

The Regional Planning Groups worked out their requirements on the basis of this general strategic plan. The result was a four-year plan, the so-called Medium-Term Defense Plan, which was ratified by the Defense Committee on April 1, 1950. This provided a rough estimate of the forces and resources the NATO powers would need for the defense of Western Europe. It proved to be considerably more than was at their disposal.

The decision to spread the plan over four years was taken not only out of consideration for the military and economic abilities of the allied powers, it also had a strategic reason. Responsible quarters in the United States already knew that the development of nuclear weapons would revolutionize warfare, and the year 1954 was regarded as the watershed between the era of wars with conventional weapons and that of nuclear warfare. Therefore, up to that time NATO was to have sufficient conventional weapons to repulse any Soviet attack by a defense organized along the lines of the Second World War. From 1954 on, United States nuclear weapons would be available in large quantities, and then a fundamentally new planning could begin.

It is worthy of note that this Medium-Term Defense Plan provided for a NATO army of ninety-six divisions, and that, even today, the actual forces available do not amount to even half that number. The fact is that, with the exception of the United States and Great Britain, the NATO powers did not realize that the cost of equipping and maintaining a modern army had risen steeply in the few years since the end of the Second World War. The smaller powers thought they could afford to raise forces of approximately the same magnitude as those existing before the Second World War. Their ideas were particularly unrealistic with regard to the air forces.

As a NATO officer at SHAPE put it, "We Europeans still thought that if we had a certain number of planes and the appropriate number of pilots to fly them, we had an air force. I can remember how the representative of one European government fought tooth and nail against a suggestion that his country's contingent should be increased by one-third of a division, but then proposed to 'round up' its air contribution by adding another fifty or a hundred planes. He hadn't the faintest idea that the costs his proposal involved would be several times greater than those necessary for a few thousand infantrymen."

Like the Congress of Vienna in 1814, before Napoleon's return from Elba, the NATO allies had been under the illusion that they had plenty of time. The crossing of the 38th parallel by the North Korean forces suddenly brought them down from the clouds of theory to the hard facts of defense requirements.

On July 25, 1950, the newly formed Council of Deputies met in London. The chairman, U.S. Ambassador Charles M. Spofford, announced that the United States would accelerate its arms deliveries, and called upon all other NATO powers to inform the Council in what form and to what degree they now proposed to increase their contributions to the joint NATO defense. The answers were available by August 31. The North Korean aggression had created a new sense of urgency.

Korea and the Berlin blockade also brought about a change in the policy of the West towards Germany. What was the use of a free German Federal Republic if it could not be defended? Every successful step in the reconstruction of West Germany, every increase in the national income, merely whetted the appetite of the Soviets. To lay their hands on so productive an area would at the the same time destroy the irritating influence of freedom and prosperity on the forcibly sovietized Eastern zone and the satellite countries. This Soviet aim has not changed to this day.

German participation in the defense of the West was first considered and declared necessary at the historic fifth session of the North Atlantic Council in New York in September, 1950. On December 18, 1950, in Brussels, the sixth session called upon the three Western occupation authorities to study the conditions for such a German contribution. This was the beginning of the end of the occupation regime.

On the following day, the Council appointed General Dwight D. Eisenhower to be the first Supreme Allied Commander Europe (SACEUR), and chose Marly near Paris as his headquarters— Supreme Headquarters Allied Powers Europe (SHAPE). It was an obvious step, because Eisenhower had been the personal embodiment of the Allied war effort, and his appointment translated an as yet abstract alliance into tangible reality.

General Eisenhower got to work at once. He arrived in Paris in January, 1951, gathered a staff from among the eight nations around him, and appointed Lieutenant-General Alfred M. Gruenther as his Chief of Staff. This international General Staff was a new experiment in military history, but under Eisenhower's leadership it was constituted rapidly. To some extent, Eisenhower could draw on the experiences of the Western European Union, which, in a smaller framework but along similar lines, had already formed a General Staff of officers of various nationalities and drawn up defense plans. Thus it was possible to start practical work as early as April, 1951. In July of that year, SHAPE moved to the headquarters in Marly. A beginning was made to turn the armies of the allies into an allied army.

The United States was the first power to place all its forces in Europe under the orders of the New Supreme Commander—on the very day of his appointment. France and the other allies soon followed suit. With this, progress was accelerated. Whereas in the first years, the fighting forces had increased only from 12 to 14 divisions and from 400 to 1,000 planes, by December, 1951, NATO could muster approximately 35 divisions, 3,000 planes, and 700 warships. Although not all these divisions were at full war strength, NATO's total strength had grown considerably. It no longer consisted merely of the combined forces of the various allies; the NATO divisions were beginning to consolidate and to increase their efficiency under unified command and in joint maneuvers. New airfields, improved communications, and better supply lines all helped to increase NATO's effective strength.

But the decisive factor was that these fighting forces from many countries now possessed a common political will. This distinguishes NATO from most alliances of the past. NATO is more than a military alliance of expediency; it is united by a common outlook which reaches from the top echelons to the youngest recruit. NATO draws considerable political strength from this unity, because this allied army, freely formed, inevitably became imbued with a spirit of freedom which soon had its effect on the peoples themselves. The soldier's preparedness to make the supreme sacrifice, which necessarily belongs to his profession and helps to form his character in peace as well as in war, has encouraged the development of a consciousness of unity among the NATO forces far more quickly than among those sheltered citizens pursuing their ordinary business. The feeling of mutual dependence is greater and more direct among fighting men, and their comradeship is more personal. The men of the NATO forces were the first to recognize that their own country could be defended only in community with the free world.

At the same time as SHAPE (on April 2, 1951) two other major subordinate commands were formed: Allied Forces Northern Europe (AFNORTH), with headquarters in Oslo, and Allied Forces Central Europe (AFCENT), with headquarters in Fontainebleau near Paris. The formation of Allied Forces Southern Europe (AFSOUTH), with headquarters in Naples, followed in June, 1951. The fourth sub-command, Allied Forces Mediterranean (AFMED), with headquarters in Malta, was formed in March, 1953.

On January 30, 1952, a Supreme Allied Commander Atlantic (SACLANT) was appointed in the person of Vice-Admiral Lynde D. McCormick (U.S.A.) He took up his command on April 10, 1952, with headquarters in Norfolk, Virginia. On February 21, 1952, the

Channel Command (CHANCOM) was set up to protect shipping in the English Channel, in the southern area of the North Sea, and in part of the eastern Atlantic bordering on the British Isles. In addition, there is the Canada-U.S. Regional Planning Group (CUSRPG), whose task it is to work out strategic plans for the joint land and air defense of the North American continent. This regional planning group is the only one still in existence of the five formed by the North Atlantic Council at its first session on September 17, 1949. It sits alternately in Washington and Ottawa, and it has no actual fighting forces at its disposal. The other regional planning groups were subsequently replaced by the four sub-commands listed above.

SHAPE, SACLANT, CHANCOM, and CUSRPG are coordinated commands under the highest military authority of the North Atlantic Alliance—the Military Committee in Washington, and its Standing Group.

The Council sessions which took place in Ottawa from September 20 to 25, 1951, in Rome from November 24 to 28, 1951, and, in particular, in Lisbon from February 20 to 25, 1952, drew the political and military conclusions from the dangerous situation which had been made clear by Communist aggression in Korea. In Ottawa, twelve experts were chosen for the Temporary Council Committee (TCC), with an executive board consisting of three members: Averell Harriman (U.S.A.), chairman, Jean Monnet (France), and Sir Edwin Plowden (Great Britain). This committee was given the task of reconciling the requirements of collective security with the political and economic capabilities of each member country. A sum of 220 million dollars was voted for the building of joint airfields, lines of communication, and a supply organization—the so-called infrastructure of NATO. With this, NATO could continue what the Western European Union had begun in 1948 at a cost of about 92 million dollars.

The Rome session of the North Atlantic Council was the first to receive a personal report from General Eisenhower, about the build-up of NATO's fighting forces and their current strength.

The Lisbon session of the Council adopted the plan put forward by the Temporary Council Committee, and the various members undertook to provide a total of 50 divisions on a war footing, 4,000 planes, and strong naval forces, by the end of 1952.

The strengthening of NATO's political organization was particularly important. The Council of Deputies of the Foreign Ministers in London was replaced by a Permanent NATO Council in Paris, to remain in session in the intervals between ministerial meetings. Its members, representatives of their governments as well as of the Foreign Ministers, were given real authority to make decisions, and their work was facilitated by a newly formed International Secretariat with a highly qualified staff. A permanent Chairman was added to the Permanent Council and given responsibility, as Secretary-General of NATO, for the work of the International Secretariat.

On April 4, 1952, the third anniversary of NATO, this office was assumed by Lord Ismay (G.B.), with his headquarters in the Palais de Chaillot in Paris. Previously Lord Ismay had been Secretary of State for Commonwealth Affairs.

The Lisbon session of the North Atlantic Council was regarded as a landmark in the history of the Alliance. The tightening of the organizational structure and the formation of a permanent political body that, with all due regard to the sovereignty of the allies, carried out supra-national tasks, gave NATO the coherence which enabled it to withstand the severe tests of the subsequent years.

When, on April 28, 1952, General Matthew B. Ridgway replaced General Eisenhower as Supreme Commander in Europe, he found fifty divisions available. Twenty-five of these, however, were provided by Greece and Turkey, which had joined NATO shortly before, on February 18, 1952. Whether the Council had counted with these forces when it asked for fifty divisions, is another matter. They were welcome new allies, but they not only increased NATO's strength, they also enlarged considerably the area NATO was committed to defend. Twenty-five additional divisions from the older member countries would have been more in keeping with the existing military situation, because in the Soviet-occupied zone of Germany alone, twenty-two divisions, with another sixty in reserve, were confronting a total of seventeen allied divisions: three British armored divisions equipped with Centurion tanks; an excellent British infantry division; four French divisions and a Moroccan division (not at full strength); two Belgian divisions (neither fully equipped); five very good U.S. divisions; and three armored regiments. In addition, there were the U.S., British, and French forces in Berlin.

Nevertheless, an important step forward had been taken. At least the Western allies were now strong enough to oppose a Soviet "offensive by substitutes," in other words, a European Korea. The Soviet Union could no longer hope to overrun the German Federal Republic with East German or satellite divisions while playing the "peace-loving" observer at the ringside. Henceforth, if the men in the Kremlin should decide to send their satellites into action, they would be taking a much greater risk. The satellite armies might be defeated by the Western powers, and then the Soviet Union would be faced with a disagreeable alternative: either to sacrifice its allies, or else to intervene itself. In the case of direct intervention, the war would automatically be extended, and the Soviets would have to expect a nuclear counter-blow. This risk, which had so far dissuaded them from launching a large-scale attack on the West, now became effective for so-called limited wars as well.

Incidentally, the effectiveness of the deterrent does not lie in any fear on the part of the Soviet leaders that cities and human beings would be annihilated. As far as these are concerned, the leaders would, like Hitler, be prepared to accept terrible sacrifices. But they are well aware that their regime would not survive a war with a Western alliance determined to strike back. Russia is a vast country, but the ruling Soviet clique is small; and it is the power of this clique which would be broken forever in the event of a nuclear holocaust.

The death of Stalin on March 5, 1953, the uprising in East Berlin and in the Soviet zone on June 17, 1953, the unrest in Poland, and the struggles for power among the rival Soviet groups greatly disturbed the Soviet Union in the following years. The dynamics of freedom began to turn against the technicians of terror, and for the first time the world was permitted a glimpse of how much the Communist system is threatened from within. For NATO, this period was less turbulent, because as long as the Soviet regime felt itself weakened, it lowered its pressure on the outside world. But not for long. Hardly had the struggle for succession been settled when, in October, 1956, the bloody repression of the Hungarian revolution and the Soviet political drives in the Near East showed the world that, despite his public attacks on the dead dictator at the Twentieth Party Congress in Moscow in February, 1956, Khrushchev was determined to perpetuate Stalin's policy.

During this period, the German Federal Republic joined the Alliance. Germany had no part in the founding and early development of NATO, but it was quite clear that the "forward strategy" called for by the fifth Council session in New York in September, 1950, could not even be contemplated without "active and willing" German participation within the NATO structure, as the joint report of the Council Deputies and the Military Committee, issued on

December 13, 1950, had pointed out. The question that remained was which particular form this participation should take.

French Premier René Pleven proposed that German troops be incorporated in a European army, under the orders of a European government appointed by a European parliament, backed by a European High Court of Justice; an army financed by a common European defense budget, equipped with standardized arms, uniformly clothed, and uniformly trained. In other words, the political unity of Europe was to be realized first.

The European nations were ready for unity: this far-reaching plan for a European Defense Community was ratified by all European members of NATO—with the sole exception of France. On August 30, 1954, after four long years—which were lost for the building up of the German Federal Army—the French Chamber of Deputies turned down the Pleven Plan. France had torpedoed her own proposals.

It was a serious situation: the whole system of Western European security was suddenly suspended in mid-air. Speaking in the German Bundestag, Chancellor Konrad Adenauer said that he had seldom been as worried as when the plan for a European Defense Community broke down. And there was good reason for anxiety. The solidarity of Europe seemed to have suffered a setback, the consequences of the confusion were incalculable, and public opinion in the United States threatened to turn away from the Old World. Great hopes had been set on the increasing strength of Germany, without which Europe could not really be defended. If there were to be no German contribution after all, perhaps it might be better not to risk sacrificing American divisions uselessly, but to return to a policy of isolationism, or, at the utmost, to confine American efforts to a peripheral defense of the European continent.

It will always be to the great political credit of Sir Anthony Eden, then British Foreign Minister, that he found the saving solution. Britain had been cool toward the European Defense Community, because she was unwilling to yield control over her own armed forces to her allies and to bind her fate irrevocably to them. But now she recognized the magnitude of the danger which threatened her if Europe were to collapse.

Eden's plan was simple. The place of the abandoned European Defense Community was to be taken by a Western European Union, namely, the Brussels Treaty of March 17, 1948, but purged of its original barb against Germany, and extended by the inclusion of Germany and Italy. At the same time, the German Federal Republic would join NATO, and the Western European Union would be incorporated into NATO, as had been planned for the European Defense Community. Eden toured the capitals of Western Europe and won widespread support for his proposals. On September 28, 1954, a Nine-Power Conference met in London. In six days it had worked out the principles of the new plan, which was given its final form at a conference in Paris, in mid-October. With this, the dangerous vacuum was safely filled.

These Paris Treaties came into force on May 5, 1955, and on May 9, in Paris, the German Federal Republic was solemnly accepted into NATO as a member state. At that moment, Germany was no longer a defeated and occupied country. The occupation statute ceased to exist, and the German Federal Republic became a sovereign state. From then on, the presence of the allied forces in West Germany was based on a free agreement with the German Federal government, as in all other NATO countries. NATO troops undertook the defense of Germany while the army of the Federal Republic was in the process of formation. All the members of NATO formally proclaimed the reunification of Germany a goal of their official policy, and recognized the government of the German Federal Republic as the only representative of the whole German people, leaving the establishment of its national borders to a future peace treaty. In return, the German Federal Republic solemnly pledged not to seek reunification or any alteration of its present borders by force.

Great Britain, France, and the United States renewed their guarantees of the freedom of Berlin, and declared that they would regard any attack on Berlin as an attack upon themselves.

With the entry of Germany, NATO reached its current membership. Since then, NATO has concentrated its activities on internal development, the increase of its defensive strength, and the establishment of still closer political and economic unity.

The continuous Soviet offensives, all pursuing the same goals albeit with varying tactics, have contributed to the awareness, among all NATO members, that morally, politically, and militarily, they must stand or fall together. The strongest Soviet attacks were directed against the modernization of Europe's defense forces; but their objective was the most transparent: the Red Army was to have a monopoly of nuclear armaments in Europe, against which any defense relying solely on conventional weapons would be hopeless from the start. With bare-faced impudence, Soviet propaganda contended that atomic bombs in the hands of the Red Army were a guarantee of peace, whereas in the hands of the free peoples preventing the expansion of Bolshevism, nuclear arms were a moral outrage and increased the danger of war.

By this time it was beyond dispute that any attempt to defend Europe with the weapons of the Second World War would be hopeless. The North Atlantic Council therefore decided to re-equip the forces of the allies with atomic weapons. The preliminary steps were taken at the December meetings of the Foreign Ministers in 1954 and 1955; after the Hungarian tragedy, at a meeting in Bonn in May, 1957; and, finally, at the first meeting of heads of governments in Paris in December, 1957. This action had become all the more urgent since in the meantime disarmament proposals of the London Committee of the U.N., adopted by a large majority of the full Assembly on August 29, 1957, were torpedoed by the usual Soviet veto. The NATO powers had voted unanimously in favor of the proposals.

To distract attention from the heavy moral defeat they had suffered as a result of the Hungarian uprising, the Soviets intensified their attacks on NATO. The new offensive was launched on a flood of diplomatic notes and personal letters from Soviet Premier Bulganin, who put forward varying proposals, in the hope of sowing dissension among the NATO countries and persuading them to negotiate separately with the Soviet Union. This new offensive failed. The recipients of these various notes and communications not only submitted them for discussion within NATO, but also worked out their replies in concert.

However, it cannot be denied that the Soviets did make some progress. They have always pursued two main aims, and still do. The first aim is to secure *de jure* recognition for the illegal status quo established in the satellite countries. Whereas only a few years ago it was generally accepted that the right of self-determination, guaranteed in the peace treaties of 1947, must eventually be realized, the world is now expected to be tactful and no longer refer to such awkward matters.

The second aim is to disrupt the North Atlantic Treaty Organization itself. Khrushchev started the ball rolling with his Berlin ultimatum of November 27, 1958. That was a frontal attack on the presence of allied troops protecting Berlin, and an attack on the freedom of the city itself. By creating an artificial crisis atmosphere (following Hitler's example), Khrushchev hoped to demoralize public opinion in the West, and then to get his own way at the coming summit conference without making any material concessions. But the principle of joint consultation within the framework of NATO now proved as valuable as it had when the peace plan for Germany was under discussion, and again during the Geneva Conference.

However, the cooperation between the Western powers still leaves something to be desired. This circumstance was frankly recognized by the NATO parliamentarians at their fifth annual meeting in Washington in November, and by the North Atlantic Council at its session in Paris in December, 1959. Some of the NATO states have not complied with the minimum obligations to strengthen Western defense, as accepted by them in Document No. 70 of the Military Committee. Progress in standardization of arms, equipment, and supplies has not been altogether satisfactory. President de Gaulle has refused to allow nuclear warheads to be stored on French territory unless he is given a say in their use. Consequently, SACEUR has been compelled to withdraw all aircraft intended as carriers of nuclear weapons from French territory. The French Mediterranean fleet has not yet been put back under NATO command. On the other hand, France accuses the United States of withholding nuclear secrets from its allies, though those secrets have been well known to the Russians for some time.

Khrushchev, playing his cards skillfully in issuing the first Berlin ultimatum, received a long-coveted invitation to the United States, which greatly increased his prestige at home. He also obtained Western consent for a summit conference—but once it had convened in Paris (on May 14, 1960), he merely used it as a platform from which to launch rude attacks on President Eisenhower because of the U-2 incident.

When the ultimatum was repeated on June 4, 1961—this time presented to the new President, John F. Kennedy, in Vienna—Khrushchev had grown much bolder. He quickly followed his note with daring action. On August 13, he caused or permitted the city of Berlin to be cut in two by a barbed-wire wall, soon reinforced by steel and concrete, in open violation of the Four Power Agreements. Here, for the first time since NATO had come into existence, the Soviets succeeded in grabbing another piece of territory.

Two weeks later, defying not only the West but also the noncommitted nations whose representatives were about to meet at Belgrade, the Soviets unilaterally broke the nuclear test ban and resumed testing. Terror and intimidation increased when Khrushchev announced that he would explode a 55-60 megaton bomb on October 30.

The erection of the Berlin wall is not only a crime against humanity; it could have the most dangerous consequences. Khrushchev—already unduly encouraged by the failure of the Cuban invasion in April, 1961—might draw the wrong conclusions from the fact that the Berlin wall was met by Western protests but not by action. He might assume that further aggressive acts would not be resisted either and—discounting Western warnings—might overstep the limits. The new offensive opened by the withdrawal of the Soviet commander from Berlin on August 22, 1962, and the abandonment of his functions to a man from the Soviet-German Army, Major-General Helmut Poppe—in breach of all Four Power Agreements—is another such move to force the Western allies to recognize the Ulbricht regime and to push them out of Berlin. Here lies the greatest danger of war, and therefore it is more imperative than ever to convince Khrushchev of the determination of the West by firm and unequivocal actions.

Nothing is gained by the prospect that Khrushchev, at a time convenient to him, might start another offensive of smiles. This is merely routine in the Soviet war of nerves, with its calculated changes of frost and heat. Perhaps these changes of tone are meant to have a favorable effect on world public opinion; perhaps, by contrast, they render threats and pressures more effective when these are applied again.

Regardless of the phase in propaganda tactics, Soviet attempts to destroy the unity of the West will never be abandoned. If the men in the Kremlin ever found a member of NATO who, out of fear or supposed self-interest, would consider abandoning the Alliance, the Soviets would find no concession too great. Success would provide them with a lever that they would use ruthlessly in an attempt to lift the whole Western alliance off its hinges.

8

European Headquarters

General Lauris Norstad, Supreme Allied Commander Europe, is a citizen of a country which did not have compulsory military service in peacetime until 1940. Then, it was introduced by a majority of only one vote; today, it is accepted without question. When he retires on November 1, 1962, and is succeeded by General Lyman M. Lemnitzer, former U.S. Army Chief of Staff, he will have held that most responsible and difficult NATO position for six years.

Norstad makes a young and vigorous impression. He is, as his name suggests, of Norwegian-Swedish origin. The son of a Lutheran pastor, he was born in 1907 in Minnesota, and he grew up there. He is a professional soldier, a graduate of West Point, and he has served in the U.S. Air Force since 1930. During the Second World War, he was at first attached to the General Staff, but later he distinguished himself on various fronts as an operational commander. In August, 1944, he was appointed Chief of Staff to the Twentieth U.S. Air Force. It says something for his unusual abilities that by May, 1950, he was Deputy Chief of Staff to the U.S. Air Force. He was also appointed to represent his branch of the service in the National Security Council, the highest advisory body of the President. After another six years of service in Europe as Commander, first of the U.S. Air Force, and then of the combined NATO Air Force, on November 20, 1956, he succeeded General Gruenther as Supreme Allied Commander in Europe.

Thus, at the age of forty-nine, Norstad became the youngest SACEUR, just as he had once been the youngest Brigadier-General in the United States. A strong personality, complete mastery of his job (he has been called "the brains of the Air Force" by his comrades), and unquestionable moral courage were the factors which contributed to this rapid rise. For example, while he was still a young lieutenant colonel, he stubbornly maintained his own opinion on a politico-military question against a full general. He expected a reproof from his own Commander, General Arnold, then in charge of the U.S. Air Force; instead, in February, 1942, General Arnold called him into the General Staff. In 1951, Norstad had a vigorous dispute with General (later Marshal) Juin of France, who as Commander of the Allied Forces Central Europe, demanded control over the air forces in his area. But Norstad, with wider vision, was unwilling to see his aircraft hemmed in by national boundaries. The dispute was settled in 1953 by giving Juin his own tactical air fleet, while as Air Deputy for SHAPE, Norstad took charge of all the air forces in Europe.

Norstad did not find it difficult to step from the position of American general to that of international Commander. And that included command over the Germans, whom he had respected as a foe in wartime, and now welcomed as an ally. This spirit of comradeship beyond all frontiers has become a matter of course with the "integrated" officers of NATO. "I am wearing a British uniform, as you see," declared the Major who led us to General Norstad, "but as a NATO officer I am only one-fifteenth a soldier of the Queen. For the rest I am French, German, American, and so on."

Thus Norstad is not "just another American general in Paris." In fact, his nationality is unimportant—or, it is important only in the sense that it is right and proper that an officer of the United States, which bears the brunt of the burden, should have supreme command. Otherwise he could just as well be of some other nationality, like his deputy, Sir Hugh C. Stockwell, for example, who is British, or his former naval deputy, who was French. What he properly is now, is Supreme NATO Commander in Europe.

The flags of the fifteen nations displayed at the entrance to NATO headquarters at Marly all turn to the symbol which unites them—the dark-blue flag of NATO with the blue-silver star in the shape of a cross. Like a many-colored rainbow, they reflect the light of freedom which radiates from this star. None of the national flags has any precedence over any other, and their positions are changed daily.

NATO headquarters consists of twenty-three buildings, put up rapidly in the summer of 1951, on a vast wooded area where the kings of France once shot pheasants. On July 24, 1951, the site and the new buildings were formally handed over to General Eisenhower by the then President of the French Republic, Vincent Auriol.

The atmosphere at this headquarters, which controls a military front of almost 4,000 miles, stretching from the North Cape to the Caucasus, is simple and soldierly. There is no display, nothing but the essentials. According to a British officer, the most remarkable thing about the buildings of SHAPE is that the heat comes up through the floor and the rain in through the roof. All the buildings are connected by two main corridors, from which smaller corridors branch off to left and right. Every door bears a sign giving name, rank, and department. The general tone is comradely, almost "civilian," and there seems to be no jealousy. Even if an officer should have his eye on a particular promotion, the coveted superior position would rarely be open to his own nationality. A communications center with its own military lines, conference and demonstration rooms, and canteens—here is the vital command center for all the NATO troops in Europe, and the fleets and air forces as well. It is here that decisions for the strategic dispositions of the troops are made, their training supervised, plans worked out, annual staff conferences arranged, including the famous "Command Post Exercises," at which problems are analyzed and, if necessary, played through in indoor maneuvers.

You get an idea of what SHAPE means when you realize that in just one of its four major sub-commands, Allied Forces Central Europe, the general staffs of the two great armies which fought each other for centuries are now united, namely, the French and German armies. In addition, there are Belgian, Dutch, Luxemburg, and Canadian units, together with British and American divisions. The Supreme Commander, General Pierre Jacquot, is French; the Commander of the allied land forces, General Hans Speidel, is German; it is as though Joffre and Moltke had joined hands to defend a common heritage.

We were led into a great room which looked like a lecture hall in a large university, but at each desk there was a pair of earphones which you could switch over either to French or to English. General Cortlandt van Rensselaer Schuyler, Chief of the General Staff of SACEUR until October, 1959, was delivering a lecture to a group of international journalists—not all of them friends of NATO by any means. Patiently and clearly, he explained the fundamental principles of the defense of Europe. When he had finished, the questions started. The then Supreme Commander of AFCENT, General Valluy, and the Belgian Lieutenant General Cumont, had come in in the meantime.

"Why are there so few French forces in Central Europe?"

Schuyler turned to the Belgian Lieutenant General. "Would you care to answer that?"

"Certainly," Cumont replied. "Because most of France's divisions are in Algeria. But we hope that some day they will be stationed here." And he pointed on the wall map to an area to the west of the Iron Curtain.

Anywhere else one would have hesitated to make such a remark in the presence of a French general, but General Valluy merely nodded his agreement. Here at NATO headquarters he was not primarily a Frenchman but a NATO officer.

New groups of visitors were gathering outside the conference hall. Someone asked who they were. "I can't tell you offhand," was the reply. "I'll have to look it up in the program." They turned out to be a mixed bunch. Among others, there were wives of U.S. Air Force officers, members of a German Christian Democratic students' organization, Socialist youths from Antwerp, German civil law students, the Norwegian parliamentary defense committee, some employees of Mobiloil in France, members of a sports association from Duisburg, Italian scouts from Bari, American businessmen and professors, and, of course, parliamentarians, officials, statesmen, prelates, and publicists from almost every country under the sun.

The Chief of the General Staff of SHAPE, and sometimes even General Norstad himself, the high commanders and their staffs, the departmental chiefs—anyone in a position of authority—is at the disposal of these visiting groups. And not only to give lectures, but also to answer questions. "That," we were told, "is part of the democratic obligation of SHAPE to Western public opinion."

The total staff of SHAPE is about 1,000, including 350 officers from 13 of the 15 member states of NATO. Two are not represented —Portugal comes under SACLANT, not SACEUR, and Iceland has no army. The United Kingdom of Great Britain and Northern Ireland is also not under SACEUR.

SACEUR is responsible for the defense of the allies against external attack throughout the area of his command, which extends from the North Cape to North Africa and from the Atlantic to the eastern frontier of Turkey. In the event of war, all land-, sea-, and air-operations would be under his command. The individual allies undertake the defense of their own territories and coasts, though SACEUR has the right to carry out operations there, too, should he consider it necessary within the general defense framework.

Only in the event of war does SACEUR have full operational command. In peacetime he commands only those units which are directly assigned to NATO: the Seventh U.S. Army, the French First Army, the British Army of the Rhine, the German divisions so far available, certain units of the Benelux countries, and the Danish, Norwegian, Canadian, Italian, Greek, and Turkish forces. Norstad has control also over the air and naval forces assigned to his command.

In peacetime SACEUR is responsible for the proper organization, equipment, and training of all the units assigned to NATO, or earmarked for NATO service. He drafts all strategic plans and submits proposals concerning matters that come within his purview to the Standing Group.

SACEUR himself receives his instructions from the Standing Group in Washington, but he also has direct contact with the allied General Staffs and, in certain circumstances, with the Defense Ministers and Premiers of the allied governments. Each allied government, with the exception of Iceland, has a liaison officer with SHAPE, known as the National Military Representative (NMR).

SHAPE has only one operational department, and that is for the strategic air forces, which are controlled by SACEUR without any intermediate command.

Norstad has three deputies, one for each arm of the services. Up to September 18, 1959, his military deputy was Field Marshal Viscount Montgomery of Alamein; today it is General Sir Hugh C. Stockwell. At the same time he is Deputy SACEUR. Naval questions are the province of Vice Deputy Rear Admiral Alexander of Great Britain, while air questions are dealt with by General Samuel E. Anderson of the U.S. Air Force.

Norstad's Chief of Staff also has a number of deputies, but they are responsible for various specialized questions which cut across the limits of the various arms. The staff of SACEUR is organized along American lines. There are nine main departments: planning and questions of principle; atomic warfare; counter-intelligence; organization and training; air defense; military projects and costs study; logistics; budget and finances; personnel questions and the office organization of SHAPE.

General Schuyler turned out to be a tall, civilian-looking man of engaging politeness, the descendant of an old Dutch family. "I'm really a New Amsterdamer," he said lightly, meaning that his ancestors came to America when New York was still called New Amsterdam.

"If we were to weaken our shield in Europe, we should be encouraging the Soviets to attack. Korea gave us ample warning of that —the Communists got the idea that they could overrun the country without any serious resistance. If the Americans had left even a token division behind in South Korea, that would in all probability have been enough, and there would never have been a Korean war at all. The situation in Europe today is much the same. If the Soviets should ever doubt that we are ready to repulse any attack by every means in our power, then disaster would be upon us."

Nothing could be as dangerous as a revival of the notorious slogan, "*Mourir pour Danzig?*" The Communists launched it in 1939 to help their ally Hitler. They hoped it would help to keep the Western Allies from honoring their solemn pledge to come to the aid of an attacked Poland. Today, of course, the appropriate slogan would be "Who wants to die for Berlin!"

"The so-called disengagement policy puts the cart before the horse," Schuyler went on. "International tension is not the result of increased armament; increased armament is the inevitable result of international tension. We began to rearm only after the Soviets had openly threatened us and we had to restore the balance. War will break out only if the Soviet Union wants it. Therefore the only way to ensure world peace is to make it quite clear to the Soviet leaders by hard facts that their plan for world conquest cannot be successfully carried out.

"We are perfectly confident that the Soviets do not yet have the military strength to destroy at one blow our strategic air forces and missiles, which are dispersed all over the world. Even if the Soviets were to launch an unexpected attack, we should still have sufficient strength to strike back with might. And we know that the Soviet leaders know it. That is the basis of world peace. Korea and Hungary are sufficient evidence that the men in the Kremlin will never hesitate to use force when it suits their purpose, no matter what treaties they may have to break in the process, provided they see a real chance of extending the Communist empire."

However, the military power of the Soviet Union is growing, and we do not know what the situation may be like in the future. For this reason, too, it is essential for NATO to build and extend its rocket bases. These bases must join SAC and British Bomber Command in maintaining an efficient deterrent in case the Soviet Union should become strong enough to put all existing NATO airfields out of action with one blow.

A Soviet attack almost inevitably proceeds as a pincer movement —a military attack from without, and a political movement from within designed to undermine the defense. We asked whether, for example, NATO would go to the assistance of a member state, say the German Federal Republic, if the Communists started their offensive with a spurious internal uprising?

"NATO takes a very cautious and respectful attitude toward the sovereignty of its members," said Schuyler. "It would intervene only if the Federal Republic formally requested it to."

General Schuyler is particularly interested in the education of youth in the international spirit of NATO. "NATO and its aims and objects should be a regular subject in all schools," he stated. When General Eisenhower was building up his staff, he regarded it as one of his chief tasks to encourage cooperation and understanding among his officers. "Let this spirit take precedence over everything else at headquarters," he declared. This, said General Schuyler, had been done, and wherever you went you would find evidence of it. But now all schools in all allied countries should work systematically to create the same spirit. If they neglected this task they would be lagging behind the times. The proper attitude had been developed in the schools run at St. Germain by SHAPE for the children of its officers and staff. The trouble in Cyprus had been a real test, but the friendship between the Greek and Turkish students had survived. And with a smile the General added, "You've no idea what that spirit can do. Why, here in the playground, you can see English children playing baseball, and American children playing cricket."

Colonel Richard Stilwell was a G3 officer; that means he was attached to the Planning and Operations Department of SHAPE. He spoke quietly and thoughtfully, and one could feel that in answering our questions he was trying to get to the bottom of each problem.

With a population of 326 million, the Soviet bloc keeps 200 divisions on a war footing. There are 135 Soviet divisions (plus 20 kept as cadres), and 65 satellite divisions. The European NATO countries, with a total population of, after all, 265 million, have just been able to scrape together 50 active divisions. "Isn't that an absurd discrepancy?" we asked. "And, what's more, isn't it militarily dangerous?"

"We certainly mustn't underrate the enemy," Colonel Stilwell began, "but, on the other hand, we mustn't fall into the opposite error and over-estimate his strength. If you count all troops, including reserves, in the United States, Great Britain, France, and the other NATO countries, you will find that the real totals aren't perhaps so far apart as you might think at first glance. However, the fact does remain that the Soviets have many more divisions on a war footing than the West."

The fighting value of such divisions also varies. Their armaments will play a decisive role, particularly their nuclear weapons. "Every future war, whether nuclear weapons are actually used or not, will be a nuclear war in the sense that all the belligerent powers will have to take the grim threat of nuclear weapons into consideration in their strategy and tactics, disposing their troops with that in mind, and organizing their countries accordingly. Since any heavy concentration of military forces may be the factor causing a conventional war to develop suddenly into a nuclear one, the Soviets are compelled to reconsider the value of large masses of troops, seeing that they offer such a tempting target for nuclear weapons."

The Colonel then went on to say that in his view, it seemed unlikely that the Soviet Union would be in a position to keep up the tremendous efforts necessary to hold several million men under arms; maintain a great force of bombers, supported by thousands of fighters and many all-purpose planes; carry out a big missile program; produce and store nuclear weapons; build and maintain a big submarine fleet, and so on, simultaneously.

Finally, there was the question of how many divisions the Soviets required to maintain order within their own frontiers. At one time, part of the forces needed for internal security were provided by the Soviet Ministry of the Interior (MVD), which had not only a police force at its disposal but also normal troop units, its own information and communications network, its own planes, its own labor camps, and even whole administrative areas under its own command. It was a sort of state within a state, and there was a certain amount of antagonism and friction between its forces and those of the Red Army, just as there had been in Hitler's Third Reich between the Brown Shirts and the SS on the one hand and the Wehrmacht on the other. The MVD was dissolved in January, 1960, and its administrative functions were handed over to the union republics, but of course the department which really mattered, the Commissariat for State Security (KGB), remained. The question is, however, whether in an emergency these forces will not have to be supplemented by army divisions.

"But to come back to the problem of military strength," the Colonel continued, "the number of divisions is not alone decisive. Their suitable deployment is also important. In other words, a point which interests me just as much as how many there are, is where these Soviet divisions are positioned. Should war break out, the divisions in the hinterland can be destroyed by our nuclear weapons, but what really gives us a headache is the twenty Soviet divisions which are already in Central Germany. They are of high quality, excellently equipped—with both nuclear and rocket weapons—mechanized, well led, and strategically well deployed. And they are right there, at our doorstep. As to the divisions in Russia itself, their mobilization would afford us a timely warning."

The important point, then, would be to decide how to react to the warning, and what magnitude our counter-move should have. Once the threat is there, recognized and analyzed by our military experts, the NATO Council must act. Our main objective would naturally be to convince the Soviet Union that the advantages of their planned attack bore no relationship to the vast sacrifices a large-scale war would involve, a war which the Soviets might themselves not desire.

In Central Europe, the West requires at least thirty divisions to hold the Soviet troops immediately opposite, in the Soviet-occupied zone of Germany, in check. In any case, the enemy would have the advantage of the first move, the offensive initiative, and perhaps the element of surprise.

"We know that the Soviets would need about ten days to increase the number of divisions available in the zone from twenty to thirty; while to increase them to sixty they would need about thirty days. This means that NATO must be able to increase its twenty divisions to thirty within ten days, and within thirty days to forty. If we are manifestly able to do that, then the other side will be forced to recognize that the risk of an attack is too great, and that they can no longer hope to seize even a limited objective in one military coup. They will be forced to realize that any attack they launch, whether they plan it as a limited one or not, will involve the danger of unleashing an all-out war."

For the first time in history, the military power at the disposal of nations is so great that the forces used to launch a hostile attack can be practically wiped from the face of the earth. This means that today we can ban aggressive warfare as an instrument of policy, not by a moral obligation not to indulge in it, but by real power. For this reason it is the soldiers above all who insist that political disputes must not be settled by military means. That is the fundamental change. Today the test of the good soldier is whether he is in a position to prevent war.

"The fighting men will be the first to face the horrors of nuclear warfare," Colonel Stilwell concluded. "Let us hope to God that it never comes to that. But if it ever should, then it will be the fighting men who will have to use the nuclear weapons; so, whether they like it or not, they have to consider the consequences carefully, because it is they who are expected to be prepared and, if need be, determined to use them. They must not allow themselves to be paralyzed in advance. On the contrary, it is part of their assignment in this new atomic age to make it possible for their peoples to have a new feeling of confidence and security. Nuclear weapons represent the protective wall behind which all of us will have an opportunity of mobilizing all moral, economic, and political resources in order to secure a peaceful solution of the problems which face the world."

In September, 1959, Khrushchev called upon the United States to agree to the complete abolition of all arms, and in a later speech to the Supreme Soviet, he declared that the Soviet Union had already demobilized over 2 million men in recent years and that it now proposed to demobilize a further 1.2 million. This statement may well be in accordance with the facts: the current Soviet Seven-Year Plan (it runs until 1965) requires enormous quantities of labor power; and that, together with the "lean years" for manpower caused by the war, may compel the Soviet leaders to reduce the number of men in their armed forces. In 1949, the number of men between the ages of 18 and 24 in the Soviet Union was 42.2 million; in 1960, it was only 28.1 million. In 1960, the Soviet economic system would have needed 4 million men born in 1949, but only 2 million were available. Only in 1965 will there again be a favorable balance between births and manpower requirements. Thus the new reduction of military personnel about which Khrushchev talked as being planned "within the next year or so" is the result of urgent necessity if Soviet heavy industry, on which the chief stress is still laid, and in particular the armament industry, is to be kept supplied with manpower.

According to Khrushchev's own statement, this reduction in personnel will make no difference to the firepower of the Red Army. Quite apart from the strategic nuclear weapons, including the H-bomb, tactical nuclear equipment has greatly increased the firepower of the Soviet divisions. Furthermore, as Khrushchev made clear, "demobilization" does not mean the same in the Soviet Union as it does in the West: both demobilized officers and men are to be kept in military training while engaged in their civilian occupations.

Thus the reduction of the military forces of the Soviet Union, about which Khrushchev talks, would not alter the fact that if it is to maintain some sort of balance, the West must strengthen its own forces, because the number of divisions on a war footing at the disposal of the Soviets will always be very much greater than those at the disposal of NATO.

General Norstad's new Chief of Staff, Lieutenant-General James Edward Moore, is a West Pointer, born in 1902 in Massachusetts. Although he has spent a great deal of his adult life on active service —he took part in the war in Europe, as Chief of Staff of the Ninth U.S. Army, from the time of the Normandy landings—one gets the impression that he looks back with particular pleasure on the years from 1953 to 1955, when he was Commandant of the Army War College in Pennsylvania; he is a man who is able to examine even the most hotly-disputed military and political problems of the day with scholarly objectivity.

Before he came to SHAPE in October, 1959, Moore was Deputy Army Chief of Staff in the Pentagon. He is well aware that the conflict between the Soviet Union and the West is a permanent state of affairs, for which there is no simple solution, and which has to be seen through with patience and determination.

In his view, the shield forces of NATO should be strengthened. "They must be kept strong enough to compel the Soviet Union to take any decision to attack on the higher scale of total war." The security of the United States itself depends on keeping U.S. troops in Europe, and the idea of "Fortress America" is altogether outmoded.

"But mightn't the Red Army, encouraged by the preponderance of its divisions in Central Europe, be tempted to start a limited war?" we asked.

"Central Europe is such a critical area for NATO that it is difficult to imagine a limited war there," the General replied. "That is something we must hammer into the heads of the Russians. We must be ready to take even bigger risks, not smaller ones, if we are to force the Soviet Union to keep the peace." And he added emphatically: "The Soviet Union will not be prepared to risk everything if its leaders are convinced that we would immediately be prepared to throw all our resources into battle."

9

The Nuclear Defense
of the West

Just so long as the Western powers had a monopoly of the atom bomb, it was a guarantee against the outbreak of a world war. The first serious threat to world peace arose when the Soviet Union—thanks in part to treason committed from ideological motives—came into possession of the secret of nuclear fission.

Why does NATO need nuclear weapons at all? We asked this question again and again. Brigadier-General Count Kielmansegg, former German military representative at SHAPE, replied, "The answer is really quite simple. First of all, because nuclear weapons do exist. Not to have them would be the first step to surrender. Second, the enemy has them. Third, NATO is just not in a position to raise sufficient troops to hold up a Soviet drive by conventional means. NATO therefore must seek to redress the balance by obtaining stronger firepower."

General Cortland van Rensselaer Schuyler, who was Chief of Staff to SACEUR until October, 1959, replied, "If we wanted to try to defend Europe against a large-scale Soviet attack without using atomic weapons, we would have to have three or four times as many troops as we have at present. That would have an adverse effect on living standards, and perhaps on the whole free economy of the West. Even if we accepted this, we should still be dependent on the good faith of the Soviets not to use nuclear weapons. Frankly, their behavior during the past ten years does not inspire us with much confidence in that respect."

At the Department for Planning and Organization at SHAPE, we were told: "Should the Soviets decide to start hostilities, we have no intention of trying to match them man for man and gun for gun. We are determined to beat off any attack with the full force of nuclear weapons. And we are confident that with our available divisions, which are armed with conventional and with tactical atomic weapons, we should be able to hold an enemy drive back long enough to allow the strategic sword forces to launch their counter-blow."

The sword, the nuclear deterrent, consists primarily of Strategic Air Command (SAC), with its eighty-two bases in the United States and in many other countries; British Bomber Command; the U.S. Sixth Fleet in the Mediterranean; and all the firing bases of nuclear missiles, including Polaris-armed submarines. This deterrent is not confined to the sphere of NATO, but is spread all around the world —if for no other reason than that both the United States and Great Britain have world-wide commitments. Thus SAC is intended not only for Europe, but also for the Far East; and, in fact, for use against any threat anywhere in the world.

SAC and British Bomber Command are under respective national control; but although they are not under NATO command, they work very closely with it. As has already been mentioned, there is a liaison center in Paris for SAC and SACEUR, the department known as SAC Zebra, and it is here that all plans and objectives are discussed at length and settled by agreement. Moreover, in the event of a Soviet attack, both the U.S. and Great Britain would immediately be involved, and they would unquestionably make use of their strategic weapons.

Every new weapon in history has produced a revolution in strategic thought and a reorganization of military forces. When firearms were introduced, they meant the end of the knight in armor; and with the invention of the machine gun, the nineteenth-century war of movement became bogged down in the trench warfare of the First World War. But the most powerful of all trenches, the Maginot Line, proved useless when the war of movement was revived with the development of the airplane and the tank. In the same way, the pattern of nuclear warfare would be fundamentally different from all preceding forms of warfare.

The rethinking required by the development of nuclear energy was so radical that it was not easy to carry out. When NATO was first formed in 1949, the atom bomb already existed, but when faced with the task of working out a strategic plan for the defense of Europe, the military were unable to rid themselves of their traditional ideas. The defense plan which they laid before the Paris session of the North Atlantic Council in December, 1950, was still based on all the classic principles of military strategy. The dominating idea was that of a long war and the defeat of the enemy by attrition. But on the basis of such calculations, and in view of the enormous conventional forces maintained by the Soviets, NATO would have needed a minimum of 90 or 100 divisions in Europe, not to mention correspondingly strong air and naval forces.

In the words of Brigadier-General Robert C. Richardson, during a discussion in the Pentagon, "We left Paris perfectly convinced in our own minds that it was out of the question for us to find the forces necessary to put that plan into effect."

Today, Richardson is attached to the U.S. Air Department for long-term planning. Earlier, he occupied a somewhat similar position with SHAPE, and before that he was with the Standing Group in Washington. During the Second World War, he commanded a tactical air group. Since the war, his work has been connected with strategic planning, first with the U.S. Air Force, and then for two years with the Joint General Staff. He has always taken an active part in the development of the North Atlantic defense community.

"If the general staff planners had really been correct in their estimates of their needs, and if it had proved impossible to find any other solution, then any attempt to defend Europe would indeed have seemed hopeless." In that case NATO would probably have fallen to pieces, and the United States would have had no alternative but to pull out of Europe entirely.

If anyone wonders why the Red Army did not attack in those confused days, the only explanation is the one already given, that the Soviet leaders, no matter how much they may have been tempted to overrun Europe, respected the nuclear strength of the United States.

A staff under the leadership of General Matthew B. Ridgway was given the job of rethinking the defense plan, and told to take into consideration the use of atomic weapons and the fact that NATO did not stand alone in the defense of the West. The result was remarkable: the new plan required even more forces for its execution than the previous one. Of course everyone was convinced that there must be a mistake somewhere, only no one could say just where.

"So we went back, so to speak, to the drawing board—'we' being a special committee of military experts, two Americans, two Frenchmen, and an Englishman. We approached the problem from an entirely different angle. We made use of an electronic brain and carried out a sort of large-scale maneuver with the aid of the computer, and we found out where the error was." It was this: No proper attention had been paid to the radical change which must take place in strategy, the structure of battle forces, and tactical operations as a result of three new factors—nuclear weapons, the extended range of aircraft (and subsequently of missiles), and the enormously increased costs of modern armaments.

All these factors developed after the Second World War; therefore no one has had any practical experience of what they will mean in action, and we are dependent entirely on theoretical considerations. But these are reliable enough to convince us that the new factors must fundamentally change the profile of war. The classic procedure in war was always that the relatively small standing forces went into action first, then came the mobilization of reserves, the organization of war production, and the harnessing of the national economies for war purposes. In other words, the war came into operation slowly, grew fiercer gradually, and often took years to reach its culmination point.

But because of the new factors, another world war would be very different. Strategic air power, rockets, and nuclear weapons might be used at once, and the great blow would probably be delivered right at the start, within the first few days, or perhaps hours. That blow would be directed primarily against the strategic nuclear and long-range weapons of the enemy and their bases, and the attack against his other forces would follow. The war might well be decided by these swift blows, if one side were successful in destroying the other's strategic arsenal while itself retaining sufficient strength to follow up its success. This does not mean that the war would thereby come to an end, but that the victor would no longer be in doubt.

The NATO countries are resolved, for ethical reasons, never to strike the first blow; it follows that, after a Soviet nuclear attack, they would need at least sufficient strategic weapons still intact to prevent a second blow. Let us assume that after the first Soviet attack, forty per cent of Western strength still remained intact; then this forty per cent must mean sufficient aircraft, missiles, and nuclear weapons to put the Soviet Union out of action strategically. To be on the safe side, there must also be enough reserves to repeat the blow several times, if necessary. For NATO's deterrent purpose, the Kremlin must be kept well aware of this ability, because if Khrushchev, or anyone else who came to power in the Soviet Union, ever persuaded himself that a nuclear Pearl Harbor would leave the West with insufficient forces to launch an effective and devastating counter-blow, then war would be certain—more likely sooner than later.

Incidentally, the nuclear counter-blow of the Western powers would not be directed against the enemy's cities. Its primary objective would be to destroy his nuclear and long-range weapons; once that had been achieved, it would not be necessary to destroy his industry and his people. The Soviet government would be forced to surrender. Should it obstinately and senselessly refuse to do so, then the mere threat of further nuclear action might well be enough to turn powerful internal forces against the regime.

In the Second World War, the destruction of the enemy's arms, troops, and war potential still posed a problem, due to the restricted effectiveness of existing weapons and the correspondingly high cost of mass attack. In a nuclear war, the capacities for destruction would be practically unlimited. In addition, the range of the carriers has increased greatly. During the Second World War, a spectacular bombing and artillery effort was necessary before any particular objective could be destroyed, and even then the chances of failure were greater than the chances of success. Today, the chances of a direct hit and total destruction are much greater than the probability of failure. This means that in modern war, firepower becomes the preponderant factor, while tactical maneuvering takes a back seat. The object will be to destroy a chosen target, not to take it. Artillery, including the bomber, the rocket, and the missile, becomes the new queen of the battlefield. The standard of comparison for strategic mass attack is henceforth firepower and not the number of men or their armaments. Just as in the last war, air superiority was necessary to hold a position or to attack, today nuclear superiority is a necessity.

"One of the consequences of this new kind of warfare," Richardson pointed out, "is that military reserves which are not available on the very first day of the conflict will have no influence on the decision. There will simply be no time to mobilize troops, once the war has started, let alone to reorganize industry and turn it from peace to war production. The only telling factors will be the fully mobilized forces available in a strategic position on the day war breaks out."

However, military reserves would still be needed for other tasks. The first and greatest of these would be to check disasters at home and get the country going again after a nuclear attack. Sufficient forces would also be needed to exploit the so-called shock period of the enemy. Otherwise, it might happen that even after he had agreed to capitulate, he might recover sufficiently to resume the war after all. One must therefore be in a position to occupy at least the strategic points in enemy territory at once, and have sufficient troops to enforce the conditions of peace.

"Leaving the question of a new world war for the moment, General Richardson, what in your opinion would be the effect of the new weapons on a limited war?"

"First of all, the concept of a limited war is a relative one. For example, the war in Korea was a limited one for us, but a total war for the Korean people, a war for their very existence. But let us agree to call a limited war one in which the two big nuclear powers are not engaged and do not use their strategic weapons. That sort of limited war has taken place on a good many occasions since 1945. Such wars are always possible when neither of the big powers has any really vital interest involved. We must certainly have sufficient conventional forces at our disposal to repulse any such Soviet or Soviet-inspired attack. Otherwise, however, in the world-wide area around the Soviet Union where the free world is determined to fight in its defense, our capacity to wage a general war is the best guarantee of peace. Our experience with NATO has already shown us that we just can't afford to keep enough conventional forces everywhere to repulse a mass Soviet attack, for the Soviet Union has the advantage in any conventional land war. But strategically we are in a position to prevent limited wars, too. Should the Soviets begin such a war, our nuclear counter-blow would inevitably follow, and with this, they would have lost their greatest advantage; we, not they, would have delivered the first nuclear punch."

But, of course, the Brigadier-General pointed out, it was imperative that the Soviet leaders be quite convinced of our determination to strike back. Should we ever give them grounds for the suspicion— no matter how ill-based—that the West would not summon up sufficient will-power to react with a nuclear counter-blow, that would be an invitation to wage limited war—which would very quickly develop into general war.

It must be added that in all this, Europe occupies a special position. It is certainly a "vital area" for NATO, and therefore under the direct protection of the great deterrent. Still, large conventional forces are also necessary here, because the enemy has already penetrated deeply into Europe, many hundreds of miles beyond his own frontiers. In this area, the West would be unable to use its nuclear weapons, because if it did, it would strike both friend and foe. Therefore NATO must be strong enough to hold back a Soviet attack with conventional forces supported by tactical nuclear weapons. If NATO were not sufficiently strong, a Soviet attack might overrun Europe, hold the peoples as hostages, live on the land, and force its industrial potential into the service of the Soviet war machine. In that case, even if the Soviet Union itself were largely devastated, the Soviet forces could be driven out only with very much greater losses and at a far higher cost than would have to be paid today to have an effective defense ready from the beginning.

There is another problem. The April, 1950, Medium-Term Defense Plan for Europe called for between 90 and 100 divisions, but later, as a result of nuclear rearmament, the Military Committee reduced this number to 30.

"In the meantime, the Soviets have equipped the Red Army with nuclear weapons, too," we pointed out to Count Kielmansegg, at SHAPE. "Does that mean that NATO must now go back to the original figure of 100 divisions for an effective defense of Europe?"

"Such a conclusion looks logical at first glance," the Count said, "but in fact it wouldn't be accurate. With a conventional weapon, you can always state clearly whether it favors the defender or the attacker; this is not the case with nuclear arms. They can do one thing or the other, according to how they are used. As a strategic long-range weapon, they naturally increase the strength of the attack, because any defense against them is still very much in the development stage. But as tactical weapons, they unquestionably favor the defense, because the defenders are, to put it simply, dug in and thus protected, whereas the attackers must come out of their foxholes and concentrate before they can attack. In doing so, they present themselves as a target."

There is another consideration. It is clearly recognized that thirty divisions, even if armed with tactical atomic weapons, could not successfully wage a long struggle against the Soviet mass armies. However, their job is merely to hold up the enemy long enough for the great counter-blow to take effect and make it impossible for him to continue waging any systematic war at all.

If, however, a long war is envisaged, in which both sides would use nuclear weapons, then thirty divisions would not be enough, and NATO would have to fall back on the larger number provided for in its earlier plans.

If the Soviet aggressor should use tactical atomic weapons, this would undoubtedly lead to war on a total scale, because their use would be a clear indication that the Soviets wanted war. And in that case they would not use tactical atomic bombs against Kassel, Hof, or Helmstedt without simultaneously doing their best to destroy the strategic sword of NATO in Europe, in America, and on all the bases around the Soviet Union before that sword could strike back. In other words, the Soviets would have to launch an all-out surprise attack which—after the historic example of 1941—is called a "global Pearl Harbor."

This is a danger which the leaders of the free world must constantly bear in mind. Every effort is made to protect the West against anything of the kind. In fact, one of the main aims of Western rearmament is to make it impossible for any such surprise attack to succeed. This is why, for example, the number of strategic airfields has been increased, and why they are dispersed all over the world. In April, 1953, NATO had hardly a score of such airfields available; today there are over 150. This is also the reason for the accelerated development of missiles and the building of bases for them. The armed forces of NATO are equipped to be as mobile as possible. A high degree of readiness is maintained, so that the NATO air forces and SAC can get their planes off the ground and strike back in record time. Aircraft carriers are used as floating strategic bases, and nuclear submarines equipped with Polaris missiles are built to be mobile carriers easily hidden under the sea. Finally, there is the Early Warning System with its world-wide chain of radar stations.

"If NATO is attacked," declared General Gruenther, Norstad's predecessor at SHAPE, at the time of the Suez crisis, "then, as surely as night follows day, the Soviet Union will be destroyed." What caused him to be so confident about this? The effect of the great nuclear counter-blow depends on three factors. The first, and the one almost exclusively discussed, is the number of nuclear weapons available. In this respect we must distinguish between stockpiling, the ever-growing number available, and productive capacity. The number ready for use at the outbreak of war will determine the weight of the first blow. Here the West still holds a certain advantage, and it will continue to do so for some time. With regard to productive capacity, however, parity has already been attained, or will be attained in the near future, by the Soviets.

The second factor is quite different. It doesn't matter how many nuclear weapons a country possesses, unless it also has the means to carry them to their targets. There must be an adequate number of aircraft and missiles to ensure delivery. Intermediate-range ballistic missiles (IRBM), are already fully operational, whereas the long-range Intercontinental Ballistic Missiles (ICBM) are still in their infancy. Here the Soviets enjoy an advantage at the moment. However, the Atlas, an ICBM developed in the United States, is already operational with the Titan and the Saturn coming up fast.

In the long run, parity in nuclear weapons and the means for their delivery is probably unavoidable. However, the situation is different with regard to the third, and perhaps most important, factor, which is geographical. Geography, and incidentally, the weather, are on the side of the West.

Let us first discuss the chances of a Soviet attack—and it must not be forgotten that the Soviets will have the advantage of the first move. They are in a position to choose the time, the place, and the strength to be put behind the first blow. In short, they have the advantage of surprise. Nevertheless, this advantage is a limited one, and, paradoxically, it is less important in the atomic age than it ever was before. First of all there is the Early Warning System, the chain of radar stations which stretches from the U.S. and Canada over the Arctic, Iceland, and Norway, and from there down to Lübeck and across Europe to the Caucasus, through Asia and across the Pacific back to the United States, i.e., all around the Soviet bloc. The Canadian-American sector of this system functions almost perfectly already, while in Europe, too, a centralized system beyond the national competences is now rapidly being established. General Norstad already has authority to coordinate, and that is an important step on the way.

With his very first blow, an attacker must do his utmost to make it impossible for NATO to reply, i.e., to deliver the counter-blow. In other words, the Soviets must destroy all the strategic bases of the West in one fell swoop. But a glance at a global map as seen from the North Pole will show that, in this regard, the Soviets are faced with an almost insoluble problem. Even if they had sufficient planes and missiles to deliver such a vast number of simultaneous blows, the attack would always trigger off the automatic Early Warning System in time to allow the West to deliver its counter-blow.

Supposing, first, that the attacking Soviets should plan to arrive at all the strategic bases in America and Europe at the same time; in that case, they would have to fly over the Arctic Ocean radar network many hours earlier than over the one which reaches from the North Cape to Turkey. This would mean that, although the strategic forces on the American continent would get a relatively short warning, those in Europe and Africa would get a correspondingly longer one, and have ample time to get into the air to deliver the counter-blow.

If, on the other hand, the Soviets were to seek to overcome this difficulty by timing their arrivals at the various warning systems simultaneously, in order not to trigger off any one prematurely, they would run into the opposite difficulty. They might catch the greater part of the strategic air forces in Europe by surprise, but those on the American continent would have ample time to get into the air. "In both cases," pointed out Count Kielmansegg, "the result would be equally unsatisfactory for the Soviets. And only these two alternatives exist."

For the West, the situation is different. Soviet geography would permit the Western powers to launch an ideal attack. Their forces could simultaneously cross all the Russian radar screens and still be, shortly thereafter, over-all strategic objectives at the same time. That is the important difference, and it represents very definite advantages to the West. As General Norstad himself has pointed out, there is nothing the Russians can do about it, neither by increasing the number of their nuclear weapons nor by changing their character and their carriers. And that would remain true even if they were in a position to concentrate three times the nuclear strength of NATO.

The Soviets know this, of course, and as they control neither the Atlantic nor the Pacific, and are not in a position to shift the continents, they seek to change the relations of power within them: Korea, Indo-China, the Near East, Africa, Cuba, and the German Federal Republic. They are doing their best to break up the ring of Western bases, and at the same time to disrupt NATO. Should they ever succeed in subverting NATO, then the steel ring which prevents them from conquering the world and subjecting it to Bolshevism would also be broken.

NATO would already be disrupted, however, if Soviet propaganda were to deceive a sufficient number of well-meaning people in Central Europe into opposing nuclear armaments. If NATO were compelled to abandon nuclear defense in Central Europe, then the U.S., British, and other allied armies would have to withdraw from the German Federal Republic and take their tactical air forces with them. At the same time, the German Federal Army would be reduced to the level of a police force and rendered useless for the defense of Germany against a Red Army equipped with modern weapons.

A completely new and revolutionary strategic factor arises with the development of the ICBM. Within an hour or less, these weapons can reach the interior of Russia from American territory, and the United States from Russian bases; and while they do not altogether abolish the geographical advantage of the West, they reduce it greatly by shortening the warning period. In a few years, each side will have a sufficient number of ICBMs, but for the moment the Soviets may still enjoy a slight lead. The United States is working to counteract this lead by keeping SAC in an even greater state of readiness.

Because of this new weapon, NATO has to rethink the whole conception of Western defense. The West, in particular the U.S. and Canada, has become more vulnerable; the situation has not changed greatly for Europe and the Soviets, which were vulnerable before. A sort of nuclear stalemate has developed, a situation in which the two sides are more or less evenly balanced in strength. Even this will not make nuclear warfare impossible, but it certainly makes it less likely. If the two big powers force a stalemate by their mutual nuclear threat, it is quite possible that the danger of limited wars with conventional arms or, at the utmost, with tactical nuclear weapons, will increase again. In these circumstances, the NATO shield assumes even greater importance. This is the significance of NATO's "Minimum Forces Requirements," which prescribes the minimum of strength NATO must maintain in Europe in order to be able to beat off a Soviet attack or reject a Soviet ultimatum.

"What will be the deployment of forces and the method of fighting when, in Europe at least, any military operations will be overshadowed from the start by the threat of atomic weapons?" we asked at the Planning Department of SHAPE.

"We have every reason to believe that the Red Army is also reorganizing and rethinking its tactics with the danger of nuclear weapons in mind," we were told. "The Soviets will certainly try to keep their forces as widely dispersed as possible in order to present the smallest possible target to nuclear attack. Of course there's a limit to it. A certain concentration of forces is necessary to break through an enemy position. That is a risk which both sides must take, if they are to have any hope of military success."

What military tactics would really be like in the event of a clash of arms in our day is anybody's guess. It seems likely that the Soviets would try to infiltrate on a broad front. This is a tactic with which they are familiar and in which they have a good deal of skill. They would probably engage our advanced troops and seek to envelop them, infiltrating into our lines so that their troops would offer no target to our atomic cannon. In this way they would hope to paralyze our tactical atomic weapons.

"The lesson of all this for us is that we must not reduce our forces. Even in future warfare, large numbers of men will be required. Each side will try to force the other to concentrate; and this can be done only by resisting the enemy's advance and exploiting any natural features of the terrain. Only when we have forced him to concentrate shall we be able to bombard him atomically."

In 1961 and 1962, several large-scale maneuvers were oriented to these new problems of tactical atomic warfare, such as an attempted enemy armored break-through on a broad front after nuclear preparation. Steel plate offers a certain protection against blast and the intense heat of atomic explosions; and even against fall-out—including the very penetrating but short-lived gamma rays. Of course tanks are not immune to near hits, but the greater their speed and firepower, the farther they can spread out. Tanks and armored vehicles are generally, therefore, among the weapons which can still be used offensively in conditions of tactical atomic warfare. The Soviet military leaders have good reason for attaching such importance to the development of their tank arm, and in particular the heavier types, T-54 and JS-3.

These maneuvers also demonstrated that in any future war, mobility would be of great importance. The NATO troops are motorized; that is to say, highly mobile on roads; and to a large extent they are also mechanized—equipped for cross-country advance by vehicles fitted with caterpillar treads. Trench warfare of the First World War will not come back, though the spade will still be a useful implement in the hands of the infantryman, because the best way for him to protect himself against atomic explosions will be to dig himself in.

Many experts, including Sir John Slessor, a Marshal of the Royal Air Force, have unanimously concluded that the best answer to the mobile power of an armored enemy is a local militia equipped with powerful anti-tank weapons, perhaps even of an atomic nature. As such a local militia would be scattered all over the country, it could quickly oppose an enemy, and, in view of the highly effective anti-tank weapons now available, probably with success. This might force him to concentrate, and in any nuclear war that would be an essential tactical aim.

There is, of course, a danger in the insistence of NATO that the first—and perhaps the fatal—blow must be left to the Soviets. Morally speaking, this is no doubt very commendable, but such an attitude concedes a big advantage to the enemy. Whereas NATO must use all its strength to prepare against an attack which can come at any time from any quarter, the Soviets can relax in perfect safety, knowing that the West will never shoot first; and they can, if they wish, apply most of their efforts to careful preparation of a surprise attack.

The concepts of "strategic" and "tactical" have changed their significance in the course of military history. Thus what would have been a strategic, and therefore decisive, victory in the First World War, would have been only a tactical success in the Second. And this development has continued. Nowadays, generally, strategic weapons are those which can strike an enemy in a decisive fashion in his own country; tactical weapons are those which serve to support battle operations and harass the enemy supply lines. For example, strategic air operations would be directed against the very source of the enemy's war potential, while tactical air operations would be those directed against his forces in the field.

Missiles and air fleets are therefore tactical or strategic according to the task which they are expected to perform. As far as nuclear arms are concerned, it is of course very difficult to draw an exact dividing line between the one use and the other. The general tendency nowadays is to make the tactical atomic weapon smaller and smaller, to scale it down to the size of tank munition or atomic hand grenades. The operational development of such weapons is already a practical possibility. In March, 1959, the U.S. Atomic Energy Commission announced that in a series of experiments in the autumn of 1958, it had exploded nuclear weapons equivalent to 100 tons of TNT, then 6 tons, and finally only 1 ton.

To give some idea of the magnitudes involved: a hydrogen bomb has an explosive force of millions of tons (megatons) of TNT and a devastation area of between 12 and 15 miles. The atomic bomb exploded over Hiroshima had an explosive force of 20,000 tons of TNT, and had a devastation area of about 2 square miles. The effect of the smaller tactical nuclear weapons will be correspondingly smaller.

One difficulty concerning these smaller atomic weapons is their disproportionate cost, which is often not much less than that of the bigger weapons. In addition, there are a number of technical problems to be solved, because, as is generally known, the chain reaction of nuclear fission begins to operate only at a certain critical volume of the fissionable material. A further problem is the production of the "clean" bomb, a weapon which will generate great heat and power when exploding but relatively little radioactivity. The radiation is normally an accompanying feature of the fission, as in the case of the uranium bomb. Of the 200 million electronic volts produced by the splitting of a uranium nucleus, about 160 million produce heat and blast as kinetic energy, while about 34 million produce radiation. (In the chemical process of burning a carbon atom, the release of energy is, by comparison, only four electronic volts.) With the opposite process, nuclear fusion—which takes place when a hydrogen bomb explodes—there is no radioactivity. The H-bomb would therefore be more or less "clean," but for the fact that radiation is caused by the atomic fuse, and also by certain by-processes. The problem is how to get rid of these.

Scientists are constantly discovering new principles which represent a scientific break-through, and with sufficent research it will be possible to produce atomic weapons of hand-grenade size both cheaply and cleanly.

The Soviet leaders know this, of course, and are directing massive propaganda against atomic weapons for the NATO forces, and in particular the German Army. The fact is that, politically, the West can afford to put small atomic weapons in the hands of its soldiers, and even of its factory workers, whereas the Soviets cannot—certainly not in the satellite states.

"You were in Hungary in 1956 yourself," the speaker continued.

"You can imagine what would have happened there if the workers of Czepel and Budapest had had atomic hand grenades to throw at the Russian tanks instead of home-made Molotov cocktails."

It is a matter of course that the German Federal Army must be equipped with atomic weapons in the same way as the other NATO forces. Brigadier-General von Butler, the German national military representative at SHAPE, put the matter very clearly: "Let us assume a defense line held first by the British Rhine Army, then a German corps, then Belgian troops, and then the U.S. Seventh Army. If the German troops were known to be without tactical atomic weapons, obviously the full weight of any attack by the Soviets would fall on their sector. And as the Red Army would be equipped with such weapons—and would certainly use them—the result would undoubtedly be a Soviet break-through."

In fact, to refuse to equip the German Federal Army with atomic weapons and train its men in their use would be equivalent to disarming it. This does not mean that, as long as there is peace, the German Army need have control over any nuclear warheads. Such warheads are already stockpiled in Europe, but in accordance with the MacMahon bill of August 1, 1946, they are kept under U.S. control. They would be put at the disposal of the NATO allies in case of war. Then, however, if the German or any other NATO troops were not equipped with double-purpose weapons or did not know how to handle atomic munition, they would be so hopelessly inferior to Soviet atomic divisions as to be practically useless. They would have only one choice: surrender or annihilation.

10

The Capital of the Free World

"His Excellency, the President of the North Atlantic Council, Mr. Feridun Cemal Erkin."

"His Excellency, the Supreme Commander of the Allied Forces Europe, General Lauris Norstad."

"His Excellency, the Secretary of the United States of America, Mr. Dean Rusk."

"His Excellency, the Foreign Secretary of Her Britannic Majesty, Lord Home."

"His Excellency, the Defense Minister of the German Federal Republic, Doctor Franz Josef Strauss."

"His Excellency, the Secretary-General of the North Atlantic Treaty Organization, Mr. Dirk U. Stikker."

Names and titles echo and re-echo before NATO headquarters in Paris as the limousines drive up, showing the flags of NATO and of many countries, bringing the members to a session of the North Atlantic Council. A breath of history is in the air, a recollection of the great days of recent European history—the Congress of Vienna and other great gatherings of the nineteenth century, the arrival of government representatives in the days of Briand, Stresemann, and Chamberlain at the Palace of the League of Nations in Geneva. Gathering here today at NATO headquarters are the representatives of the modern powers who have joined together in the great peoples' community which is called NATO. The flags of the fifteen nations line the drive. In the center, above the entrance, is the flag of NATO. Protocol is not always so formal, only in April and in December, when the ministers themselves come together for their annual meetings.

For eight years the Palais de Chaillot, a provisional construction of wood and metal built into the high structure of the palace proper, served as the political headquarters of NATO. Jacques Carnus, the architect of the palace, designed it in the summer of 1951 for the sixth plenary session of the United Nations. At its meeting in Lisbon in February, 1952, the North Atlantic Council accepted the offer of the French government to house the NATO organization there for the time being. During the still-born summit conference in May, 1960, the Palais de Chaillot, obstinately long-lived, like most provisional arrangements, served as press center for the conference. It has now been broken up into its separate parts, but it can be said in retrospect that this simple roof over NATO's head witnessed a memorable development.

In the spring of 1960, NATO—the General Secretariat, the International Staff, and the delegations of the member states—moved into its permanent headquarters at the Porte Dauphine near the Bois de Boulogne. The new headquarters is a large, functional building, constructed in the shape of an A, with wings almost a hundred yards long. There are 1,000 rooms in the building; the session hall of the Council itself can seat 550 people. In the part which is open to the public, there are a bank, a post office, a travel bureau, a bookshop, and a cinema. Just as in the early days in the Palais de Chaillot, there is always a great coming and going here. In addition to the hundreds of members of the international staff and the national delegations, there are daily visitors from all parts of the world. For example, there were 10,000 visitors in 1960. They arrived in groups of a dozen to over 100, people of many countries and many tongues. And few of them come just as tourists; most want to know more about NATO and its work; and here, as at SHAPE, prominent NATO men are at their disposal for lectures, discussions, and questions. It is no mean supplementary burden for the staff, but they all feel that the extra work is worthwhile, and that it bears fruit.

"I think it's a good thing that so many visitors come here," said Paul Lieven, a member of the Information Department who usually receives the visitors. "One could wish there were even more, in fact. Because when they come here they see NATO as a living reality."

Certain areas are open to the public, but the entrance to the offices is closely guarded, and a pass is required to go in. There are no exceptions. The employees on duty at the reception center still talk about that day in December, 1957, when President Eisenhower arrived for a session of the North Atlantic Council at the Palais de Chaillot and, due to an oversight on the part of his secretary, was not provided with the necessary pass. No exception was made even for him. Of course, the man certainly looked like the President of the United States, but, as a detective confided to us, he might have been a double. Eisenhower submitted to the formality and waited patiently until the security officers had made out a provisional pass in his name.

Even General Norstad—and we witnessed such an incident—has to show his pass when he enters the building. And so does the master of the house himself, the Secretary-General of NATO and chairman of the North Atlantic Council. From May 15, 1957 until March 4, 1961, Paul-Henri Spaak, now Foreign Minister of Belgium, was the Secretary-General, succeeding Lord Ismay. On April 21, 1961, Dirk U. Stikker took over, appointed by the North Atlantic Council which met in Paris, on April 18.

"If I had ever come across the slightest indication of any aggressive idea in NATO, I should immediately have resigned," Spaak assured us when he received us in his office. His manner of talk is precise, avoiding emotional emphasis, almost as though he were disdainful of seeking persuasion by any means but cool logic. This renders his remarks all the more compelling, because one senses his passionate conviction, held in check by the discipline of the trained jurist. In appearance he reminds you a little of Churchill—the same powerful head, the same combination of intellectual ability and practical action. From 1935 on, he was a member of the Belgian government, and after the outbreak of war he became Foreign Minister. He continued to occupy this position in the cabinet of Premier Pierlot of the government-in-exile, and retained it when, in 1947, he became Belgian Premier. Today he has returned to the service of his country.

Spaak is a Socialist, and this puts him in a strong position where the British Labour Party and the German Social Democratic Party are concerned, both of which often disagree with him in matters of foreign policy. There are not many people who can see, as uncompromisingly and clearly as he can, the threat which hangs over Europe from Bolshevism, and the obligation to resist that threat, even by force of arms if necessary.

Of his own accord, Spaak plunged into the middle of all the most burning problems of the day: the nuclear armament of NATO forces, the reunification of Germany, disengagement, and so on.

"Everyone wants peace," he said. "If anyone is a pacifist from religious or moral conviction, that is a position I can understand and respect. In that case one must be opposed to militarism in any form whatsoever, and wish to abolish the armed forces altogether. But once you accept the necessity for an army at all, you must also accept the necessity of equipping it with the most modern weapons, if it is to be of any use at all. You can't send soldiers into battle armed with obsolescent weapons and therefore without hope of victory over an enemy equipped with modern arms. Let us suppose that a statesman—myself, if you like—were the president of a country whose army was equipped only with conventional arms, and his government received an ultimatum from the Soviets, whose army is, of course, equipped with nuclear weapons. In such a case, I, or anyone else in a similar position, would have no alternative but to accept the Soviet ultimatum. We should just have to capitulate. In the circumstances, no one could take the responsibility for anything else."

Spaak returned to this point again and again. "The artillery of the Second World War is so out of date now as to be almost on a par with medieval culverins. With such batteries you couldn't do a thing against modern bombing attacks—not to speak of rocket bombardment. In order to counteract the supersonic jet bomber, you must have missiles with atomic warheads. Could you, or anyone, expect people to let themselves be blown to smithereens by bombs without using the only weapons which are effective against them?" And he added, "Furthermore, there's nothing like inadequate arms and equipment for undermining the morale of the defense, and such a state of affairs would be a positive invitation to the Soviets to attack."

We asked whether he thought the West should oppose Khrushchev with greater determination. Should it, for example, accept Khrushchev's dictum that no one had a right to interfere in the internal affairs of his satellites? Surely the Soviet Union was under an obligation, imposed upon it by binding international agreement, to allow free elections in the satellite states?

"Unfortunately, we are to some extent the victims of our past errors," Spaak replied. By giving the Soviets a free hand for so long, and doing nothing to stop their advance, the Western powers put themselves into a position where their legal rights were overshad-

owed by the *fait accompli.* Governments which have been formed in
the satellite states are now presented as legitimate, even though they
have to be maintained by force. In these circumstances, it is much
more difficult for the West to compel the Soviet Union to recognize
its treaty obligations than it would have been in the years immediately after the war.

Spaak spoke with particular vigor on the problem of "disengagement," the creation of a so-called neutral zone to keep the East and
West blocs apart. To accept this proposal would be to fall victim to
a dangerous illusion. "What should we do," he demanded, "if, after
the adoption and implementation of the Rapacki Plan, Soviet troops
marched back into the neutral zone? Should we then decide on a
nuclear counter-blow? On a third world war in which the United
States would be exposed to nuclear attack at home, just because of a
treaty breach and even before a shot had been fired? To say the
least, that would certainly be a very difficult decision. And that is
why, in my opinion, the West cannot possibly accept the Rapacki
Plan or anything of the sort. Incidentally, what hypocrisy it is to
pretend that the two blocs would be isolated from each other by a
neutral zone a few hundred miles across, when the range of rockets
already operational today extends over thousands of miles. They are
quite capable of attacking and perhaps destroying a country beyond
such a zone without a single soldier crossing a single frontier."

The danger does not lie in the fact that the armies of the West
and the East are within contact of each other, and therefore it
would be illusion to suppose that to draw them a little apart would
result in a reduction of tension. For fifteen years now, East and
West have been in such close contact in Europe, and yet—apart from
one or two minor incidents—Europe has always been the quietest
spot in the East-West conflict. If ever an armed clash did occur—
it is difficult to recall an example offhand—both sides hurried to
settle it, because the West does not want a war at all, and the
Soviets did not want a war at that moment.

"Responsible NATO military experts are positive that any neutralization of Germany would be both strategically and tactically
dangerous," Spaak went on. "If Germany were neutralized, it would
be technically impossible to defend the rest of Europe—even if the
Americans did not promptly withdraw their forces to the United
States. In that case the Benelux countries would have no alternative
but to declare themselves neutral, too. And that would probably
mean the end of all NATO attempts, successful so far, to bring the

advance of Bolshevism to a standstill by organizing joint resistance. That is the reason why the German problem is so serious and so important."

In 1914, and again in 1939, a withdrawal of the opposing forces might perhaps have contributed something toward the preservation of peace. But in those days the range of modern artillery was only from twenty-five to thirty miles. Today it would be senseless. In any case, wars do not break out because of some border incident, but because a government wants war.

Militarily speaking, "disengagement" would give the Soviets overwhelming advantages. NATO's operational basis in Europe has already become very narrow, as a result of the Soviet drive westward, and any further narrowing by the creation of a neutral zone would make the task of defense hopeless. The Early Warning System would have to be taken even farther back, and the forward bases for rocket defense abandoned.

The Soviets, on the other hand, would still have the endless land mass right back to Vladivostok as their operational base, and even if their forces were stationed further east than at present, they could be back again at the Iron Curtain in a very short time, ready to march across it into Western Europe.

"I find it incredible that any European could risk compelling the United States to change its present policy, on which the security of Europe depends," Spaak said emphatically. "At the present time, the U.S. is keeping watch on the eastern borders of the free world. Anyone contemplating an attack on Western Europe today knows that such an attack would immediately mean war with the United States." His voice became more urgent: "For my part, I am convinced that the presence of American troops before the Iron Curtain is the decisive factor for the preservation of world peace. Do we want to surrender that great advantage and frivolously adopt a new policy of illusions which must inevitably lead to the withdrawal of the Americans, first from Germany and then from Europe?"

The most difficult thing to understand, he said, would be the existence of any opposition to NATO in Germany. "Germany above all ought to be grateful for the existence of NATO, particularly since all NATO countries have recognized the importance of reunification and have adopted it as their own aim." However, it is difficult to see this reunification coming about as the result of any confederation between the German Federal Republic and the Soviet-occupied zone. All experience since 1945 has shown how dangerous it is for any democratic government to attempt to cooperate with the Communists. Poland was a case in point, and so was Czechoslovakia. The Communists flouted all democratic rules. And sooner or later—probably very quickly—any such association would lead to the Bolshevization of the whole of Germany. "But, quite apart from that," Spaak continued, "even if the West and the German Federal Republic were prepared to agree to any such federal solution, the Russians would not."

Turning to the question of Berlin, he said, "Without formally belonging to NATO territory, Berlin is a NATO outpost, and the one most threatened at the moment. The Germans ought to appreciate NATO more than anyone else, because, after all, Berlin was saved by NATO. Without NATO's guarantee, Berlin would long ago have fallen into Soviet hands."

The Secretary-General of NATO, who is chief of the staff of experts known as the International Secretariat, is not merely an executive. He is in a very strong position, because since the reform based on the December, 1956, report of the "Three Wise Men," he is also chairman of the North Atlantic Council, even when it meets at ministerial level. He has the right to put proposals on the agenda, and it is his duty to see that the decisions of the Council are put into effect. His sphere is by no means confined to technical matters; his proposals may embrace the whole present scope of NATO, and even concern the future shape of the alliance. Such prominent personalities as Lord Ismay, Paul-Henri Spaak, and Dirk U. Stikker were chosen precisely because the office is so important.

The Secretary-General has direct access to all NATO institutions and to all member governments. In the event of a dispute between members, he is empowered to offer his services as a mediator; and he may, if the parties to the dispute agree, set up machinery to investigate, effect a compromise, bring about a conciliation, arbitrate, and produce a settlement, or take any steps calculated to facilitate a settlement. An example of such a situation was the long-drawn-out and involved dispute between Great Britain, Greece, and Turkey over Cyprus, which threatened to develop into a danger for NATO itself. The Secretary-General contributed greatly to the final settlement. He has also intervened in the fishery dispute between Great Britain and Iceland.

It is the job of the International Secretariat to prepare and organize the work of the NATO Council; what makes it so interesting is that it has actually developed into an international authority. Its members come from the fifteen NATO states, but they are supra-national officials, not responsible to their own governments, only directly to the Secretary-General, who is responsible for them to the Council. In France, as in all other NATO countries, they enjoy diplomatic status on the basis of a Council decision taken in Ottawa on September 20, 1951, and subsequently ratified by all member states. This status gives them all the usual diplomatic privileges, including legal immunity and exemption from taxation. The premises of the International Secretariat, like those of the North Atlantic Council and of all the authorities and committees established by it, are extra-territorial. Some of these officials have been lent to NATO for a fixed period by their own governments. Others are employed directly by NATO because of their particular expert knowledge and experience. Thus, in the course of time, a truly international civil service will develop.

The highest-ranking assistant of the Secretary-General is the Deputy Secretary-General. Since June 6, 1962, the former Italian Ambassador to Norway, Guido Colonna di Paliano has occupied this important post. His predecessor was Alberico Casardi, now Italian Ambassador to Belgium.

Three main departments dealing with the most important spheres of NATO activity are directly under the supervision of the Secretary-General. Each of these departments is headed by an Assistant Secretary-General. The head of the Political Department is Robin William J. Hooper, who formerly served on the British Embassy staffs in Paris, Lisbon, and Baghdad. Immediately prior to his acceptance of this important NATO post, he was Departmental Chief to the Permanent Under-Secretary of State for Foreign Affairs in London. The head of the Economic and Finance Department is François-Didier Gregh of France. The head of the Department for Production and Logistics is Johnson Garrett of the United States.

The structure of the Political Department under Robin Hooper is typical of the close integration which prevails. Two political directors, Dr. Alexander Böker for general questions, and D'elle Gorce of France for special questions, are subordinate to him. W. Newton of Great Britain is in charge of the Research Department. Robin Hooper is also in control of the Information Department, which is under John E. McGowan of the United States, and the Press Section, which is under the Press Officer, D'Yberville-Fortier of France. Citizens of almost all the fifteen nations of the alliance serve in the various departments.

For information concerning all scientific questions within the framework of NATO's activity, the Secretary-General can call upon his Science Advisor, who is at present Professor William P. Allis of the United States. Professor Allis is at the same time the chairman of the Science Committee of the North Atlantic Council. It is his job to facilitate the closest possible cooperation in the scientific field between the various NATO departments, the corresponding authorities of the member states, and the various international organizations.

The Personnel and Administration Service, which is also under the Secretary-General, is responsible for general personnel administration and for the drawing up of the International Secretariat budget. The department of the Financial Controller is, in accordance with its tasks, independent.

Finally, the Secretary-General controls the Office of the Executive Secretary, which is in the charge of Lord Coleridge, who is at the same time the Secretary of the North Atlantic Council. It is his job to supervise the technical running of the Council's work and that of its committees, including preparation of agendas, keeping minutes, drawing up reports, drafting the Council decisions, and supervising the preparations for their execution. He appoints the secretaries for the Council committees and coordinates their work. He is also responsible for the Civil Emergency Planning Office, which is in the charge of the Senior Civil Defense Advisor, Aldo Cippico.

Thus the International Secretariat is organized along cabinet lines. As in Great Britain, there is only one responsible "minister," the Secretary-General himself; the other members of the government are subordinate to him as deputy or assistant secretaries-general, or in other high official posts.

As Deputy Secretary-General, Alberico A. Casardi was the highest official of NATO after the Secretary-General. Casardi is a typical Italian diplomat, dignified and rather reserved at first. In the course of a conversation he invariably warms up and becomes more animated. He was born in 1903. In 1955 he was observer for his country at the U.N. in New York. In course of our conversation, he said that although NATO certainly came into being as the direct result of the Soviet threat, it would be in danger of withering away if it remained nothing but a military alliance. "It must become more than that," Casardi insisted. "It must have a real aim. It must become a community of peoples." The preservation of human dignity, the defense of a free way of life, a state based on the rule of law, democracy, and the development and extension of economic cooperation—these goals are so important that people at the Porte Dauphine often speak of NATO II, the political, economic, and cultural community, side by side with NATO I, the military alliance.

"Formerly," said Casardi, "cooperation was perhaps easier because alliances were more a matter for the governments than for the people. Today, public opinion has to be won over. People must be convinced that the policy which their government is carrying out— a policy which necessarily has its repercussions in the economic and social spheres—really serves their best interests.

"Of course, for this purpose NATO would need a bigger apparatus than it has at present. People must learn much more about NATO, about what it is, and what its aims are." Without the support of an informed public opinion, the West would find itself constantly on the defensive, and the Soviets would be able to drive forward along the line, psychologically, politically, and economically. "First and foremost, a common policy must make it impossible for the Soviets to play off one NATO member against another."

Thanks to NATO, the Soviet advance was brought to a halt. Democratic countries are patient and their governments peaceable; the danger is that the dictators may mistake this patience for weakness. Whenever they do so, they will inevitably go too far, and the free world will find itself faced with war or surrender. Hitler reached these limits when he took over Czechoslovakia in March, 1939. His next move meant war, which ended in the destruction of his regime. It is interesting that once again Czechoslovakia represents this limit of tolerance. The democracies accepted its subjugation, but their reply was the North Atlantic Alliance. So far the Soviets have respected this warning, and the peace of the world has been preserved. But once again a totalitarian ruler is in danger of misinterpreting patience as weakness. The walling-off of East Berlin was the first act of aggression in Europe since NATO was founded in 1949—a fateful portent of things to come. Should Khrushchev fall victim to his own propaganda and believe that he can intimidate the West and compel it to tolerate further Soviet conquests—for example, the seizure of West Berlin—then the consequence would be incalculable.

"Far more people should be taught to see through the falsehoods of Marxist sophistries," we said. "Again and again we find that democratically minded people, particularly the young, are helpless when faced with the dialectical tricks of the Communists. NATO ought to hold courses on the mysteries of Marxist-Leninism."

"What we really must do," said Casardi, "is to strengthen the psychological counter-warfare of the West. Many countries are already doing a great deal in this respect, but we need a centralized apparatus in NATO. The difficulty is that the consent of fifteen governments first has to be obtained. However, we must not forget that NATO is not the only alliance against Bolshevism. The United States has additional obligations; it is simultaneously a member of NATO, SEATO, the U.N., the Pan-American Union, and so on. In my own country, former Premier Alcide de Gasperi was a great believer in the effectiveness of psychological warfare, and he was always saying that if it was possible to organize joint military defense, to integrate economic policies, and to take a joint line politically, then we should certainly be able to pool our resources in organizing psychological warfare."

Wouldn't it be sensible if the Ministers of Culture of the various NATO countries would hold a conference to discuss questions of cultural policy within the framework of NATO? Anglo-Saxon countries, of course, do not formally have such ministers, but they could send prominent representatives of the cultural life of their countries.

"I'm afraid the time isn't yet ripe for such a proposal," replied Casardi. "Most countries are very jealous of their cultural independence."

For example, the German Federal Republic has no Ministry of Culture, because the federated *Laender* are jealous of their own rights in the matter. But at least public opinion has been strong enough to persuade the various ministers of culture of the federated *Laender* to meet and discuss educational and related questions. Such an enlightened public opinion should be created in the NATO countries generally. That would be a promising way of implementing Article 2.

Among the free peoples of the world, difference of language, customs, and culture are not insurmountable barriers. On the contrary, they are stimulating. "Let us put it another way," said Casardi. "Among free peoples, coexistence—to use that expression—is the natural order of things; it is a matter of course. But what the Soviets mean by coexistence is that the West should have little contact with the Soviet satellites, while the Soviets must have a free hand to subvert the institutions of the free peoples."

11

The Work of the
International Secretariat

François-Didier Gregh looks at NATO from the economic point of view. That is his job as Assistant Secretary-General for Economics and Finance, with the rank of a Deputy Secretary-General, and he brings a great deal of expert knowledge and experience to his task. He is a jurist by profession and an economist by avocation. Even during the war, when he was an active member of the Resistance, he was in charge of the economic department of the Free French Government under General de Gaulle. After the war, in 1949, he became Director of the Crédit Lyonnais, and in 1953 he was with the Bank for Economic Construction and Development in Washington in charge of Asian and Asia-Minor affairs.

In his lively manner, Gregh went straight to the heart of the matter: "Public opinion—or what is regarded as such—is putting constant pressure on governments and parliaments to cut down military expenditure. But that just isn't feasible. It must not be permitted, because it would weaken the position of the West. The Soviets believe with almost religious zeal in the world revolution. They are proud of their Red Army, and think they could survive a war. The knowledge that the Western powers will never start a war already gives them a great advantage."

Gregh takes a realistic view of the Soviets' economic situation. They have made progress, he admits. Not by leaps and bounds, but systematically, based on earlier endeavors which are beginning to bear fruit. During the past fifteen years, they have extended their educational system to encompass broad masses of the people, and have had notable successes. Their technical schools and universities are turning out scientists, engineers and technicians at a faster rate than those in the West.

If Stalin had said thirty years ago that the Soviet Union was seriously planning to overtake the West economically, the world would have laughed at him. "A few years ago," Gregh pointed out, "it would not have been thought possible that the Soviet Union could ever appear in Argentina as a serious competitor of the West. Nevertheless, that is the situation today. Oil is being bored in Argentina with Soviet drilling machinery and Soviet credit. And you know how vigorous the Soviet economic offensive is in the Near East. Without exaggeration, we can speak today of a general attempt of the Soviet economic system to penetrate the world. And the economic offensive is followed by political influence; witness the difficulties the United States is having even in some parts of South America."

The Soviets gain that advantage by setting their conditions solely according to political considerations, while the West considers the laws of economics. This, of course, is also in the interest of the receiving countries who must build their economies on a profitable basis. When any competitive contract comes up, the free countries of the world bid against one another. There is nothing wrong in that; it is a good thing. But in the economic struggle with the Soviet Union, it is a drawback. "Take one example—Iceland. The economic life of Iceland is based almost entirely on fishing; so the Soviets offered to take thirty per cent of the total catch. Obviously, the West couldn't stand by and do nothing, so our Secretary-General spent five whole months on the problem. The result? He finally managed to obtain economic assistance for Iceland from just two countries, the United States and Germany."

Of course, it very often happens that disillusionment rapidly follows the first period, in which Soviet assistance is joyfully accepted—unless the country has in the meantime succumbed to the grip of the Soviets. The following bitter observations are credited to Nasser on his return from Moscow in the fall of 1958: "The first time, the Russians help willingly. The second time, they impose crippling demands before they make any further deliveries. And the third time, they only impose conditions and make no deliveries at all, unless it suits their political plans."

Developments in India and China also concern NATO, Gregh

said. Despite his formal neutralism, Nehru unquestionably leans more toward the West than the East, but he has to cope with one tremendous problem—the rapid increase in population, which is so great that large new investments have to be made every year merely in order to maintain the current per capita income. Internal resources are not sufficient to ensure even this, and though Nehru has raised loans from time to time to draw on the savings of a people not accustomed to saving, he needs outside help. He always has been able to count on a certain amount of aid from the West, but loans from this quarter have to be paid back with interest—however low—over a period of fifteen years. The Soviets boast that, with the exception of 1921–22, they never accepted foreign assistance. Of course, they make no mention of the fact that during the war they received vast deliveries, not only military but also economic, totalling 11 billion dollars, from the United States.

"In any case," Gregh went on, "they are now inculcating the same principles in their satellites. 'Foreign aid leads to slavery,' they tell them. And 'slavery' as interpreted by the Russians means greater independence from Moscow."

In conclusion, Gregh spoke of a plan he had drawn up. It is based on the Eisenhower proposal that the unexpended balances of the military budgets in the West be used to assist the underdeveloped countries economically. How would it be, Gregg suggested, if all NATO countries were to contribute a fixed percentage of their military budgets to a joint fund? At the rate of 2 per cent, this would provide an annual sum of 1 billion dollars. The original proposal of 2 per cent has since been whittled down to .25 per cent, which would still provide 125 million dollars. But even this meets with some resistance.

The misgivings of most member states largely concern the protection of their sovereignty. They still shy away from giving NATO's international bodies more authority than they think is absolutely necessary. Again and again, Gregh warned of the grave economic threat to the West. The Soviet Union is in a strong position. Its territory is rich in natural resources, and its economic system so strictly controlled that it could exist almost without imports. On the other hand, living standards are still so low that it could absorb practically any quantity of raw materials and food from the underdeveloped countries. Its rapidly developing production allows it to export industrial commodities, including arms. In other words, while NATO is hampered at every turn because the agreement of fifteen member states has to be obtained before it could move at all, the Soviets have their hands free, and therefore often can take the initiative, particularly in the underdeveloped countries.

"Anyone can see what military aggression is," Gregh continued, "but an economic offensive is quite different and by no means easy to recognize. The ordinary citizen just doesn't notice it."

But that is what is at issue here: a long-term plan, which couples an economic offensive with the military threat. The men in the Kremlin hope to bleed the Western countries white by forcing them to over-extend themselves, both to keep up with Soviet armaments and to counter Soviet pressure in the underdeveloped countries.

"Behind it all is the Leninist-Stalinist dogma that the so-called capitalist world is incapable of increasing its production beyond a certain limit; its collapse can therefore be brought about by driving it beyond that limit. Marx's doctrine, that capitalism can survive as long as it is in a position to produce at all, has long since been buried and forgotten by the new doctrine."

The fact is that in the ten years from 1949 to 1959, the NATO countries increased their production by thirty-five per cent. Most of their currencies are again freely convertible, trade has been freed of a good many restrictions. Because of this, the NATO countries have been able to triple their armament expenditures, and at the same time give far greater aid to the underdeveloped countries than the Soviet Union did.

"However, we must make good use of our resources, because the Soviets have so strengthened their war machine that in order to keep pace with modern nuclear and rocket weapons, we must rapidly reorganize our own armaments. Shouldn't we perhaps consider a much greater rationalization of resources within the framework of NATO? Perhaps even a strict division of labor, so that in future each country would be given those tasks for which it is best qualified, and freed of those which others can perform better?"

It has been said that NATO should not undertake tasks which are already being satisfactorily performed by various other international economic organizations. Gregh agreed. "But the task I have in mind happens to be one which none of those organizations does carry out, namely, to make a systematic study of the Soviet economic offensive and devise ways and means by which it can be counteracted."

It has to be counteracted because it is an attempt to conquer the world by economic means and thereby destroy that freedom which the NATO countries have banded together to defend.

And it is a matter of some urgency. Defense against the Soviet economic offensive, and the provision of aid for the underdeveloped countries, are joint tasks. Unfortunately, not much had been done so far. Spaak said so quite openly at the conference of NATO parliamentarians in November, 1958: "I can assure you that during the past few years I have listened to so many speeches, and delivered so many myself, on the desirability of bringing Western aid for the underdeveloped countries under one cover, that I must confess they are beginning to make me feel quite sick." And he added rather bitterly that although Article 2 was still a favorite subject for a speech, it had never taken on any real life. In Europe, Communism had been halted because it no longer had anything to offer; but in the underdeveloped countries it was still a temptation. Everyone knew that, Spaak pointed out. Everyone recognized the nature of the problem, and even agreed about the remedy, namely, for the West to adopt a common policy in the matter, but for some reason or other, it seemed impossible to get any action.

"Our countries have realized that one day they may be called upon to fight together against a common enemy; but they don't yet understand that they must learn to live together." Yet here lies the real core of the problem, because it is very likely that future attacks would be launched in the economic and social spheres rather than the military. The West has joined forces in face of the Soviet military threat. The same means would just as successfully ward off the Soviet economic threat.

The job of the Production and Logistics Department of NATO is to contribute to the rationalization of armament production in the NATO countries; in other words, to ensure that the allied resources are properly utilized so that in the end NATO has a modern, efficient, and well-balanced force. What are the most recent proposals for a new weapon? What are the most modern methods of production? How can the industrial capacity of the NATO countries be most effectively used? What is the best long-term planning for NATO's defense production? How do the plans of one NATO country dovetail with those of the others? These are the kind of questions the NATO governments put before the department; therefore most of the officials are highly qualified experts in the production of heavy armaments.

Johnson Garrett, who has been in charge of the department as Assistant Secretary-General since November, 1960, is an American. He graduated from Princeton, then held important positions with Pan-American Airways and the First National City Bank of New York. From 1952, he was head of the Paris branch of that bank, as well as treasurer of the American Chamber of Commerce in Paris. His department firmly believes that the best solution of the problem would be to set up a joint production program for the whole of NATO. Theoretically, the most favorable moment for the introduction of such a plan would have been the beginning of 1949, but at that time most European governments were primarily interested in getting their industries running again as quickly as possible; they did not have sufficient energy to go in for any large-scale reorganization plans. And psychologically they were not prepared for any such scheme, either; they were still anxious to maintain their own sovereignty and make their own independent decisions about the arming and equipment of their forces. Unfortunately, some of them still think that way.

Consequently, efforts to coordinate the production of conventional weapons have met with little success. Even the attempts at standardization, which is the task of the Military Agency for Standardization (MAS) in London, under the direction of Lieutenant-General Poncelet, have been restricted to such matters as spare parts for vehicles, munitions, explosives, arms, electronic apparatus, and some technical data and methods. It therefore looks as though one shall have to wait until much of the present equipment is obsolete before it will be replaced by standardized types in any significant quantity.

But the situation with regard to ultra-modern weapons is quite different. Most NATO countries don't manufacture them, and when something beyond the resources of any one country has to be developed and produced, then close cooperation is automatic. One of the first examples was the light fighter-bomber and reconnaissance plane, Fiat G-91, which has been produced jointly by a number of European countries since 1954, and was adopted by SACEUR in 1958 as a standard NATO model for use in the extended battle area. It is being produced continuously. Another joint project is the development of a naval reconnaissance plane, the French Breguet 1150, with a very long range. As a NATO prototype, it will be known by the name "Atlantic."

Valuable work is being done by NATO's Defense Production Committee (DPC) in Paris, by the advisory group of Aeronautical Research and Development (AGARD), by the Scientific Air Defense Technical Committee (SADTC) of the NATO command in Europe, to mention only a few. In addition, there are many committees to which only some of the NATO countries belong. FINABEL, for example, was created by the chiefs of the land forces of France, Italy, Germany, and the Benelux countries.

Joint planning and production is making good progress in connection with rocket construction, and the U.S. does its utmost to make sure that its NATO partners in Europe, especially on the continent, are given all scientific and technical data. An American anti-aircraft rocket, the Hawk, which is especially effective against low-flying planes, is the first item to be produced jointly by five countries. Another is the air-to-air missile known as the Sidewinder, which will be produced in Germany, Norway, Denmark, Holland, Greece, Turkey, Belgium, and Portugal. The procedure for such joint NATO projects has been laid down by the Council. Twenty projects are under preliminary consideration, among them a vertically-starting reconnaissance plane and an anti-submarine torpedo.

Johnson Garrett is convinced that before long all NATO countries will take part in one or another form of these joint production schemes. A sizable part of the weapons and military transport available in Europe still comes from the U.S. Spare parts are needed, and it is more economical if all countries pool their requirements. Sometimes it is even worthwhile to produce such parts in Europe. For this purpose, NATO has formed the Spare-Parts Maintenance Board, which is carrying out this task with great success.

Another job of NATO's Production and Logistics Department is the supervision of the infrastructure program. The term infrastructure is used to cover all fixed military installations such as headquarters buildings, airfields, ports and harbors, oil depots, pipelines, radar network, communications, and long-lines organizations, etc. It is, so to speak, the physical basis of NATO's armed forces.

What each country needs for its own requirements it pays for, but there is also a "joint infrastructure," for example, installations erected at the request of the Supreme Commanders for general NATO use. As it would be unfair to place the burden exclusively on the countries in which such installations happen to be situated, these costs are divided according to a carefully worked out formula. The calculation is made according to the advantage which each nation derives from the installation and according to the ability of each nation to pay. The U.S. contributes between forty-two and forty-eight per cent. The host country provides the site and the necessary services; in exchange, the installation will become its property when NATO no longer needs it. These projects are invariably welcomed by the host countries (and almost all NATO nations have such installations), because they bring economic advantages. Some countries, which are industrially less developed, have gathered valuable technical experience in the building, for example, of oil pipelines and supply depots.

How does such a joint infrastructure installation come into being? Let us assume that the Commander Allied Air Forces Northern Europe with headquarters in Kolsaas, Norway, requires a new airfield for his NATO squadrons. A formal request is sent by him to General Norstad, who then has the proposal examined, both locally and within the framework of his general plans, while NATO's International Staff discusses the proposal technically and financially. If SACEUR decides in favor of the proposal, a request goes forward to the Standing Group in Washington, which in turn examines it from the standpoint of military urgency and passes it on to the Military Committee. A similar request goes to the Infrastructure Committee of the North Atlantic Council, which finds out whether the proposed airfield is really of common advantage and must therefore be jointly financed. The reports of these two committees are placed before the NATO Council at its next meeting.

Should the Council decide in favor of the proposal, then all NATO members are automatically under an obligation to finance it according to the agreed scale. Norway as the host country undertakes the supervision of the project, provides the necessary land, and presents the plans to the NATO military authorities for approval. However, no capital may be invested in the project until the Infrastructure Payments and Progress Committee has given its approval. When this is done, all NATO nations are invited to bid for the contract. The building operations are supervised by technicians from the International Staff, representatives of the Supreme Commander, and of the user nation. After all these bodies have submitted a final report, the airfield is accepted and taken over by the Infrastructure Committee, but not until an International Board of Auditors has released a certificate confirming that all expenditures were found acceptable and in good order.

The whole procedure is very conservative, perhaps a bit exaggerated; but a great deal of money is involved—something like 3 billion dollars was granted by the Council in eleven installments between 1949 and 1953. With this money, over 200 airfields, some 5,000 miles of oil pipeline and vast storage capacity were built, many thousands of miles of telephone wires, overland and underwater cables laid, and radio relay stations established. Large sums were also spent for piers, breakwaters, and the like, as well as fuel-oil stations and munitions depots for the naval forces. A far-flung radar network, the Early Warning System, and a wireless network on the new "forward scatter" model, immune from jamming, are also under construction.

"The full development of our science and technology is essential to the culture, to the economy, and to the political and military strength of the Atlantic Community," declared the heads of government of the NATO nations in Paris in December, 1957, at a time when the impression made by the first Soviet sputnik was still fresh. It was this realization that led to the formation of the Science Committee of NATO and the establishment of the office of the Scientific Advisor to the Secretary-General, a post now held by Professor William P. Allis, who succeeded Professor W. A. Nierenberg, of the University of California in Berkeley.

Cooperation between the allies must begin with basic research, not only with production. And a good deal of the secrecy which has surrounded and hampered research for defense purposes must be abandoned, since the Soviets have in all probability already discovered for themselves a good many of the secrets which the NATO powers are still jealously hiding from each other. The allies now have several joint research institutes—such as the SHAPE Technical Air Defense Center at The Hague and the SACLANT Antisubmarine Warfare Research Center at La Spezia—and NATO proposes to encourage still others to be set up. In 1960, fifteen institutes received financial support in order to hold seminars for highly qualified specialists. One of them was the University of Grenoble which held a summer course in theoretical physics at Les Houches. Two hundred scholarships had been awarded to both undergraduates and postgraduates for studies abroad, and the number was greatly increased in 1960. The NATO research grants, initiated in 1960, had 110 applicants. After being screened by national authorities, a

NATO advisory board chose twenty-six projects, most of which required cooperation between several member countries—such as, for instance, the charting of the currents in the Farö-Shetland channel and the Straits of Gibraltar. Six guest professors will be exchanged between Europe and the U.S. They will be selected by their own countries, and will be completely free in their choice of subjects, working out their curricula together with the universities to which they will be accredited. One might call these exchange professorships NATO Professorships for International Peace, on the model of those of the Carnegie Endowment for International Peace. The Council of Europe has a similar program, and it would be advisable to coordinate the two.

In this context, one should also note the plan to found an Atlantic Institute which would conduct basic research and analyze the shared historical, sociological, and economic problems of the NATO countries. Whether the institute should be in Europe only, or whether there should be a second one in the United States, are matters still to be decided. General plans have already been drawn up, with the assistance of the European University in Brussels, and a committee has been formed to deal with the preliminary work. The project received the approval of the NATO Conference in London in June, 1959. The funds to finance this scheme have not yet been raised, and this burden need not fall wholly on government; private sources might well contribute, perhaps along the lines made familiar by the great American foundations.

The military organization of the North Atlantic Alliance has a joint educational and training center, the NATO Defense College in Paris; the Atlantic Institute could become an academic center for the intellectual, political, and economic aspects of the North Atlantic community.

Groups of visitors who come to Paris to learn something about NATO are usually received by the Information Director of the Press Section, and the atmosphere is frank and informal. One of the officials of the Information Directorate is Paul Lieven, a man of Baltic extraction who emigrated to Canada in the nineteen-twenties. He is a democratic Grand Seigneur of the house of the Princes of Lieven, with a mastery of many European languages, and his inherited Baltic spirit of hospitality pairs excellently with the liberal generosity of the New World. Many thousands of visitors to NATO headquarters have been glad to make his acquaintance.

"What is your personal impression," we asked Paul Lieven, "of what the visitors who come here think about NATO?"

"Undoubtedly the vast majority approve of NATO," he replied. "Perhaps a tenth of them are determined opponents, some others are either doubtful or refuse to commit themselves." But only a few of those who are opposed to NATO have Communist sympathies.

The task of the Information Directorate is to inform the general public about the aims and achievements of NATO, and important events within the Atlantic community. For this purpose it makes use of publications, films, radio and television, lectures, books, and exhibitions. Unfortunately, the funds allowed for this purpose are unbelievably meager. In 1958, for example, the total departmental allotment was less than a hundred thousand dollars. In 1959, this sum was approximately doubled, but had to cover special expenditures such as those made in connection with the tenth anniversary of NATO. Cultural exchanges among the various member countries, cooperation between scientists and teachers, conferences of journalists, publicists, religious groups, and others with an influence on public opinion—all must be encouraged in order to create the desired spirit of NATO solidarity.

In particular, the International Secretariat should be given liberal facilities to combat the psychological warfare being waged ceaselessly against the West. Day and night, a never-ending stream of aggressive propaganda against NATO pours out into the ether from Soviet stations, and NATO has not a single station with which to reply. A staff should be formed to supply Western newspapers and public opinion with immediate answers to all Soviet attacks and charges, and counter-arguments to all Soviet propaganda.

If the Information Directorate and the Press Section are not yet equipped to do so effectively, that is not the fault of NATO, but rather of the fifteen governments whose representatives form the North Atlantic Council. It is up to them to see to it that sufficient funds and means are set aside for this important purpose.

12

NATO and
Emergency Planning

"The German zeppelins of the First World War were the progenitors of civil defense," declared Sir John Hodsoll. Sir John was Senior Civil Defense Advisor at the International Secretariat in Paris. He holds the rank of Commander in the Royal Air Force, and is one of the very early fighter pilots—he was a Royal Naval flyer in 1914, at a time when there was as yet no air force. Although he has been flying for forty-five years, he has never been shot down, "surprisingly enough," as he added drily.

"In comparison with the V-1, V-2, and blockbusters of the Second World War, you might think the zeppelins and bombing planes of the First World War were not to be taken seriously; but in relation to the weight of bombs dropped, the rate of casualties was much higher than during the Second World War, primarily because air-raid precautions were in their infancy. The psychological factor was also important—people ran out into the streets to watch the fun —and, in fact, a number of zeppelins were shot down. But the casualty rate among the civilian population was 100 dead to every ton of high explosive—they were already pretty good bombs, and they were dropped with considerable accuracy."

The corresponding losses during the Second World War were only one dead per ton of high explosive; and even when the V-1s and the V-2s (the precursors of our present-day rockets) became operational, the rate of casualties was only seven and nine per ton, respectively. The slow V-1s, or doodle-bugs, as they were called in Britain, often were shot down by fighters over the Channel or by General Pike's coastal barrage; but there was no defense against the V-2.

In view of the comparatively heavy bomb casualties of the First World War, the British authorities gave a good deal of thought to the problem of defending the population from air attack. Sir John, who retired from the Royal Air Force in 1932, began to study the problem with growing interest as the danger of a new war increased with the advent of Hitler. In 1935, the government appointed him Under-Secretary of State for Air Raid Precautions; from 1938 to 1948, Sir John was Inspector-General of Civil Defense for the United Kingdom.

The object of civil defense is to preserve the morale of the civilian population and to keep the casualty rate as low as possible. This is a matter of importance for the men at the front as well, because an army whose homeland is destroyed must sooner or later itself be defeated. Within NATO, the civil defense obligation comes under Article 3 of the Charter, in which the signatory powers undertake to develop their own and joint defense against armed aggression.

As Sir John pointed out, in the event of war the Soviets will undoubtedly do their utmost to wreak devastation behind the lines. The primary task, therefore, is to ensure that whatever happens, government will survive and be able to continue its work; that its instructions will reach the populace, and that it will be obeyed. In other words, even in the midst of nuclear devastation, the government must remain master of the situation.

In this respect, all countries are faced with essentially the same problem. Where lawful authority ceases to function, the field is open to dictators and illegal exercise of power. All Western governments therefore must be prepared to invoke emergency powers. Traffic and communications must be maintained under all circumstances. The government must always be in a position to give instructions and to make known its decrees. Emergency broadcasting facilities must be available, since the radio and telephone networks might be destroyed by nuclear attack. Our complex society is based on electricity; but gas and electricity supplies could be cut off; therefore batteries must be stored for local use and household radios. Provision must also be made for maintenance of contact between the central government and provincial and local authorities. Finally, reserve headquarters must be prepared for the government and its ministers, members of parliament, and officials.

"Let us assume that the attack does not leave us time to get the entire government out of the capital. In that case, a number of headquarters must be held in readiness to which responsible leaders, and in particular well-known statesmen and leaders of public opinion, can go in order to take up the reins of government."

Decentralization is the dictate of our era. Some NATO countries are already well prepared. In the German Federal Republic, for example, there are the ten *Laender* governments, and Berlin; in the U.S., there are the fifty states, and in France there are numerous Departments with their own administrations. The regions set up in Britain are somewhat arbitrary, Sir John thought, but they would serve their purpose. These subdivisions would have to take over the responsibilities of government for their powers if central administration broke down. All such eventualities call for advance planning.

"Even during the last war, the regional authorities, right down to the County Councils, had a sealed letter which would have transmitted full governmental powers if the central government had been destroyed by casualties or invasion."

The role of civil defense in a total Western defense plan is increasingly well understood, but despite this, far too little is being spent on it. "The important thing is to get the idea of emergency planning accepted," said Sir John. "That isn't by any means the case at present. The resistance of the governments is enormous, because they fear the idea might meet with opposition from the civilian population. European countries have long accepted the need for armies, navies, and air forces, even in peacetime; these are traditional. But if you tried to get them to accept an emergency program which would interfere with their private lives—to build civilian shelters, store adequate supplies, construct decontamination facilities —everyone would believe that war is imminent."

The first step therefore must be to persuade the public that such emergency planning, like military defense, is as necessary for peace as for war—that it is an important part of the deterrent, and therefore contributes to the avoidance of war. The more thoroughly a country prepares to defend its civilian population, the less the Soviets can hope to defeat it rapidly by inflicting crippling losses.

It is also necessary to convince the public that there is a defense even against nuclear bombs, and that it is therefore meaningful to seek safeguards against danger. The governments must have the courage to grasp this nettle. Protection of the civilian population cannot be assured with administrative measures alone. Special laws are necessary; governments must be willing to draft them, and parliaments must be willing to pass them. If they lack courage now, they will be helpless if war should come. Prevention of a catastrophe requires careful planning, and cannot be improvised at the last moment.

Some governments fear that the opposition might exploit public resistance to civil defense, but Sir John believes that the opposite would be true: if a government does nothing, the opposition can argue that so long as there is no civil defense, there can be no question of voting money for armaments.

"What advice would you give the populace, Sir John? How can people prepare themselves for the possibility of nuclear attack?"

"The important thing is to keep sufficient food in the house. A reserve of drinking water is also necessary, because normal supplies might be contaminated. And then, of course, people must be trained to help themselves; there must be supplies of candles, matches, batteries, and bandages."

"Is there much sense in all that if an atom bomb explosion makes everything radioactive?"

"This is an enormous danger which must not be belittled. On the other hand, it is also true that if one is not in the center of the explosion, one can protect oneself against the dangers of radiation more easily than is generally believed. The hard gamma rays are the most dangerous because the most penetrating; but they dissipate fairly rapidly. The other rays contaminate, but they do not penetrate."

"Would it be necessary to protect larders with leaden walls?"

"No, that isn't necessary. Ordinary tins are impenetrable to most of the rays, and even a loaf of bread wrapped in cellophane would be protected. One cannot disintegrate radioactive fallout, but it can be washed off and rinsed away with water."

The government itself must store supplies for the so-called survival period, which is reckoned at about a month from the first great atomic blow, though it could be longer or shorter. NATO proposes that a six-months' supply should be stored, but so far this has remained a counsel of perfection. A month's supply is ready; it is to be increased gradually to the optimal amount.

One must not underestimate the importance of self-help to civilian defense efforts. Under the leadership of local doctors, min-

isters, and public officials, the citizenry can accomplish a great deal
—as was shown during the air raids in World War II. Established
voluntary organizations, such as the Red Cross, can also play a significant role.

But in the final analysis, it will be possible to deal with an
emergency only if the preconditions have been met which only the
state can meet—if competent individuals and organizations are given
the means to act.

More would be needed than food and water. One would need
equipment to fight fires and to protect against radiation, medical
supplies, and transport, to mention some essentials. These materials
would have to be readily accessible in numerous locations; otherwise,
the possibility of self-help will have been foreclosed.

The construction of shelters is an essential part of civil defense.
Given the rapidity of weapon development, which could make large-
scale plans obsolete before they have been realized, the enormous
financial outlays necessary for a modern, complete shelter system can
hardly be justified. What is needed is a simple building plan which,
though still expensive, would be financially feasible and objectively
useful. The biggest problem is the radioactive dust which is scattered by any atomic explosion at ground level. Such dust would remain dangerous for days, and perhaps even weeks. Therefore it would
be necessary to equip all homes, institutions, factories, etc., with a
room which is protected against radiation. It must be done everywhere, because, should nuclear rockets be used, it will hardly be
possible to give people any early warning. A basement shelter,
with a ceiling shored against collapse, and sealed against atomic,
bacteriological, and chemical contamination, would offer adequate
protection—beyond a radius of about 400 to 500 yards from the explosion center against an atom bomb of the Hiroshima type.

In a wider sense, every means of countering enemy air attack belongs to civil defense: defense rockets of the Nike-Hercules, Nike-
Ajax, and Nike-Zeus types, the whole world-wide system of air-raid
warning, and the appropriate air forces, in particular the fighter-
interceptors.

"The actual period in which strategic nuclear weapons are used
may not be very protracted," said Sir John. "War might not even
start with their use at all. It is conceivable, however, that it would
end that way, if one side found itself being driven into a corner in
ordinary war with conventional weapons." The leaders of emergency
planning must necessarily give a good deal of thought to the way

war is likely to be waged and how long it is likely to last. The Soviets seem to be reckoning with the possibility of a long-drawn-out conventional war; how else can one explain the fact that they are building such a large submarine fleet? Its only purpose can be to squeeze the lifeline across the Atlantic Ocean between Europe and the United States.

In view of the probable short warning period, one may question whether there is any sense in the proposals to evacuate large cities. As a matter of fact, there still is; because even in a surprise attack, it is unlikely that large towns would be the first target. From the military standpoint, the primary targets would be the nuclear and missile bases. Cities would only be second- or third-line objectives.

An evacuation must be a carefully planned operation, in order to avoid chaos. Unless an evacuation is ordered by the authorities, it would of course be the duty of every conscientious citizen to stay in his own home—if only from self-interest, because masses of footloose people in the open would be helpless against radioactive fallout, military operations, hunger, cold, sickness, and panic.

One might expect that the Soviets would seek to spare the workers, perhaps in the hope that they might turn against their own governments. But the Soviet leaders do not regard the workers of the West as proletarians at all, but as lower middle-class, or petty-bourgeois elements—people who have been "corrupted" by high living standards and thus lost their Communist class-consciousness. The Soviets would find some satisfaction in turning the workers into real "proletarians"; and the misery which would follow upon a bombing of cities would be an effective means. Let no one be under the illusion that humanitarian considerations prevent the Soviets from exploding atom bombs over open cities. They would, in fact, hope to use the survivors as allies of the Soviet advance, just as, after the Second World War, they first used and then began to rule the populations of the satellite countries. Ultimately, the choice of nuclear targets by the Soviets will depend upon their expectation of the speed at which they could overrun Europe—whether they could hope to exploit its industrial potential.

"Should this emergency planning be centrally controlled throughout NATO?" we asked. "The expense is pertinent. It could prove enormous, and perhaps it would be desirable to spread it evenly over all the countries."

But Sir John was of the opinion that circumstances varied so between countries that this would not be workable. In any case, most of them would refuse to carry out such measures except in their own way. "The leaders of the fifteen NATO countries meet every year to obtain a general impression of what is being done in this respect. It would be useful if the military took more interest in the problem, since it is a vital matter for them, too. At present, most of them say that civil defense planning for an emergency is an excellent thing, but not if done at the cost of military preparations."

Civil defense preparations are carried out in a variety of ways. For example, in Portugal the backbone of civil defense is the Portuguese Legion; in some other countries it is based on the fire brigade organization, and so on. An attempt to bring about uniformity would therefore meet with difficulties. However, there is a Senior Emergency Planning Committee for Civil Defense, and all NATO countries are represented on it. Its aim is to coordinate activities and act as a clearing house for information. Every year it issues a progresss report, and publishes recommendations for improvements in planning. Among other things, it has prepared a basic list, setting out the foodstuffs, materials, and equipment the various countries should keep in store for emergency use.

In another conversation, we asked Sir John whether there had been any recent developments in civil defense.

"Well, one could certainly say that Khrushchev has stimulated interest in the problem. We have reports from the United States to the effect that since the failure of the summit conference, there has been a big new wave of interest in civil defense matters."

Even stronger was the impact when the Soviets unilaterally resumed nuclear testing and exploded the 55-60 megaton bomb on October 30, 1961, thus making it clear that they had used the moratorium merely as a propaganda weapon until they were ready for further testing. At once, people became more "shelter-conscious" than ever before.

"There has also been an important new development during the past few months," he went on, "namely, a new international fallout warning system from one NATO country to the other. This is an integrated system for collecting information and passing it on to both civil and military authorities. In the event of a nuclear explosion in one country, all others would receive immediate warning. This innovation has been worked out by the Civil Defense Committee under my chairmanship, and the new system will be tested during SHAPE exercises.

"In fact, we can say that there has been progress over the whole field of civil defense; slow progress perhaps, but quite steady. One of our main jobs is to persuade the public that it is possible to do something effective in the way of civil defense even in this atomic age; and, as a matter of fact, a great deal can be done. Nevil Shute's bestseller *On the Beach* was completely defeatist, a manifesto of the 'No Hope School.' The book was not based on scientific fact at all. Fallout rapidly loses its lethal qualities, and after about 200 miles it is more or less harmless. Even the deadly gamma rays don't last. A hundred roentgens at one o'clock would be, let's say, only fifty at two o'clock. And there is no fallout at all if the explosion takes place high up. But the fundamental problem is still to arouse public interest."

In most countries the Home Secretary, or Minister of the Interior, is in charge of civil defense. It would be a good idea if these fifteen NATO ministers came together for a conference to consider the whole state of emergency planning throughout NATO, and at the same time to give an impetus to still more vigorous work on this important field of defense.

Such a conference could be in the form of a North Atlantic Council session. Since every NATO government can choose its representative, this could be a meeting of officials responsible for civil defense. Thereby it would be possible to obtain Council decisions on the subject that would be binding on NATO as a whole. If these decisions would be taken by the men actually in charge of civil defense, they would have the full weight of expert opinion behind them, and there would be reason to hope that emergency planning, which is an essential part of the defense of the Western world, would receive an impetus as great as that operating in the sphere of military preparations. In fact, many experts feel that civil defense will begin to make real progress only if NATO assumes supervision, on the model of the annual review in military affairs. As long as this is not the case, it would be advisable for all NATO countries to build priorities for civil defense emergency planning into the general defense structure.

In a future war, civil defense would in any case have to be closely integrated with military defense, and joint planning is essential. However, an organizational merger would not be desirable. Unless there are urgent reasons to the contrary, civil defense must remain a civilian matter, both for psychological reasons and in order not to burden the military with additional tasks.

If a hydrogen bomb were to explode over a large city whose

authorities had made no preparations, the casualties would be crippling. Advance planning can reduce the casualties considerably. One must not overlook that, in the event of a Soviet attack, the Red Army first would have to move against the strategic bases in Europe, the U.S., and all around the Soviet Union; and that this reduces the likelihood of atomic attack on open cities. In any case, the situation cannot be judged apart from military developments. NATO would deliver a counter-blow, and this would reduce the likelihood of a second or third atomic attack.

No matter how great the losses in such an attack, the democratic constitutions would live on in the consciousness of men, and thus retain their political reality. Democracy is a natural form of life which would always arise again, unless the Red Army could prevent it by force. Even if only a part of the population would survive a war, the democratic constitutions of Britain and the U.S. would survive and start to function again.

The government of the Soviet Union, on the other hand, could not hope to survive a nuclear war. The Bolshevist system would break down as soon as the coercive apparatus were destroyed. This is, perhaps, one of the strongest guarantees of world peace, and at the same time an essential factor of the deterrent. The fear of devastation and death is felt by the people of Russia, but they are powerless to prevent war. The leaders, however, who hold the power of decision, fear collapse of the regime. Their primary interest is in maintaining their own power, and they are clever enough to realize that their rule would not survive the holocaust of an atomic war. It is therefore essential that they not be left in the slightest doubt that an attack on the free world would be answered by a nuclear counter-blow.

Ultimately, every totalitarian state is in danger of falling victim to its own agents, who, in order to curry favor with their masters, tell them what they want to hear. For example, Hitler believed the reports of his agents in the U.S., that a war with Germany would release a crippling wave of sabotage; and he accepted the assurances of his Foreign Minister, Ribbentrop, that Britain would never fight. Similarly, Communist agents today doubtless assure the men in the Kremlin that the West is infiltrated by friends of the Soviet Union, and ready to fall. Khrushchev and his assistants must be robbed of this illusion—and war be prevented—by a continuous demonstration of the West's resolve to defend its freedom.

13

The North Atlantic Council

"What would happen if the Soviets attacked tomorrow? How quickly could the NATO Council meet and decide on the counter-blow? In other words, how long would the moment of paralysis last?" We put the question to the German Ambassador in Paris, Herbert Blankenhorn, who until he was relieved by Gebhardt von Walther in April, 1959, was the permanent German representative on the North Atlantic Council.

"As you know," he replied, "since the Lisbon conference of 1952, the Council is in permanent session. The delegates of the fifteen nations are in Paris all the time."

"But supposing that, for once, they happened not to be in Paris? Or that, simultaneously with a Soviet attack, the NATO ambassadors were kidnapped or killed by Communist terrorist groups?"

"Their deputies have the same powers as the delegates themselves. The NATO Council always can meet within an hour."

"But in an emergency, even an hour might be a very long time—too long, perhaps."

"This question is raised frequently. It has been suggested that plenary powers should reside in an authority that could act at once in an emergency." But that is a delicate political question; it depends on the several governments' willingness to transmit power to make the ultimate decision before the event.

"But recall the situation in the U.N., when the North Korean Communists attacked in 1950: the counter-move was made within twenty-four hours, when President Truman alerted the U.S. forces. Only then did the Security Council meet and pass the resolution which led to joint action. Of course you can never exclude the possibility that Soviet atom bombs might come like a bolt from the blue. So far, however, wars have always been preceded by a period of increasing tension."

"But isn't it true that we are living in a state of permanent tension with the Soviet Union?"

"Yes. Nonetheless, there are always certain indications when the Soviets are planning something special. Our counter-intelligence has succeeded in isolating some thirty or forty significant factors; and presumably even the Soviet leaders would need a certain period of psychological preparation. Of course, one cannot rely on this. It is also not possible to foretell just how long the tension period would last."

But, should the Soviets launch a surprise nuclear attack, the *casus foederis* would exist by this very act, and all subsequent declarations would be mere formalities.

"In practice, the U.S. Strategic Air Command and British Bomber Command, neither of which are under NATO, would be in action within a matter of minutes. Their respective orders would come from the President of the United States and the British Prime Minister. The countries under attack would, of course, strike back at once—on the basis of the natural right to self-defense, as recognized in Article 51 of the U.N. Charter. If the attack were launched in Europe, General Norstad as SACEUR would immediately give the necessary orders for defense. Shortly thereafter—unless Paris were under nuclear bombardment—the North Atlantic Council would meet and grant retrospective authorization."

The North Atlantic Council, the supreme organ of the fifteen allies, is a powerful assembly. The simplicity of its procedures should deceive no one. Other than the biannual formal meetings already mentioned, meetings take place when necessary. The Council meets most formally when the heads of the allied governments come together to represent their peoples. So far, this has happened only once, in Paris in December, 1957.

In 1961, the Foreign Minister of Portugal, Franco Nogueiro, was President of the Council; in 1962 it has been the Turkish Foreign Minister (since June 11), Mr. Feridun Cemal Erkin. However, the Secretary-General of NATO always presides, even when the session is at ministerial level.

The powers of the Council remain the same, regardless of who is in attendance—heads of government, ministers, ambassadors, or their deputies. The ambassadors usually meet twice a week, and always on Wednesdays.

"A new community has formed among the diplomats of the Western world," Blankenhorn said. "They speak freely about world problems, not merely about issues which directly affect their own countries. This comes about very naturally. They meet often and casually, and when something happens in one or another capital— the visit of a high Soviet diplomat, for example—one will later call in his colleagues and discuss the matter."

Ambassador von Walther confirmed this conversation in his study at the Porte Dauphine: "This is a complete reversal of customary diplomatic behavior," he said. "I have never encountered such cooperation. Here, one does not represent only one's own country; one also helps to shape the joint will of the alliance." These were the impressions of a diplomat with thirty years' experience in the Foreign Office. Von Walther was in Moscow under Count Schulenburg, the last German Ambassador to Russia before the war, and returned there with Chancellor Adenauer on the occasion of the first postwar visit of state.

Every Tuesday, the Committee of Political Advisors meets, composed of deputies from the fifteen delegations. The Assistant Secretary-General for Political Affairs is in the chair. Until July, 1960, this was Sir Evelyn Shuckburgh; his successor is Mr. Robin Hooper. "This committee has increasingly become a second forum in which opinions are freely exchanged," Sir Evelyn told us. "Here the deputies, quite informally, let each other know what their governments think about current problems; and on questions that are not of sufficient importance to warrant the attention of the Council, this Committee hammers out a common policy."

Sir Evelyn is now in the British Foreign Office as Under-Secretary for European Affairs and Regional Organizations. We talked with him in Paris, shortly before he took over his new responsibilities.

"How would you sum up your feelings about the past two years, Sir Evelyn?" we asked.

"Our deterrent power is made up of three elements: the forward shield forces; the retaliatory striking force; and, perhaps the most important of all, the political unity of the alliance. Only if this unity is preserved, and demonstrably preserved, will the other two elements of the deterrent remain convincing. And we are certainly not in a weak position politically; in fact, the feeling of unity among all the members of NATO has become stronger than it was in the past. We must now plan ahead for the next ten years."

"How should NATO plan ahead, Sir Evelyn?"

"There are two ways of doing so: we might improve the machinery of NATO; or we might widen the subject matter with which NATO has to deal. This could prove difficult, of course, since the consent of the governments concerned might have to be obtained. However, a suggestion has been made that NATO should also tackle economic problems. This has been under discussion in the form of long-term economic planning for the underdeveloped countries. As to the first alternative, improving the machinery of NATO, quite a lot could be done. Of course, the political will to use the improved machinery must exist, because without that the best machinery in the world would be useless. We must always remember that NATO is an inter-governmental organization. If it is used, it can become of tremendous importance. But if it is not used, it will wither away."

The Council has more than twenty standing committees and a great number of working groups, so that there is no single working day on which members of the various delegations do not meet. Going over a problem together at an early stage, before opinions have hardened, makes it easier to find a compromise between the various interests involved. Something develops which one might call the concert of the Atlantic powers.

Since NATO is an alliance of sovereign states, the decisions of its Council are adopted unanimously, and this unanimity of fifteen members must be gained before the Council can act. This is not always easy, and without the good will of the allies it would be quite impossible. One can imagine the difficulties if a democratic government, to secure the passage of a bill, would need the support not only of a majority, but of all parties.

Of course it would be easy to point to this and that instance when the Council was unable to reach agreement; there are questions which cannot be settled at the time, even with the best will in the world, because social, economic, and political factors are all against it. For example, it would be a good thing if all the NATO fighting forces were uniformly equipped, but almost all the member countries already have large investments in arms and equipment, which it would be economically impossible to scrap. Therefore this is a problem which can be solved only gradually.

Algeria was a political example. It was a problem which directly concerned NATO, because the three northern departments belonged to NATO territory, but the conflict was not readily adjudicated. It required political developments which needed time and patience, economic changes, and greater insight both in Algeria and in France —until one day a solution emerged, as it did in Cyprus.

When one considers all these difficulties, the undoubted success of NATO becomes all the more remarkable. It is an encouraging sign that use of the veto has not developed in the North Atlantic Council as it did in the Security Council of the U.N. This is not a matter of judicial intent, but of political style. The U.N. Charter does not contain the concept of the veto. As in the NATO Council, decisions of the Security Council require unanimity. Nonetheless, up to 1962, the U.N. has been subjected to a veto on one hundred occasions—whenever the Soviet Union, by its opposition, has been able to block proposals agreed upon by all other members. The veto, in sum, is an attitude—a refusal to negotiate.

In the North Atlantic Council, differences of opinion are negotiated until agreement is reached. Decisions are usually arrived at without formal voting; the situation in which single nations, especially the stronger ones, might seek to impose their will, simply does not arise. Naturally, such a procedure requires patience and a willingness to make concessions. The spirit and practice of the Alliance has promoted just this attitude.

Consultation is the preferred technique for the articulation of joint policies. Whenever the Soviet leader pours a flood of letters, notes, or ultimatums over the governments of the Atlantic community—in the hope that they may be divided and persuaded to negotiate singly—consultations in the NATO Council shatter this hope. Khrushchev's visit to the United States, the Foreign Ministers' conference in Geneva, the threat to Berlin; a summit conference, the Rapacki Plan, disarmament; the abandonment of nuclear tests, rocket bases, German reunification, non-aggression pacts—an endless series of problems, most of them a potential threat. Each of them was dealt with by consultation. On certain questions, particularly with regard to relationships with the Soviet bloc, the larger NATO powers for some time now have done nothing without prior consultation, in order to obtain the advice and support of their allies.

The United States in particular has set a good example. As Paul-Henri Spaak said to us: "The United States is the most reasonable of the big powers. There is no important question that the Americans would not be prepared to put forward in the Council, in order to hear and consider the views of all, including Iceland and the Grand Duchy of Luxemburg." He added that it was difficult to believe that France, Britain, or Germany, or indeed any other power, if they were as influential, would behave so considerately and generously.

There have, however, been some exceptions. In 1959, Prime Minister Macmillan did not consult his allies before he went to Moscow, and he thereby set off a chain reaction of single-country conversations with Khrushchev. President Eisenhower's invitation to Khrushchev also came as a surprise to the allies. Both countries said later that these conversations had not signified a change in policy; but they did initiate a new approach to negotiations with the Soviet Union, and were of sufficient import to have warranted prior consultation.

The NATO Council is a sensitive instrument—a kind of political seismograph that records the slightest political tremor anywhere in the world. Although NATO is geographically limited, it is affected by events everywhere. For example, the conferences of African and Asian states are taken note of, and political committees work on resultant problems. A crisis in Indonesia, a revolution in Iraq, a rising in Tibet, a threat to Laos or the Shah of Persia, tension between India and Communist China, revolts in Cuba and the Congo—all such matters are studied immediately. In this context, NATO's close relationship with other organizations of the free world, such as the CENTO Pact, SEATO, and the Pan-American Union, is particularly important.

Consultation confers influence on the small countries, and authority on the powerful. That authority extends beyond NATO problems: a policy statement by one major power, on a topic such as relationships with the Soviet bloc, often will express the NATO position.

The practice of consultation developed pragmatically. Article 4 of the North Atlantic Treaty provides for consultation, but only in the case of imminent attack. The allies soon realized that this was inadequate. Council reports in 1956 and 1957 called for increased consultation in order to coordinate policies. After those declarations, there were no further incidents like the Suez crisis. It would still be necessary, however, to grant NATO ambassadors free access to major government offices in their own countries, and thereby opportunity to keep themselves fully informed.

Serious differences of opinion within NATO often have been a consequence of inadequate or delayed consultations; this was the case when Great Britain and France "went it alone" over Suez; when Great Britain delivered arms to Tunis against the desire of the French; and in connection with various problems raised by the Algerian war. Inadequate consultation generally indicates a reduction in the sense of solidarity, itself a consequence of reduced tension.

Consultation is also the means by which the Alliance can be extended on the basis of the Treaty. The members must always study the interests of the Alliance as a whole. As Dr. Schwarz von Liebermann, Deputy Director in the Political Department of the International Secretariat, put it: "The guiding idea is that the enlightened self-interest of the individual ally is also that of NATO. The converse is also true, because the interests of the member states are served by a strong alliance. We are committed to the Atlantic community because we are committed to the future of our own countries."

What does it actually mean when NATO announces that the Council has approved Western disarmament proposals; that it urges, on the basis of its annual review, that all members accept certain objectives for the following year; that the Council has accepted the annual budget for SHAPE? What is the national and international binding force of decisions by the NATO Council? There is as yet no clear answer to this question. But in NATO, legal clarity is less important than the feasibility of decisions and their practical consequences. In NATO's present stage, it may be more fruitful to trust the power of developing custom than to create strict legal obligations.

The question was raised in May, 1957, with a proposal to make consultation within NATO obligatory. The late U.S. Secretary of State, John Foster Dulles, rejected the proposal. He pointed out that his country was a member not only of NATO, but of three dozen other alliances. If only for reasons of time, the U.S. Government therefore could not undertake to place every emerging problem before NATO. But at the same time, Dulles instructed his department that the U.S. Government would always be prepared to discuss any problems within NATO. It therefore seemed gratuitous to press for formal obligations.

Consultation is a mutual process; it also involves an obligation for those who are consulted. In his report to the Fourth Annual Conference of NATO, in November, 1958, Paul-Henri Spaak said, politely but firmly, that the smaller allies had not as yet understood this point. As an example he mentioned his own country, Belgium, which had no particular interests in the Middle East, and therefore no policy. "But," he declared, "as soon as we say that we are open to consultation, because we know that we are affected by any conflict in the Middle East, we have involved ourselves. Our responsibility begins the moment we ask for consultations; it becomes even greater when we take part in them and put forward our own point of view; and that is something new in the foreign policy of many states."

The smaller powers must realize what they are doing when they ask that the great powers discuss their policies in advance and ascertain whether their allies are in agreement. Some countries seek to evade their responsibility by remaining silent. But what does diplomatic silence mean? Does it mean yes, or does it mean no? The uncertainty leads to misunderstandings.

A great power could say: "We have explained our policy, and no one has expressed disapproval. Therefore we assume that everyone is in agreement." But those who have said nothing might then object: "Oh, no; we did not express our approval." Such ambiguity must be eliminated if consultation is to have any real value. Consultation is not an end in itself; it is a means to the formulation of policies that will be accepted by all and be binding on all.

As the supreme political organ of the North Atlantic Alliance, the Council is superior to the Military Committee and the Standing Group in Washington. The Council makes the political decisions; military activities take place within their framework. For example, the Council examined NATO's defense plans and laid down guiding principles for the organization of NATO's fighting forces. Among the important problems in which the Council has the final word are the coordination of air and naval defenses, military equipment, logistics, and armaments production—in sum, all questions which involve important political decisions.

On the other hand, the Council is responsible for providing the military leadership with the manpower, equipment, and infra-structure needed to defend NATO territory. National defense policy also comes within the scope of the Council.

In these decisions, the Council must strike a balance between military necessity and economic feasibility. The fundamental value of economic stability also guides the Council's annual reapportionment of infra-structure expenses among the allies.

The Annual Review, which provides the basis for these major decisions, is the Council's most important task. Every year, the fifteen member states submit their reports which provide a review of what each country has done in the past year, both militarily and economically, and sets out its plans for the next three years. Each country opens its books for inspection by all—a procedure without precedent in European history. Neither in peace nor in war have governments ever before allowed any other power insight into the details of their economic affairs. These various reports are examined closely and subjected to criticism. The object is to determine whether each member has, in fact, stretched its capacity to the limit, to maximize its military, economic, financial, and political contribution.

"In practice," a member of the staff told us, "the budget of Denmark, for example, is submitted to a committee—an Englishman, a Norwegian, and a German. The Danes listen and reply to whatever criticism the committee may have. The same procedure is followed with all annual reports, and finally there is a joint meeting of the fifteen member states. The particular value of this procedure is that each country does its best to pull its weight and maintain its reputation in the eyes of all the others."

This Annual Review is not a one-time event; it extends over the whole year. The procedure itself is not new; it can be compared with the drawing up, discussion, and acceptance of a national budget. In the latter case, the several ministries or departments submit their proposals, which are then adjusted to each other and incorporated into the total budget. NATO's Annual Review coordinates fifteen national budgets into a single defense program.

Every defense plan is a long-term undertaking; but no democratic government can bind itself for more than the limited period of its own mandate. Therefore NATO plans for a three-year period, but the goals set for each country on the basis of the Annual Review represent firm obligations only for the first year. For the second year, they are provisional, and for the third, they are estimates, subject to revision. The annual revaluation, and addition of another third-year estimate, create a continuous planning process.

At its Paris session in December, 1959, the Council adopted a proposal of the U.S. Secretary of State, Christian Herter, to draft a ten-year plan for the general work of the Alliance; this will also affect future defense planning.

One of the chief difficulties in preparing the Annual Review is to get comparable returns from countries with disparate military and social systems. The questionnaire has only sixteen schedules, but it has 200 pages of definitions and instructions, designed solely to facilitate the provision of accurate and comparable data. Gradually the member countries are adapting their traditional systems to NATO guidelines.

NATO has adopted the calendar year as the basis for its calculations. Experience has shown that it is practical to conclude the Annual Review in November or December, with special regard to the U.S. military aid program, which is important for many NATO countries. The U.S. President traditionally presents his budget to Congress in January, and the fiscal year begins on July 1. This permits inclusion of the current NATO commitments in each American budget.

The Annual Review proceeds by stages: from January to March, a questionnaire is drawn up on the basis of previous experience, and methods of procedure are agreed upon; from March to July, the various commanders put forward their proposals, and military experts visit the capitals of the member states; from July to October, the national armament programs are discussed and analyzed, and a concluding report is drafted, which the several governments examine in November. Then the NATO Council meets at the ministerial level and fixes the obligatory commitments.

Once the completed questionnaires have come in, they are distributed to all concerned: the delegations, the Standing Group, the Commanders-in-Chief, and the International Staff. Then the process of analysis begins. The military experts discuss their own particular problems: are their troops adequately equipped? Have they sufficient striking power? If they think it necessary, they press for an increase in the armed forces. The economic and financial experts examine the economic and financial capacities of each country. In the first years of the Alliance, it was hoped that it would be possible to find a formula whereby this capacity could be described in comparable terms, but this proved impossible. Today, therefore, one simply tries to take each country's weak points into account.

On the basis of the questionnaires, the NATO military authorities make their recommendations: how to strengthen the fighting forces of the Alliance, modernize its equipment, increase its power, improve its air defense, develop an efficient warning system, and so on. Furthermore, each year it is decided how to assign the forces of the member states. Category 1 means that they are directly at the disposal of NATO, and that even in peace they are, in certain respects, under the control of NATO commanders. Category 2 means that, although they remain under the orders of their own government in peace, in the event of war they come under NATO command at once. Category 3 consists of forces to be summoned only upon outbreak of war, and then placed at NATO's disposal. Category 4 includes forces that will remain under national command even in the event of war.

The question of conscription is also dealt with in the Annual Review. SHAPE has repeatedly declared that a two-year period of military service is the absolute minimum required to train men in the use of today's complicated weapons; but so far, only the United States and Turkey have instituted this period by law. Great Britain proposes to abolish conscription altogether, and rely exclusively on a small professional army. The period of compulsory military service in the German Federal Republic was first fixed at eighteen months, but under strong pressure from the Opposition it was then reduced to twelve months. General Bruce C. Clarke, during a discussion at U.S. Army Headquarters in Fort Monroe, said: "This is an expensive way of building up an army, because no sooner are the men half trained and just becoming useful for serious military purposes, when they are sent home again." Only when the Berlin crisis had reached another climax on August 13, 1961, was the service extended—first to fifteen, then to eighteen months. Belgium has also reduced the length of military service to one year. The best interests of defense are not served by such short military service.

The adoption of the Annual Review is one of the most important jobs of the Council. Thereafter, it is the duty of the various governments and parliaments to provide the necessary means in their national budgets.

The NATO Council can be compared to the Congress of the original thirteen states of the Union of North America in 1777; or to the Diet of the German Federation as it emerged after the Napoleonic Wars. The history of both these countries provides a signpost for the future of NATO. As they developed representative institutions so, in the course of time, NATO should establish an "Atlantic Parliament" of directly elected representatives from allied nations. Such a parliament would be a natural development of our era, in which the people take an active part in the forging of their own destinies. It would also be the most effective way to give NATO a more vital reality in the consciousness of men.

The basis for such a parliament is already in existence in the form of the Parliamentary Union of the Atlantic States. Members of the parliaments of all allies belong to this body, and meet at regular intervals to discuss NATO problems. The Union has a small steering committee and maintains a permanent secretariat in Paris; it conducts its work as though it were a NATO parliament. It deals with all questions of interest to NATO; it has special committees for political, military, economic, cultural, and scientific questions; and it adopts resolutions and makes recommendations, which it lays before the North Atlantic Council and other leading NATO bodies. For example, its Fourth Conference, in 1958, dealt chiefly with the question of joint consultation. It recommended close cooperation with other alliances in the Western world; and it called upon the NATO Council to reject the flagrant violation of international law by the Soviets in Berlin.

The Fifth Conference took place at the invitation of the U.S. Congress in the House of Representatives in Washington, from November 16 to 20, 1959. It confirmed the previous decision with regard to Berlin, and declared that "no solution is acceptable which threatens the security, the freedom, and the right of self-determination of West Berlin, or threatens its ties with the German Federal Republic." The conference also adopted recommendations on questions of interest to the Western alliance, including the unity of Europe, disarmament, European security, the situation of the peoples of Eastern Europe, and various military, economic, scientific, and technical problems. An equally wide field was covered by the Sixth Conference—held at NATO headquarters in Paris, November 13–18, 1961—including a "resolution on the Soviet-created crisis of Berlin."

Today, in almost all NATO countries, private associations further the idea of the Atlantic community. In 1954, an international organization, the Atlantic Treaty Association (ATA) was formed. In 1960, at its Sixth Annual General Meeting in Oslo, the ATA—which represents the rank and file of the Atlantic peoples—gave vigorous support to all NATO policies.

An Atlantic Parliament could develop from the Parliamentary Union and the Atlantic Treaty Association. It would not have to be in permanent session; a few meetings a year would suffice to provide a democratic representation ground for NATO and its peoples.

14

Fontainebleau, Headquarters
Allied Forces Central Europe

Headquarters of the Allied Forces Central Europe is situated in Fontainebleau, royal capital of the united Frankish empire in Carolingian, and perhaps already in Merovingian, times. The lilies of the French kingdom were succeeded by the golden eagle of Napoleon's empire, which in turn was replaced by the tricolor of the Republic. Queens of all the dynasties of Europe and three empresses moved through the halls and gardens of the ancient palace; Italian, Spanish, Portuguese, English, and German influences mingled with the French, to make Fontainebleau the magnificent palace it is today.

The old soldier who guides tourists through the palace is a Bonapartist—he might be a character from Rostand's *L'Aiglon*. To him, this is not a mausoleum of past glories, but the center of living history, the home of a tradition which did not die when the Emperor departed. Today, the people of Europe whom he tried to unite by force are assembled in this palace, to defend their common heritage. At Headquarters in the Cour Henri IV and in the Aile-des-Princes, an alliance seems to have formed among the victors of Austerlitz and Leipzig, Jena and Waterloo. The tricolor flies there in harmony with the Union Jack of Britain, the Black, Red, and Gold of the German Federal Republic, and the flags of Belgium, Holland, and Luxemburg. And to the naval, military, and air force uniforms of all these countries are added those of the United States, Canada, and the other NATO countries.

A Frenchman, General Pierre Jacquot, is Supreme Commander Allied Forces Central Europe (AFCENT); a German, General Hans Speidel, commands the land forces (LANDCENT); a Dutchman, Vice-Admiral G.B.M. van Erkel, the joint naval forces (NAVCENT), and Air Chief Marshal Earl of Bandon of Britain commands the joint air forces of Central Europe (AIRCENT). The Second Tactical Air Force, stationed in Mönchen-Gladbach and commanded by Air Marshal Sir Humphrey Edwardes-Jones, and the Fourth, stationed in Wiesbaden under the command of General Smith (U.S.), both come under Sir Harry.

General Speidel has two army groups under his command: the Northern Army Group (NORTHAG) under Lieutenant-General Sir Archibald James Cassels (G.B.), with headquarters in Mönchen-Gladbach; and Army Group Center (CENTAG), under General Bruce C. Clarke (U.S.), with Headquarters in Heidelberg.

"The military fully recognize the primacy of political control," declared General Speidel. "More than that: we welcome it."

The General received us in his office in the Aile-des-Princes. As a historian and economist, a Doctor of Philosophy and a lecturer on the Philosophical Faculty at the University of Tübingen, General Speidel is a scholar as well as a soldier. His historical perspective gives him insight into political events. We could readily see the qualities that have gained him confidence within NATO. He commands not only German divisions, but also French units, the British Army of the Rhine, the U.S. Seventh Army, and Canadian, Belgian, Dutch, and Luxemburg troops.

Speidel, born in 1897 in Württemberg, volunteered for the army in 1914, and remained an officer in the *Reichswehr* throughout the inter-war period. During the Second World War he was Chief of Staff to Corps, Armies, and Army Groups. After the attempt on Hitler's life on July 20, 1944, he was arrested, and not released until after the German collapse. In the first postwar years he did research at his old university, Tübingen; in 1951, he was a technical expert and delegate at the negotiations for the European Defense Community and subsequently NATO; since 1955, he has been in the Defense Ministry. He took over his command at Fontainebleau on April 1, 1957.

There is nothing peremptory about General Speidel; his manners are in the European, and particularly the South German tradition, with a strong Austrian influence—it is no accident that he feels a particular sympathy with men such as Prince Eugene and Field-Marshal Radetzky.

It was of course to be expected that the Communists would attack any German officer appointed to a NATO command; and as Commander of NATO's land forces in Europe, General Speidel was a natural target. But such propaganda has not diminished the loyalty and regard of his staff. A comradely spirit prevails among these NATO soldiers, and they are indifferent to the nationality of their leaders.

The relationship between France and Germany was a matter for some speculation, but in practice their cooperation here in Fontainebleau has been a particularly happy one. The rule-of-thumb experience of history has proven accurate once again: fought-out enmities lead to close friendships.

The relationship between General Speidel and his Chief of Staff, Lieutenant-General Albert Crahay, who commanded the Belgian contingent in the Korean War, is excellent. The same was true for Crahay's predecessor, the Belgian Lieutenant-General Cumont, a man of keen mind and refreshing frankness, who is now a member of the Military Committee in Washington.

The operational sphere of AFCENT stretches from the Seine to the Iron Curtain; from the North Sea, the mouth of the Elbe, and the Baltic, to the Austrian frontier in the Alps. It defends the Benelux countries, the German Federal Republic, and Northern France: 200,000 square miles of territory inhabited by 100 million people—in peace, the heart of Western European industry; in war, the first great objective of the enemy. Three great gates lie open into this area, and there are no natural obstacles: the North-German plains; the valleys near Kassel, Eisenach, and Hof; and the valley of the Danube. At the shortest point, the distance from the Iron Curtain to the Rhine is only 100 miles.

The Soviet divisions stationed along the Iron Curtain are of high quality. Twenty of them are actually in the Zone, and a large proportion of them are armored. The modern Soviet tank, the forty-five-ton JS-III, is armed with a 122 mm. gun. Each Soviet infantry division also has 350 tanks and self-propelling guns, as well as helicopters, the MIL-4 and the YAK-24, which can carry fully equipped men. Furthermore, the Red Army has special artillery divisions and nine airborne divisions. The troops in the Zone are equipped with rockets and tactical atomic weapons. They are organized as an expeditionary force and are all at full strength, with never more than 10 per cent of their personnel absent at any time. Behind these front-line divisions, there are further divisions stationed in the satellite countries and on Soviet territory.

Of course, the number of divisions is not the only thing that counts, and the Central European area is only one strategic sector of a much bigger front. It is important to realize that the Soviets could not, as they did in the last war, throw all their strength in here without leaving other places along their long frontiers critically exposed. This was one of the things we discussed in connection with SHAPE. If the Red Army were to take the offensive today, it would have to protect its frontiers on many fronts simultaneously, and allow for the fact that the strategic sword of the NATO powers would deal ruthless blows. The NATO shield has its own specific tasks within the framework of this general defense, and it would fulfill them.

However, there is still a good deal to be done. The British troops stationed in Central Europe are of high quality, but the divisions have been watered down. The French divisions which were for so long in Algeria must be retrained for nuclear warfare. The German Federal Army is still in the process of formation, and its arms and equipment are not yet as modern as could be wished. Of course, all this could be remedied fairly quickly, if the European members of NATO would decide that the seriousness of the situation demands radical measures.

"If you were Commander-in-Chief of the Red Army, would you advise Khrushchev to attack the NATO forces?" we asked a high-ranking officer in Fontainebleau.

"No, I certainly wouldn't," he replied. "The Red Army is not strong enough for a total war, and the risk that I might not be able to prevent the destruction of my troops and of the Soviet Union would be too great."

Fortunately, the Soviets are not without their troubles. There is, for example, the demographic problem. Since 1960, the generation born during World II has been coming up for military service, and the annual contingents are falling away rapidly. For four or five years, there will not be enough recruits to go around, and the Soviets are compelled to adjust to this development. A standing army of several million men cannot be thinned down by a fifth; if the attempt is made, nothing will work smoothly. If a gun needs a team of seven men, it cannot operate with five; it is better to withdraw every sixth or seventh gun. In addition, Khrushchev needs a large labor force in industry. The Supreme Soviet, on January 15, 1960, therefore decided to reorganize the Red Army. Its main aim is to keep men on active reserve in the Army and put them into industry, as we have already pointed out.

The satellite armies vary in quality. The People's Army of the Eastern Zone is in all probability too burdened with involuntary recruits to be valuable for large-scale action. At most, the Soviet military authorities would be able to integrate battalions with their own undermanned divisions. In addition, the Red Army has to perform many non-military tasks. It is the power behind the scenes that keeps the satellites and Russian peoples in check. This job requires a great deal of manpower; if the Red Army were to conquer Europe, there would be another dozen countries to be held in subjection, and under circumstances in which the troops would be in constant danger of infection from the Western mentality.

"But all that would take place in war and under martial law, which would facilitate matters. If they were victorious, the Soviets would not need to worry unduly about what happened afterwards."

"True," the AFCENT officer continued, "but even so I cannot see any grounds on which the Soviet Army would press for war now. If I were Soviet Supreme Commander, I should have my hands full making sure that nothing happens in Hungary, that the Poles continue to work, and that all goes well in the other satellites. The Germans in the Eastern Zone would fill me with misgiving all the time. After all, I would be the man to be made a scapegoat by Khrushchev and the political leadership, if anything went wrong."

Like all the other staffs, the Central European Command is an integrated one. What is the difference between an integrated officer and a national officer? Quite simply, the former is no longer under the authority of his own government as regards his military duties, but subordinate to his NATO superiors.

On the other hand, the NATO forces are not a unified army as the forces of the European Defense Community would have been. They consist of national contingents supplied on a national basis; and therefore even an integrated officer has, as Count Kielmansegg put it, "national underpinnings"; in pay and discipline, for example, he still depends on his own country.

We asked one of the German officers in Fontainebleau: "What

would happen in wartime if, say, a German division were to be pressed back into Denmark or Belgium? If it is cut off from Germany, who would supply it?"

"All units carry some supplies," he replied, "enough for about three days; and supplies for one month are kept in reserve. Long before these are exhausted, replenishments should be streaming across the Atlantic from the United States. These arrangements are already in force for U.S. troops, and similar arrangements are now being made for German troops. Of course, it isn't easy for Germany to build up a new army rapidly and at the same time lay down reserve supplies, which represent a big capital investment. Eventually, however, the necessary reserves ought to be stockpiled."

G-4, Transport and Logistics, is what formerly was called the Quartermaster's Department. G-4's job is to provide the troops with all they need to carry out their assignment, and to free them from all hindrance. The staff of G-4 is integrated, but as supplies are a national responsibility, it has no authority; it can recommend, but it cannot command. A NATO officer pointed out that G-3, which is the operational leadership, is closely linked with G-4. In G-3, the will of the Supreme Commander is translated into operational planning. But in order to translate this into action, G-3 needs the aid of G-4; the operational leadership must know what troops, weapons, and reserves are available, and how quickly they can be provided.

A considerable improvement in the supplies situation has been brought about by the introduction of the so-called cross-servicing system: when necessary, a NATO commander can call upon one country to supply another with whatever it requires. But this system is handicapped by the lack of standardization within NATO, whose forces still use a variety of non-interchangeable equipment.

Standardization has so far been achieved only in the infrastructure, especially in the airfields, depots, and long-lines communications system. The new pipelines laid through Denmark and France to the Rhine also are standardized. Two kinds of oil fuel are pumped through them, *Jet* for the jet planes, and *Mogas* for the tanks and heavier transport.

"Air defense must be integrated and standardized," declared Brigadier-General Ernst Kusserow, who is Deputy Coordinator for Air Defense, Central Europe, at Fontainebleau. The German Federal Republic can be crossed by plane in fifteen minutes. In such circumstances, even the fastest jet fighters are almost too slow, because it takes them four minutes to get into the air, and seven minutes before they reach top speed. Every day, the radar screen shows us Soviet aircraft flying towards the Iron Curtain, and then our fighters have to go into the air, to hold them back.

"What would happen if it were the real thing? How would you recognize in time that it was the real thing, if it really were?" The problem is difficult. Formerly, there had been a scale: twenty planes was a minor threat, fifty a medium threat, 200 a major threat. But today, one plane carrying a hydrogen bomb would represent a much greater threat than 200 carrying ordinary high-explosive bombs.

"When may one take action against a plane?" we asked.

"When it commits a hostile act," General Kusserow replied. But just what does a hostile act consist of? Does it mean flying over NATO territory? Before long, enemy bombers won't need to; they will be able to discharge their stand-off bombs fifty miles or more behind the Iron Curtain, and then turn away. When should one respond to such a threat? If one waits until the attacker crosses into NATO air space, it will surely be too late. The preliminary radar warning makes it possible to pick up an enemy plane before or at the Iron Curtain. But suppose the flight was a routine exercise? Or suppose that at the last moment the attack is countermanded and the planes turn away at the frontier, while the defense rockets are already on the way? Would this start the large war? What one really ought to do is to draw a line well beyond the frontier and parallel to it, and announce that any plane which crossed it would be regarded as committing a hostile act and risk being shot down without warning.

The order for defense can be given only by the commander of the particular sector. So far, this question of when to shoot has prevented the French from agreeing to an integrated air defense command, even though they agree that the problem must ultimately be solved.

We had opportunity to discuss this with Air Chief Marshal Sir Harry Broadhurst, then Commander Allied Air Forces Central Europe. Sir Harry is a man with years of combat experience in Africa and Europe. "There has been one very important change recently," he began, "and that is the rapid development of Soviet missiles. They are making our airfields increasingly vulnerable, and ultimately they will make them obsolete. You see, unfortunately we are well within range of Soviet medium and even short-range rockets. What that means I can best illustrate from an experience of mine in North Africa during the last war: Rommel was shelling my air-fields at close range. Loss of life was negligible, and my men could always find adequate shelter, but the splinters and fragments hurled in all directions by the exploding shells wrought havoc among my aircraft. They were being put out of commission at such a rate that the airfields were unusable and I had to pull my planes out and base them farther back. Later on, exactly the same thing happened in Normandy, when the Germans were shelling our airfields at 3,000 yards' range. Once again there was very little loss of life, but so much damage to aircraft that the airfields had to be abandoned. You can imagine what's going to happen in the future with these modern weapons. Why, even weapons of the size of the Honest Johns and the Corporals are pretty nasty things."

"In your opinion, Sir Harry, is there any answer?"

"Yes, I think there is: to put planes into the air the way you do from a carrier—by catapulting them off. Ultimately, of course, the answer will be the vertical take-off. But until it becomes operational, we shall have to get by with catapulting. In addition, we might also use what the Americans call *Jato* to speed the take-off and make it practically vertical."

"Few people realize," Sir Harry went on, "that within the whole Second ATAF operational field, the warning period is about a minute and a half; or, in other words, the flying time of Soviet guided missiles or rockets. For this reason the warning system must be integrated."

"How do you feel about our present strength, Sir Harry?"

"Oh, I'm not so worried about that. And a great consolation is that in recent months, German combat readiness has become very apparent. This is particularly true now that the first German Air Force wings are completely combat-ready, and trained for an atomic strike. They would certainly know how to deliver the goods if necessary, and that is an essential contribution to our defense. But as to integrated air defense, there are still certain difficulties. However, on the working level, the French are now cooperating; and, by the way, the French Air Force has just won the reconnaissance competition. And a jolly good show, too! The fact that the Nike-equipped battalions of the various allied forces are now approaching combat readiness is another reassuring factor in estimating our defensive capacity. There is one problem though, and that is to get hold of the necessary launching sites.

"There is one danger we must always beware of, though," Sir Harry concluded, "and that is the Maginot mentality—you know, just sitting behind a supposedly impregnable defense line, and doing no more about it. Should the Soviets attack, we could not content ourselves with mere defense; we should have to strike, too."

No one at Allied Forces Central Europe doubts for one moment that the Soviet's powerful navy is intended for offensive purposes. Whereas in the Second World War the Soviets did nothing at sea, and were probably in any case not in a position to do anything, their present-day naval strength in the Baltic, at Murmansk, in the Black Sea, and in the Pacific, is considerable. These fleets are modern, independent of one another in part, and capable of operating at long distances from their bases.

Protection of the seas around Central Europe is in the hands of several commands. Whereas the land and air forces of Europe Center are the strongest of any NATO sector, the Commander of the Allied Naval Forces Central Europe, the Dutch Vice-Admiral van Erkel, has only very few craft at his disposal. The central North Sea is included in the sphere of responsibility of the strategic forces of SACLANT; Channel Command protects the western North Sea and the English Channel from the Dutch-German frontier to Ushant; the Atlantic area from Ushant to the Franco-Spanish frontier is again under SACLANT. Protection of the Mediterranean Sea adjacent to the French coast is in the hands of the Mediterranean Command in Malta, as well as of the French fleet operating under national command. And the defense of the Baltic exits, including Schleswig-Holstein, has been made the business of the Allied Forces of Northern Europe.

The most immediate naval threat to Central Europe is posed by the powerful Baltic Fleet of the Soviets, with Riga, Reval, Königsberg, Kronstadt, and Libau as first-class naval bases. The commander, Admiral Charlamov, has over forty other admirals under him, and forces consisting of 5 cruisers, 53 destroyers, 259 minesweepers, 230 fast torpedo boats, 133 anti-submarine boats, 115 landing craft, and 56 depot ships. The importance that Moscow attaches to this fleet can be seen from the fact that it has also 112 submarines, whereas the Arctic Fleet stationed at Murmansk, and the Black Sea Fleet have only 100 submarines each, and the Far East Fleet at Vladivostok only 120. The Soviet Baltic naval forces also include 1,350 naval planes, most of them fighters, but also bombers, transport, and reconnaissance planes.

Further, with the completion of the Leningrad-Murmansk Canal, the Baltic Fleet could be reinforced, if need be, from Murmansk during the seven ice-free months of the year—although, of course, in the event of war this canal could be blocked or destroyed.

A fleet of this size could give powerful support to the Red Army launching an invasion along the Baltic coast. Khrushchev made it clear that he was determined to use this weapon as a means of pressure in the Cold War when he demanded "defense considerations" with Finland, in October, 1961. For a typical reversal of the facts, he alleged a "threat" by Germany and her allies; what he really meant was a Soviet threat—not only against Germany and Finland, but against all Scandinavian countries, including neutral Sweden.

Also, if Soviet submarines should succeed in breaking through into the North Sea and the Atlantic, they might cut the Atlantic lifeline on which Europe would depend for survival.

"Should the Soviets attack," declared Vice-Admiral Henrik Bos, who was Commander of the Allied Naval Forces in Central Europe until the late summer of 1960, "they would probably first try to attack Själland with combined naval and air forces, using parachute troops, in order to get control of the Sund and Belt. Thus the Baltic would not be a purely naval arena in the event of war; our naval, army, and air forces would have to work closely together."

The military command over this area was split up for a long time, the German North Sea fleet was under Europe Center, the Danish fleet under Europe North, and the German Baltic fleet under Europe Center in peacetime, under Europe North in the event of war—but this unsatisfactory arrangement has now been amended. Adopting a plan recommended by General Norstad, Germany and Denmark agreed to have this important theater placed under a newly created Allied Command Baltic Approaches (BALTAP) unified command for naval, land, and air forces, under a Danish commander reporting to Allied Forces Northern Europe (AFNORTH) in Oslo. On December 8, 1961, it was announced that Lieutenant-General Tag Andersen of the Royal Danish Air Force had been assigned to this post by SACEUR, with Major-General Peter von der Groeben of the German Army as Deputy Commander. There are four subordinate commands under BALTAP. The German North Sea and Baltic naval forces are united with the Danish fleet under an admiral, the Danish Army in Jutland and the German division in Schleswig-Holstein under a general, one commander to be a German, the other a Danish officer. The commander of the armed forces of the Danish isles Själland, Bornholm, and Funen also comes under BALTAP.

The fourth is an air command too, mainly from Danish forces; this, however, is of less importance, because the powerful Second Allied Tactical Air Force under the command of AFCENT covers this area —although only up to the latitude of Hamburg, which might not be quite far enough north for tactical missions. While the new arrangement still has some problematic features, it is likely to work well, if there is close cooperation between Europe North and Center.

The Central European front is perhaps the most endangered part of the whole Western defense line. Here the powerful Soviet bloc, with its endless supply possibilities, bulges dangerously into the heart of Europe; and here NATO needs its most effective defensive organization. We discussed this point with the French Air General Maurice Challe, who was Commander-in-Chief at Fontainebleau from April, 1960 until January, 1961.

"It seems to me that the most important thing is to strengthen the European community," he said. "After that, of course, comes the standardization of weapons and equipment, and, indeed, of all our material. We need NATO depots, and not merely national depots, if all our allies are to be assured of supplies."

"You are an air force general, *mon général*, so what do you think of the relationship between land and air forces?"

He replied forcefully, "A perfect understanding is necessary. There must be complete cooperation between all the fighting forces down to the last detail. I am very conscious of that, because my own command has always consisted of both land and air forces. The shield forces must be strengthened," he went on, and he pointed to the Iron Curtain on the map before us. Behind that line, the Soviet divisions were building up. To bolster the shield of NATO is both a political and a moral obligation; and the European community, as the core of the whole defense, must be strengthened too —in close cooperation with the United States, of course, whose strongest overseas army is stationed here. The *entente parfaite* to which he referred applies not only to the land and air forces, but to all the joint allied forces in Central Europe.

15

Great Britain and the
Benelux Countries

In order to appreciate the contribution of Great Britain to the defense of the West, we must look far beyond the limits of NATO. The three divisions that make up the British Army of the Rhine, the squadrons of the Royal Air Force attached to the Second ATAF at Mönchen-Gladbach, British Bomber Command, and the Home Fleet at its European bases, are by no means Britain's only contribution. "There are 100,000 British troops east of Suez," we were told by Frank Mottershead, then Under-Secretary at the Ministry of Defense —from Aden to Kenya, from Singapore to Hong Kong, Malaya, and the British possessions in the Indian and Pacific Oceans. In the South Pacific, the dominions of New Zealand and Australia, tied to the motherland through Crown and Commonwealth, are united with her in the struggle against Bolshevism. Through the ANZUS Pact, they are allied with the United States; and through SEATO, with France.

The Dominion of Canada is a member of NATO in her own right.

That India, now independent but still a part of the Commonwealth, has not gone over to the Soviet bloc, is largely owing to her long years of Western influence, chiefly through Great Britain. Had New Delhi followed the example of Peking and gone over to Bolshevism, the effect on the other Asian and African peoples would have been incalculable. Pakistan, whose educated strata feel themselves to be not only the heirs of Islam but also of Hellenism, has even become Britain's loyal ally. Pakistan is also a member of the Commonwealth, and connected with NATO through the CENTO Pact (called the Baghdad Pact before Iraq's withdrawal), together with Iran, Turkey, Great Britain, and, by association, the United States.

Through SEATO, Great Britain is allied with Thailand and the Philippines, and here too she takes part in the defense against Bolshevism. The resultant reduction of Soviet pressure on Europe is to the direct benefit of NATO. Finally, British warships still sail all the oceans, and the formidable Royal Air Force encircles the globe.

It is not surprising that such widespread obligations often create tensions, and the achievement of the British people—not only in the military sphere—in a time of growing and often fanatical nationalism, is all the more admirable. Naturally, the Soviets systematically do feed old colonial resentments, and these are sometimes a burden. But Great Britain's contribution to the free world can be gauged by imagining the end of the Commonwealth. The Kremlin realizes this, as is shown by the constant efforts to separate Great Britain from NATO and persuade her to play a lone hand.

As the British Ambassador in Bonn, Sir Christopher Steel, pointed out, "One should not forget that Great Britain did a great deal towards bringing NATO into existence. Western European Union was a good beginning. NATO used it as a basis, and after the collapse of the European Defense Community in 1954, the way was open for the acceptance of Germany into the North Atlantic Treaty Alliance."

Sir Christopher knows Germany well; before the Second World War, he was attached to the British Embassy in Berlin. At the end of the war, he became a member of the Military Government, latterly as Deputy High Commissioner. In this respect he may be said to continue a family tradition, because his wife's father, Sir Sidney Clive, was British Military Governor in Cologne in 1919.

Great Britain's defense budget is sizable—approximately $4.8 billion for 1962–63, according to the forecast of the 1962 White Paper on Defense—an increase of more than $180 million over the previous year. This represents 7 per cent of the national product. It is one of the biggest defense budgets in the North Atlantic Alliance.

"Defense is the decisive thing," said Sir Christopher. "We take the view that NATO is primarily a military alliance and not a new League of Nations. But of course such an alliance brings a good deal

of close political cooperation with it, and in the end—as envisaged in
Article 2 of the NATO Pact—a closer economic and cultural community."

Sir Christopher, who is well acquainted with the alliance from
the years when he represented his country in the North Atlantic
Council, believes that Britain's request to join the Common Market
will also strengthen the solidarity of NATO.

The headquarters of NORTHAG in Mönchen-Gladbach was
originally the command center for the British Army of Occupation,
and even today it is headquarters for the British Army of the Rhine
and the Royal Air Force (Germany). But the NATO function now
predominates.

This headquarters, the biggest of its kind in Europe, is in effect
a town with a population of 1,500. It was built between 1952 and
1954, on an area of about 1,500 acres in the Rheindahlen Forest.
Headquarters is grouped around a main administration core of 3,000
offices, which has become known simply as the Big House. In addition, there are 100 barrack blocks—quarters for 1,800 married couples
and their children and 1,000 civilian employees, three churches, four
schools, ten clubs and messes, a theater, a cinema, a shopping center,
and a guest house. And, because it is originally British, there are
cricket pitches, football fields, golf courses, and tennis courts—no
less than twenty-eight of the latter.

"All that counts with us is soldierly competence," declared General
Sir Dudley Ward, then Commander-in-Chief of NORTHAG, when
he received us in the study of his house, situated in the center of
the wooded camp area. "When anyone says 'we' here, he doesn't
mean 'we British' or 'we Germans,' but all of us in our joint headquarters."

Sir Dudley's Chief of Staff, Major-General R. W. Eubank, is also
British, but he could well be an officer of one of the other nationali-
ties there. One of the two Deputy Chiefs of Staff is Brigadier-General
Kurt Brandstädter, a German, and the other a Dutchman, Major-
General G. H. Christian.

The Northern Army Group consists of four corps, each of which
is called the first in its own country: the First Belgian Corps at
Cologne-Weiden, the First British Corps at Bielefeld, the First
German Corps at Münster, and the First Dutch Corps at Apeldoorn.
In addition, there are four independent Canadian brigades, and 1,600
Luxemburgers, who are brigaded with the Belgians. The corps, like

the divisions, are nationally homogeneous, and integration begins only at Army Group Staff level.

"This is more efficient than if we were to mix the divisions without any real necessity," said Sir Dudley. "Though, of course, each Corps Staff must be capable of taking over the leadership of any division, irrespective of its nationality. Here this is no longer a problem. It doesn't worry me that each group has its own peculiarities, because they involve no special difficulties for tactics and operations. Communication is excellent. We all have the same ideas, and in our build-up we are in any case gradually coming closer to a general brigading."

"Then standardization is making progress, Sir Dudley?"

"Standardization is important, but it isn't my chief problem here. You know the difficulties involved, and I've neither time nor energy to expend on them. I must also admit that there are good reasons for some national differences."

"But doesn't the variety of equipment cause a good deal of trouble? For instance, when one division is equipped with British Centurion tanks, and the others with American M-47s and M-48s?"

"It doesn't affect our firepower, but it leads to some supply problems; you can't interchange munition and spare parts at need. It hampers tactical mobility to some extent."

Sir Dudley also had something to say about the vexing question of light *versus* heavy tanks: "Everyone wants a powerful tank which is as light as possible—that is to say, the lightest for real effectiveness in the field. And that's bound to be a fairly heavy tank. A commander must be in a position to force the enemy to concentrate his firepower, and he certainly can't do that with tanks which are so vulnerable that an anti-tank man with a bazooka can shoot them up effectively from a distance."

Of course, lighter tanks are more mobile, but mobility isn't everything. "Wars aren't won just by maneuvering. The utmost a commander can gain by maneuvering is the advantage of position."

"May I suggest, Sir Dudley, that you are paraphrasing a famous axiom of Frederick the Great—'battles win wars'."

"Certainly, no campaign was ever lost or won without a decisive battle."

Tanks are of particular importance for NORTHAG, because the area it has to defend is the North German plains, which would allow the Soviets to deploy their tanks on the widest possible scale.

Although there was still a great deal to do, Sir Dudley was confident that his Army Group would be in a position to carry out its assigned tasks. "Provided our divisions are armed with tactical atomic weapons, well coordinated and deployed in positions of our own choosing, we shall be able to pose a difficult problem to the enemy," he declared in conclusion—which struck us as a typical piece of British understatement.

Like General Norstad himself, Sir Dudley wore two hats: he was not only Commander-in-Chief of NORTHAG, but also Commander-in-Chief of the British Army of the Rhine and of all British forces on the Continent, including those in Berlin. The same applies to Lieutenant-General Sir Archibald Cassels, who succeeded him in 1960. The Army Group insignia is a gold axe on a blue ground, called the Franzisca—a weapon meant to be hurled. "In 451, the West won the battle on the Catalonian fields with this weapon," General Brandstädter explained. The Franzisca was the tactical weapon of its day. The allied armies of the Goths and the Romans hurled them among the mounted masses of Huns, felling horses and spreading confusion. The Franzisca broke the overwhelming superiority of a foe theretofore considered invincible.

Before long, the Northern Army Group will have an integrated signals battalion, its own transport pool, and a mixed staff battalion.

The Second ATAF was formed in April, 1952, as one of the two air forces in Central Europe charged with the tactical air defense of this area. The British Army of Occupation provided the basis for the Second ATAF. By January, 1959, integration with Belgian, Dutch, and German units had progressed so far that the staff of the Second ATAF could be turned into a NATO unit.

The combination of "national" and "NATO" organization may be confusing at first glance, but it is quite simple. It rests on the fact that the equipment, training, and supplying of the troops, even when they are at the disposal of NATO, remain national tasks. For Great Britain, these are carried out by the Royal Air Force (Germany). But in the event of war, and in peacetime maneuvers, NATO takes over the operative command through the integrated staff of the Second ATAF.

"In my view, the best way to arrive at a common understanding is to work together," said Air Marshal Sir Humphrey Edwardes-Jones. "Each officer who comes to us has his own job to do and he does it irrespective of his nationality."

Sir Humphrey joined the staff of the Second ATAF as early as

1952, and in 1957 he took command. He is no mere administrator; he has been in the Royal Air Force for over thirty years, and for two years he was a test pilot. His sun-tanned face and his physique show that at the age of fifty-four he is still devoted to active sports. He is a keen golfer and tennis player, and when he can find time, he flies to Kiel to get in a little sailing.

He went up to a map of his operational area. Colored buttons indicated the air bases: red, those belonging to the RAF; green, the Belgian bases; black, airfields already operated by German airmen. The white buttons indicated airfields which are still in the planning stage.

"The units of the four nations in the Second ATAF are more or less the same strength. At the moment, the list would read: Belgium, Holland, Great Britain, and Germany. But of course, it's not only the number of machines and men that counts, but their performance."

Formerly, there were 28,000 British men; today there are 13,000, equipped with nuclear weapons. So far, Germany's contribution consists of the Thirty-first Fighter-Bomber Wing at Nörvenich, and the Seventy-first Day-Fighter Wing at Ahlhorn. Before long, they will be reinforced by the Thirty-fifth and the Seventy-second Fighter Wings.

The British Javelin all-weather fighter and the Hawker-Hunter both reach the speed of sound and are armed with air-to-air guided missiles. Even the excellent Canberra bomber, which was taken over by the United States and produced under license as the B-57, very nearly reaches the speed of sound. As soon as its nuclear equipment is ready, it will represent one of the most powerful tactical units in existence. In order to evade the enemy's radar defenses and anti-aircraft rockets, the Second ATAF has adopted a low-flight tactic— as has, at least in part, the American Strategic Air Command.

"With its present equipment, the RAF is ready for immediate action, and capable of dealing with anything the enemy is likely to put up against it," declared Sir Humphrey.

For reconnaissance in the warning zones, there are Swift FR-5s and Hunter-6 fighters at forward air bases, whose squadrons can be in the air, ready for action, within five minutes. Further Hunter fighters can be in action within half an hour.

"Our bombers and the other reconnaissance planes are not normally held in such a high degree of preparedness," we were told. "But they, too, must be able to get into the air quickly at any time. At the last maneuvers, they took just nine minutes. If we have advance notice, as we would in the event of crisis, they could get into the air even quicker."

In the Second ATAF, not only the headquarters staff is integrated, but also some subordinate commands: the Tactical Operational Centers (TOC) for the fighter-bombers in Goch and Sundern, and the Sector Operational Centers (SOC) for the fighters in Brockzetel, Udem, Niew Milligen, and Glons. National dividing lines begin at wing level, but even there, coordination is so close that in an emergency, any one could replace the other. Thus the Second ATAF demonstrates the feasibility of an integrated European air defense apparatus—and Sir Humphrey is convinced that it is essential. On January 7, 1961, his place was taken by Air Marshal John Grandy, a man with wide experience in Europe and Southeast Asia.

The reduction of British troops in NORTHAG and in the Second ATAF is a result of the general defense reorganization which has been going on in Great Britain since 1957, as part of a five-year plan. The plan lays great stress on strategic weapons and the modernization of all equipment. On the other hand, manpower is being reduced from 700,000 to 400,000. By 1963, the British Army is to consist of between 165,000 and 180,000 men, the Royal Navy of 88,000, and the Royal Air Force of 135,000. By then, the armed forces will consist only of professional soldiers serving a minimum of six years. The objective is a small but modern and mobile fighting force with tremendous firepower.

Great Britain, as the third atomic power, already has a considerable stock of atom bombs, and the production of hydrogen bombs is making good progress. In 1958, the first units of Bomber Command were equipped with nuclear weapons. The present carriers will be progressively replaced by the newest V-series types, the delta-shaped Vulcan and the Victor, which both compare favorably with the American B-52 Strato-fortress for speed and altitude. These are being fitted with stand-off weapons—the Blue Steel and the Skybolt—which can fly swiftly towards their objectives long before the planes come within range of enemy anti-aircraft rockets.

Britain's strength rests on, among other things, the fact that her people are prepared to look hard facts in the face, and that the government is therefore not afraid to express them. For example, in February, 1958, the White Book of the Ministry of Defense declared bluntly that it was impracticable to attempt to protect the country as a whole against nuclear attack, and that the available fighters must therefore confine themselves to the defense of strategic bomber bases. For this purpose also, Britain developed her own weapons, for example, the Lightning fighter (English Electric P1B) which reaches twice the speed of sound and is to be armed at first with Firestreaks and later on with an improved type of air-to-air guided missile capable of coping with the much faster planes of the future.

For a time, the Lightning was referred to as "the last manned fighter," in the belief that within a few years, anti-aircraft defenses would consist exclusively of guided missiles. But this view has now been abandoned, in realization that for a long time to come there will be jobs which only manned planes can do, such as to intercept hostile or unidentified planes. They are also essential for use against bombers equipped with anti-radar devices and/or stand-off bombs.

In May, 1958, the RAF took over its first rocket base for modern anti-aircraft defense, chiefly as a test and training station. The English Electric Thunderbird and the Bristol-Ferranti Bloodhound have approximately the same performance as the U.S. Nike and Hawk homing rockets, respectively. While the Thunderbird is devised for a high degree of mobility, the semi-mobile Bloodhound, assisted at the take-off by four solid-fuel rockets, is intended primarily for fixed sites. With a ram of fifty miles, it is thought to outdo all other known ground-to-air rockets.

The all-purpose TSR-2 is being developed as a tactical plane for army support, and in about four years, when it is operational, it will replace the Canberra bomber. Although the TSR-2 will fly faster than sound and be big enough to carry nuclear weapons, it will require only medium-length starting and landing facilities. It will be able to fly beneath the enemy's radar screen, and it will also be equipped with air-to-air missiles.

Aircraft are of increasing importance for the Royal Navy, Britain's senior service; the big naval engagements of World War II were decided less by the firepower of the big ships than by air attack from carrier-launched planes. British aircraft carriers are therefore being equipped with the most modern jet planes. The first Scimitar jet fighter-bombers were put into service in 1958, and they carry nuclear weapons. In 1960 came the first all-weather Sea Vixen, equipped with Firestreak guided missiles. Great Britain has also developed the first all-weather helicopter, the Wessex, which promises to develop into a very effective anti-submarine naval plane.

After a long and honorable history, the British Navy has discarded battleships; the last of a long line, the Vanguard, which "never fired a shot in anger," has now been sent to the breaker's yard. The backbone of British naval power today is the carrier task-force, battle groups which are well able to defend themselves against sea and air attack, and, above all, against the biggest Soviet threat, the submarine. At present, Britain has three large and ten medium aircraft carriers. Among the most modern are the Hermes, the Victorious—which was reconditioned in 1958 and is now one of the best-equipped aircraft carriers in the world—the Centaur, and the Albion. All of these vessels are equipped with angled decks, steam-operated catapults, landing mirror, audio landing aids (all British inventions), and, of course, modern radar equipment. There are five other air-craft carriers in service with various Commonwealth navies; Australia has two, Canada two, and India one. The sixteen British cruisers, fifty-seven destroyers, and 115 frigates can also look to the navies of the other Commonwealth countries for support.

During the past five years, twenty-four new antisubmarine vessels, eight anti-aircraft frigates, and thirteen submarines have been launched, while many of the already existing vessels have been modernized. The first British atomic submarine, the Dreadnought, also has been completed.

Thus the British Navy has become smaller but more mobile, and better adapted to the demands of nuclear warfare. So far, the Soviets have not built any aircraft carriers, and their strongest weapon is the group of submarines intended to cut Europe's Atlantic supply line. Britain's medium aircraft carriers, with their escorts, are specially designed to protect the Atlantic convoys from submarine attack.

Two aircraft carriers, two cruisers, and a considerable number of destroyers, frigates, and submarines are always on patrol in European, Atlantic, and Mediterranean waters. They are subordinate to SACLANT and to the Channel and Mediterranean commands of NATO, and they work in cooperation with the naval forces of the other NATO allies. The British East-Asia Fleet with its base at Singapore is independent, well balanced, and ready for any naval task. It has two aircraft carriers, including the Bulwark, which carries landing forces of marines. The various units operate singly or in groups, but they come together regularly for maneuvers. This fleet also serves to fulfill the obligations of Great Britain in the Far East and in Southeast Asia, pursuant to the SEATO and CENTO pacts. In addition, a number of British frigates patrol the Persian Gulf and the neighborhood of Hong Kong for the protection of shipping.

The Army is most affected by the defense reorganization and

gradual reduction taking place in Great Britain. But there are already worried Englishmen who doubt whether such a small army can possibly be adequate to all obligations. It would hardly suffice when, as a result of the balance of nuclear terror, conventional forces begin to recover their importance.

However, according to the 1959 British White Book on Defense, among the 280,000 men to be demobilized, there are over 100,000 non-combatants engaged in training and administrative tasks. Like the Navy, the Army is to be smaller but more mobile and better trained. Its firepower certainly has increased. Two units have already been equipped with Corporal guided missiles, and they will be attached to BAOR. By 1962, all equipment from World War II is to have been replaced. A large number of the reliable Centurion tanks are already operational, and a new heavy tank, the Conqueror, is to go into service soon.

The battalion is the basic unit of the British Army. Depending on the task at hand, they are organized into divisions of varying strength and equipment. The biggest field army at the moment is the British Army of the Rhine, with 55,000 men. There are 100,000 men in the Middle and Far East, and a brigade of infantry is an expeditionary corps in East Africa. They are supplemented by colored troops such as the King's African Rifles and the Gurkhas. A staff network in all British possessions can undertake the operational direction of the troops at once, in case of need.

In order to meet its far-flung obligations without having to keep permanent garrisons everywhere, the British Army holds a strategic reserve in England, part of which is always ready to go anywhere. Among them is a brigade of parachute troops, and these units can be transported rapidly by the highly efficient Transport Command of the Royal Air Force, which is now equipped with the big Bristol Britannias.

The 1962 White Paper on Defense points out that Britain's contribution to the Western strategic deterrent is by itself enough to make a potential aggressor fear that retaliation would inflict destruction beyond any level he would be prepared to tolerate. It acknowledges that her duty in NATO is to contribute not only to the formulation of an agreed strategy but to make available a fair share of the forces to fulfill that strategy. And it adds: "We accept that the provision of adequate forces to support the strategic objectives of NATO must continue to be one of Britain's primary responsibilities as far as we can see into the present decade."

Belgium, Holland, and Luxemburg, united by the Congress of Vienna in 1814—until the Belgian Revolution of 1830—are again moving together: economically through the Benelux Customs Union, and politically through Western European Union and NATO. They have joined the Coal and Steel Community and the Common Market, and are setting Europe an example by moving toward union.

Owing to their geographical situation, these three small countries have often been the battlefield of Europe. In the nineteenth century, they were neutral countries between England and France; in the twentieth century, between Germany and Britain. Today, under the threat of Soviet aggression, they have become a bridge between allies.

Belgium, which abandoned her traditional neutrality in order to join NATO, has always pressed urgently for close integration. It is perhaps no accident that Paul-Henri Spaak, whose insight about the common fate of Europe has prompted his passionate advocacy of European unity and the development of the Atlantic community, is a Belgian statesman.

Belgium has always been ready to make a substantial contribution. Her defense budget amounted to no less than $380 millions in 1958; and then her young and vigorous Minister for National Defense, Arthur Robert Gilson, secured an increase to $400 millions. With this budget, Belgium maintained a standing army of 120,000 men. For 1961, however, to help absorb the losses suffered by the events in the Congo, a drastic reduction of all these figures became necessary. Defense expenditures had to be reduced by some $50 millions, and non-essential personnel, as Gilson declared, would be dropped from the armed forces without, however, reducing combat readiness.

Such austerity measures were of course unavoidable. With the loss of the Congo, inhabited by 14 million people in an area of over 900,000 square miles—almost eighty times the size of Belgium—Belgium was deprived of $300 to $500 millions in annual income, according to figures prepared by the Bank of Brussels. Investments and other property have been estimated as high as $8 billions.

The loss of income represented between 2.5 and 4.2 per cent of the gross national product. While this is sizable, it is, on the other hand, no more than Belgium's recent annual rate of growth, and most Belgians are therefore confident that their country will weather the storm.

The First Army Corps, which is at the disposal of NORTHAG,

consists of an infantry and an armored division, and, in addition, certain specialized groups: parachutists, rocket detachments, and units trained for nuclear warfare, artillery, engineers, signals, supplies, medical service, and military police.

Within seven days of mobilization, two reserve divisions would be available for defensive operation, and within thirty days, for full-scale operations. Four battalions are already mechanized and equipped with American M-41 tanks and M-75 armored cars. There are also an airborne regiment and field security troops.

Belgium is rapidly adapting her Army to the requirements of modern warfare. The period of compulsory military service had been reduced from eighteen months to twelve, as in some other NATO countries, but to offset this, the Army is to have a greater number of long-service volunteers. The proportion of professional soldiers was always high—about 50 per cent—and now the Belgian military authorities have started to recruit men for highly technical expert training—"NATO technicians," they are called. Selected young volunteers (the average age is eighteen) who sign on for from three to five years, will receive basic military training for one year and then be educated for technical specialties. To ensure that they retain and develop their specialized knowledge when they return to civilian life, they are simultaneously prepared for some civilian job related to their army specialties; and in order to make the transition easier for them, they receive a special demobilization bonus of about $2,000. The Defense Minister hopes that, thanks to these arrangements, within about three years the Belgian Army will be composed one-third each of ordinary service men, professional soldiers, and NATO technicians.

The new program has proved attractive to young Belgians, and the number of volunteers in the first year (1959) was so large that the authorities were in a position to set high standards and select men of suitable character and technical ability. Unfortunately, this program is proving to be so high in cost that it is doubtful whether the country will be able to maintain it.

Belgian divisions are being grouped into brigades or special units; the new infantry divisions will consist of 13,000 men, and the armored divisions of 11,000 men. So far, the Belgian Army has relied on conventional artillery, but after the reorganization, six or more batteries will be equipped with Honest John or Corporal missiles.

After World War II, the Belgian infantry was equipped with a variety of arms from various sources, but recently Belgium, like

Great Britain, has made great efforts toward standardization. Her own armament industry turns out excellent weapons; for example, the Belgian automatic FN rifle has been adopted as the standard NATO infantry weapon. Used as an automatic weapon, it can fire 700 shots a minute. The Energa rifle grenade can also be used with the FN rifle. The Belgian Sten and Vigneron works also turn out first-class machine pistols and light machine guns.

The greater part of the Belgian Air Force is attached to the Second ATAF—five wings and one reconnaissance squadron. The two Belgian fighter-bomber wings are equipped with American F-84s; and the two day-fighter and all-weather wings with Canadian CF-100 and British Hunter Mark 4 and 6 planes; but all these aircraft are to be replaced by up-to-date models as quickly as possible. Belgium will acquire F-104 Starfighters and has joined Germany, Holland, and Italy in the common program for production of this multi-purpose plane in Europe on license. One hundred million dollars were set aside by the Belgians for this purpose. In addition, Belgium has certain available reserves, as well as a number of aircraft which have remained under national command. The air bridge which Transport Command (using chiefly American C-119s, DC-4s, and DC-6s) set up between Belgium and Leopoldville during the Congo crisis in the summer of 1960 was instrumental in saving the lives of many innocent people.

During World War II, Belgian airmen formed a special detachment of the Royal Air Force, and the Belgian Air Force of today, which is a development of that wartime body, is on the same footing as the Army and Navy. In the first years after the war, Belgian pilots and air personnel were trained with the British, Canadian, and U.S. air forces, but today the Benelux countries combine for training purposes.

The Belgian Navy is relatively small—it has only 4,000 men—but the coastline is only about forty miles long. Two destroyers and forty minesweepers, most of which were provided by the United States, are kept in service.

Belgium has a particularly good officers corps, proud of its long tradition. Caesar's famous words, *fortissimi sunt Belgae*, which stood at the beginning of Belgian history, are still valid today. Belgian officers are expected to live up to high standards, and promotion requirements are unusually strict. The almost spartan military tone is reflected by the fact that the highest military rank is that of Lieutenant-General. Only the King holds the rank of full General, as

Commander-in-Chief of the Army. But even he wears the uniform of the Lieutenant-General.

The Defense Minister secured an increase in the defense budget by convincing the parliament that Belgium must fulfill her obligations if she in turn expects aid from her allies, in particular the United States. But beyond that, he desires an improvement in the structure of NATO and a closer integration of its forces.

He pointed out that integration and greater specialization were essential, for both political and economic reasons. For a country of 9 million inhabitants, it is, for example, a heavy burden to purchase 200 jet planes, whose cost exceeds the annual defense budget, and know that in case of war, they would not suffice to defend Belgian air space. Gilson realizes that only a systematic division of labor within NATO is the answer. Each member should specialize in its area of greatest competence—for instance, build up an efficient land army, and rely on its allies for complementary fighting forces.

"NATO's organization must definitely be improved," Gilson declared. "For us, this is a condition *sine qua non,* and the only way to solve the economic problem. It is in fact a basic requirement of our policy."

Unlike Belgium, Holland has a relatively long, broken coastline, and a great seafaring tradition. Before the Second World War, her colonial empire embraced about 700,000 square miles, inhabited by 65 million people. Today it still amounts to perhaps a quarter of that area.

The Dutch Navy, with its modern ships, is a considerable fighting force. It is part of the NATO naval forces, one section under the Channel Command, and the other under SACLANT. Its aircraft carrier, the Karel Doorman, is only 18,000 tons, but jet planes can land and take off on its flight deck. The Dutch Navy also has two light cruisers, thirty-four destroyers and frigates, ten submarines, fifty-two minesweepers, and sixteen auxiliary vessels. The Dutch Naval Air Arm consists of 160 planes, including jet fighters, long-range bombers armed with torpedoes, and aquaplanes. The new cruisers and destroyers are fast and well equipped; the 120 mm. guns of the destroyers are fully automatic, and can fire fifty shells a minute. The cruisers are armed with 150 mm. guns, and are now being equipped with guided missiles. The anti-submarine rocket of the Dutch Navy was designed and developed in Holland. The two latest Dutch submarines have a triple hull, in order to allow them to go down to greater depths, and they are equipped with ultra-modern torpedoes and firing apparatus that are effective even at great depths.

Thus the Dutch Navy can provide an effective anti-submarine task force; in addition, it has sufficient vessels to carry out important mine-sweeping and mine-laying operations. Two overseas naval stations provide for the defense of Dutch overseas possessions: one in New Guinea and the other in the Antilles. Naval air squadrons are based at these two stations, together with special groups of marines, 200 to 400 strong, depending on their tasks.

The Dutch Army has consisted of four infantry divisions and one cavalry brigade, and this framework has been retained. There are 35,000 men, or two divisions, on the active list, together with various specialized units. The greater part of this force is at the disposal of NORTHAG. One of these divisions is at full war strength and ready for action. The other is a skeleton division and is gradually being filled out. The two staffs are already at the disposal of NATO. The men are stationed on Dutch territory, but go to Germany to take part in the combined maneuvers of Army Group North.

"Two or three battalions took part in the last maneuvers," said Lieutenant-Colonel H. M. Dijkman, Chief of Operations in Department G-4 (Logistics). "Cooperation with the German troops was good and comradely."

During the course of 1960, a limited fighting group of the Dutch Army was stationed in Germany. In addition, an anti-aircraft group equipped with Nike missiles was stationed in the Münster area to strengthen the defense ring.

Since the adoption of the brigade organization, the Dutch Army is built up like the U.S. Army. The Dutch Defense Minister, M. S. H. Visser, is a civilian, but he is supported by two Under-Secretaries who are both, as a rule, soldiers. One of them was formerly Deputy Chief of the General Staff. There are Chiefs of Staff, one for each arm, and the senior takes the chair but has no superiority over the others.

"Doesn't that arrangement create difficulties?" we asked a highly placed Dutch officer.

"No," he replied, "because in practice they are always in agreement." And with a smile he added, "If three high officers of the Army, Navy, and Air Force could not agree among themselves, we should regard it as a sign of incompetence."

A Dutch division consists of seven infantry battalions, two tank squadrons, and three battle group staffs. Three battalions are placed at the orders of these staffs, which have only operational tasks; logistics remain in the hands of the division.

The Dutch Air Force is similar in strength and equipment to the Belgian—fifteen squadrons, with 350 planes. Two wings of fighter-bombers and two of day fighters, together with three fighter squadrons and one reconnaissance squadron, are assigned to the Second ATAF. They are to be equipped with F-104 Starfighters.

With its 312,000 inhabitants, Luxemburg represents just one military district. There are a regimental staff and two battalions, one of which is active and provides the field companies and the guard company. The second is a training battalion. In the event of war, Luxemburg would provide 3,000 fighting men equipped by Belgium. The country has no tanks and no planes. The contingent assigned to NORTHAG is attached to the Belgian forces.

Apart from the military contribution of the Benelux countries, their modern, highly developed industries represent a valuable reinforcement of NATO's potential, and, at the same time, a very attractive objective for Soviet conquest. The ports of Amsterdam, Rotterdam, and Antwerp are valuable doors which must be kept open to receive supplies coming from the United States across the Atlantic.

In recent years, two statesmen of the Benelux countries have been Presidents of the North Atlantic Council. In 1958, it was the Luxemburg Premier M. Joseph Bech, and in 1959, Dutch Foreign Minister J. M. A. H. Luns. Together with the Belgian statesman Paul-Henry Spaak, and his successor as Secretary-General, the Dutchman Dirk U. Stikker, they have made it clear to the world that NATO is not an affair for the big powers only, that, indeed, it owes its special moral stature to the fact that the smaller states, including the Benelux countries, are among its most loyal members.

16

France and the
North Atlantic Pact

"The only patriotism that comes into question for us today is loyalty to NATO."

These words were said by General Paul Henri Romuald Ély, when, as Chief of the General Staff of National Defense, he occupied the highest military position in France. (At present, it is held by Jean Olié.) Ély is a tall man with fine, almost ascetic features. He began his military career in 1915 as an eighteen-year-old Army volunteer. Later, as a major, he was attached for five years to the famous Deuxième Bureau, the counter-intelligence department of the French Army. After the rapid collapse of France early in World War II, he took part in the Resistance. In May, 1954, after the conclusion of the fighting in Vietnam, he was appointed Commander-in-Chief and Plenipotentiary by the then French Premier Mendès-France, and in this capacity he had the thankless task of dismantling France's position in Indo-China, and pulling out her troops.

General Ély has been called "the conscience of the Army." During the political crisis in May, 1958, when the French Government and the French Army clashed, he resigned his position as Chief of the General Staff. General Charles de Gaulle, with whom Ély has a good deal in common, called him to this even more responsible position, which had been created by the new Constitution. The

Chief of the General Staff of National Defense is directly subordinate to the Minister for the Armed Forces, and his primary task is to coordinate the activities of the Commanders-in-Chief of the the Army, Navy, and Air Force. Ély, who represented his country in the Washington Standing Group for four years, is familiar with the work in NATO.

"No country can stand on its own today," he said. "Even the neutral countries owe their freedom indirectly to the existence of NATO." The threat that hangs over the West is aimed at the whole of Europe, and all the continental peoples are well aware of this. "In centuries of struggle—with you, gentlemen, if you will permit me to put it that way," smiled the General, "France, like Germany, has learned to think in terms of continental defense. Today both are faced with a common danger of far greater dimensions."

It is understandable that the Anglo-Saxons have no such clear understanding of the situation, because they have never suffered actual invasion. Involuntarily, they think in the first place of the problem of strategic defense against the military power of the Soviets. But for France and Germany, it is a total threat to their lives in every form—political, economic, and cultural.

"To put it bluntly," Ély continued, "it is a world-wide threat, a permanent war with all possible means. The Soviets never take any step which does not serve their ultimate aim of world-revolutionary conquest. Even if it is only a question of appointing a new consul in North Africa, it all fits in."

In the past, in order to wield political influence in development areas, one first had to build up a large apparatus; today that is no longer necessary. The Soviets and their helpers distribute small wireless sets, and then can reach large numbers of people whose total vocabulary may be only a hundred words. This propaganda, which is part and parcel of the cold war, does not cease day or night.

The problem of Algeria belongs in this context. "Our task there," he said, "lets us in for a good deal of misdirected criticism. Many people still don't understand that we are not waging a war of colonial domination."

Since those words were spoken in May, 1959, President de Gaulle has shown by his courageous plan of September 16, 1959, which was adopted in the National Assembly by an overwhelming majority, that the French are not fighting to maintain colonial rule in Algeria. In the previous year, soon after he was elected President, he gave the other French possessions in North Africa full freedom to decide their own fate by referendum. All, with the exception of Guinea, chose to remain attached to France; and Guinea was given its freedom at once. General de Gaulle offered the Algerians the same choice, and he has proved to the world that he meant this offer seriously and was determined to carry it through, supported by the great majority of the French nation, against the resistance of the French extremists in Algeria.

Algeria was a moral test for the French people. After the Second World War, France also had her "economic miracle." In consequence, her people have enjoyed a high standard of living, and were inclined to regard their comfort as a matter of course. But then French conscripts of all classes were being sent to Algeria, where their duties were onerous. They lived for months in active-service conditions, with little leave, and they were often engaged in heavy fighting. But the French Army in Algeria did not merely wage war; it also ran the political administration. Even the guidance of the far-reaching Constantine plan for economic reconstruction lay largely in its hands.

For many years, France spent billions of francs on developing and opening up Algeria, and establishing an educational system. Without the assistance of France, there would have been no hope at all of ever creating tolerable living conditions and attaining political freedom. Algeria is a poor country, Moslem unemployment is high, and the population grows quickly. The rebels draw strength from this misery, which provides a hotbed for revolutionary radicalism. If France had simply washed her hands of Algeria, if she had thrown independence upon the country before a leadership capable of governing it had matured—as the Belgians did in the Congo, under pressure of a public opinion shrewdly fostered by the Soviets—the result might well have been disaster. Algeria might have fallen an easy prey to the Soviets, and that could have been the beginning of the Bolshevization of Africa. The Algerian people do not know what a Communist regime means, and if they were to learn from experience, it would be too late to find out.

General Ély pulled a number of strategic charts from a file. Arrows indicated the likely direction of any Soviet drive. "Just take a look at these," he said. "From Red China via Tibet, and from the Soviet Union in the direction of Pakistan, Afghanistan, and Persia—everything aims at one point: to the Indian Ocean, to the Mediter-

ranean, to Egypt and Abyssinia, and finally to the whole of North
Africa." All these areas, like Berlin, Quemoy, and Hungary, are "war
arenas" for the Soviets.

Ély continued, saying that the century-long discord of the peoples
of Europe, and in particular France and Germany, had been a
tragedy, and fortunately has now come to an end. France and Germany in particular have much in common intellectually and in
everyday life. The General Staffs grew out of the same tradition;
and, trained by similar problems, they think along similar lines.

"What do you think of the problem of European air defense,
mon général?"

"Now that a plane can fly across any European country in a few
minutes, separate national air defense systems are impossible," the
General replied. The facts are obvious; there were sharp discussions
in NATO until, on September 22, 1960, General Norstad and General Ély were able, after long and difficult negotiations, to come to
an agreement on the full integration of the European warning
network.

General Ély returned to the attitude and intentions of the Soviets,
and declared that the Western powers must be prepared to expect the continuation of permanent and total war against the
West. "It may well be that the Soviets don't want a war with weapons—having come to the conclusion that they couldn't win it—but
they are determined to press forward and conquer by an all-out psychological war." The General added emphatically: "No country can
hope to achieve anything for itself or the alliance by trying to reach
a separate agreement with the Soviets. It would always be a bad
agreement, and would favor the other side."

Towards the end of our interview our discussion turned to the
"thinned-out" zones.

"Disengagement would always be exclusively to the advantage of
the Soviets," the General declared, "regardless of how far they would
agree to withdraw their forces; whether 100 or 200 miles, they could
be back in a day or so, while the Americans would be on the other
side of the Atlantic. It would mean handing Europe over to the
enemy."

France has almost a million men under arms today—750,000 in
the Army, 150,000 in the Air Force, and 68,000 in the Navy. For her
internal security she has between 60,000 and 70,000 men in the
garde mobile, which is equipped by the Defense Ministry but or-

ganized and directed by the Ministry of the Interior. In addition to this force, which is organized on military lines in battalions, there is the *gendarmerie*, and in Paris the *garde républicaine*, which can, if necessary, be sent to other towns.

Originally, five divisions of the French Army were placed at the disposal of NATO—the French First Army in Southwest Germany and France, which comes under the Central Army Group (CENTAG). Nine or ten further divisions were to be at the disposal of NATO on short notice. Today, however, the French First Army, under the command of Major-General Pierre-Marie Josef Roy with headquarters in Trier on the Mosel, has only two divisions, both much reduced in strength: an infantry division and an armored division. The other divisions are there as skeleton units. However, with the return of the French Army from Algeria, this can now be changed quickly.

There are French naval units under NATO command in the Channel and Eastern Atlantic Commands, and French air units attached to the First Tactical Air Command (First CATAC) with headquarters in Lahn, which is a part of the Fourth ATAF on the southern sector of the Central European front.

France could mobilize two or perhaps three supplementary divisions on short notice. For mobilization and territorial defense, the country is divided into nine *régions militaires*.

It should not be overlooked that the French Army is the only European army that has been in action and gained practical experience during the long years of the Algerian war.

The speaker was Brigadier-General Alain Le Ray, military attaché at the French Embassy in Bonn, who had but recently returned from three years' service with the parachute battalions in Algeria. France had suffered heavy losses in officers and non-commissioned officers in Indo-China, but a new group has come to the fore under the hard conditions of that war.

"Of course," he went on, "the fight against the rebels in Algeria was not anything like 'the war of the future.' Both sides were fighting with conventional weapons, and flew mostly in piston-engined planes rather than jets. However, the basic experience of men in action is much the same; our divisions there have had battle experience."

The French Army had to be built up from scratch after the Second World War, with material, equipment, and clothing from British and U.S. supplies; but French production gradually took over. The

French armament industry produces particularly good light tanks, planes, helicopters, and various special weapons. For example, the new light tank AMX is an effective, highly mobile weapon. It weighs only fourteen tons; its 75 mm. gun is only about six feet from the ground, but is capable of piercing the armor of a thirty-two-ton tank at a distance of about a mile. The AMX takes about 100 gallons of fuel, which is said to be enough to keep it in action over rough terrain for thirteen hours, or for over 200 miles on surfaced roads at a speed of over forty miles an hour. The AMX is a valuable French contribution to the problem of providing a suitable medium tank for the armament triangle of Germany, France, Italy. French anti-tank weapons are also among the best of their kind, and the guided anti-tank rocket SS-10 has been adopted by the German Army.

French artillery always has been excellent, with a tradition reaching beyond Napoleon, back to Louis XIV. Today, the 105 and 155 mm. guns are the backbone of French conventional artillery.

In addition to membership in NATO, France also belongs to SEATO, because of her interests in Southeast Asia. Her still considerable overseas possessions are grouped in two strategic zones: Equatorial and French West Africa, and the Indian Ocean, Madagascar, and the coast of Somaliland. France also maintains a station on the island of Noumea in New Caledonia, and another in French Central Africa. The French-trained native troops in these areas have chiefly police functions.

The task of the powerful French Navy is to protect communications between the motherland and these overseas possessions, and to facilitate ocean traffic in time of war. In addition to these national tasks, it takes part in the NATO defense of the West. The modern French Navy consists of two battleships (two more are under construction, together with a helicopter carrier), six cruisers, ninety-two destroyers and frigates, eighteen submarines (fourteen more on the stocks), 160 minesweepers, anti-submarine vessels, and a variety of small ships, auxiliary vessels, and so on. The Rhine flotilla, which consisted of speedboats, guard boats and landing boats, has been handed over in part to the German Army.

The French Navy is being modernized and enlarged: 185,700 tons were built or laid down between 1946 and 1957. In order to relieve the budgetary difficulties of the country, no further work was put in commission in 1958, but in the following year, a further 60,000 tons was earmarked for construction. The Navy Council estimates that if France is to fulfill her far-flung obligations, she must have a navy of at least 540,000 tons. According to the original building program, this tonnage is to be available by 1970.

French aircraft carriers in service today, some of them of British and U.S. origin, carry U.S. supersonic jet bombers such as the Chance-Vought Corsair, British jet fighters like the Venom (renamed the Aquilon in the French Navy), and conventional fighters of the Avenger type for use against submarines. Then there are helicopters, the Alouettes of French manufacture, which can go down on the sea at need. Two further carriers are under construction. Like the new British and American carriers, they are equipped with all modern improvements, including angled flight decks, steam catapults, and landing mirrors; they can carry sixty planes, including supersonic bombers and fighter-bombers of the Étendard IV type made by Dassault, and anti-submarine fighters of the Breguet Alize type. Anti-submarine precautions are of great importance for the French Navy; all big convoy ships carry helicopters and torpedoes with homing devices. Long-range supersonic audio detection devices also have been developed. The cruisers, and some of the 2,750-ton destroyers under construction, will be equipped with anti-aircraft guided missiles of the Mascala type.

The French Naval Air Arm is to receive 250 planes to operate from carriers. At the moment it has only eight such squadrons. The land-based air forces are equipped with fighters, long-range reconnaissance planes, transport planes and helicopters; and they too are to receive 250 modern aircraft. In addition, there will be modern naval training planes and sea-rescue planes.

The French aircraft industry is exceptionally modern and progressive. Its fighter-interceptors and fighter-bombers, the Super Mystère, Trident, Mirage, and Griffon, are excellent designs; and the Super Mystère, driven by a turbo-jet, develops supersonic speeds in level flight. It is being built for the French Air Force by Dassault in Argenteuil, which is carrying out a preliminary order for 250 planes.

The Griffon II of Nord Aviation is an experimental plane built to try out a combination of turbo-jet and ram-jet power. Within one minute of take-off, it can reach a height of 16,000 feet, and its top speed is reported to be twice the speed of sound. Its radar equipment is particularly interesting—the data are transferred to an optical sight that shows the pilot the distance and position of an enemy plane. At the same time, a radar-operated comptometer gives the pilot the most favorable range and the best moment to fire.

Another remarkable design also being produced by Dassault is the Mirage III, a fighter-interceptor that can also be used as a fighter-bomber. In addition to a turbo-jet with an after-burner developing a push of 4.400 kilopond, it also has a rocket-assisted take-off developing 1,500 kilopond, which allows it to get into the air within 600 or 700 yards. At top speed it is one and a half times as fast as sound, but it can throttle back to the relatively low speed of 160 miles an hour, so that by using a parachute brake it can land on a runway of about 800 yards. Thus the Mirage can be used from very short runways and even from improvised airfields, where its light weight and low-pressure tires come to advantage.

The Mirage IV is a fast, long-range bomber with two aggregates, capable of carrying nuclear weapons. For France's future *force de frappe*, a strategic and tactical striking force to be equipped with nuclear weapons, an even more modern Mirage is to be developed. It will weigh between forty and fifty tons, and be driven by two Super-Atar turbines that will give it a top speed of more than twice the speed of sound.

Under de Gaulle's leadership, the Fifth Republic is making fundamental changes in the structure of national defense. The military has been reorganized; emergency legislation has been extended in order to give the French Government wider powers; the Army has been modernized; and defense has been given a broader basis. French experience with the opponent's military and political methods in Korea, Indo-China, and Algeria, have influenced these changes.

The boundaries between war and peace have become more fluid today. National defense can no longer confine itself to the purely military field. Revolutionary coups, actions against security and national unity, the introduction of spies and agitators, demoralization of the army, psychological manipulation, terror as a political weapon —all these are part of the Soviets' total war, against which the West must develop its own defense.

Since immediate intervention might be necessary, on January 7, 1959, the French Government promulgated a decree called *mise en garde*—a preliminary to mobilization or martial law. The Government will have the power to declare the existence of this emergency without the preliminary approval of parliament.

"The threat is permanent," declared the French Minister for the

Armed Forces, "and therefore the defense must always be ready. Aggression can take the most varied forms, and therefore there must be complete unity of action between the civil and military authorities. Aggression can come as a surprise attack with nuclear weapons; defense therefore cannot await the transformation of our technical and economic potential into an operational force."

Measures have also been taken to maintain the authority of the state in case of emergency. If, for example, the President, the Premier, and the Senate all were prevented from exercising power, it would pass into the hands of the Minister for the Armed Forces. Should Paris be put out of action as an administrative center by nuclear attack, power will pass into the hands of the provincial authorities—which is something revolutionary in centralist France.

Because national defense is no longer a question for soldiers alone, the newly created National Defense Committee consists of the Prime Minister, the Minister of the Interior, the Finance Minister, and the Minister for Foreign Affairs, in addition to the Minister for the Armed Forces. General de Gaulle is not merely Supreme Commander in name, but also in fact. He decides strategic problems of defense, and the Minister for the Armed Forces implements these decisions. The office of Defense Minister has been abolished.

National defense has been strengthened by these measures but others caused embarrassment to de Gaulle's allies. For example, he withdrew the part of the French Fleet that had been placed under NATO's Mediterranean Command at Malta, and returned it to national command. France needed it, de Gaulle declared, to take care of her commitments in North Africa, which (with the exception of the three Northern Departments of Algeria) is not covered by the North Atlantic Treaty.

More serious has been President de Gaulle's refusal to permit nuclear warheads to be stockpiled on French territory unless France is given some share of the control, such as the United States has conceded to the British Government over American warheads stored in the United Kingdom. Because of this refusal, General Norstad had to withdraw three tactical wings, consisting of about 250 planes, from France and station them in Britain and Germany. Another difficulty has fortunately been removed: France has now consented to place her radar and other warning devices under the control of SACEUR. On September 28, 1960, the North Atlantic Council ratified this agreement, reached between Generals Norstad and Ély only six days earlier. The agreement provides further for the integration of French wings stationed in Germany and in the eastern frontier areas of France with those of the other allies under the command of SACEUR, and this includes not only interceptor aircraft but also anti-aircraft units and ground-to-air rockets.

Another important step forward was taken when France decided to reorganize part of her armed forces in accordance with the exigencies of atomic defense, as recommended by NATO. The First and Third French Divisions, as well as a brigade of the Fifteenth Division, all stationed in Germany, were announced to be among the first to be converted. In September, 1960, the French Government accepted an American offer of weapons with nuclear capability for its NATO-assigned forces in Germany, and shortly thereafter arrangements were completed for a joint nuclear training program. The defense of Europe has thereby become stronger. In the future, an invader would have to face a solid front of NATO forces, all having nuclear capability.

All these agreements were reached after France had successfully manufactured and exploded her own atomic bomb. On February 13, 1960, at the testing grounds at Hamoudja near the Reggane oasis in the Sahara, a plutonium charge was exploded on a 300-foot high steel mast, generating a power equivalent to sixty or seventy kilotons of TNT, or more than three times as much as the Hiroshima bomb. The plutonium was provided by three reactors in the French atom center Marcoule, each producing 100 kilograms of the precious material from natural uranium. This was the two hundred and fiftieth atomic explosion that had taken place in the world. The second bomb, exploded close to ground level on April 1, 1960, was of only twenty-kiloton caliber. This was the beginning of the French program for the production of smaller weapons for tactical use. In addition, France has decided to manufacture fifty atom-bombers of the Mirage IV type, a nuclear-powered submarine, a rocket-firing warship, as well as carrier missiles.

As a result of these achievements, the international prestige of France has undoubtedly increased, and from the point of view of joint defense this is to be welcomed.

Being now a member of the "Atomic Club," France will no doubt be consulted in the future when nuclear tests or disarmament are discussed. Also, some joint control over American warheads to be stored on French soil, so far denied France on the basis of the

McMahon Act, might possibly be reconsidered by the United States. If this were done, it would raise this problem for NATO: whether the other partners ought not to be given a say in the matter, by making NATO the "fourth nuclear power." As a matter of fact, this was officially requested by General Norstad in December, 1960, and the American Secretary of State at once offered to release 100 Polaris missiles and, in case of war, five submarines capable of carrying this weapon, for sale to the North Atlantic Council.

From the point of view of the chief aim, the preservation of peace, nuclear weapons in the hands of NATO would certainly be desirable, because they would emphasize the determination of the West and diminish the danger of a Soviet attack. Of course, NATO in such a case could hardly avoid placing the decision for the immediate counter-blow against a surprise attack into less than fifteen hands, preferably into the hands of one man, and that would logically be the SACEUR, perhaps in agreement with the Secretary-General of NATO.

President de Gaulle's insistence that France must have a *force de frappe*, a nuclear striking force of her own, has raised the question of whether this was intended to indicate a gradual withdrawal from the alliance. The French Government, Parliament, leading officers, and de Gaulle himself, have vigorously denied it. What France wants, they declared, is certainly not to "go it alone," for there is general realization that this, in the face of the Soviet threat, would be disastrous. France needs her allies as much as they need her. What she wants, rather, is to exercise greater influence within the Alliance; and her influence will grow with the increase of her military power and the progressive consolidation of her economic and political system. This is to be welcomed. But it has nothing to do, of course, with setting up a directorium, say, by a number of powers within NATO or with the hegemony of one or more allies over the others.

"What we must under all circumstances avoid," one of the former representatives to the NATO Council declared emphatically, "is to permit different kinds of membership within the Alliance. There must be no partners of higher or lower rank than the others."

Neither would it be advisable to back away from such "integration" as has already been achieved. Integration has proved its value, not only by kindling a supra-national spirit but by its practical effect in bringing about a more powerful defense. The clock cannot be turned back. Any attempt to return to the patterns of past alliances between nations jealously guarding their sovereignty would be perilous in the highest degree. For within the North Atlantic Alliance, the reversal of integration would mean disintegration, and that, surely, would not be in the true interests of the European community or any of its members.

Politically naive?

17

Under Four Flags

Just as the Northern Army Group (NORTHAG) and the Second ATAF based at Mönchen-Gladbach defend the northern sector of the Central European front, so to the south of Sieg and Eder stands the Central Army Group (CENTAG) with headquarters in Heidelberg, and the Fourth ATAF with headquarters in Ramstein in the Palatinate.

The forces of four nations are united in the Fourth ATAF: the French First Tactical Air Command, the Canadian First Air Division, the U.S. Seventeenth Air Force, and German air units under Air Commander South. The Tricolor, the Maple Leaf, the White Star, and the Iron Cross are fraternally united here. Altogether the Fourth ATAF has 50,000 men and 1,500 modern planes, distributed over twenty-five airfields. In addition, there is a radar system for air control and warning.

Headquarters is integrated. The Commander-in-Chief is an American, his deputy is a Frenchman, Lieutenant-General Raoul V. Marias, and Chief of Staff is Air Commodore H. M. Carscallen of the Royal Canadian Air Force. So far, there are not many German officers on the staff, but when the integration is completed, there will be 40 per cent Americans, 24 per cent French, 20 per cent Germans, and 16 per cent Canadians.

The Commander-in-Chief of the Fourth ATAF was General Frederick Harrison Smith, Jr., a man with a great deal of flying experience. In the Second World War, he saw active service in both the Pacific and Europe, and after the war he was, among other things, Chief of the General Staff of Strategic Air Command. This time he came to Europe directly from U.S. Air Training Command, which gives its trainees a very thorough grounding in both theory and practice. General Smith realized that the next war will not be a push-button affair, but fought by trained men who understand the values for which they are prepared to sacrifice their lives. He was at the same time national Commander-in-Chief of U.S. Air Force Europe (USAFE).

NATO will have full operational command of the air forces placed at its disposal only on the outbreak of war; the activity of the Fourth ATAF in peacetime, therefore, is less concerned with formal commands than with coordination and cooperation, in order to integrate all national differences on a common plane of efficiency and striking power. Integral planning and joint maneuvers are the two chief factors that help towards this end. Plans have been worked out to cope with any possible enemy attack, and the aim of all operations is to make these defensive plans as effective as possible. There is hardly any time of the year when the Fourth ATAF is not preparing, carrying out, or thoroughly discussing the results of a joint exercise.

The main body of the French Air Force, First CATAC, is 17,000 strong, and almost half of its effectives are officers or non-commissioned officers. It provides NATO with eight wings and about 400 planes. Among them is the French Mystère IV-A (the Second Wing stationed at Dijon is equipped with this plane), the U.S. F-84-F Thunderstreak, and the corresponding U.S. reconnaissance plane RF-84-F Thunderflash, the F-86-K Sabre jet, and the F-100 Super-Sabre jet.

The Commander-in-Chief of First CATAC, Major-General Jean Marie Accart, is an outstanding flyer with the exceptionally high record of 5,500 flying hours, some gained with the French Air Force in 1939–40, others from 1943 to 1945. In 1954, he joined the staff of General Ély in Indo-China. General Brohon is also a first-class staff officer who represented his country for four years in the Standing Group in Washington, and for another year in the Planning Department of SHAPE. Before he took over his present post on October 1, 1958, he was Chief of Staff of the French Air Force.

Apart from his NATO command, General Brohon is national commander of the French air forces in Germany. As such, it is his job to ensure that, in pursuance of the decision of the North Atlantic Council of September 28, 1960, French forces are kept fully integrated and at the disposal of the Commander-in-Chief of the

Allied forces at any time, with the proviso that they may open fire on an attacker only at French orders—a proviso that seems to have more theoretical than practical significance.

The Canadian First Air Division, with headquarters in Metz, is a high-quality force of 6,000 men and twelve fighter wings stationed in Marville, Gross-Tänchen, Zweibrücken, and Baden-Söllingen. In recent years, Canadian airmen have often taken first place in the competitions between the allied forces, and in 1959 they won the Guynemer Trophy against strong United States, British, French, Belgian, and Dutch competition. Apart from winning the team prize, they also won first place for individual performance.

The Maple Leaf is regarded with great respect in Europe. The Canadians have demonstrated that they will be second to none in carrying out the chief task of a fighter unit: to train their guns and rockets on the enemy and destroy him.

All the Division's planes were built in Canada, including the CF-100, an all-weather, long-range fighter-interceptor used by four of the wings. The other eight wings are equipped with the CF-86 Sabre fighter, but this plane will gradually be replaced by the new Lockheed F-104 Starfighter, which is now being built in Canada under license as the CF-104. Some of the Sabre jets used by the German Air Force, and some of the Super-Sabre jets of the Belgian Air Force, were also built in Canada, and the Canadian Air Force trains the pilots to fly them and the mechanics to service them.

This has also helped to facilitate the regular transfer of squadrons from their own bases to airfields run by other allies. When, for example, a squadron of Canadian Air Force fighters from the First Squadron stationed in Marville lands on the Dutch Air Force field near Amsterdam to take the place of a Dutch squadron—which is in the meanwhile playing a similar guest role in Marville for a couple of weeks—it is tanked up, armored, and serviced by Dutch Air Force ground personnel and flies for a while wing to wing with Dutch planes; this then not only helps to consolidate the prevailing comradely relationship, but it also improves military integration and increases the joint striking power of the allies.

The First Air Division practices firing, including the use of rockets, in Sardinia, from airfields and training areas provided by the Italian Air Force, and also over large areas of the Mediterranean.

A fighter group is kept in constant readiness—armored, tanked-up, thoroughly checked. Both ground personnel and pilots never venture far from their planes; they may be playing bridge or baseball, but the switchboard is always manned, and the moment the alarm sounds, they are ready to scramble. The Canadians have an excellent radar warning unit, their own long-lines system, and a supply base in Great Britain.

The Canadians are well liked by the local population; for example, the highly successful ice hockey team in Zweibrücken is regarded with as much pride by the local Germans as though it were their own. But the Canadians are something more than popular strangers; people know that Canada is in the front line today, exposed to enemy attack across the Bering Straits or over the North Pole. In case of war, Soviet bombers and rockets would pass not only through the Iron Curtain but also through the "DEW Line," the Distant Early Warning System in the Arctic. That in such circumstances Canada, which is one of the founder members of NATO, is prepared to send her forces to help defend Europe, is a real show of fraternal solidarity within the North Atlantic Treaty Organization.

The headquarters of the American air forces that are at the disposal of the Fourth ATAF is in Ramstein in the Palatinate. In order to provide more effective operational leadership, the experienced staff of the Seventeenth Air Force, under the command of Major-General Gabriel P. Disosway, was transferred in November, 1959, from Wheelus in Libya to Ramstein. Here the Major-General took command of all the tactical air units of the United States stationed in Germany and France. They are now under the command of Major-General Henry R. Spicer.

The Seventeenth U.S. Air Force provides the biggest contingent to the Fourth ATAF, and at the same time it is the strongest unit of USAFE, one of the sixteen major commands of the U.S. Air Force, whose operational area extends in the form of a sickle from the North Cape, around the British Isles, over Europe and North Africa, around to Pakistan and Ceylon. Apart from the Seventeenth, there is also the Third U.S. Air Force stationed at Ruislip near London, the Three Hundred Twenty-second Air Division stationed at Evreux in France, the Three Hundred Sixteenth in Morocco, and the Second at Dharan in Saudi-Arabia. USAFE also supplies the U.S. units that are attached to the Fifth ATAF in Italy and the Sixth in Greece and Turkey, and many others—in all, 1,500 establishments in thirteen countries. USAFE even has its own radio and television network.

The Headquarters of USAFE, Lindsey Air Station, is in the

former Gersdorf Barracks near Wiesbaden. It was built under Emperor William II, and its coat of modern paint does not disguise its origin from a more settled period.

USAFE is geared to defense; it is always on the alert and ready for action. It has fighters, fighter-interceptors, bombers, reconnaissance planes, transport planes, and control wings for radar guidance —twenty different types in all. But the fighters represent the major part of its forces. There is the Super-Sabre fighter-bomber F-100, which flies faster than sound and can be used against tactical ground targets or to win command of the air in the event of an enemy attack. Then there is the fighter-interceptor F-86-D, the Sabre jet, known to its pilots as "Bloodhound" because it finds its way to the enemy by radar and destroys him with a salvo of rockets—often without even having set eyes on him at all. But since February, 1959, this type is being gradually replaced by a still more up-to-date plane, the F-102-A Delta Dagger, so-called because of its triangular shape. It is an all-weather fighter equipped with twenty-four homing rockets of the Sidewinder and Falcon types, and also the nuclear Genie. Its electronic guidance system is so highly developed that it can be flown unmanned from the ground. The Five Hundred Twenty-fifth Fighter Squadron stationed at Bitburg in the Eifel, and the Four Hundred Ninety-sixth of the Eighty-sixth Wing stationed at Hahn have already been equipped with these new Delta Daggers.

An even more modern type is now being developed, the F-106 Delta Dart, but it is still in the prototype stage. On December 16, 1959, it set a new world speed record with 1,435 miles an hour.

There is already a squadron of the big F-101 Voodoo planes stationed in England. These have a maximum speed of 1,125 miles per hour and can carry an H-bomb. The atomic tactical bomber B-66 Destroyer is also stationed there.

The F-104 Starfighter developed by Lockheed in the United States held three world records for planes that were operational in 1958: speed of 1,404 miles per hour, altitude of 91,243 feet, and rate of climb. In 1959, these figures were increased to more than 1,500 mph. and 103,395 ft. It ascends at the same speed that it reaches in horizontal flight. The Starfighter was the first manned plane to fly faster than the earth turns—flying from east to west, it overtakes the sun. This "flying bullet" is so fast that the utmost precision is necessary in its construction. The slightest deviation from trim would create such air pressure in flight that the plane would soon spin uncontrollably on its own longitudinal axis. The characteristic of this F-104 is its short, thin wing, which extends only about seven feet on each side of the fuselage. The plane weighs 7.7 tons unmanned, and is about fifty-four feet long. The wing edge is as sharp as a knife, and the greatest wing thickness is only about four and a quarter inches.

In setting the speed record, the pilot did not dare to fly at maximum speed, because heat developed by friction would have become dangerous, even with a cooling system so powerful that it could produce ten tons of ice a day. Despite its very high speed, the F-104 can land on relatively short runways at relatively low speed, thanks to a new system of slipstream stabilization. It is armed with two Sidewinder rockets that home onto the warmth discharged by a jet plane. The F-104 can also carry nuclear weapons. In addition, for its own defense, it is armed with an M-61 Vulcan 20 mm. gun firing up to 6,000 shots a minute.

The F-104 is an all-round plane which can be used as a day fighter, a night fighter, an interceptor-fighter, and a fighter-bomber, not only for close front-line support, but also at long range. The F-104-B variant, which has two seats one behind the other, is particularly suited for training purposes. A further variant is being built for reconnaissance. The new German Air Force is also being equipped with the Starfighter—F-104-G, which has been built to specifications and has an even more highly developed electronic system, as well as other improvements.

In a sense, the Starfighter can be said to have been in action already. At the height of the Quemoy crisis in September, 1958, a number were loaded into C-124 Globemaster transport planes and flown out to reinforce the Thirteenth Pacific Air Force off Formosa. Thanks to the radar network provided for them by the Russians, the Red Chinese discovered the presence of a new type of plane flying at twice the speed of sound; and perhaps this, together with the uncanny accuracy of the Sidewinder rockets discharged against a number of ultra-modern MIG-17s, had a soothing effect on their belligerence.

USAFE also has tactical atomic rockets at its disposal: the Thirty-eighth Tactical Guided Missile Units stationed in Hahn, Bitburg, and Sembach, which are ready to take to the air at any moment, day or night, in any weather. Since the summer of 1959, the TM-61 Matadors are being replaced by the newer TM-76 Maces, which have a range of over 600 miles.

As the Rhine is only seven jet-flying minutes from the Iron Curtain, the warning system here is of great importance. In the opinion of experts, given sufficient energy and means, it would be possi-

ble to surround the Soviet Union with a world-wide electronic
warning system that would sound the alarm the instant the Red
Army discharged an intercontinental ballistic missile.

In the meantime, dispersal is one means of protecting our forces
from surprise attack; this will be increasingly feasible as vertical-start
and catapulted planes come into wider use. Here "at the front," so
to speak, it is especially clear that a joint and therefore effective
European air defense is essential; given the shortness of the warning,
even at best the counter-blow against enemy bases will always be a
substantial part of defense.

A section of the American air force in England that belongs to
the Third Air Force of USAFE would, in an emergency, be under
the direct command of the Supreme NATO Commander in Europe,
General Norstad, and not that of the Fourth ATAF.

The U.S. Air Force maintains several units in Europe and Africa
that do not belong to USAFE, in particular the strategic air commands in Britain, Spain, and Morocco. The Seventh Air Division of
SAC, with headquarters at Ruislip in England, is dispersed over
fourteen airfields, while the Sixteenth in Spain and Morocco, with
headquarters at Torrejon, is dispersed over five bases.

The European section of the world-wide air transport command
(MATS) with bases in Prestwick, Scotland, and Lajes in the Azores,
is also independent of USAFE.

"Our forces must be ready for action day and night," declared
General Clyde D. Eddleman, Deputy Chief-of-Staff of the U.S.
Army, speaking at his headquarters. Until March, 1959, he was
Commander-in-Chief of the Seventh U.S. Army. From then until
the beginning of September, 1960, he was Commander-in-Chief of
U.S. Land Forces Europe (CINCUSAREUR) and Commander of
Army Group. Within half an hour of an alarm, half of his men
would be at their posts; another 35 per cent would have joined them
within another two hours. At no time would more than 15 per cent
of his effectives be on leave or otherwise unavailable.

With its two corps—two armored and three infantry divisions—
an anti-aircraft brigade, three armored regiments, and about thirty
field artillery batteries and their supply organization, the Seventh
Army is an impressive force. It is highly mobile, capable of acting
over any terrain, armed with both conventional and nuclear weapons,
and based on an excellent supply organization whose efficiency has
been provided time and again in maneuvers. American divisions rep-

resent the hard core of this Army Group. They are fully trained, fully equipped, and at full war strength. Representatives of NATO countries therefore like to watch the annual maneuvers. It costs $1.2 billions a year to keep this army going, or one-eighth of the total U.S. Army budget.

Since the reorganization of the American forces, only the armored divisions have retained the three-regiment form of organization; the infantry divisions and the airborne troops have "pentomic" organization—they are brigaded into five nuclear-equipped groups, each of which is capable of acting independently for long periods, even if cut off from command channels and supply bases. The nuclear fire-power of the Seventh Army is based primarily on three weapons: a gun, the 280 mm. atomic cannon; a rocket, the Honest John; and a ground-to-ground guided missile, the Corporal. Despite its imposing appearance and its weight of eighty-five tons, the atomic cannon is highly maneuverable; it can be towed at over thirty miles an hour, and in amphibious operations it can readily be landed anywhere without special preparations. Its accuracy is greater than that of corresponding conventional artillery of the Second World War. Atomic munition is also available for the 203 mm. howitzer.

The Honest John has a range of about twenty miles, and the Corporal a range of about seventy-five miles. The more modern Sergeant now has a range of up to 175 miles. The Redstone rocket, which is already operational and in service with the Seventh Army, has a similar range, and a speed several times faster than sound. It is a development of the German V-2 and was part of the rocket that put the first American satellite Explorer into orbit on January 31, 1958.

The atomic cannon does not make the conventional gun superfluous. The 105 mm. and the 155 mm. howitzers are not out of date, and the 203 mm. and 280 mm. guns are made to take conventional shells. The experts think that it would be a mistake to rely exclusively on atomic shells. An army must always use the weapon best suited to the job at hand, and not shoot at sparrows with elephant guns, lest it trip over its own weapons.

A particularly useful development is a self-propelling gun-carriage capable of taking both a 175 mm. anti-tank gun and a 203 mm. field howitzer. The combination is lighter and swifter than previous types, has a higher rate of fire, and can be got into position within five minutes.

The new infantry divisions are each supported by fifty army

planes, twice as many as formerly, and they will also have a greater number of helicopters, particularly for use as transport behind their own lines. Some of the guns can be transported by air, and the 105 mm. howitzers can be landed on the battlefield by means of a parachute.

The M-48 and M-60 tanks with diesel drive are to be built with a bigger command cupola and equipped with the British 105 mm. cannon. Since the Centurion tanks of the First British Corps will also have this gun, this represents an important step towards standardization. The M-60 has been in serial production since April, 1960.

In order to be ready to go into action at any moment, the Seventh Army since 1955 no longer replaces individual officers and men, but relieves whole units at a time, thus maintaining inner cohesion. The procedure is known as Operation Gyroscope. When it was first introduced, whole divisions were relieved, but now the procedure is confined to one group at a time, because a newly arrived group will assimilate rapidly the valuable experience of the two divisional groups already on the spot.

The Seventh Army is the main contingent of American land forces in Europe, but not the only one. There is the special unit Southern Europe Task Force (SETAF) in upper Italy, which is equipped with rockets and guided missiles; U.S. troops stationed in Berlin; and a widespread apparatus for administration and supplies. As for all NATO forces, the supply system is on a national basis, and all supplies come from the United States. For this, a special command has been formed, U.S. Army Communications Zone Europe (COMZ), with headquarters in Poitiers and Verdun as rear and forward supply bases.

Since the spring of 1959, the Commander-in-Chief of the Seventh U.S. Army has been Lieutenant-General Garrison Holt Davidson. "It was like a homecoming for me," he said, because he had already commanded the Seventh Army during the war in southern Europe. During the Korean campaign, he was Chief of Staff to the Eighth Army. The Headquarters of U.S. Army Europe (USAREUR) is in Heidelberg. Together with USAFE it is subordinate to the Supreme U.S. Command Europe (USEUCOM) at Camp de Loges near St. Germain-en-Laye, whose Supreme Commander, known as CINCEUR in this capacity, is General Lemnitzer.

Apart from the Seventh U.S. Army and the French First Army, two German corps belong to the Central Army Group, the Second Corps in Ulm under the command of Lieutenant-General Max

Pemsel, and the Third Corps in Coblenz under the command of Lieutenant-General Heinrich Gädcke. So far, no joint staff has been established for these two corps, and they are brigaded in the NATO structure of the Seventh Army. Their direct superior for national tasks is the operational staff of the German Army under the Inspector, Lieutenant-General Alfred Zerbel.

The frontier along the Iron Curtain guarded by the allied forces in the Central Army Group, 500 miles long from the Austrian frontier to the Harz, is a symbol of what the West is defending. Hundreds of watchtowers loom from Czechoslovakian territory, and along the frontier triple rows of barbed wire up to nine feet high, sometimes electrically charged, turn the unfortunate country into one vast concentration camp. Many houses, even whole villages, along the frontier have been evacuated and razed. On the western side, the scene is very different; men and women go about their affairs freely, and the local peasant peacefully plows his land right up to the frontier post.

But it is a frontier which has to be watched carefully in order to be ready for any surprise that might be brewing behind that gloomy barrier. A special group of the U.S. Seventh Army, three regiments strong, works in close touch with the German frontier defense force and the border police, and is ready to go into action at once. These armored cavalry regiments, as they are called, the Second, Eleventh, and Fourteenth, are highly mobile and well equipped for that mountainous terrain, where the eye cannot sweep unhindered over the countryside. Five-man motorized patrols are on the move day and night between the frontier camps and the forward observation posts. Military planes, usually of the L-19 type but including a number of bigger L-20s, are also constantly available. Helicopters can rapidly bring the commanders to otherwise inaccessible areas.

The light reconnaissance tank M-41 is now being replaced by the more powerful M-48, which will greatly increase the fighting strength of these forces. Although their primary task is to keep watch, the men know that in their exposed position they would be the first to offer resistance in the event of any attack by land; and for them the Iron Curtain is not a newspaper phrase but a daily reality.

Thus on a sector like this, immediately opposite a well-armed and well-equipped country of the Eastern bloc, whose government is particularly subservient to Moscow, an *entente parfaite* is more than ever necessary, not only in theory but in daily practice; it embraces the men of four nations—France, Canada, the United States, and Germany—and the various arms deployed here irrespective of nationality. And what one desires above all here is that before long it might be possible to bring more of those French units now in North Africa back to reinforce the defense.

A closely knit radar network which the enemy cannot put out of action covers the whole area. Here, 4,000 men, specialists of the Five Hundred First Tactical Control Unit, with headquarters in Ramstein, operate the electronic eyes and ears of the free world. They listen day and night and look deep into the camp of the potential aggressor, setting up an invisible shield far ahead of the tangible shield of the NATO armed forces. If the enemy ever drives forward, he will have been picked up by the watch and control system, with the word passed on long before the men of the armored cavalry regiments see a single foe. The U.S. officers and men engaged in this tremendously important work all are well aware that in performing it they are at the same time being watch and ward on the frontiers of their own country. Thus the joint military defense is an expression of a close moral and political alliance, and the latter operates to strengthen the former.

18

The New German Army

The frontiers of the German Federal Republic run directly along the Iron Curtain for a distance of over 1,000 miles: from the three-nation corner where Czechoslovakia, Austria, and Bavaria meet, to the Privall peninsula near Travemünde. Strategically speaking, one must add the 600-mile Baltic coastline that today is controlled by the Soviets.

This German frontier is the heart of Western defense. It is the task of the new German Army, the *Bundeswehr*, together with its NATO allies, to protect this geographically and strategically most exposed sector of the Western front. But over and above this, the problem of defense is one for the whole German people—because if ever this front collapsed, it would not be merely the end of the Federal Republic, but the end of all hope of freedom for the Germans unfortunate enough to live in the Soviet-occupied zone. Thus what the *Bundeswehr* does—its training, its exercises, its efforts—is a matter of interest not only to the military but to all Germans.

"The object of the *Bundeswehr* cannot be to form part of the strategic striking force and to take part in the strategic deterrent," said German Defense Minister Dr. Franz Josef Strauss. "The sword, the strategic bomber force carrying nuclear weapons and the guided missiles with nuclear warheads, is wielded by Great Britain and the United States. The military task of the *Bundeswehr* is to strengthen the shield forces, to help provide them with the minimum of striking power which the responsible commanders of NATO deem necessary. Of course, the deterrent effect of the Western alliance does not reside exclusively in its strategic weapons; the shield forces contribute to it, too—to an increasing extent, because modern weapon developments will soon provide the infantry with tactical nuclear weapons."

By far the greater part of Germany's armed forces are at the disposal of the Allied Forces Central Europe, but its small Navy and the land forces of Military District I (Schleswig-Holstein Hamburg), are part of the unified command "Baltic Approaches" and thereby of the Allied Forces Northern Europe with headquarters in Kolsaas near Oslo.

When the *Bundeswehr* will be completed in 1965, it will be 500,000 men strong and will have another 500,000 in reserve. Upon the request of NATO, the original goal of 350,000 men—200,000 men in the Army, 100,000 in the Air Force, 25,000 in the Navy, and 25,000 in the territorial defense force—will be considerably exceeded. In the summer of 1962, the figure was already 350,000 men.

"The object in building up the *Bundeswehr* is not to replace the Allied forces," declared General Adolf Heusinger, speaking on the tenth anniversary of the founding of NATO, "but to strengthen the joint defense of Europe." In view of the tremendous concentration of Red Army forces against the West, the defense of Germany without allies is as unthinkable as the defense of Europe without an appropriate German contribution.

General Heusinger is Chairman of the NATO Military Committee in Permanent Session in Washington. Until April 1, 1961, he was Chief of the German Federal Armed Forces Staff (Inspector-General). From the very beginning, he has played a great part in building up the *Bundeswehr*. In 1951 he was military adviser to the German Federal Government at the negotiations for the formation of the European Defense Community. In 1952, he was appointed to direct the military section of "Department Blank," from which the Defense Ministry subsequently developed. In 1955, he became Chairman of the Military Advisory Council, and in 1957 he was placed in charge of the department for all the armed forces.

Adolf Heusinger was born in 1897 in Holzminden, and as a young man he took up the profession of arms. In 1915, at the age of eighteen, he was a *Fahnenjunker*, meaning officer cadet; and before long he became a company commander. After the First World War he joined the *Reichswehr*, in which he received a very thorough all-round training, even by the exacting standards of this 100,000-man army of the Weimar Republic. In 1932, he was promoted to the rank of captain, and became a staff officer in the Reichswehr Ministry. During the Second World War, he was Chief of Operations in the High Command, and he held this post until he was arrested and charged with complicity in the attempt on Hitler's life on July 20, 1944. He is a man of wide education and culture who did a great deal to gain confidence for the new *Bundeswehr*.

At present, General Friedrich A. Foertsch is Inspector-General of the *Bundeswehr*. He is an excellent soldier, a career officer in the *Reichswehr* at the time of the Weimar Republic, and a man of wide interests and great erudition. He knows the Soviet Union well—one might even say intimately, for he spent ten years in several forced labor camps as a prisoner of war.

Before taking over as Inspector-General, Foertsch had held the important NATO post of Deputy Chief of Staff for Plans and Operations at SHAPE under General Norstad. "NATO's deterrent power must remain credible to the Soviets, also in the long view," he told us. "The Russians' sense of time—perhaps due to the Asiatic influence—is very different from ours. They think in decades when we are thinking in terms of months or years." The shield forces, Foertsch said, are an essential part of the deterrence in Russian eyes, and thus the *Bundeswehr*, as part of the NATO shield, is becoming an important factor in the preservation of peace.

This army of the Federal Republic is conceivable only within the framework of NATO. The Alliance had already taken shape when the Federal Republic was founded in 1949, and before serious thought had been given, either in Germany or among the Allies, to the possibility of a new German Army. However, the fact that the original NATO members were defending not only their own territories but also that of the defeated and disarmed Germany—for reasons of military necessity, but also from a growing sense of moral responsibility—could not remain without its effect. As the military threat grew, it became clear that free Europe was indefensible without the inclusion of German territory; and during the Berlin blockade, victor and vanquished stood shoulder to shoulder and became allies in defense of their joint freedom.

This marked a turning point for the German people. After everything they had experienced under the totalitarian regime of Hitler, they were left with a deep longing for peace. Exhaustion and resentment may have played a certain role, but for the great majority, the desire for peace was real. This was proved when the idea of rearmament was not accepted without a hard spiritual and political struggle—not until it became clear to the German people that renewed military service and rearmament were necessary precisely in order to fulfill their longing for peace and freedom. In the end, the idea prevailed that a people desiring peace and liberty must be ready to make sacrifices.

Thus the love of freedom stood sponsor at the birth of the *Bundeswehr*. The new German Army was born in the spirit of the Atlantic community, a community to which Germany has belonged throughout her history. It is therefore not surprising that the German soldier so quickly embraced an international outlook, and won the confidence that is the basis of any alliance, from the soldiers of other nations.

It is obvious that the fighting forces of a state based upon the rule of law will be different from those of an authoritarian or a totalitarian state. This does not mean that the political forms of democratic procedure, whereby power goes from the bottom to the top, can be transferred to the armed forces. In all armies, authority must move from the top downwards; this is the very essence of an efficient organization. However, it does mean that, as a part of the executive, the armed forces are firmly in the hands of the political rulers. In the *Bundeswehr*, supreme command is vested in the Federal Minister of Defense. In the event of war, it passes into the hands of the Federal Chancellor himself.

The *Bundeswehr* command and the commands of the three service branches are organized as general staffs, but they are also sections of the Defense Ministry, and, like the other Departments—Law, Administration, Housing, Finance, Personnel—subject to the Minister and his permanent Under-Secretary. Thus the Defense Minister is not only the superior of all the civilian employees of this Ministry, but of all military personnel.

The General Staff of the *Bundeswehr*, under the direction of Inspector-General Foertsch, works out the principles of military leadership, training, organization, and logistics for the three services and the territorial forces as a whole; the staffs of the Army, Navy, and Air Force, each headed by an Inspector, adapt those principles to their particular spheres. The same applies to the Army Medical Corps and the Sanitary services. The Inspector-General has authority over them all.

The supreme authority watching over the *Bundeswehr* is Parliament. A law passed on March 19, 1956 incorporated the Defense Committee of the Federal Diet into the Constitution (Article 45a) and clothed it with the constitutional rights of a commission of inquiry. A Defense Representative was appointed to protect the constitutional rights of service men, along the lines of the Swedish *Ombudsman* (Article 45b). Vice-Admiral Retd. Helmuth Heye, a member of the postwar German Parliament since 1949, has held this position since October, 1961. Any aggrieved member of the *Bundeswehr*, whatever his rank, can approach him directly and lodge a complaint. It soon became clear that there was very little chicanery or abuse of authority in the new German Army, and the great majority of the 350 to 400 complaints made to the Defense Representative each month refer to such matters as excessively long separation from the family, housing problems, children's education—administrative problems of a new organization. Although such matters do not fall within the scope of the Defense Representative, he does his best to help. Only a small number of the complaints refer to alleged violations of fundamental rights; and when such cases are inquired into, the officers are invariably cooperative.

Finally, by virtue of the law of June 23, 1955, the Federal President appointed a personnel investigation committee for the armed forces, a body consisting of thirty-seven members of democratic integrity, to inquire into the character and antecedents of officers from the rank of colonel upwards. Its clearance was necessary before any officer could be accepted, in order to make sure that no high officer tinged with a National Socialist record should be permitted to enter into the new German Army.

The *Bundeswehr* had to start from scratch in 1955, just as, a decade before, the state, society, and economic system had had to do. Everything had to be created anew, from the appropriate legal provisions to the staffs, including the men, their training, equipment, stations, and headquarters. The Federal Republic was completely disarmed, and its industry fully converted to peacetime production. Ten years' development in armament technique and strategic thinking had to be made up for. No new men had been trained, and most of the officers who had served in the Second World War were old for their ranks; as for junior grades, they remain scarce to this day.

Considering the psychological difficulties of the first years, the opposition to everything military in postwar Germany, and the widespread idea that the soldier was at best a necessary evil, it is remarkable that the *Bundeswehr* has managed to establish itself at all in such a short time, and that planned developments have been carried out more or less on schedule. This achievement would not have been possible without the devoted cooperation of everyone from the top leadership to the youngest recruit.

The necessity of starting anew also had its advantages. It freed the Army from many fetters: the rigidity of an inherited structure, the hampering effect of worn-out traditions, the burden of obsolescent weapons difficult to scrap. The new Army was at liberty to plan for up-to-date requirements. This was more than a matter of organization, equipment, tactics, and strategy; it applied equally to morale. The new *Bundeswehr* needed a new spirit which would combine the best traditions of the past with the requirements of changed times.

The core of this is what is known in the *Bundeswehr* as "inner leadership." It is closely connected with the name of Brigadier-General Count Wolf von Baudissin, who elaborated the new concept since 1952 and introduced it into the armed forces.

The goal of inner leadership in the *Bundeswehr* is, to quote a much used phrase, "the citizen-soldier." This is a comprehensive formulation, involving a respect for human dignity and the constitutional rights of the individual, and as much freedom as is consistent with good discipline. It also means that the ordinary soldier must be taught to make decisions on his own, if need be; that he must be encouraged to welcome responsibility, to show initiative, and to exercise self-discipline; and to accept authority freely and of his own accord. He must be brought to see that the *Bundeswehr* is *his* army, the protective shield of *his* state. And he must also be taught the political and moral meaning of the order of society he is called upon to defend.

Some people might say that such an education is really a matter for the home, for the school, and for society itself. The *Bundeswehr* would not disagree; and its task would be made very much easier if all the young men who came into its ranks were already conscious of their responsibility as citizens. Unfortunately, this is not always the case. And even when it is, the young citizens in uniform must be encouraged by the *Bundeswehr* to consolidate and develop their attitude as free citizens of a democratic society.

The earnestness with which the *Bundeswehr* approaches this task, which goes far beyond the military sphere into political theory, social science, history, and ethics, impresses everyone who has an opportunity of seeing "inner leadership" in action. A special Inner Leadership Council of people prominent in public life has been set up to counsel and advise. Courses for both officers and men have been carefully prepared, and their objectivity and impartiality are impressive. The whole curriculum is open to public inspection at any time. A School for Inner Leadership has been established at Coblenz, headed by Colonel Claus Hinkelbein; its high scientific level and the spirit that prevails there could be taken as an example by other institutions of political education.

"The present generation of young people is just as willing as its fathers were to accept authority," declared the late Lieutenant-General Hans Röttiger, the creator of the new Army. "But the scale of values has changed. Performance transcends rank and status today, and to that extent one can say that the present generation of recruits is more critical. This naturally puts higher demands on the officers. An officer must consolidate his authority by his own ability and personality. At the same time, the ordinary soldier is ready to give more, and to prove himself in the army as in his civilian job."

The new spirit prevails throughout the *Bundeswehr*—not only in the outward forms of an unexaggerated salute, ease in relations with superiors, the absence of senseless ritual—but also in the atmosphere. Of course, the officers still give the orders, and the men still obey them, but the spirit behind it, far from any so-called "cadaver obedience," is a willing acceptance of authority and a relationship of mutual confidence.

It would be a great mistake to equate this freer relationship with slack; the opposite is true. The old-style barrack drill is gone, but from the military point of view, it had long been out of date—in fact, it was an anachronistic survival from the days of Frederician linear tactics, which depended for their success on the absolute accuracy of moving automatons, obtainable only by blind obedience. Already in the Napoleonic wars it broke down against the onrush of the revolutionary armies; and today even the command relationship of the Second World War is inadequate. In a future war (which let us hope will never come), soldiers may often be entirely on their own, because the introduction of tactical atomic weapons will make larger concentrations of men suicidal. The operative units of modern warfare are likely to be the lone pilot in the fighter-interceptor, the handful of men in the jet bomber, the machine-gun crew in its hole in the ground, the lone grenadier with his anti-tank weapon, the small crew of the tank. In such circumstances, men must master their weapons, and be trained with heretofore unheard-of thoroughness.

In such a war, it will no longer be sufficient for the soldier merely to obey commands. He will have orders, a battle assignment—but given the incalculability of battles, these orders may sometimes become useless. Any man may find himself in a situation that will call for independent action on the basis of a general plan.

It is clear that this responsibility will make demands on the determination and the initiative of the individual soldier such as were previously made only on officers. And here lies the proof that freedom and a willingness to accept responsibility will be positive military requirements of our new tactics and weapons.

The most important German contribution to the defense of the West unquestionably is made by the new German infantry divisions —though this is not to belittle the importance of the Navy and the Air Force. The new German infantry is increasingly developing into an important part of NATO's shield forces. The general defense plan is to push the front line as far forward as possible. This is not only in Germany's interest, but also in that of her allies, because the shield protects the anti-aircraft belt, the airfields, the navigation aids, long-lines system and supplies organization, and, above all, the radar warning screen, without which the strategic sword would be blind on this sector. Moreover, Soviet advances into Europe have left a narrow operational defense base.

The *Bundeswehr* will be able to fulfill its task only when at least the twelve divisions to which the Federal Republic obligated itself in the Paris Agreements are fully trained and equipped. But considering that recruitment for the new Army did not begin until 1955, progress has been rapid. On July 1, 1957, General Norstad and the Commander of the Allied Land Forces Europe Center, General Hans Speidel, solemnly took over the first staffs and trained units of the *Bundeswehr*. Since then, the number of German divisions placed at the disposal of NATO as "ready for limited action" has risen to nine. The units are transferred to NATO as soon as a division has sufficient effectives, training, and equipment to go into battle. The twelfth division is expected to be ready in the course of 1962.

The equipment of the new Army with modern weapons, which is planned for the final phase, has not yet been carried out everywhere. The first material, particularly transport and weapons, was provided chiefly by the United States, since Germany had no inventory and no armaments industry. The U.S. Army authorities gave 1,100 tanks of the M-47 type for the new German armored divisions. Gradually these will be replaced by the more modern M-48 type, of which Germany will have 600 by 1961.

A new type of tank, even better suited to European requirements, is now being developed jointly by the armament industries of France, Italy, and the Federal Republic. One French and two German prototypes are already under test. The final model will be between thirty and thirty-five tons, and by giving up heavy armor it will have a high speed and great mobility. It probably will be armed with the new British 105 mm. tank gun, which has a long range and great penetrating power, and has already been adopted by the Americans. In times when even the strongest armor can be pierced by anti-tank weapons, the advantage lies with a tank that has speed, mobility, and low construction.

It is possible that Anglo-German cooperation may lead to the development of a joint tank with a weight somewhere between the forty-five tons favored by the British and the thirty tons preferred by the Germans. The new British medium-range rocket Blue Water has also been offered to the *Bundeswehr*, and discussions are proceeding for the development of a joint long-range guided missile. If necessary, the nuclear warheads could be placed in NATO hands for safekeeping. Other material and equipment for the *Bundeswehr* is being bought by the Federal Government from its other European allies, as, for example, the automatic FN rifle from Belgium. Munitions have been ordered from Turkey, Israel, and Portugal.

So far, German industry has provided chiefly clothing, transport, portable firearms, engineering equipment, and optical, electronic, and mechanical precision instruments. The Dornier Works have produced the first military plane since the war, the single-engined Do-27, used by the new German Air Force for communications and medical services. It has proved itself to have good all-round qualities. The job of bringing the new German aircraft industry into line with modern developments has been facilitated by the production under license of the U.S. F-104 Starfighter and the French Fouga-Magister and Noratlas aircraft.

"The year 1959 brought particularly onerous tasks to the *Bundeswehr*," declared Major-General Joachim Schwatlo-Gesterding, Commander of the Territorial Forces. "It had to introduce the new brigade formation, in addition to training and posting men to newly formed units."

In effect, this means that almost every unit has been reorganized. Once the process is at an end, which it very soon will be, the *Bundeswehr* will be a modern army of great striking power, prepared to ward off nuclear as well as conventional attack.

Reorganization was urgently necessary. The United States began to reorganize its own armed forces in 1955; Great Britain followed suit in 1957, on the basis of the Defense White Book; and other allies, including France, followed their example.

The reasons which compelled NATO to equip its forces with tactical atomic weapons have already been set out. An army with conventional weapons would be in a hopeless position from the start against an enemy not only superior in numbers but also equipped with tactical atomic weapons.

Provision of the *Bundeswehr* with tactical atomic weapons will not mean that henceforth it will be able to fight only an atomic war. The concept of the graduated deterrent means that limited aggression could be met and repulsed with conventional weapons. So far, the German forces have no atomic warheads at all; they are all in the hands of the American authorities, who alone can dispose of them. However, it is essential that the *Bundeswehr* be trained in their use now; its organization, equipment, and training must be geared to whatever type of war the enemy thrusts upon it.

There is another factor: Since any future war probably would not be fought on fixed fronts, but be a mobile battle over wide areas, the need will be for swift, effective units in small commands. This is one of the aims of the new organization. The division is too large a unit for the purpose. Formerly it was the smallest unit for combined operations; today even the brigades consist of mixed units, the light-armored brigades 3,800 strong as well as the armored brigades 2,700 strong. This means that the brigade can now be used for any military task. Even in peacetime, it is in battle order; in war, it could operate alone for several days without connection to its supply bases.

But the division does not become superfluous; on the contrary, it gains in leadership functions. Generally, it consists of three brigades, but, depending on the task, a greater number can be put together on the unit system.

The manpower of companies and battalions has been reduced by a quarter, but firepower, even with modern conventional weapons, has increased by 20 per cent. Greater mobility has also been attained, because the infantry is either mechanized or motorized. The motorized units still fight on foot, but they are carried to the battle in trucks. The mechanized battalions usually fight from their own light-armored vehicles, which carry 2 cm. guns and machine guns. These mobile, caterpillar-tread vehicles can keep up with the tanks, and they offer their occupants some protection, even against radiation.

The brigade is equipped with conventional arms; the double-purpose weapons that can fire both ordinary shells and atomic warheads are retained at divisional and corps level. Only the NATO Supreme Commander controls the atomic warheads, and he may release them only at the orders of the U.S. President. The graduated deterrent here finds its expression in graduated armament.

"The aim of our brigade organization is to get the last ounce of fighting power out of our forces," declared a spokesman for the German Defense Ministry, Colonel Baron Freytag von Loringhoven, now with the NATO Military Committee in Washington. Considering that the German Army is so far only 200,000 men strong and yet consists of twelve divisions, the proportion of fighting men is high. But balance must be maintained between fighting and supply units. In war, a division would need between 1,500 and 1,700 tons of supplies daily; and the more modern its equipment, the greater its requirements. A modern quick-fire weapon can fire 1,000 rounds a minute, which gives some idea of the quantities of ammunition needed every day. This has been taken into account, now that the strength of the Army was increased.

In one respect, the German Army is in a special position; almost all of the allies have troops under national commands in addition to those assigned to NATO. That is essential for countries like the United States, Great Britain, France, Belgium, and Holland, which have interests to be defended outside the NATO areas, or which, because they lie outside the front area, may have to defend their country against air- or water-borne thrusts far behind the lines. Neither of these contingencies applies to the German Federal Republic. All its territory lies within the NATO area, and in the event of an attack, it would immediately be an arena of war for the NATO forces.

Therefore all German forces are placed at the disposal of NATO as soon as they become operational. Only the territorial forces for home defense—30,000 men eventually—remain under German command, even in the event of war. One of their most important tasks is to give the fighting men operational liberty. Roads, railways, rivers, bridges, and airfields would have to be guarded, as well as vital industries, power stations, hydraulic works, and radar stations. In the event of war, these would be enemy targets which would have to be protected against sabotage and parachutists. If damaged, they would have to be repaired. It might also be necessary to erect barricades and blow up bridges. For this purpose, engineers are needed. Military police would have to maintain order and keep the roads open for military traffic. The territorial forces would also be given police powers to deal with emergencies and plunderers. And one would have to ensure that base supplies reach the corps supply units.

Even in peace, the territorial forces relieve the mobile regular troops of all location-bound tasks. They maintain connections with the *Land* governments, local authorities, and the press; take over guard duties, and generally support the NATO troops on German territory. "Territorial defense is, so to speak, the fixed chess board on which the divisions move," said Brigadier-General Cord von Hobe on behalf of the Federal Defense Ministry.

Although the territorial troops will not fight on the front line, they receive battle training to enable them to deal with invasion and sabotage. In other words, they are not a militia, but fully trained troops with special tasks. The personnel can be transferred readily to the fighting forces.

In the final analysis, effective defense rests on the cooperation of the populace. As a spokesman for the territorial defense force put it, "Do you think we could protect industrial plants against sabotage if the workers were indifferent or hostile?" The days are past when the defense of the country could be left to a small percentage of the population. Indifference and lack of vigorous preparations are a danger to peace, because they are a temptation to the enemy. The Soviets carefully study the attitude of the civilian population in all Western countries, and take it into account in their plans. A moment might come when this could be the factor that tips the scales—to peace or to war.

From its very inception, the *Bundeswehr* has placed itself in the service of the people. The new Federal President, Heinrich Lübke, was therefore speaking in the name of all Germans when, in 1960, he declared in his New Year's address, "The *Bundeswehr* has stood the test in the eyes of the people. I therefore wish to take this occasion to thank all our soldiers, and in particular the young National Service men, and to express my appreciation of their services."

The community of free nations, so long the aim and hope of the best in all nations, is most willingly realized today among the soldiers. It is not by chance that the most bitter Soviet attacks on Germany today are directed against the *Bundeswehr*; it is becoming a force that, by its will to defense, its democratic stand, and a spirit transcending nationalism, is serving the cause of liberty.

19

The New Luftwaffe

Towards the end of the Second World War, the German Air Force, or *Luftwaffe*, was inferior in strength to the air power of the Allies, but its most modern planes were technically far ahead of the best that could be put into the air against them. For example, the jet Comet Me-163, designed by Alexander Lippisch and built by Messerschmitt, reached a speed of over 600 miles an hour in May, 1941. Its rate of climb was almost 500 feet a second, which is impressive even today; climbing at an angle of between 50 and 60 degrees, it reached a height of 48,000 feet in 210 seconds. Of the 350 Me-163s, several fell into the hands of the West and of the Soviets. With planes based on these models, American pilots succeeded in breaking through the sound barrier two years after the end of the war. The Messerschmitt 262 was also a plane of which both British and American pilots spoke with great respect. A wing under Colonel Johann Steinhoff, based on Achmer near Osnabrück, was operational in the autumn of 1944. Steinhoff today is a General in the new German Air Force. Then there were the revolutionary German weapons known as the V-1 and V-2, which after the war contributed much to the development of rockets and ballistic missiles.

Talking to us in Northwood near London, Air Vice-Marshal Oulton said: "We respected the *Luftwaffe* when it was our enemy, and we are glad that it is our ally today."

The new German Air Force will be a tactical weapon; it will defend the air space of the Federal Republic and give close support to the ground forces. In view of the closeness of the Iron Curtain, it would not be militarily useful for the Federal Republic to establish strategic air bases and build a strategic bomber fleet.

Dr. Strauss, the German Minister for Defense, said that the tasks of the new German Air Force will be: first, to engage the tactical air force of the enemy; second, to carry out reconnaissance flights for all tactical purposes; third, to assist in the air defense of European air space; fourth, to give close support to the ground forces; fifth, to provide air transport. Anti-aircraft units will also belong to the Air Force, as well as batteries of the Nike and Hawk anti-aircraft missiles, and light anti-aircraft units equipped with electronically controlled 40 mm. anti-aircraft guns, to be replaced later by ground-to-air guided missiles. The first German ground-to-ground missile units will be equipped with Matador rockets; later, these will be replaced with more modern types, as for example, the Mace.

So far, the new German Air Force has placed five fighter-bomber wings, a fighter wing, a reconnaissance wing, and a transport wing at the disposal of NATO. Twenty-eight wings are planned in all.

"But is an effective air defense possible at all?" we asked Brigadier-General Johann Steinhoff. During the Second World War, Steinhoff notched up over 300 air victories, until he finally crashed and was seriously injured. He enjoys great esteem among both his own comrades and the flyers of the allied nations. Today he is Permanent Representative of Germany on the NATO Military Committee in Washington.

"There are people who say that every penny we spend on air defense is a penny wasted," he replied, "but in my opinion they're wrong. When it comes to the crucial point, we may not be able to prevent the Russians from penetrating our air space, but at least we can deny them command of the air. The fact is that the Russians have over 20,000 planes, and they would use them if it came to war. It was therefore right for us to buy Nike anti-aircraft missiles—and the more we buy the better. They deal with fighters and bombers flying at great heights, while the Hawk rocket takes care of low-flying planes. And then, of course, we have anti-aircraft batteries still equipped with conventional guns. So long as there are no guided missiles for short-range use, our 40 mm. conventional anti-aircraft guns are a good deal better than nothing. In any case, the Russians themselves are producing a great mass of anti-aircraft weapons, because they are convinced that the development will be towards low-flying attacks."

As the new German Air Force is starting from scratch, one of its most important tasks is the training of young pilots. This is in the hands of Air Training Command at Fürstenfeldbruck near Munich.

"The objective of our present training scheme is to meet critical needs by 1962, and we shall achieve it," declared Major-General Hannes Trautloff, then in charge of Air Training Command.

"Do you really think an effective air force can be built up in such a short time?" we asked.

The General considered the question. "Yes, I think so. Of course, the *conditio sine qua non* is that we get the best types of young Germans for the job—physically, mentally, and morally. The men we need must be willing to take responsibility and be capable of initiative." The young pilots are entrusted with valuable planes; each one represents a large investment of public money. Even more important, men's lives are at stake—and will be to the utmost should the Soviets ever attack.

"Just as the gallant pilots of the Royal Air Force saved their country in 1940, so a handful of young Germans may one day save Germany and the whole of Europe, fighting wing tip to wing tip with their American, British, and French allies," said the General.

Irrespective of the tremendous development of technique and electronic control, the decisive factor is still the pilot. "The sword is thrust by those who sit in the planes," he went on. "All depends on their getting into action in time, and their ability to make correct decisions in those few seconds that may mean the difference between victory and defeat."

Many people in Germany still don't realize the seriousness of the situation. Economic prosperity, the comfortable life it makes possible, and the great work of reconstruction tend to deceive them. When planes fly over inhabited areas, particularly holiday places and spas, complaints will come from local mayors. People write the authorities to ask what they intend to do about the nuisance.

"When they complain, perhaps it would be a good idea to ask them whether those were Soviet planes or ours," suggested the General with a grim smile. "And then point out to them that so long as the noise is made by ours, it can't be made by theirs. Perhaps we'd hear fewer complaints then."

"What do the young people think about the new air force?"

"The schools and youth groups which come to visit our airfields and training centers are usually enthusiastic. It isn't merely a question of technology. Flying creates comradeship, and that appeals to young people. The sporting and technical aspects reinforce the attraction. But, above all, it's the far-flung international contacts that catch their imagination—airmen have friends everywhere and among all peoples."

Air Training Command has eighteen schools dispersed all over Germany; its total strength is about 23,000 men, or a full division. Their job is exclusively to train. Everyone passes through their hands, from the youngest recruit to the accomplished pilot. This is a national command, because the training of pilots is a national task.

"Are the pilots given their battle training here, too?" we asked.

"No, only their flight training. The tactical and operational part comes later. And that's just as well, because the amount of time at our disposal is very limited. Of course, the officers are given an all-around idea of tactical problems. For example, they learn how a ship is fought, how a tank is used and what it can do, how a gun is fired. However, their practical battle training comes when they have joined their units."

While we were talking to a group of officers, the steady whine of jet planes could be heard from outside, and through the great window of the control tower we could see the T-33s coming in to land, one after the other. Most of them landed as though veterans were at the controls, but one or two appeared less certain. They were so fast that as their wheels touched the ground, a small bluish cloud of burned rubber rose from their tires. Each plane rolled along the runway for a while and then, with a sudden howling of its engines, rose into the air again. Behind it, the next plane came in to land, and another in its wake. It was an impressive piece of air choreography.

Later on, we made the acquaintance of the pilots. They strode out onto the airfield as though they had taken to heart the inscription over the doorway: "Through these portals pass the best qualified jet instructors in the world."

The Lockheed T-33 Shooting Star is the training plane. It has a speed of well over 500 miles an hour, and it flies at a height of nearly 50,000 feet. "It's a very reliable machine," one of the instructors at Fürstenfeldbruck assured us. He has two pupils in his care. "And two's enough, if you're really going to give them everything you've got," he said. "When they come to us they can fly ordinary piston-engined jobs, but jet flying requires a good deal more. However, after twelve hours, a pupil is allowed to take up a jet plane on his own."

The T-33 is not fast enough to break through the sound barrier, but even 500 miles an hour puts a strain on an inexperienced pilot.

The instructor demonstrated this to us in a test flight. In looping, for example, describing a vertical circle in the sky, the centrifugal force causes the weight of the body to increase about threefold, and some effort is necessary to lift one's own arm. It is not difficult to imagine that at still greater speeds the pilots are held so tightly in their seats as to be almost immobile.

"We'll touch down for a while in Kaufbeuren," our instructor said over the intercom.

"How do you make sure there's no one beneath you?" we wanted to know, because in the T-33 you can see ahead but not below.

"I'll show you," he replied, and he promptly turned the plane over on its back. Heaven and earth swiftly changed places, and we had a full view of the airfield. In fighting planes, this maneuver is unnecessary, as their radar instruments allow them to see what is beneath them. Within a few minutes, we had landed, taken off again, and were back at a height of over 20,000 feet. Below us, the snow-covered peaks of the Alps stretched one behind the other like stage scenery, and before long we reached Lake Constance. If we had been flying to the east, the Iron Curtain would by this time have been dangerously close.

"I think the Germans are wise to start off right away with the best planes," Major-General Timberlake had said to us. He was referring to the German purchase of F-104s, but the same applies to other equipment.

Cooperation with the British and the Americans is excellent. Up to December, 1954, most airfields, including Fürstenfeldbruck, were in the hands of the occupation authorities. During that period Fürstenfeldbruck was called "Firsty," and it still is.

Today, U.S. Colonel William J. Choniski is no longer commander of the station, but liaison officer. "We're just here as advisers," he explained. "About thirty teams for training, flying, airspace control, early-warning system, and so on. Our main job is to help the Germans stand on their own feet as quickly as possible."

"And how are things going?"

"The Germans are doing well. They have *esprit de corps*, and they work hard. We do our best to transmit our experience, but we're delighted to see their determination to catch up and then get on with the job themselves."

The German officers also assured us that cooperation was all that could be desired. "They help us as though we were fellow Americans," they declared. "You might say we're one big happy family here. Not only do they give us all we ask for, but they're always racking their brains to discover any other way in which they can help us."

"How are the boys who come here as flyers?"

"Absolutely first class. The talk you sometimes hear about the present generation not being as good as the last, or even earlier ones, is just nonsense. On the contrary, they're frank and they have an agreeable ease of manner. They come to grips with things without inhibitions, and they're neither awkward nor obstinate. It's difficult to get in wrong with them; and you'd have to try very hard to spoil them."

"And the comradeship of the air?"

"The recruits like it best in their own units because that's where comradeship is closest. I think that what chiefly impresses them is that, although each man is just one of a big community, they're still treated as individuals."

Fürstenfeldbruck is well known today. Until recently, pilots of other nations, in particular those of the NATO allies, were trained here—2,000 since 1954—at a cost per jet pilot of $75,000.

"Without the help of the Americans, we could never have built all this," said Colonel Hrabak, Commandant of the flying school at Fürstenfeldbruck. "And I'm not thinking merely of material assistance, but also of the mechanics capable of servicing a jet plane, and the electronic craftsmen—the sort of thing that just wasn't available in Germany."

Nine-tenths of Germany's youth get only elementary school education. German elementary schools are good, but the training isn't enough for modern life, either in industry or the *Bundeswehr*. The Soviets are well aware of the importance of modern technical training, and turn out more engineers and technicians a year than the United States and Europe together. In consequence, another requirement for the defense of the Federal Republic is that higher education should be extended to a much greater proportion of the population. We discussed this point with the Commandant of the flying school at Kaufbeuren.

"The modern air force officer must be a technician," he said. "It's no longer enough to memorize data—to know what power an engine can develop, what frequency a piece of apparatus works on, and so on. He must be a bit of a physicist and a bit of a chemist."

Modern pilots must understand complicated processes such as

radar, without which jet flight is inconceivable. "I witnessed the first great radar-guided bombing raid on Berlin," said the Commandant. "It took place on November 22, 1942, on a night when the clouds were so low and heavy that we thought the city was safe from attack. But radar gives the pilot a picture of the landscape and the blocks of houses beneath him even through 100 per cent cloud cover. His screen shows him all he needs to know."

The school at Kaufbeuren trains for flying and long-range communications, electronics, the use of arms, handling of munitions, flying safety, television, intelligence, and supplies. It has a staff of 1,200, including teachers, mechanics, ground personnel, and guard troops, and between 1,800 and 1,900 pupils, of whom about 400 are officers or officer-cadets.

"We have adopted American methods because they're good," the Commandant explained. "They are systematic and thorough. During the war, we had a tendency to improvise, but the Americans are quite right when they say you waste time and money that way."

Colonel Hrabak in Fürstenfeldbruck made the same point: "The principle of all American training schools is 'safety first.' Avoid accidents whatever you do. The British are prepared to take what they call a 'calculated risk.' Of course, if you fly at all, there's invariably an element of risk, but the Americans do their best to remove it from their training schools and to leave it to the operational units. But that also has its disadvantages. When young men pass out from their training and go to their units, they have to fly machines they've never flown before, and then they just have to take risks their school training has taught them to avoid."

The Commandant was also impressed by the excellent relationship with the Americans. He told us of his astonishment when he took over the school from Colonel Richard Picton of the U.S. Air Force, and the latter had said to him casually: "You call me Dick or Pick, and I'll call you Wern." Once he got used to it, he said, the relationship worked well. And when "Wern" came to the United States, he and his colleagues felt they were being received with warm and sincere comradeship. In their mess, the American officers had put up portraits of the outstanding pilots of the First World War, von Richthofen, Boelcke, and Immelmann, as a compliment to their German guests.

The Officers Training School of the German Air Force is now in Neubiberg under the command of Brigadier-General Richard Heuser. "Actually we should like to train them even more thoroughly than we do," we were told, "but we have a very tight schedule, and the Air Force awaits the officers we train. It wants as many as possible, as soon as possible. The chief shortage is in the younger pilot officers: we miss the group that wasn't trained between 1945 and 1955. The men who had just been commissioned in the last year of the war are between thirty and thirty-five, and that's too old for training as a jet pilot. Most of our trainees here are around twenty-one, but we have a few who are older, up to twenty-eight."

The parachute or airborne regiments, as they are called today, are part of the Army. There are cogent arguments in favor of this, and others against. From the standpoint of air tactics, they are infantrymen who use the airplane and the parachute as a means of transport. On the other hand, of course, the engagement of the enemy by airborne troops requires the closest possible cooperation with the Air Force. These units are not a special arm; they are made up of companies and battalions taken from the ordinary Army, who are given supplementary training as airborne troops. We met some of them.

"What are you?"
"Jumpers!"
"Are you happy?"
"Yes!"
"Are you scared?"
"No!"
"What do you want?"
"To jump!"

This was a ritual between a sergeant and his men, conducted at the tops of their voices in the fuselage of a Noratlas transport plane, barely audible above the noise of the two engines that came in through the open side doors. There were ten parachutists standing on each side of the fuselage, in the charge of Sergeant Smichowski of the Airborne-Troops Training School at Altenstadt-über-Schongau in Bavaria. The men had received the order to prepare to jump. At a sign from the sergeant, they hooked themselves to the static line that would open their parachutes automatically when they jumped.

The atmosphere was tense; you could see it in the faces of these young soldiers—hence the odd ritual, learned from the Americans. Everyone now was ready, some eager to jump; nevertheless, the idea of plunging out into the sky made the heart of even the most experienced beat a little faster. For the last time, each man tested the position of his neighbor's parachute and the state of his harness. Then they stood ready, their hands on the static rope, waiting for the final signal.

Lieutenant Böneker looked towards the pilot. The Noratlas was down to a height of about 1,300 feet and rapidly approaching the dropping area. Then the pilot lowered his hand, and the light at the side doors glowed green. The Lieutenant gave the order to jump. A last probing glance from the Sergeant, a friendly slap on the back, and they went, the one to the right, the other to the left, in quick succession. We watched them through the back window. For a moment or two, the silk of their parachutes fluttered, then it bellied out, and they floated safely down to the ground, swaying gently in the air as they descended.

The dropping area was small, not more than a few hundred yards across, and bordered by trees on three sides. Wind direction and strength had been calculated before the drop, but it can change suddenly. The parachutists must guide their descent; it is one of the things they learn in training. They can brake their fall by pulling on one side of the parachute, or they can let themselves drift in the breeze. As our plane turned away, we saw the parachutes falling one after the other into the dropping area, making dark green patches on the lighter grass. Ten minutes later we were back at the airfield in Kaufbeuren, and the Noratlas waited on the runway to take up another group.

"Why aren't your men called parachutists any more?" we asked Lieutenant Böneker.

"Because the expression isn't adequate. We are airborne troops; the parachute is only one way of getting down, and we use it only when necessary. When circumstances allow, the plane touches down; that's simpler. But of course, one doesn't always find a neatly laid out airfield behind enemy lines, and then one jumps."

The Noratlas from which the parachute jumps were made is the transport plane Nord-2501, of French manufacture. Its construction is particularly suited for parachute drops, because the fuselage is underslung, with the wing span overhead, so that in jumping there is no danger that a parachute will get caught up in the wings.

So far this is all training, but the active wings are gradually being formed, and their transfer to NATO is going forward satisfactorily. Nörvenich, for example, twelve miles to the west of Cologne, is not a training center, but an operational base from which the new German Air Force will take part in the joint defense of the West under NATO; the atmosphere is already that of a front-line airfield. The present Commandant is Lieutenant-Colonel Gerhard Barkhorn, Commodore of the Thirty-first Fighter-Bomber Wing. He is still young for such an important command—in his early forties—and he has retained something of the cheery forthrightness of the young fighter pilot. But he receives the deep respect and authority that derive from good performance. He is also one of the most decorated fighter pilots of the Second World War, with over 300 confirmed air victories, and was himself shot down on no less than eleven occasions, escaping safely each time.

"Whose orders are you under here, Colonel?"

"For supplies and reinforcements, Air Force Group North of the *Bundeswehr*" now under Major-General Werner Panitzki in Münster. But the operational orders come from NATO.

This means in the last analysis, from SACEUR.

The Commandant's office was a small, bare room; almost the only furniture was a large table and a steel safe. There was no room to walk about. There were four telephones, a wall full of maps, and a cartoon cut out of a newspaper showing a stork with a baby slung from its beak being safely "talked down."

"Are you ready to take to the air at any time?" we asked.

"We have to be. That's our job. Our aim is the same as that of Strategic Air Command: a third of our strength ready for instant action, and in the air within a quarter of an hour. We haven't quite got that far yet; it still takes us twenty minutes, unless we receive a preliminary warning and the machines are ready—then we can be in the air within five minutes."

"Just what would happen if matters ever became serious and you got the order to go into action?"

"We get such orders every day. They're routine. We know exactly what we have to do for each stage of preparedness. Perhaps we receive a certain code word, and that means planned objectives; we fly towards them, but not directly; the flight pattern is turned around by 90 or 120 degrees. There would not be much difference if it were the real thing—except, of course, that we should get the order to shoot. If you are interested in the technical side of it, the delta form comes over the teleprinter."

"The delta form?"

"Yes, that's an instructions formula that tells us what we have to do. For example: a) nature of task—say, armed reconnaissance; b) which squadrons; c) which plane or planes; d) what armaments; e) any information concerning the target; f) T.O.T., which means time over target; g) time of return; h) any special instructions. And so on."

"Can you give us some idea of what sort of task you might be called upon to perform?"

An order for an armed reconnaissance to discover whether the enemy has planes capable of carrying nuclear weapons, say, MIG-17s or MIG-19s, or YA-28s stationed at a particular airfield. The instructions come out of the teleprinter with several copies—one for the navigational department, one for target fixing, another for the meteorological office, and so on. Here at staff we quickly survey the order, calculate the distances involved, decide how much fuel a pilot needs, what additional information if any we can give him, what armament he must carry, how much ammunition, and so on. Then everything goes to Battle Headquarters, and from there to the squadron concerned. When everything is ready, the leading pilot gets his copy and makes his own preparations."

One could see that Lieutenant-Colonel Barkhorn was proud of his wing, but he immediately added: "Of course, we're still in the building-up phase. We're doing our best to become a full member of the defense, but we've not got that far yet."

The F-84-F Thunderstreak and the reconnaissance plane RF-84-F are among the standard types of the German Air Force. They are not ultra-modern, and need a long runway to get into the air, but they are good machines, which stood up well to the MIGs in Korea. At their top speed of 750 miles an hour they come very near the sound barrier, and in a dive they can break through it. They have a remarkably fast rate of climb, a ceiling of almost 50,000 feet, and a range of 1,800 miles, which can be increased by refueling in the air. They are armed with six heavy machine guns, and they can also carry rockets. To see one of them racing along the runway is an impressive sight. They look a bit heavy, but then suddenly they rise very steeply, leaving a trail of smoke behind them, and disappear into the sky.

"Which plane would you prefer for the jobs you have to do?" we inquired.

"Unquestionably the F-104-G Starfighter. Particularly because it is to be developed and equipped for low flying as well—that is to say at about 1,000 feet. The ultimate objective is about 250 feet. We start our training at about 1,000 feet and 300 miles an hour. Of course that means a high fuel consumption and correspondingly reduces our range, which is about 750 miles at 40,000 feet. But tactical planes must be capable of low flying, too. For minor jobs, we are going to get the Italian G-91. It's a great advantage that we can get by with two types."

"Are there other NATO allies in Nörvenich?"

"No, this is a purely German wing. We used to have British, American, Belgian, and Dutch advisers, but now only the British are left, apart from one or two Americans, chiefly technicians from the Curtiss-Wright and Republic companies, which provided our planes."

As a young fighter pilot in the last months of the war, Lieutenant-Colonel Barkhorn flew an Me-262, the first operational jet fighter. According to him, it was the "same sort of job" as the present models, though more primitive. His own basic training during the war was, naturally, with piston-engined planes, but he is not among those who think that this is necessarily the proper way to start. "I think the best thing would be to put trainees into a two-seater model of a front-line plane with an experienced pilot to accompany them," he said. "We have already proved that in this way a fledgling pilot needs only an hour more of training than his colleague who has been piston-trained."

The Commodore concluded by saying that, above all, the new German Air Force must have the moral support and encouragement of the population. "The thing I wish most for," he declared, "is that people would realize how essential our defense is. We are ready to go into action at a moment's notice, but we must be given the feeling that the people we are training to defend really want us to defend them, and that they're behind us with all their hearts."

We also talked with the Chief of Staff and the Chief of Operations, and they too stressed that the wing was still concentrating chiefly on standards. It was the first German wing to become operational, and a good deal of time was still taken up with experimentation. The experiences of the last war were only conditionally valid; new forms and methods had to be tried out.

They had started off with the old form of flight organization—two or three squadrons and a supply group. "But gradually we noticed that this no longer suited modern requirements. From the operational standpoint, the job has become much bigger. For example, nowadays we have to reckon with about eighty missions a day. During exercises, we have to report back the state of the wing every twenty minutes to the Tactical Operations Center. In addition, there is much more radio work, safety precautions, and so on; and therefore, if we're to get our planes into the air quickly, and get good results, we need a strong operations center."

As far as reconnaissance is concerned, it is assumed that it will respond to enemy activity. "We get instructions from TOC, the forward ATAF post. The orders may refer to anything—a reconnaissance flight, a control flight, or an attacking mission. We're told what we have to do; how we do it is left to us. We need to know our objective; we choose the procedure and weapons."

Technical developments demand such a complicated organization that it should be kept as stationary as possible, and the wings transferred infrequently.

So much for the immediate problems. But the future also requires thought. The fundamentals of air fighting have changed, and that affects the new structure of the German Air Force.

"Today the wing is no longer the battle unit, or even the squadron, but, strictly speaking, the individual plane. We are retaining the wing as an organizational unit, but that is really more a question of comradeship and morale; it no longer has any tactical significance. We must reach the organizational point at which any individual plane, no matter where it is stationed, can land at any other airfield, be refueled, readied for battle, and sent up again. In other words, we need bases that are stationary supply centers—a cross-servicing system. Here in Nörvenich we should be able to service any plane and send it into the air again with a new mission set by our Tactical Operations Center. Similarly, our planes should be able to land anywhere and be sent into action again, without loss of time."

20

The New German Navy

Just as the Soviets have subjugated half of Europe, so they have also burst out of Kronstadt Bay into the Baltic itself and established a dominant position. The whole southern coast almost up to Lübeck, 600 miles, is now in Soviet hands. Today the Red Fleet is the strongest in the Baltic, and it is supported by the naval forces of Poland and the Eastern zone.

In order to establish and consolidate their position in the Baltic states, the Soviets killed, deported, or recolonized millions, and uprooted 400,000 Carelian Finns from the part of Finland captured by the Red Army in 1939 and seized again after the Second World War. Just as the Soviets regard the annexed territory as a base for aggression against the free countries of Europe, so the Baltic serves for a drive into the North Sea for an attack on NATO's Atlantic lifeline.

"There are good reasons why the Soviets try to turn the free Baltic into a Red inland sea," declared the German Minister for Defense, Dr. Strauss, in his report to the Fourth Annual Conference of NATO parliamentarians on November 19, 1958. Success would mean that, in the event of war, the still free Baltic countries would have to submit to a Soviet ultimatum without even the possibility of defending themselves. If the Red Navy were to succeed in breaking out of the Baltic into the Atlantic, the Soviets could interfere with the movement of supplies for Europe; they could directly threaten the great American centers of industry and population with medium-range rockets fired from the sea.

The strength of the Baltic Fleet is one measure of the Soviets' aggressive plans. Along the entire coast they have established bases and supply depots, and built roads to link them with their own industrial centers. For example, the canal system being cut in the Soviet zone to provide a direct inland waterway from the Bohemian-Moravian industrial area to the triangle of harbors, Rostock, Warnemünde, and Wismar is of great military significance; so is the planned pipeline from Baku to Frankfurt on the Oder; and, indeed, all such Soviet undertakings.

One cannot speak of an even approximate balance of naval forces in the Baltic today. NATO forces there do not have the strength necessary to meet a challenge. The Soviets would like to make this a permanent condition, and advocate a so-called neutralization of the Baltic—prohibition of access to all warships except their own and those of the other littoral states. This would mean that in the event of attack, NATO naval forces would be prevented from coming to the assistance of Denmark or Germany. Moscow wants to maneuver these states into a position where they could neither defend themselves nor be defended, and this Soviet propaganda calls "the Baltic a peaceful sea"!

If they succeeded, the West would be excluded from the Baltic even in time of peace, and that would mean that the Soviets could control it with a fraction of their present naval strength there. The surplus ships could be used elsewhere, for example, to increase the strength of the Soviet Arctic Fleet at Murmansk, whose wartime task would be to threaten Europe around the North Cape and to cut the Atlantic lifeline.

It has always been an aim of Russian policy to turn the Baltic into a *mare clausum*. Peter the Great had it in mind when in 1703 he gave orders to build a town on the marshland at the mouth of the Neva, which, as Petersburg, became the capital of the Russian Empire. After the third dismemberment of Poland under Catherine the Great, Russia pushed forward as far as the River Memel. Stalin seized Poland and a great part of Germany because the Soviets were no longer satisfied with access to the Baltic; they wanted access to the open seas beyond it.

The new German Navy, working closely with the Danish armed forces, has various assignments and has a very important job within the framework of NATO defense. In war, it would have to prevent Soviet naval units, in particular submarines, from breaking into the Atlantic. It would have to harass the seaborne supplies to Soviet land forces along the Baltic coast and to repulse Soviet air, sea, and land operations against the Danish islands. But even in peace, the NATO allies cannot afford to let the mastery of the Baltic go to the Soviets by default.

At the end of 1961, the new German Navy consisted of six destroyers, six groups of minelayers, and landing craft supported by speed and escort boats; in all, a total of 174 warships and 21 auxiliary vessels. The three American destroyers, six training frigates from Britain, and two supply ships from France, were borrowed or purchased. More modern destroyers, the *Hamburg* and the *Schleswig-Holstein* among them, are being built in German shipyards. In the next few years, the German Navy is to be strengthened by twelve submarines of between 300 and 350 tons, an as yet indeterminate number of smaller submarines for anti-submarine defense, minelayers, coastal and ocean-going minesweepers, various coastal defense vessels, a training ship, a sailing training ship, and a considerable number of auxiliary and supply ships.

In addition to a planned total of 22 squadrons of various craft, the German Navy will have two Naval Air Wings. We were assured that in view of the special tasks of the German Navy and the increasingly important role of submarines and the naval air arm, both these weapons would receive special attention in future naval rearmament programs.

The German naval forces in the North Sea would probably be used primarily for escort duties, though such tasks might be overshadowed in the first phase of a conflict by the operations of the German Navy in the Baltic.

"The destroyer will probably be the biggest unit in the new German Navy. In view of the special tasks likely to devolve on us, we have decided against bigger ships, and we shall confine our building program to small and medium-sized ships. Today our tasks are no longer strategical, and the seas of the world are no longer our operational area. Our job is to make a certain tactical contribution in the North Sea and the Baltic, within the general framework of the Atlantic Alliance."

The speaker was Rear-Admiral Rolf Johanesson, the Commander-in-Chief of the new German Navy, and the scene was the bridge of his flagship, Destroyer Z1, during the naval maneuvers in the Baltic. The Z1 is a U.S. destroyer that saw service during the Second World War, the first of six to be turned over to the German Navy.

The limitation of tonnage to 3,000, as accepted by the Federal Republic in the Paris agreement, had to be modified before long.

NATO needs a modern and efficient German Navy, and this means, among other things, guided missiles, which for technical reasons can be installed only on bigger vessels. And if the auxiliary ships are to work efficiently, they too must be bigger. At NATO's recommendation, therefore, Western European Union has finally raised the maximum limit to 6,000 tons. In November, 1960, the 4,800-ton training ship *Deutschland* was launched. Further, the Federal Republic will have to be given permission to manufacture acoustic, magnetic and remote-control mines, since these will be the chief means of blocking the exits from the Baltic to the North Sea.

We made the Admiral's acquaintance during a torpedo exercise for which his flagship was serving as a target. One after the other, "enemy" ships raced up to us. Long lines of light bubbles indicated the path of the practice torpedoes, which were adjusted so that if they scored "hits" they would pass harmlessly under our keel.

These new German escort vessels are not big—870 tons with a full load—but they are smart, fast, and maneuverable. We had seen them from close up earlier in the day, while watching gunnery practice—2 cm. and 4 cm. guns firing tracer bullets at moving targets.

Suddenly, one of the torpedo trails snapped before reaching us. "A diver," commented the Admiral. Immediately a smoke buoy was fixed to mark the spot. "A man will go down tomorrow and fish it up again. We owe that to the Treasury; the things are expensive."

Later we met Admiral Heinrich Gerlach, the Commander of Naval Group East, and asked: "Isn't the Soviet Baltic Fleet overwhelmingly superior to our forces?"

"Well, we're not altogether alone, you know. There are the Danish naval forces; and behind them, the naval forces of the other NATO powers. Above all, we have a limited task. Our objective would be to prevent the Soviet fleet, and in particular its submarines, from entry into the North Sea and the Atlantic."

"Then the task of the combined NATO fleets is comparable to the task of the British Navy against the German Navy during the First World War?"

"In one sense, yes. The Imperial German Navy could have made a decisive contribution to the German cause only by breaking through the British blockade from the North of Scotland to Bergen and reaching the Atlantic. The British therefore rightly claim that the Battle of Skagerrak, or Jutland, as they call it, was a British naval victory. Tactically, it was a German victory, because the British fleet suffered heavier losses; but strategically, the British achieved their objective. It mattered little to Britain that our Navy was still able to operate in the North Sea off her own shores, so long as the British Navy could seal off our forces and confine them to that area. This they did successfully, both before and after the Battle of Skagerrak."

The maneuvers of the German naval forces in the Baltic are no secret to the Soviets. The western Baltic is a free zone, and Soviet ships, disguised as harmless fishing boats or merchant vessels, shadow and photograph every movement. Sometimes they even send warships, which cruise alongside the German and Danish ships for hours, as for instance during the NATO autumn exercises in 1960.

Admiral Gerlach then made some interesting comments on the Soviet Navy: "Its staff work is thorough but a little rigid; individual commanders, particularly the lower commands, are not given enough freedom of action." If one can upset their plans, the whole operation comes to a halt. They have to start again from above. In their over-all planning, the Soviets are efficient, but it all takes a good deal of time."

To close the Baltic for the Soviets means at the same time to keep it open for the NATO naval forces, and this task gives the German and Danish naval forces a significance which transcends coastal protection and defensive action.

"If we can guarantee to keep open the Baltic," wrote the Inspector of the German Navy, Vice-Admiral Friedrich Oskar Ruge, in a study entitled *Sea Power and Security*, "then the influence of the great naval powers will extend into the Baltic, to the 600 miles of coast in Soviet hands, most of which is well suited to amphibious landings. The Soviets will have to take that into account, and adopt measures to protect themselves against tactical and operational landings, regardless of their likelihood. This will tie a large number of Soviet divisions to the coast. The defender never knows where such an attack might come, and is therefore compelled to divide his forces. A concentration of all Soviet forces against Western Europe, though sometimes seen as a threat, is therefore hardly possible—the transport problems are insoluble, and the Soviets must be prepared for an attack wherever their country lies open to the sea."

Thus the presence of naval forces in the Baltic could also influence land operations in the event of a Soviet attack in Central Europe, because they would relieve pressure on the still-undermanned NATO front along the Iron Curtain.

Admiral Gerlach is NATO Commander of Allied Naval Forces

East (BSO), and as such he is subordinate to the Supreme Command Allied Naval Forces Northern Europe, with headquarters in Kolsaas.

The relationship between men and officers on board ship is comradely. A common cause, proximity, and mutual dependence strengthen the sense of community. Moreover, all ranks and ratings, from commanding admiral down to youngest sailor, get exactly the same food. When we were luncheon guests of the three admirals on board the *Sirius*, the menu was pickled pork, sauerkraut, and potatoes. "It's good enough for me," said Admiral Karl Adolf Zenker. "I hope the men think it's good and ample enough for them."

Admiral Zenker was the first Commander-in-Chief of the Combined Naval Forces North Sea (BSN). He is now in charge of naval training at Kiel. As was always the case in the German Navy, officers and men come from all parts of the country, not only from ports and coastal areas. For example, Admiral Zenker is a Berliner, as is his successor, Admiral Hubert von Wangenheim, one-time commandant of the Officers Training School at Mürwik. One can hear the accents and dialects of all parts of the country aboard German naval vessels; in divided Germany, that variety is an element of unity.

The Communists direct a great deal of propaganda against the *Bundeswehr* and malign the naval, military, and air commanders. But we were assured by the counter-intelligence officer attached to the Schleswig-Holstein Military District that the leaflets, their contents predictable, are handed over by the men to superiors or consigned to the wastebasket.

A so-called freedom broadcasting station claims to be on the territory of the Federal Republic and to be run by officers and men of the *Bundeswehr*. However, the naval radio branch ascertained that it actually operates from the Soviet Zone, in the neighborhood of Magdeburg. The vehemence of this propaganda is a measure of the importance the Soviets attach to the new German Navy.

The Naval Operational Staff under Vice-Admiral Ruge controls the Fleet Command, Fleet Base Command, Naval Training Command, the Ships' Commission Command. All floating, flying, and amphibious naval units are under the Fleet Command, grouped in special arms: Destroyer Command, Minesweeper Command, Speedboat Command, Naval Air Command, and so on. The naval air arm is organized into squadrons consisting of from six to ten units. For battle operations and maneuvers, however, the German Navy is already part of NATO, through the North Sea and Baltic Commands. Logistics is in the hands of Fleet Base Command. The general supply establishment also includes base and depot commands subordinate to the various sectional commands.

In 1959, a floating supply system was organized, and supply vessels began to carry fuel oil and other supplies to ships at sea. As this system develops, the fleet units will become less dependent on shore-based installations, and their mobility and operational range will correspondingly increase.

In accordance with NATO practice, logistics, as distinct from operations, is on a national basis, but special agreements provide for mutual assistance under certain circumstances. We inquired about this:

"If the German Navy were cut off from its own land bases, could it obtain supplies from other NATO naval bases?"

"Certainly," replied Admiral Gerlach. "Without the slightest difficulty. For one thing, its armaments are largely foreign. And the greater part of the rest is readily interchangeable."

The young seaman's first contact with the Navy is through Naval Training Command, to which he is attached during the first few months of his service, usually in one of the naval training battalions at Wilhelmshaven, Glücksburg, Glückstadt, and Brake. After basic training, he goes to one of the Command's special training schools. Special training continues throughout a sailor's career.

As Rear-Admiral Werner Erhardt told us, "You can judge the importance of Naval Training Command from the fact that, at any given time, about half of our naval effectives are undergoing training. From young cadet to experienced staff officer, everyone goes back time and again for advanced work."

The Armed Services Act of March 19, 1956 provides that long-service men be given an opportunity to prepare for some civilian occupation. This also comes under Naval Training Command. The work of the various technical branches of the new Navy is closely related to a large number of civilian occupations. Apart from such specifically naval matters as shipbuilding, surveying technique, and cartography, the Navy trains coppersmiths, turners, toolmakers, fitters, smiths, welders, riveters, cooks, bakers. There are also technical occupations in radar and radio, meteorology, electro-mechanics, machinery and aircraft construction, and so on, which have their counterparts in civilian life, as well as such general occupations as bookkeeper, photographer, medical attendant, storekeeper, buyer, and even musician.

Officer cadets are trained in the Officers Training School at Mürwik near Flensburg, which was founded in 1910 under Kaiser Wilhelm II. "What we aim at," we were told at training headquarters "is best summed up in the expression *navale generale*. We try to give our cadet trainees everything they need in the way of knowledge on board, including grounding in the natural sciences and history."

This part of the training is theoretical rather than practical. For example, cadets are taught the nature of electricity rather than the use of electrical equipment. After that, they receive practical naval and technical training on board a training ship—in home waters, on windjammers, and, on cruises in foreign waters, aboard conventionally driven vessels.

At the underwater-arms school in Mürwik, the young officer cadets are first introduced to naval battle tactics by the use of models serviced by electronic equipment which simulates conditions at sea. The trainees sit at the same kind of radar and sonar screens as they will find when they join their units. For example there is an "attack teacher," a British device designed to impart the art of submarine hunting. It is exciting to stand in the control room and watch the swift movements of the anti-submarine speedboats and the evasive maneuvers of the submarine seeking to escape attack. This equipment saves many weeks of training at sea, and a good deal of money. Training installations are expensive, but less so than the operation of a speedboat at sea. There is also a torpedo-firing trainer, another British invention, which reproduces all the factors met with at sea, including the unsteady platform, diminution of visibility by spray, and so on. Finally, there is an even more complicated apparatus known as the Action Speed Tactical Teacher, for introducing trainees to the combined maneuvers of entire squadrons.

"All naval flyers come under Naval Command," we were told by the commandant of the naval flying station at the Holtenau base. "Their job is to give air support to naval operations, to reconnoiter, and keep good look-out for submarines, medium altitude air attack, and so on. Thus they are not a part of air defense, and they therefore do not belong to the Second ATAF. Both the Americans and the British have been very helpful," he went on. "They lent us their airfields, and many of our men were trained for between eighteen and twenty-one months at Pensacola, Florida. Others were trained at Lossiemouth, Scotland and at Eglinton, Northern Ireland."

At the air base in Schleswig to which we were taken by a Sycamore helicopter, we met some of the young naval flyers who had been trained at Pensacola. The youngest was just twenty-one. He was full of praise for the thorough training he had received and for the friendly atmosphere he had found. "I have been up to 45,000 feet in one of our Seahawks," he declared proudly. "You feel a bit lonely at that height."

The Seahawk is the jet fighter of the German Navy. There are also Gannets, turbo-prop models with contra-rotating propellers mounted one behind the other. These planes are intended as submarine hunters, and in addition to the pilot they carry an observer and a wireless operator. In accordance with their job, their speed is not very high.

The German Navy is forming two naval air wings, the first in Schleswig, with twelve Seahawks and ten Gannets, and the second in Nordholz, with three Seahawk groups. In addition, there is an Air-Sea Rescue Group equipped with helicopters of the Bristol-Sycamore type, Albatross amphibian planes, Pembroke transport planes, and one or two other types.

Every year, an average of over 60,000 vessels of all nations pass through the Kiel Canal, almost ten times as many as pass through the Suez or Panama Canals. On its bank stands a magnificent monument with a tremendous tower like a ship's bow. Every ship that passes dips its flag in salute. It is the German Naval Memorial, erected in Laboe near Kiel in the 1920s and paid for from funds collected by the German Navy League. It was dedicated to the memory of 35,000 officers, petty officers, and men of the Imperial Navy, whose names are recorded in a book kept in an underground hall inside the monument. In 1954 the monument was rededicated to the seafolk of all nationalities who lost their lives during the two world wars. Today, the monument is a symbol of peace, in meaningful location on the Kiel Canal, which Stalin demanded for Russia at the Teheran and Yalta Conferences, in order to get entry to the North Sea. The Soviet plan was frustrated by the opposition of Great Britain, but not abandoned. Now the new German Navy, in alliance with the other land, sea, and air forces, stands perpetual guard under the international command of NATO.

21

Northern Europe

In Northern Europe, NATO has a very long front: almost 1,800 miles, from Schleswig-Holstein northwards to Spitzbergen far beyond the Arctic Circle. The distance from NATO's northern headquarters (AFNORTH) in Oslo to the northernmost point of Norway is as far as from Oslo to Moscow, or from Oslo to Rome.

Only three of the five Scandinavian states, Norway, Denmark, and Iceland, belong to NATO. They were neutral during the First World War, and again during the Second, until Hitler occupied Denmark and Norway. They know, therefore, that the desire to remain neutral is no longer enough, and that without the support of NATO they would be helpless in the face of Soviet demands.

"It is the security system of NATO that gives us, here in Western Europe, the possibility of choosing our position, and the strength to prevent its imposition by force." This was said by Halvard Lange, Norway's Foreign Minister, in the Storting, or Norwegian Parliament, on January 20, 1959.

Sweden was again spared in the Second World War, and her strong and well-equipped army never went into action. In the first years of the cold war, a special responsibility devolved on her, and the Swedish people did not hesitate to stand by their obligations. In 1948, she offered her war-weakened neighbors, Norway and Denmark, an alliance, the Nordic Defense Union. It was clear, however, that Sweden did not have the economic strength to help as effectively as the United States to build up their defenses, and this finally persuaded them to join the North Atlantic Alliance.

Today the Swedish people harbor few illusions; most of them are aware that they owe their freedom more to the existence of NATO than to a precarious armed neutrality. If, nevertheless, Sweden sets her face against joining NATO, it is out of consideration for the fourth Scandinavian state. Finland has a strong Communist Party, depends politically, geographically, and economically on her power-ful Soviet neighbor, and struggles to preserve her political independ-ence. According to the terms of the peace treaty Moscow imposed on the Finns in 1948, they have to provide bases for the Soviets not only in time of war but "whenever there is a threat of aggression," which means in effect whenever it suits the Kremlin—as Khrushchev was careful to demonstrate to the Finns, as well as to the rest of the world, in 1961.

If Sweden were to join NATO, Soviet pressure on Finland un-doubtedly would increase, perhaps beyond Finland's ability to resist. But there is no doubt that Sweden, like Austria and Switzerland, belongs to the Western World, historically, culturally, and politically, and in the event of a Soviet attack would defend itself by force of arms.

Soviet military might casts a grimmer shadow over the Scandi-navian countries since Moscow lost hope that neutralism would make these countries as dependent as Finland. It is estimated that the Soviets have twenty-eight divisions and 6,000 planes on this sector of the front alone.

The ice-free Soviet ports along the Kola coasts, Murmansk and Polarnoia, are protected by powerful land, sea, and air defenses, and if the Soviets ever attempted an invasion of Norway by sea, these would be their bases. In the event of war, Soviet submarines would try to get out into the Atlantic to cut Europe's lifeline, and perhaps attack the United States by rocket. It thus would be vital for the Western World to prevent such a breakthrough, but without Nor-way and Denmark it would be impossible.

In Central Europe, the main burden of defense lies with the land forces, but in Northern Europe, defense by land and sea is equally important. Norway is a bigger country than the United Kingdom, but her total population is only 3.5 million. Because of her long and broken coastline—something like 12,000 miles, if you count the in-numerable fjords which penetrate deep into the interior—and her 150,000 islands, she cannot be defended by land forces alone. Strong naval and air forces are also necessary. In October, 1960, a new naval building program was laid before the Storting.

"This new program provides for the construction of many small modern naval vessels," declared Vice-Admiral Erling G. Hostvedt, the Commander-in-Chief of the Norwegian Navy. "When they are operational, they will be kept so dispersed that they could not be destroyed by a sudden Soviet nuclear attack. We must have a fleet ready for action at all times." And then he added: "We can't afford to bluff; what we have must be real."

This "reality of power" is also demanded by SACLANT, in whose operational scope the seas around Norway fall. The combined allied naval forces are necessary to defend the Far North, because the long, deep fjords of Norway would offer Soviet submarines excellent hiding places from which they could prey on Atlantic shipping and communications. At AFNORTH Headquarters in Kolsaas, great importance is attached to the presence of the U.S. naval task force in the waters between Iceland and Norway. This special task force, combining land, sea, and air forces under the command of Admiral Storheill, is necessary because of the great distances involved. Kolsaas headquarters are too far away from the scene.

Strategically speaking, Norway is divided into two parts—the South, where, together with Denmark and Germany, she guards the Baltic exits, and the Far North, which is a bastion against Murmansk and Polarnoia. The two areas are connected by only one main road.

The sea and air forces, as well as the brigade (with headquarters in Heggelya) which make up the Task Force Northern Norway, know that they would be the first to be hit by any Soviet attack. Should the Red Army strike through Finland, the mission of these forces would be to hold the Lyngen line, a fortified defense in depth laid out by the Germans during the Second World War. The Lyngen Fjord penetrates so deeply that the land front is not more than twenty-five miles wide. The same troops must also defend the country from invasion from the sea, and protect the northernmost NATO airfield in Bardufoss.

The terrain is favorable to defense, but considering the tremendous Soviet power concentrated here, many Norwegian military experts welcome the idea of support from allied troops. Unfortunately, Norway is not yet prepared to allow them into the country except in wartime or during NATO maneuvers. The one active Norwegian brigade in the North consists of picked men, and in the event of war it could rapidly be enlarged to divisional strength. Despite the difficult terrain, it is highly mobile. In case of attack, the Norwegian troops would quickly occupy their fortified positions in the hills and mountains. Moving on skis, drawn by jeeps and Canadian Weasels—caterpillar-tracked vehicles specially designed for use in Arctic conditions—they would be ready for action even in the Arctic winter.

It is close to another 400 miles from the Lyngen line along the winding coastal road to the point where the yellow frontier posts of Norway face the red and green posts of the Soviet Union. At this advanced post of the free world, a frontier battalion is stationed, with headquarters in Höybuktmoen near Kirkenes. On both sides of the frontier, the country is without roads and consists of marshland, swift rivers, rocks, and thick scrub. In winter it is shrouded in Arctic darkness. At one time it was believed that this area, Finnmark, was indefensible, but could not be attacked, either. However, the great offensive preparations being made by the Red Army on the other side of this barren frontier have led to the abandonment of this comforting theory.

The Soviets are well aware of the tremendous importance of this wild and beautiful Arctic area. They have labored tenaciously to blast roads and railways in the rock of the Kola peninsula. They have built barracks and great shipyards where part of the growing Red Navy is being built, day and night. Modern airfields can accommodate 1,500 planes. The important Soviet base of Lkstari is only about twelve miles beyond the Norwegian frontier. It has rocket firing bases. There are torpedo posts along the coasts, and eight Soviet divisions stand ready not far away, with another fifteen divisions around Leningrad.

The northern frontier of Finnmark, over which the sun does not rise at all for two months of the year, lies farther north than Alaska and extends farther east than Istanbul. This province is thinly populated, but larger than Belgium and Denmark put together, and it must not be abandoned to the enemy. In the event of war, the Soviets would certainly move across Finnish territory and drive forward along the road built and fortified by the Germans during the last war. But then they would be faced with the Lyngen line—unless they should try to outflank it by violating Swedish neutrality.

"Southern Norway is chiefly threatened from the south, from the continental mainland," said Major-General Ørnulf Dahl. A firm front line held from the Elbe to North Jutland, and the protection of the Baltic outlets are vital for South Norway. Since the Sixth German Division became operational in Schleswig in the summer of 1960, the situation has improved. Norway has about 30,000 men under arms—20,000 in the army, 6,000 in the navy, and 4,000 in the air force. Including the Home Defense, their total armed strength could be raised to 270,000 in the event of war. The period of national service in the army is sixteen months, for the navy and air force eighteen months, and fifty hours a year in the Home Defense Force. All men capable of bearing arms have to do military service, and in the event of war they will all take part in the defense of the country.

The country is divided into sixteen regimental districts. There are sixteen infantry regiments, two independent battalions, and certain detachments for other arms. The task of these districts is largely administrative and to prepare for mobilization. In the event of war, eight brigades would be formed—in other words, units of combined arms. There are two divisional skeletal staffs, one with each of the active brigades, certain specialized field units, and a territorial organization for local tasks.

The Norwegian Army is small, but efficient and well trained. The particular strength of the defense system rests, as in Denmark and Switzerland, on a "people in arms." Apart from the years of the German occupation, 1940 to 1945, when military service was in abeyance, there is no age group that did not receive training, and even the men of those years are part of the territorial Home Defense Force, which is strengthened by the inclusion of volunteers. The members of this force all keep their weapons at home and ready for immediate use. In the event of war, they would continue their civilian jobs but would also be available for local military action. Members of the Home Defense Force also man part of the coastal fortifications and the anti-aircraft batteries.

Military preparedness in Norway is not bedevilled by party politics. As in Switzerland, national defense is a matter for the whole people. Voluntary associations of sharpshooters, no less than 1,800 groups with 130,000 members, encourage military preparedness; and the women of Norway have their Lotta League, which trains them for first aid, communications, and other auxiliary services, so that in the event of war they could support the armed forces.

The Norwegian Air Force consists of eight wings with about 200 planes. The fighter and fighter-bomber squadrons are equipped with F-84-Gs, F-86-Fs, and F-86-Ks. In addition to reconnaissance groups, training squadrons, and transport units, there are also four helicopter units and four communications units. The anti-aircraft batteries are grouped into four divisions, and their guns are gradually being replaced by guided ground-to-air missiles. The first Nike anti-aircraft battery was made operational in 1959.

Ten NATO airfields have been built, among them Sola, Garde-moen, and Lofoten in northern Norway. At AFNORTH Headquarters in Oslo there is an integrated air staff consisting of Danes, British, and Americans, as well as Norwegians. The British contingent is particularly strong.

Large areas of Norway are still wild and awaiting pioneers. So far, only about one twenty-fifth of the total area of the country has been made arable. The rest consists of forests, virgin land, rock, and glacier terrain, dotted with lakes and criss-crossed with rivers. But this sparsely settled land is inhabited by a people of great creative ability, which has produced such men as Björnson, Ibsen, Hamsun, Grieg, Munch, and Nansen, and made a significant contribution to the culture and civilization of the West. Modern Norway did not come into being until 1905, when she broke away from Sweden. Nevertheless, there is consciousness of a long history. Norway is an integral part of the Scandinavia which produced the Normans and the Vikings who founded states and helped to shape the features of Europe—in northern France, England, Iceland, Greenland, and southern Italy. They were the creators of a Russian empire, and the first discoverers of America. Norman Sicily was the first modern state in Europe. Through their great scion, the Hohenstaufen Emperor Frederick II, they lent a creative impulse not only to law and politics, but to art and science, to Christianity, and to the Holy Roman Empire, and paved the way for the Renaissance.

In February, 1949, the Soviets tried to prevent Norway from joining the North Atlantic Alliance by offering her a "non-aggression pact." They have not given up, and are doing their utmost, alternating threats and promises, to break the political morale of this little country, which is so decisive for the defense of the free world. The Soviets exploited the U-2 incident of May 1, 1960, and their shooting down of an American observation plane, RB-47, on July 1, 1960, to send notes to Norway couched in such insolent terms that the Norwegian Government announced it would not reply to them at all. When it is not indulging in threats or abuse, Soviet propaganda does its best to persuade the Norwegians of the advantages of a neutralist policy, which, of course, would favor the Soviets exclusively. But the Norwegians are not only a gallant people, they are also intelligent, with a firm grasp on the hard facts, and well aware that they can retain their freedom only in alliance with the other free peoples of the world.

The burden of building up an efficient defense rests more heavily on Norway—large but thinly populated—than it does on a highly industrialized country. As Major-General Harald Löken, Deputy Commander-in-Chief of the Armed Forces, pointed out: "We had to start all over again in 1945. And our new naval building program will require still further large sums." Then there is the modernization of Norway's arms and equipment, which will be very expensive. Modern means of transport, helicopters (of particular importance in the Far North) and planes (the Starfighter F-104 is under consideration) will mean heavy outlays, and the defense budget for 1960–61 was more than $200 millions. In addition, NATO, between 1951 and 1958, contributed nearly a billion dollars to help rearm Norway, and its contributions continue.

Norway now has a Nike anti-aircraft battery, an infantry battalion equipped with Honest John rockets, and a Hawk anti-aircraft battery for dealing with low-flying planes. However, the atomic warheads necessary to make these modern weapons really effective may not, by Norwegian law, be stored on Norwegian territory in peacetime. Many experts wonder whether, in the event of an enemy attack, the nuclear weapons could be there in time. Medium-range rockets are also not allowed on Norwegian territory. When we raised this question at the Foreign Ministry in Oslo, we were advised that the Norwegian Government had to take "the Scandinavian balance" into consideration, and in particular the very exposed position of Finland towards the Soviet Union.

Another obstacle to joint defense planning is that at present it is not possible to establish permanent bases for the allied forces. Some left-wing objections were raised even to the establishment of supply depots, though these are essential in view of the great distances involved in the area. The Social-Democratic Premier, Einar Gerhardsen (who barely escaped with his life from a Nazi concentration camp during the war) took a firm stand in their favor, however, and he was supported by his own party and the great majority of the Norwegian people. The Norwegian Labor Party, to which both Foreign Minister Lange and the Premier belong, has declared itself in favor not only of such depots but of co-opting German officers onto the headquarters staff at AFNORTH in Oslo. Supply depots have now been set up, and military attachés exchanged between Oslo and Bonn. The atmosphere at AFNORTH Headquarters among the officers of many different nationalities is as warm and comradely as it is everywhere else in NATO.

"The fate of my country is bound up with the North Atlantic

Treaty Organization," declared Hersleb Vogt, the Norwegian Ambassador in Bonn, adding, "and with the fate of all its members, including Germany."

It is understandable that the five years of occupation cannot be effaced overnight from the memory of the Norwegian people, but at least they know that the German Federal Republic of today is a very different country—a changed Germany which has suffered a great deal herself and now sets her honor on creating that confidence on which the joint defense of freedom must rest.

Denmark is the bridge to Central Europe. Strategically, the country is of great importance, because it straddles the exits from the Baltic into the North Sea. The Belt and the Sund are, so to speak, the Bosphorus of Northern Europe, while the straits from the Kattegat to Skagerrak are the northern Dardanelles. Just as Turkey and Greece deny the Soviets passage from the Black Sea into the Mediterranean, so Denmark, Norway, and the German Federal Republic deny them passage from the Baltic to the North Sea and beyond.

On her own, Denmark could never stand up to a Soviet attack. Upon completing her defense reorganization in the spring of 1960, the Danish Navy consists of eight light destroyers, eighteen torpedo boats, six submarines, eight minelayers, twelve minesweepers, and nine coastal defense vessels. In addition, there are supply and auxiliary ships. But even with this increased strength, the Danish Navy is outnumbered twenty-fold by the Soviet Baltic Fleet. And while NATO maneuvers are invariably carried out under the assumption that an enemy attack is being repelled, Soviet maneuvers are usually planned as large-scale invasions.

Although Denmark has a long coastline on the North Sea which, from its geographical position, the Danes call the West Sea, there is only one useful harbor on it, Esbjerg. Primarily, the country may be said to face the Baltic; in that direction lie the chief economic concentrations; the industries, intensive agriculture, and the largest population centers. Copenhagen, on the extreme eastern edge of Zeeland on the Sund, with its 1.2 million inhabitants, is the most populous city in Scandinavia; about one-quarter of Denmark's total populace lives there. The second largest Danish town, Aarhus, which has a fine harbor and is an important shipbuilding center, is also on the east coast.

Accordingly, the main weight of Denmark's defense lies eastwards. The Danish North Sea Fleet is indeed rather insignificant;

far the greater part of Denmark's naval strength is concentrated on the east coast, to protect the 500 Danish islands and guard the straits leading from the Baltic into the Kattegat. The two main Danish naval bases are at Frederikshaven and Korsör. Like the new German Navy, the Danish Navy has purely tactical tasks and does not require big ships, which would be unsuitable in any case for her narrow waters. Because of the irregular depths, the frequent mists and fogs, and the difficult currents which depend more on wind than on tide, the Sund and the Belt are among the navigationally most difficult stretches of narrow water in the world. Detailed knowledge of local conditions is needed to negotiate the straits safely, even with the help of buoys, markers, and lights, which would, of course, all be removed in the event of war. The waters would also be defended by minefields, booms, nets, coastal batteries, and air patrols. Soviet warships attempting to force their way through the Great Belt would have to count on being attacked at least fifteen times by fast torpedo boats racing out from their hideouts among the innumerable islands along the route.

This refers to a Soviet attack with conventional weapons. But the Soviets do not bother with the conventional-*versus*-nuclear-weapons argument which in the West leads to so many disagreements. They will use both if it suits them, and NATO has to take this into account. The defense of Denmark therefore demands that all NATO land, sea, and air forces in Northern Europe be equipped with nuclear weapons.

The Soviets must know that if they use tactical atomic weapons, the NATO forces will reply in kind, and that the use of such weapons would make it much easier to deny them passage through the narrows into the North Sea.

Denmark has a population of 4.5 million and a standing army of 45,000. In the event of war, this figure could be quickly raised to 200,000, including the well-organized Home Defense Force, which numbers 65,000 volunteers. Compulsory military service has existed for over a century. Young Danes are called up at the age of seventeen—between 13,000 and 20,000 every year. The country is divided into eight military districts, the two chief ones being Zeeland, together with the Jutland peninsula, and the Isle of Funen.

As part of defense reorganization plans, the length of military service, formerly sixteen months, has been shortened to twelve, with a further two months for refresher training. To ensure that this will not affect the fighting power of the armed forces, all democratic political parties have agreed that long-service volunteers shall be recruited in addition—4,000 for the army, 1,000 for the air force, and another group for the navy.

The peacetime strength of the Danish Army is to consist of two and one-third mobile infantry brigades, a battalion stationed on Bornholm and equipped with light tanks, two units equipped with Honest John rockets, and a Nike rocket anti-aircraft battery. In addition, there will be the appropriate staffs and auxiliary units, including heavy artillery and a logistics apparatus. There will be a total of three divisions, one of which is fully equipped and has already been placed at the disposal of NATO. The Danish Air Force is to consist, apart from rescue and transport units, of three fighter-bomber squadrons, three all-weather fighter squadrons, and a reconnaissance squadron, each of sixteen machines. They are at present equipped with F-84-G fighter-bombers and Meteor Mark II night fighters, which operate from Aalborg, Vaerbose, Copenhagen, and four other NATO bases. Danish Air Force training is assisted by British, Canadian, and American instructors.

Reorganization plans provide also for an extension of the territorial defense system. Fifteen infantry battalions as well as fifteen batteries of light artillery are already available to protect specially threatened objectives such as airfields, ports and harbors, bridges, and strategic islands that the regular forces might not reach as quickly as Home Defense. These territorial units are, as their name implies, locally based, made up of men in the neighborhood of the objects to be guarded or defended. They have all served their time in the regular army and they can be mobilized within a matter of hours, since their equipment and arms are also stored locally. The mobile reserves of the regular army are also to be reinforced. This dispersal of forces as well as depots serves at the same time the requirements of survival and defense in modern war.

Like Norway, Denmark is financially assisted by her allies in her rearmament effort. For example, in April, 1959, the U.S. Government agreed to meet half the costs of building twenty-three Danish warships, chiefly fast patrol vessels, minelayers, and motor-torpedo boats, and it has also provided a quantity of Nike rockets for the anti-aircraft defense of the capital, without payment.

Land and sea are indissolubly connected in the defense of this small country, no part of which is more than twenty-five miles from the sea, and whose coastline, owing to its great indentations, is more than twice as long as that of Great Britain. The army, navy and air force are therefore compelled to work very closely together. Any Soviet attack on Denmark, even if it came from the Baltic, would be a land, sea, and air war. The Soviets would put in landing troops and undoubtedly use some of their nine parachute divisions to occupy Denmark swiftly and thus come into possession of the Baltic outlets to the North Sea, at the same time driving a wedge between Central and Northern Europe. Simultaneously, the Red Army would stage a breakthrough near Lübeck, concentrating on the Elbe and Trave junctions, which represent the dividing line between AFNORTH and AFCENT.

Long discussions about the command structure, split up in many ways in this area, fortunately came to an end in November, 1961. Under the unified Baltic Approaches Command which reports to AFNORTH in Oslo, the following NATO forces are brought together: the Danish NATO troops in Zeeland (LANDZEELAND); Danish troops in Jutland and two German divisions in Schleswig-Holstein (LANDJUT); the Danish and the German Baltic and North Sea Fleets (NAVBALTAP); and the Danish Air Force (AIRBALTAP).

Thus Danish and German troops are working side by side. The fact that a solution was finally found in this difficult area, which had troubled NATO experts for a long time, is proof that any problem, if approached in the NATO spirit of cooperation and mutual understanding, can be solved reasonably, by agreement. This is encouraging for the future alliance of the North Atlantic peoples.

The difficulties to be overcome were largely of a psychological and political nature. For Denmark, as for Norway, to give up her neutrality represented a break with a long tradition. When the Second World War ended, not many Danes would have believed such a thing possible. A serious Soviet threat was necessary before the change in outlook could take place. Then, in 1949, the Danish Parliament voted by a majority of four to one to join the North Atlantic Alliance. But until now, the Danes have been unwilling to allow foreign troops on their territory in peacetime. Where German soldiers are concerned, deep-seated memories of the time of occupation are to be overcome; but not even British, American, or French troops are allowed.

However, there is little doubt that before long, as the democratic reputation of the German Federal Republic is consolidated, there will be a change in this respect, too. After the war, 40,000 Danish troops were stationed in Germany as part of the forces of occupation, and they were renowned as the most polite of all occupation forces. Consequently the relationship between them and the German civilian population was good. Many young Danes saw for themselves that National Socialism in Germany has given way to a different spirit, and this undoubtedly contributed to the solution of the problem of German depots on Danish soil. The exchange of military attachés between Copenhagen and Bonn is a further step to closer cooperation between the two countries within the framework of NATO.

The shock suffered by the Danes when Hitler's forces occupied the country on April 9, 1940, has made them sensitive to the disquieting parallels in the present situation. The Scandinavian states had been threatened by the National Socialist regime, and in June, 1939, to document his "peaceful" intentions, Hitler offered a non-aggression pact, which the Danes accepted. One year later, Hitler's forces were in Copenhagen. Today the people of Denmark know that the interval between a similar treaty with the Soviets and a Soviet coup or invasion, might be just as short.

Denmark is a country with a high level of civilization. She is the only Scandinavian country whose line of kings has been uninterrupted for a thousand years, and for centuries she was the hub of Northern Europe. At one time she even conquered and ruled the greater part of England.

"Denmark was once a great power," said Minister Helge Knudsen when we met him at the Danish Embassy in Bonn. "We are no longer that, so we must gain within what we have lost without." It is the aim of the whole Danish people to further this inner greatness. They are a broad-minded and progressive people, and the possession of property, including real estate, is widespread among them. The level of elementary education is the highest in Europe. Denmark is a land of free men, and it is socially so stable that Communist propaganda finds very little response. The Danes know what they have to lose, and they also know that they can defend it successfully only in alliance with the other NATO nations. They realize that this cannot be done without sacrifices, and their political parties are in agreement that these sacrifices are worthwhile and must be made.

22

Headquarters Allied Forces Southern Europe

Headquarters Allied Forces Southern Europe (AFSOUTH) is in Bagnoli near Naples. The road to Bagnoli goes through a tunnel under the Posilipo almost at the exact spot where, in the days of Augustus, Marcus Cocceius Nerva ordered a cut to be made through the spur. On the way, you pass the grave of Virgil, and the new buildings of the university founded in 1244 by the German Emperor Frederick II. Thousands of years of Western history are incorporated in "Neapolis," the "New Town" of Parthenopeia, City of the Virgin, which was already old in the days of Virgil, having been founded by Ionian Greeks around the year 500 B.C. For centuries before the town became Roman, it was the intellectual hub of Magna Graecia in Southern Italy. It was here, at the Battle of Vesuvius in 553, that the last king of the Ostrogoths, Teja, was defeated by the general of the Byzantine Emperor Justinian; and in the church of Santa Maria del Carmine lie the bones of King Konradin, the last of the Hohenstaufens, who was beheaded in the market place of Naples at the order of Charles of Anjou. Many peoples have ruled here— Greeks, Romans, Vandals, Arabs, Normans, Spaniards, Austrians, and French—and some of them are now joined in the free alliance whose southern headquarters is near Naples.

The familiar sight of the flags of NATO and the Allies creates a different impression here, against the bright sky of Naples, than at Marly, Kolsaas, Portsmouth, or Fontainebleau. One feels that the brightness emanates not only from the hot southern sun but from a consciousness of liberty never so intense as where, thousands of years ago, it flowed from the Hellenic spirit.

The present Chief of Staff of AFSOUTH is Major-General Robert W. Ward of the U.S. Army, who in August, 1960, succeeded Major-General W. G. Yeager. Ward is a man of considerable battle experience, having seen action in the Tunisian and Italian campaigns. Later, he served as Chief of the Plans, Policy, Organization, and Training Division of the General Staff at the U.S. War Department. From 1952 to 1955, he was with SHAPE; then he became Deputy Chief of Staff for Plans at Far East Command Headquarters.

General Yeager received us in his office. Half of one wall was covered by a relief map. "It's a pretty long front," he said, "1,500 miles from the western Alpine passes to the Caspian Sea."

Seen from this southern angle, the Iron Curtain looks like a left flank, separated from the Mediterranean by the Alps and neutralized Austria.

"This isn't a uniform front with a deep hinterland and almost unrestricted approaches, as in Central Europe," the General went on. "It's a relatively narrow coastal area, bordered by mountains and lacking military depth. Strictly speaking, it consists of four more or less independent operational areas—Northern Italy, Greece, Thrace, and the Caucasus."

Separate headquarters for each of these areas had been considered, but that would have meant too large a staff. Today there are two land headquarters, at Verona and at Ismir, both subordinate to Naples. Seen from the air, of course, the whole Mediterranean constitutes a single front. For the air force, the main goals are to get the earliest possible warning and strongest possible defense against attack.

Commander-in-Chief of AFSOUTH is Admiral James Russel. Allied Land Forces Southern Europe (LANDSOUTH) are under the command of an Italian, General Aurelio Guy, whose headquarters are in Verona. Those in LANDSOUTHEAST are under the command of Lieutenant-General Harry P. Storke whose headquarters are in Ismir. The commander of the Allied Air Forces South (AIRSOUTH) is Lieutenant-General Ralph P. Swofford, who has the Fifth and Sixth ATAF under him; the Fifth is commanded by Major-General Luigi Bianchi at Verona, and the Sixth by Major-General Edward W. Suarez of the U.S. Air Force, at Ismir. In the event of war, Admiral Russel would also have the Naval Striking and

Support Forces Southern Europe—in other words, the U.S. Sixth Fleet—under his command.

We asked Lieutenant-General Richard C. Lindsay, Swofford's predecessor: "Supposing you were the Supreme Commander of the Red Army on the European front, what would you do?"

The General went up to a large map showing the world from the North Pole. "The Soviets have driven a wedge deep into Europe," he said. "The Red Army now stands well over 600 miles beyond its own frontiers, deep in German territory. That represents a terrible threat to us. But one mustn't fail to see the consequences it has for them, too." He put his open hand on the map, wrist over the German Federal Republic, thumb on Turkey, fingers stretched out over Norway. "A hand," he said, "that grips the whole of Soviet-occupied territory in Europe. If I were the Red Army Commander and received an order to attack, I wouldn't be happy with the situation."

The General has had personal contact with the Russians—for example, at the Yalta Conference in February, 1945, when he was Chief of the Joint General Staff at the Pentagon.

"At best, one can persuade the Soviets not to pursue their aims for the time being; and for that you need superior power. Their aims, however, will never be abandoned."

He then gave us a short review of the situation. First, the Italian theater: The Soviets couldn't send more than ten divisions through the Alpine passes and the Gorizia gap to Friuli and the Po Valley; the supply problem alone would prevent it. Moreover, those passes are well defended. A large number of the crack Italian divisions are stationed in upper Italy, together with the U.S. South European Task Force (SETAF), which consists of 6,200 men equipped with Honest John and Corporal missiles complete with atomic warheads. Before they could attack, the Soviets would have to violate either Austrian or Yugoslav territory, and one must assume that respect for international law or Austria's neutrality would not prevent them. Perhaps they would try to replace those governments with puppet regimes which would then allow Soviet troops to pass through, but in that case, the country in question would no longer be neutral.

In the General's view, the Soviets could also send ten divisions from Bulgaria through the Monastir (Bitolj) and Varda gaps, again by violating Yugoslav neutrality and driving across towards Macedonia and Salonika.

In the event of an attack on upper Italy, NATO would be warned by a violation of Austrian or Yugoslav territory. But Thrace lies open

to attack from Bulgaria, and the Soviets could drive forward unhindered by any natural obstacle, perhaps employing sixteen divisions. There is no doubt that they regard this as the critical area of
the southeast European front. Even if they wanted to send their submarines into the Mediterranean, they would have to mount their
attack on the Bosphorus and the Hellespont through Thrace.

Of course the Soviets could send their submarines through the
Dardanelles into the Mediterranean in peacetime, but in the event
of war, they would be cut off from their bases, because the 1936
Treaty of Montreux returned sovereignty over the Dardanelles, which
up to then had been controlled by an international commission, to
the Turks. Since then, Turkey has asserted her right to fortify the
Straits, and control warships passing through, despite heavy Soviet
pressure. Turkey rejected the Soviet demand for shared control of the
Straits, as well as the proposal of August 7, 1946, that the Straits be
permanently closed, except by special permission, to the warships of
all powers whose territory does not border on the Black Sea.

"In any case," the General went on, "the Straits would be easy to
defend in wartime."

Here in the south, NATO is faced with the special problem that
smaller countries are economically weak and find the burden of military defense onerous. This is true particularly of Turkey, which has
felt the strain of rapid economic development, and southern Italy.
To help here is a NATO obligation.

The forces now available for the defense of Southern Europe are
considerable. When the first Commander-in-Chief, Admiral Robert
B. Carney, took over on June 21, 1951, his headquarters was the U.S.
Mount Olympus in the Gulf of Naples. His staff consisted of seven
officers, and he had no forces at his disposal except the U.S. Sixth
Fleet. Today the greater part of the Italian Army is under the Commander-in-Chief Allied Forces Southern Europe (CINCSOUTH),
as are the armies of Greece and Turkey. Here are forces ranging from
Italian Alpini on skis to sabre-brandishing cavalry in south Turkey;
from the atomic rockets of SETAF in northern Italy, and the nuclear bomb-carrying planes of the U.S. Sixth Fleet, to the mule-borne
guns of the Greek Army in Macedonia; from the jet fighter-interceptors of the various air forces to anti-submarine craft in the Mediterranean.

An important part of the South European front is the sea, 3,000
miles from Gibraltar to the coast of Syria. The sea represents the
main traffic and supply line from Western Europe to the United

States, and must be kept open if the defense forces are to remain mobile and ready for action. Command of this sea also means protection of NATO's southern flank, while a loss of the Mediterranean would leave NATO's southern European land forces exposed to unpredictable Soviet attacks.

The operational area is about 100,000 square miles. AIRSOUTH has two tactical air forces under its command, the Fifth ATAF with headquarters in Vicenza, which consists of the Fifty-sixth Italian Tactical Air Force, and the Sixth ATAF with headquarters in Ismir, consisting of the Twenty-eighth Greek Tactical Air Force in Larissa, the Turkish First in Eskisehir, the Second in Ankara, and the Third in Dijabarkir.

"You can see from the map that, giving them a range of 400 miles, Soviet fighters stationed in Tiflis, Burgaz, or in the Crimea could reach almost any point in Greece and Turkey," General Lindsay said. "And most of the planes held in readiness in the arc from Albania over Bulgaria and Roumania to the southern part of the Soviet Union are modern jets with a high performance, comparable to NATO equipment."

The MIG-5 Fagots, which fought well in Korea against the U.S. F-84s and F-86s, have now largely been replaced by MIG-17s and MIG-19s—the Frescoes and the Farmers, as they are called in NATO; and it may be assumed that before long these will give way to the all-weather YAK-25, known to NATO as the Flashlight, which has two jet turbines, a comparatively long range, and a maximum speed of about 720 miles an hour, just below the speed of sound. The Soviet medium bomber TU-16, the Badger, has a speed of over 600 miles an hour and is about equivalent to the U.S. B-47. It could reach any objective within the South European operational area.

If the Soviets decided to attack from the Caucasus, Thrace, or upper Italy, they would have large land forces for the purpose. Their Black Sea Fleet doubtless is strong enough to carry out amphibious landings on a considerable scale, and at least one of their nine airborne divisions is stationed on this front.

Our interview with Admiral Robert P. Briscoe was probably one of the last he gave before he retired after forty-four years of service in the U.S. Navy, on January 1, 1959. Admiral Briscoe was born in Centerville, Mississippi, in 1897. He saw active naval service in both world wars; in the first as a young petty officer, and in the second as Admiral. He must be counted among the builders of the modern U.S. Navy. His long acquaintance with Greece and Turkey—from

1919 onwards he spent a number of years in Ismir and knew Kemal
Pasha personally—served him well in his South European command.

The interview was friendly and informal. "We are confident that
we can hold our fronts," he assured us. "As far as Turkey is concerned, I'm not worried about the defense of the Straits. And that
applies to the Caucasus, too; if they tried to break through there,
they would find it a long and difficult passage to Ankara and Istanbul."

The greater danger threatens from Syria—not from the Syrian
forces, which Turkey could deal with easily, but from the use of
Syrian territory as a deployment area. The Soviets could use both
revolutionary and military means to try a drive through Iran, Iraq,
and Syria; and there the Turkish frontier is wide open.

The situation in the Mediterranean has changed considerably in
the last ten years. At one time it was a friendly, land-locked sea; now
there is a danger that more and more of the littoral countries will fall
into the hands of the enemy. Albania is a Communist country this
side of the Iron Curtain. Egypt, Syria, and Morocco—not to mention
Algeria, Guinea, and the Congo—have all become problematical.

The regional geography favors the West, because rugged mountains and the possibility of bringing up supplies by sea favor the defense, to which NATO is oriented. On the other hand, the land
forces of the three allies are so widely separated that it is difficult
for one to go to the other's aid, except on the Graeco-Turkish frontier.

The important thing would be the defense in the mountains,
where it would be easiest to hold up a Soviet attack; and the military
agree that the passes could be held with tactical atomic weapons—
another proof of the defensive importance of these weapons. By dis-
couraging the attacker, they might prevent war. At the same time,
the possession of atomic weapons means a strengthening of morale
for the defenders. Of course the Soviets could use parachute troops,
but their sphere of operations would be limited.

"The Russian Fleet in the Black Sea may be strong," said Admiral
Briscoe, "but as long as we can keep it bottled up there, we need not
fear it."

Doubtless the Soviets have airfields in the Crimea, and the possibility of amphibious attacks exists. They might be tempted to land
to the north of Istanbul, in order to take the Bosporus fortifications
from the rear. However, this would put them in a dangerous position. If necessary, NATO would have to adapt the Turkish land

bases on the Black Sea for air and naval use. One thing should be quite clear: if the Soviets should ever start a war, it must not end as in Korea. It would have to be won, and a purely defensive attitude, a new Maginot Line outlook, would not win it.

Rear-Admiral Harry Smith of the U.S. Navy, Deputy Chief of Staff, Logistics, and Administration since November, 1959, saw action during the Second World War in the Marshalls and Gilberts, at Lae and Salamaua, in the Coral Sea, at Midway and Guadalcanal, in the Aleutians, and at Okinawa. After the war, he commanded the cruiser *Helena*, flagship of the Commander of the Seventh Fleet. But his experience is even wider than that; when he returned from the Far East, he was in charge of Project Mercury space recovery operations. In his present post he succeeded Rear-Admiral Ignatius L. Galantin, who, like Smith, saw service in the Pacific during the Second World War and took part in all the important operations.

We went straight to the point when we saw Admiral Galantin at Naples: "Can the Soviets reasonably hope to get their Black Sea Fleet out into the Atlantic?" He immediately admitted that this was one of the decisive questions for the whole southern front, but pointed out:

"The Straits are well defended. How could the Soviets get their ships through them? Perhaps in bad weather or under cover of darkness? Provided the West stays watchful, that wouldn't be easy against coastal batteries, minefields, planes, and, if necessary, atomic weapons."

Nevertheless, the Soviets are strengthening their Black Sea Fleet because, like the West, they have realized that command of the sea is essential. Their chief difficulty is that they cannot reinforce one fleet with the other, with the exception of the Baltic and Murmansk forces. But they try to make a virtue of necessity by turning each of their four fleets into a strong, independent striking force.

"Sea power is the condition for keeping Communism in check," said the Admiral confidently. The title of the Western alliance has often been criticized, but the Admiral finds "North Atlantic Community" a very appropriate name because, as he says, it indicates that the sea is the focal point of the alliance.

"What happened in Hungary in 1956 showed you how important the sea is," he declared. "How much easier it would have been for the West to have helped and defended Hungary if her geographical situation had not cut her off from the sea! And the fact that Yugoslavia can afford to take a more independent attitude toward the Soviets may not be unconnected with her possession of a coastline."

While for land strategy, inner lines of communication are advantageous, the opposite is true for the sea. Inland seas—even the North Sea, if it can be blockaded—are dangerous for a fleet, whereas high seas offer protection and superiority. Thus during the two world wars, Great Britain had the naval advantage over Germany because she had the outer position; the U.S. secured it in the war against Japan; and today the West has it against the Soviets.

Admiral Galantin summed up the situation by saying that militarily, the South European Command was in a position to take care of any attacker. The only real anxieties were of a political and economic nature. These lay outside the military scope, but were of great importance to him. This is the area in which the free world would have to do more to alleviate problems.

The compass needle of the two-engined naval plane which took us from Naples past the slopes of Vesuvius, over the temples of Paestum and over Calabria, to the Ionian Sea, pointed steadily in the direction of the U.S. Sixth Fleet.

"That's a great help," said the pilot. "You've no idea how easy it is to miss a whole fleet in the Mediterranean, even if you start off knowing its exact position and your own course." When we first spotted her from about 1,000 feet up, even the great U.S. aircraft carrier *Forrestal* looked tiny, and it seemed impossible that our plane could land on that small deck. But the pilot knew his job. We landed, and the steel hawser brought us to a standstill within 100 feet.

The Sixth Fleet is, of course, a U.S. striking force; but in the event of war, it would come under NATO command, and in peacetime it is assigned to NATO for planning and maneuvers. For this purpose it has its own staff on land, attached to AFSOUTH in Naples. But, like all NATO contingents, the fleet is a national responsibility with regard to supplies and administration. The fleet is therefore directly subordinate to the Commander of U.S. Naval Forces Europe (USNAVEUR, formerly U.S. Naval Forces Eastern Atlantic and Mediterranean, or NELM). Admiral H. Paige Smith of the U.S. Navy, who has his headquarters in London, is Commander-in-Chief of these forces, directly subordinate to the Chief of Naval Operations in Washington.

"The Sixth Fleet has no bases in the Mediterranean," said Admiral Charles D. Griffin, Squadron Commander-in-Chief. "Our supply base is the United States itself, and everything we need comes straight to us by sea."

We were received by the Admiral and Captain Allen M. Shinn, commander of the *Forrestal*. They told us that the Sixth Fleet spends half its time carrying out maneuvers in the Mediterranean, and the other half in the hundred or so ports and harbors scattered at various points along the littorals of this million square miles of water. It makes two circular tours per year, visiting the eastern Mediterranean in the spring and autumn and the western Mediterranean in summer and winter. The ships are rotated regularly, so that the composition of the fleet changes completely every four or six months. The only exception to this arrangement is the flagship—usually a heavy cruiser —which is likely to stay for two years. It is the only unit of the fleet with a fixed base in Europe, at Villefranche near Nice, apart from a few supply ships based in Barcelona and Naples. The Sixth Fleet is one of the two largest ocean-going U.S. fleets, the other being the Seventh, in East Asian waters.

An HUP-2 helicopter carried us from the *Forrestal* to the flagship.

"If the Sixth Fleet could survive even for a few hours, in the event of a Soviet attack, all my planes would be in the air and would have delivered their nuclear weapons to their assigned objectives," declared Admiral Charles R. Brown, then Commander of this fleet. "And if we could manage to hold out for twenty-four hours, we would have a very good chance of surviving altogether, because in that time the big nuclear strike would presumably be over, and if the enemy planes hadn't found and destroyed me by then, they probably wouldn't have much left over to hit me with."

The Soviets were Red Fascists, the Admiral declared. They respected one thing only, and that was power. The Sixth Fleet therefore contributes to the peace by making it more difficult for the Soviets to choose war. Past experience has shown that whenever the West has stood up firmly to the Soviets, as for instance at the time of the Anglo-American landings in Lebanon and in Jordan, the Kremlin had taken note of the warning and heeded it. At the same time, such demonstrations of Western strength impressed the Arab peoples, who value courage and determination.

The same had been true at the beginning of the Korean War: the Soviets had sent out planes against the U.S. fleet, and those planes had been shot down. There were protests, but for the rest of the war, no Soviet plane had come anywhere near the U.S. fleet.

"On the first day of a war, Soviet planes would be the main danger to our fleet," declared the Admiral. "In any war, if the Soviets attack the Sixth Fleet, it will be with planes and submarines. Their submarines would have to find us, then break through our protective escort of destroyers. Experience gained at maneuvers suggests that submarines operating within a range of 100 miles would take at least a day, and perhaps two, to get within striking distance of an aircraft carrier. And if one can detect their approach, by radar or aircraft, while they are still about 20 miles away, there wouldn't be much to worry about, even if they were fast. A homing rocket with an atomic warhead is a very effective weapon against submarines."

But in a long war, in the Admiral's opinion, the submarine would become an even greater danger than the plane. The main threat would be to the supply lines between the United States and Europe. Merchant ships are the natural objective for submarines. As a case in point, the Japanese could have got much more out of their submarines if they had used them for attacking merchant shipping, instead of sacrificing them against warships.

"And there's another lesson we learned from World War II," the Admiral went on. "It's a mistake to wage war by stages. If the Germans had been able to launch all their operations simultaneously, they might have forced the decision."

The same applies to the Soviets today: they could not afford to concentrate their operations on a single objective. If they did, they might score tactical success, but they would suffer devastating nuclear strikes from all other areas. And yet they are not strong enough to strike everywhere at once.

When we met Admiral Brown again in June, 1960, as Commander-in-Chief of Allied Forces Southern Europe, he returned to the ideas he had broached aboard the Sixth Fleet.

"The great struggle of our age is not merely military and political; it goes much deeper than that."

Khrushchev had just torpedoed the summit conference, and in the Far East and many other parts of the world, the Soviets were poised for new offensives against the free world.

"There are three main factors which characterize modern despotism," the Admiral continued. "First, it denies the existence of God. And from this follows the second axiom, that man has no inherent rights. If he is just a part of nature and a mere product of society, how can he have fundamental rights or a dignity of his own? Thus the third axiom comes into play, that the state is everything, and man, as an individual, is nothing. But if the state is the sole source of man's rights, then the state can take them away whenever it feels inclined.

"A free society, on the other hand, such as we are pledged to defend, recognizes God as the Creator who has endowed man with inalienable rights. No earthly institution may take them away from him. From this follows the sacredness of the individual and the inviolability of man's dignity. It is the duty of governments, therefore, to protect the rights which God has bestowed on us."

"So the present conflict is really just one phase of the age-old struggle?"

"What is going on today is nothing new. But, mark you, it's not The Revolution we're faced with, as the Communists would like people to believe; on the contrary, it's a permanent counter-revolution, because throughout the centuries there have always been men who strove to deprive their fellow men of their basic rights."

The conversation then turned to NATO and the various criticisms that have been levelled against it.

"If you examine NATO," the Admiral went on, "you will undoubtedly discover many shortcomings, and even mistakes. But then if you compare it with the past, I think you will come to the conclusion that NATO is the most remarkable, perhaps the greatest, peacetime alliance the world has ever known. In spite of all the criticisms —some of which may be justified—we can be certain that, whatever may still have to be done in the future, NATO will do it."

"What should one think of Khrushchev's nuclear threats against NATO countries neighboring the Soviet Union?" This was shortly after the Soviets had shot down the U-2 plane flying from Turkey to Norway.

"The answer is really quite simple," replied the Admiral. "It's already provided for in Article 5 of the NATO Pact: Any attack against one of our members is an attack against all. That's precisely what the alliance is for."

This is the essential fact in the present situation, and it is one that the Soviets are never likely to overlook. It is precisely for this reason that the fighting forces of so many different countries are joined together along the South European front under the command of Headquarters Naples. And for the same reason, the U.S. Sixth Fleet cruises around in the Mediterranean—to preserve peace and defend freedom of all countries on both sides of the Atlantic, wherever free men have joined together to uphold their rights.

23

Graeco-Turkish Defense

Among nations, enmities fought out to the end often lead to friendships. The history of Turkey for centuries was the history of a long and bitter struggle with the Greeks. In the Middle Ages, the Turks attacked the Graeco-Roman Empire in Asia Minor; later on, they fought against European Greece. The long Turkish victory was sealed with the fall of Constantinople, ancient Byzantium, in 1453. Henceforth the Turks ruled Greece, and it was only in 1830 that this country, with the moral support of all the classically educated nations of the West, won back its freedom.

But that was by no means the end of the Graeco-Turkish strife; it again came to war in 1896, after a Greek rising in Crete. Greece was defeated, but ultimately the island of Crete was reunited with the motherland. In the first Balkan War in 1912, the two countries were at grips once more, and again in the wars of 1920 and 1922, when, in counter-offensive, the Turks recaptured Smyrna, which had been given to Greece by the Peace Treaty of Sèvres in 1920. With assistance from the League of Nations, the Lausanne Treaty of 1923 turned the forcible expulsion of the Greeks from Asia Minor, where they had been settled for thousands of years, into an exchange of populations—1.25 million Greeks against 220,000 Turks. Greek bitterness about these tragic events led to the overthrow of the monarchy. The Treaty of Ankara of October 30, 1930, heralded the end of enmity, and a new phase in the countries' relationship.

The Soviet threat hanging over Greece and Turkey lent impetus to the Truman Doctrine of March 12, 1947, which gave both countries military and economic aid. In 1952, they joined the North Atlantic Alliance.

Old wounds were reopened during the dispute over Cyprus—a dispute that also greatly strained relationships between Greece and Great Britain. Today, it is only of historical interest. By the Treaty of Zurich of February 11, and of London of February 19, 1959, the representatives of Great Britain came to an agreement with Archbishop Makarios for the Greek Cypriots, and Doctor Fazil Kücük for the Turkish Cypriots; representatives of the Greek and Turkish governments also signed this definitive treaty. The establishment of the new independent Republic of Cyprus on August 16, 1960, gave new strength to the free world, because it closed a dangerous breach which, like any quarrel within the alliance, might have threatened NATO interests.

"Our cooperation with the Turks within the framework of NATO is excellent," we were assured by the chairman of the Hellenic National Defense Staff, Lieutenant-General Athanasios Frontistis, whom we visited in his headquarters in Athens. It was a few weeks after the conclusion of the NATO autumn maneuvers, during which Turkish and Greek units had worked very closely together in Thrace. Units of the U.S. Sixth Fleet had also taken part, including the 16,700-ton rocket cruiser *Canberra*, which serves chiefly as an antiaircraft ship. Her accurate, radar-guided Terrier rockets are held ready for action at a moment's notice. Amphibious landing operations were carried out in the neighborhood of Alexandropolis by the allied forces.

"We happen to know our enemy very well indeed," went on the General. "Whoever allows himself to be deceived by the Soviets is lost. You have to show them that you're strong. That's the only way to impress them, and therefore the only way to prevent war. We were once at odds with Germany, and that was a difficult struggle. But it's all over now, and there are no longer differences between us. We are friends. That's impossible with the Soviets." And he added: "We have no alternative but to support NATO with all we have, because as far as we are concerned, everything is at stake in this struggle: the fundamental principles of freedom, justice, and human dignity, which were born on our soil."

General Frontistis had a distinguished record during the Second World War, and subsequently in the civil war against the Communists.

"NATO has still not fully grasped the significance of the psychological war the Soviets are waging," he said. "At the moment, it looks as though they are concentrating primarily against Berlin, but tomorrow it may be Greece, and the day after that some other objective—but it all goes according to the same master plan. What I'm wondering is when we are going to coordinate all our efforts properly to meet the threat. If we closed our ranks with greater determination, the enemy would not be able to pick on one weak spot after the other."

General Frontistis regards a "forward strategy" as essential, above all in the Balkans. "If the Soviets should attack, it would be a great error to pursue a passive policy and confine ourselves to defensive measures."

In the General's opinion, the contribution made by Greece to the common struggle—her men and her territory—could be better utilized if the Allies would lend a hand. Modern armaments should be supplied just as quickly as the Greek forces can assimilate them.

"We need highly mobile forces which could drive forward with lightning speed, withdraw just as quickly if necessary, and then drive forward again," we were told in Athens. "We must have widely dispersed forces which a Soviet attack could not destroy."

The total strength of available Greek forces is about 150,000 men, including 25,000 in the air force, and 17,000 in the navy. With the exception of certain coastal defense forces, they are under NATO Mediterranean Command at Malta. The Greek Army consists of three corps. The First in Saloni and the Second in Kozani are ready for action at any time. And since the summer of 1960, the strong Twentieth Armored Division, with headquarters at Salonika, has been ready. It is a fine division, equipped for the most part with American M-47 tanks.

The Royal Hellenic Air Force consists of the Twenty-eighth Tactical Air Force, the Thirtieth Air Supply Command, and the Thirty-first Air Training Command. The tactical units are under the Allied Sixth Tactical Air Force, with headquarters in Ismir. The Deputy Chief of the General Staff of the Planning Department is Major-General L. Parissis, a Greek officer. In recent years, the Greek air force has been thoroughly modernized. Jet planes have taken the place of the conventional piston craft, new airfields have been laid out, a modern radar network has been built up, and communications have been greatly improved. The Greek air force today is largely equipped with F-84-F, F-86-D, and F-84-E planes, and there are RF-84-F planes for reconnaissance. Many Greek pilots were trained in the U.S. Recently, all-weather fighters and Nike anti-aircraft batteries have been taken into commission.

Two battalions equipped with Honest John rockets are on the spot to strengthen the defense of this area, which is so important for the defense of the free world. The regular troops are supported by numerous trained reservists, some of them with battle experience—if necessary, up to 400,000 men. And behind the fighting men stands a whole freedom-loving people.

Today Greece, an economically poor country, spends 27 per cent of her budget on defense, and that means for the defense of the free world. It would be impossible to increase that proportion without weakening the social structure of the country, and that, of course, would play directly into the hands of the Communists. The NATO allies must therefore come to her aid. Eastern Macedonia, western Thrace, and the two classic gateways from the north are the danger spots for Greece and for NATO. And the Aegean Sea right down to Crete is of great strategic significance, because it is here that the Soviets would try to drive down into the Mediterranean to Italy, southern France, and North Africa. Polaris rockets could do useful service here, as a warning and a deterrent; and, in the event of a Soviet attack, to ward it off promptly.

Even when you leave Europe proper, you are still in the same historical and cultural ambient, and because of the NATO alliance you feel the essential unity even more strongly. There is Ismir, the one-time ancient Smyrna, one of the towns that claim to have been the birthplace of Homer. It was there that we met the Commander-in-Chief of the Sixth ATAF, Major-General Tansel, a Turk, who received us in his light and airy office at headquarters. Since August, 1960, he has also been Commander-in-Chief of the Turkish Air Force.

He proved to be a polite, amiable, and highly educated man. Generally, Turkish manners are pleasing: formal courtesies are always exchanged at the beginning and end of any conversation; it is not a waste of time, but a good habit which helps to ease personal relationships.

General Tansel knows Germany well. During the 1930's, he was a test pilot in Germany and flew the Fokke-Wulffs and the Messerschmitt 109. It was on his recommendation that the Turkish Government decided to buy them for the air force.

"You know, we flew well over 400 miles per hour even then," he said with a smile.

Turkey keeps three army groups on a war footing; the first is at the Dardanelles, the second in South Turkey, and the third on the eastern frontier opposite the Caucasus. The total strength of Turkey's armed forces is 400,000.

"Thanks to her physical structure, Turkey is not so vulnerable to nuclear attack as some countries," pointed out the General. "The terrain is largely mountainous, settlements are dispersed, and in consequence there are not many targets to be destroyed by nuclear weapons. In the east, the country could be defended with comparatively light forces, particularly if they, too, were armed with nuclear weapons and could thus deny the enemy the concentrations he would need to storm mountain fastnesses."

As we were leaving, General Tansel told us that we should have a look at the Turkish air base in Eskisehir. "It's one of our three air bases, and it's our first for jet planes." The next morning, we landed at Eskisehir after a short flight from Ismir. The First Tactical Air Fleet consists of two wings; it uses the T-33 for training purposes, though, as we noticed, there were already a number of F-84s and F-86-As available. Between 1951 and 1956, some Turkish pilots were trained in England; about half of them are trained in the United States, and some have attended U.S. training schools in Germany. Training in Turkey, as in Germany, is given in English, and the Turkish language is used only to explain unfamiliar English terms.

Ground personnel and part of the staff are trained wholly in Turkey. Training is thorough, starting off with take-apart models, whose parts—engine, steering, cockpit, and so on—are studied before the trainees go on to practical training.

A young Turkish pilot, Captain Nedim Asil, was told to take us up for a flight in a T-33 jet. He spoke excellent English, and after flying with him we could see what the U.S. instructors meant when they said the Turks are good pilots.

"Has the Turkish Air Force any particular contact with the U.S. Sixth Fleet?"

"Of course, and if it called for any special air support, our planes would be in the air at once."

The Commandant of Eskisehir airfield told us that his planes are always in a state of readiness. "Whatever the Russians do, they will always find us in the air to meet them." The Turks are not afraid of their mighty neighbor. The Soviets have their agents in Turkey, and the Turks know what is going on in the Soviet Union. One thing is certain: Soviet spies have no easy job in Turkey, and cost the Soviet Government a great deal. The Turks have little patience with Communism, and when they come across a Communist, they know how to deal with him.

"We always try to keep one step ahead of the Russians in preparedness," the Commandant assured us. "We are, of course, not political, but we keep a very keen eye on all Soviet moves from the military standpoint." And he added drily: "Every time they launch one of their 'peace offensives' we step up our own preparedness—just in case."

The Commander-in-Chief Allied Land Forces in Southeast Europe (LANDSOUTHEAST) since the middle of August, 1960, is Lieutenant-General Harry P. Storke. He has both Greek and Turkish divisions under his command, which together make up 53 per cent of the total NATO Army. His operational command extends from the west coast of Greece on the Adriatic to the Caucasus. His predecessor, Lieutenant-General Paul D. Harkins, also American, had assured us when we talked with him at Ismir that this was a case of "United we stand, divided we fall." Harkins was originally a cavalryman and was a personal friend of General Patton, who appointed him Deputy Chief of Staff to the U.S. Third Army in 1944.

"What do you think about the strength of NATO in your command, General? Is it enough to do the job?"

"In the present build-up, yes," he replied. "The combined Greek and Turkish divisions are strong enough to hold back the enemy, though he would certainly be in a position to bring up reinforcements. By means of a big offensive, he could separate the two armies in Thrace, but then he would be compelled to mass troops, and thereby give us targets for our nuclear weapons."

General Harkins expressed the opinion that, valuable and necessary as they are, atomic weapons cannot replace troops. If the Soviets were to start a war, strong land forces would be necessary to repulse them and win.

General Harkins and his staff maintained good military contact between the Greek and Turkish forces even during the Cyprus crisis. In short, in peacetime, the job of a NATO commander has something of the diplomat about it. He sees to it that the forces assigned to him are equipped, trained, and deployed to be ready for action at any time, but he does not give them any direct orders. Rather, he approaches their national commands and provides leadership and coordination on the basis of mutual confidence. Thanks to the fact that both the Greek and Turkish authorities cooperate willingly, the results are good. In the event of war, however, the NATO commander would have operational command of the troops, as he does during maneuvers.

"Never take counsel from your fear," is the motto at Ismir, and it struck us as a good one, to be kept firmly in mind whenever the Soviets try to blackmail with threats and attempts to intimidate.

NATO does not ask either Greece or Turkey to send any of their forces beyond their own frontiers. This is chiefly on account of the greater need for internal security, since both countries border on the Iron Curtain—on Albania, Bulgaria, and the Soviet Union itself— which means intensified infiltration. Turkey has a longer common frontier with the Soviet Union than Norway, and, in addition, over 700 miles of Black Sea coast open to amphibious action.

But the Turks are tough soldiers and can stand a great deal of hardship. During the Korean War, 9,000 of the 16,000 U.N. troops who fell into Communist hands died, owing to the abominable prison camp conditions. But of the Turks who, after the Americans, contributed the most numerous contingent, only 700 were taken prisoner at all, and of those not one died. When the U.N. forces broke and fled in the face of the great offensive of the North Koreans and Red Chinese, flinging away all that impeded their retreat, the Turks never parted with their rifles, and never suffered demoralization. Although they were not motorized, it was they who brought up the rear in November and December, 1950, and delayed the advance of the enemy.

An American doctor told us the following anecdote. Treating a Turkish soldier, he was anxious to discover whether a certain nerve was injured and made a number of tests, including pin pricks, to which the Turk did not react at all. To make him understand what was meant, the doctor took the needle and stuck it lightly into his own hand, making a gesture of pain and withdrawal. The Turk then took the needle away from him, and with a contemptuous gesture thrust it right through his hand, observing, "Me Turk!"

The equipment of the Turkish Army is almost entirely American. Its tank is the U.S. M-47. The famous Turkish cavalry, including three brigades in the rugged mountainous area along the eastern frontier, was motorized and mechanized during the course of 1960, in order to turn it into a highly mobile force along the lines of the American pentomic divisions. However, where the terrain favors their use, mounted detachments are still available. As in Greece, artillery drawn by mules has its uses in the more mountainous parts of the country.

The strength of the Greek and Turkish armies is in accordance with their respective populations of 8 million and 25 million. The Greeks maintain one army, the Turks three, consisting of about eighteen divisions. A large proportion of Turkey's troops are stationed in the Dardanelles area, including six divisions on a war footing, four cadre divisions, and an armored brigade. A second armored brigade is stationed on the south frontier. The Turks are thus well capable of withstanding any Soviet offensive which is not on an all-out scale. What the Turkish Army needs urgently is more artillery, more tanks and, above all, tactical nuclear weapons.

The critical area in the Turkish defense system is the Skutari Peninsula, where, in the event of war, the Soviets presumably would attempt an amphibious landing, to take the Dardanelles fortifications from the rear. The Turks therefore keep the main part of their fleet in the Black Sea. Their biggest unit is the destroyer, but they do not need larger units in the Black Sea, any more than the Germans do in the Baltic. Their chief need is for minesweepers, escort boats, anti-submarine frigates, and the like. The Turkish Navy is now as strong as the Greek. The Aegean Sea is no longer entirely Greek, and it is therefore reasonable that naval parity should prevail.

Greece and Turkey are the two easternmost countries in the NATO southern front. They are particularly valuable allies because their forces would oppose a Soviet advance and at the same time threaten the Soviet flank. Conversely, NATO is an indispensable protection for them both because on their own they could not resist a Soviet attack for long. The Red Army could at any time concentrate the necessary forces to overrun these two countries, but today the men in the Kremlin know that any attempt to do so would trigger a NATO counter-attack.

Two American friends put an L-20, a small, one-engined courier plane, at our disposal for the flight from Ismir to Ankara; and within three hours—after a flight over barren, reddish-brown mountains, in which we could discern the rectangular outlines of camps and ancient settlements—we arrived in the Turkish capital.

Before we began to keep our various appointments, we went to the Kemal Ataturk mausoleum, where we signed our names in the Golden Book and laid a wreath in memory of the great man to whom the new Turkey owes her spirit and structure. A brief ceremony was held in the presence of a group of Turkish officers and the German military attaché, representing the German Ambassador. The mausoleum is a large, simple but impressive monument, designed with the assistance of German architects in a somewhat severe modern style, lacking all ornament. It was unveiled in 1953, on the fifteenth anniversary of Kemal Ataturk's death. Some idea of the great political influence which his memory still represents can be obtained from the events of May 27, 1960, and the following months, when the Turkish Army, under the leadership of General Kemal Gürsel, took power in the country in the name of its modern founder.

Although it is an ancient city, Ankara also owes its appearance to Ataturk. It was probably founded by Hittites in about 2000 B.C. The Galatians, a Celtic race, gave it the name Ancyra. Alexander the Great was once within its walls, and so was the Emperor Augustus, whose temple with his legacy engraved on marble slabs is still in existence. This *Monumentum Ancyranum*, which is an historical source of great value, was not rediscovered until the sixteenth century. When Ataturk transferred the Turkish capital from Istanbul to Ankara in 1923, he probably had strategic considerations in mind, since on the European side Istanbul is too exposed to attack by Turkey's hereditary enemy, Russia. At that time, Ankara was only a small provincial town; today it is a big modern city, with a population of 230,000.

Our discussions in the various Turkish Ministries and in the German Embassy underlined the strategic significance of the country. Turkey has to keep fairly strong military forces to the northeast, on the Caucasian frontier, but the real threat is not likely to come from there, since it would offer few rewards to the Soviets. The much greater danger is that they might overrun Iran, or revolutionize it, and drive through Syria in the direction of the big Turkish air base at Adana.

In addition, there is Thrace, and the danger of an amphibious landing to threaten the Bosporus and the Dardanelles. The Soviet objective there would be to get their Black Sea Fleet out into the Mediterranean. For this the Soviets would need to capture the Straits, and the logical line of attack would be through Bulgaria. We were assured that the Soviets have such plans and would sooner carry them out today than tomorrow, because it would be a natural manifestation of their aggressive character.

As for a possible attack from the southeast, from the area of the oilfields which supply not only Turkey but the whole of Europe, Turkey is the only protective bulwark—perhaps supported by Iran, which does not belong to NATO, but is a signatory of the CENTO Pact, an agreement representing, so to speak, an extension of NATO to the east. Subversion in the Arab lands, the Communist efforts at rabble rousing, the furious campaign against Islamic rulers who refuse to bow their necks to the Communist yoke, and in particular against the Shah of Iran, are all evidence enough. Experience has shown how easy it is to blow up oil pipelines. Such a coup could cripple supplies to the whole of Europe.

Syria is important primarily as a possible Soviet approach point. The Turks know the country well, for it was once under their rule; and they also know that the Syrian Army is not particularly strong.

Afghanistan occupies a key position on the board. She is a neighbor of the Soviet Union, but has not yet fallen into Soviet hands, and therefore should be supported. If she fell victim to the Soviets, this would create a direct threat to both Pakistan and Iran, with the danger of a breakthrough to the Indian Ocean. Even such help will represent no guarantee; a good deal will depend on the attitude of the king, who is said to be a shrewd man, well aware of the dangers involved in any Soviet penetration or infiltration.

Owing to Western political errors, the Soviets have already gained some influence over Afghanistan. The country needed help for its economic development; when the West proved unhelpful, the Soviets stepped into the breach, and this began a development unfavorable to the West which could have been prevented. Even today, it is not yet too late. The Afghans are an independent and warlike people, but economically backward. However, with some assistance (and the German Federal Republic has come forward), it should be possible to raise the standard of living. Economic development is the precondition for an efficient army.

The word "chain" was used more than once in our discussions: each NATO country is a link in a chain that must not be broken, and each country is a link which depends on all the others. Iran is also under pressure from the Soviets, who do their best to exploit every internal difficulty. The Shah, a frank and sincere friend of the West, incorporates in his person both the home and foreign policy of his country; he is therefore the natural target for every possible revolutionary activity. At home, however, the Shah's position has undoubtedly been strengthened by the birth of an heir, although the general situation is complicated by tension between Iran and Egypt in the Israel question.

Continuing the natural strategic line, one arrives at Pakistan, which is also a signatory of the CENTO Pact and a bulwark of the free world. But Pakistan is harassed by a number of acute problems, including some of a social and economic nature. Since the bloodless coup carried out by the Army on October 27, 1958, however, increased efforts are being made to resolve them. The land reform program of January, 1959, imposed restrictions on large estates and provided for the distribution of many millions of acres of arable land to landless tenants and agricultural laborers. Although relations with India still remain somewhat strained, owing particularly to the Kashmir question, the frontier violations committed by the Red Chinese in 1960 brought the two countries more closely together than in the past.

Turkey also is a valuable bridge between Europe and Islamic states such as Afghanistan, Pakistan, and Iran, which feel themselves akin to Turkey because of their common religion. On the other hand, modern Turkey regards herself as practically a European state. For example, the younger generation in Turkey is almost ignorant of the Arabic alphabet, because Kemal Ataturk replaced them with Roman characters. However, despite this pronounced Westernism, Turkey has not broken off her old historic and cultural relationships with the world of Islam. Her presence in NATO, in the Council of Europe, and in the European Economic Council, and her membership in the CENTO Pact is therefore of great advantage, not only to the Atlantic-European world, but also to the Islamic world of the Near and Middle East.

The Soviets are, of course, doing their utmost to prize Turkey out of the Atlantic Alliance, using their traditional policy of threats and promises in alternation, because a "neutral" Turkey would greatly increase the chances of success for their aggressive plans in the Black Sea, the Near and Middle East, and the Western Mediterranean. The U-2 incident of May, 1960, was immediately exploited by the Soviets to hector Turkey and demand that her territory not be used for "spy flights." So much for the threats. How quickly the tune can change is seen from the fact that on June 28, less than two months later (though the details were not published until September), Khrushchev delivered a markedly amiable speech for Turkish consumption, extolling the advantages likely to accrue to Turkey from "a policy of neutralism," and stressing the desirability of improved relations between Moscow and Ankara. Of course, the objective is the same in the one case as in the other, and the two "treatments" are likely to be used regularly and alternately for an indefinite period, it being always the objective to demoralize Turkey, disrupt the Atlantic Alliance, and turn NATO's southern flank. Perhaps the events of May 27, 1960, and the political differences within the Revolutionary Committee persuaded the Soviets that the time was ripe for a new soft-pedal approach—despite the fact that in its very first announcement, the Committee for National Unity formed by the Turkish Army stressed the unswerving loyalty of the country to NATO and the CENTO Pact.

Even the rebellious students and officer cadets who demonstrated against the previous regime, who did so much to pave the way for the Army take-over, were not remotely demonstrating against Turkey's obligations to NATO; and they were certainly not demonstrating in favor of the Soviets. In fact, the whole Turkish people have confirmed what Brigadier-General Ereld Cardiff, Chief of the SHAPE Information Center, said to us: "The continued and urgent necessity for the existence of NATO is fully recognized in Turkey." The answer given to Khrushchev by Kemal Gürsel as head of the new Turkish Government confirmed this once again. The General declared that Turkey's alliances were all of a purely defensive character, an insurance against any potential aggressor, not directed against any other country. Khrushchev can hardly be in doubt as to which country Turkey regards as a potential aggressor.

On the return flight we flew over Troy, the site of Priam's ancient fortress city whence, according to Virgil, the history of Rome began. Soon we reached the Sea of Marmara. Ahead of us was the Bosporus, and beyond that, the Black Sea. Circling twice over Istanbul, we finally landed.

Modern Turkey is a land of contradictions. Jet planes left their white trails across the sky while below them caravans made their way slowly as of old, some of them still using ancient Roman highways. High up on the balconies of slender minarets, the muezzins still call the faithful to morning and evening prayer in the age-old chant, while below the old mullahs squat peacefully on the steps of the mosques and children gather eagerly around the traditional storyteller to listen to the old and ever new tales of Aladdin and the beautiful Princess Suleima. Swiss, French, and German legal principles have been adopted, but go beyond the center of the town and you will find the ancient Sheriac law still being administered. Glaring neon signs advertise American Wild West films and modern thrillers in Roman lettering, but in the nearby shops where men bargain over carpets and coins, they still use the old Arabic characters. On the streets you can see some women dressed in the latest Western fashion, and other women as closely veiled as they were in the days of the Prophet. There are smart modern racing cars using the same roadways as ancient caravans drawn by sedately stepping camels turning their heads haughtily from right to left. It is a country from which coffee came to the West, but for a long time—in order to save foreign currency—it was forbidden, and many Turks have got used to drinking home-grown tea.

But what about Istanbul, which is no longer the capital of Turkey —the Istanbul which was once Constantinople, which was once Byzantium? The city seems to have shrunk within the thick but crumbling walls, but one still feels a breath of past Imperial glory in its streets; in the Hagia Sophia of Justinian, which since the days of Ataturk is no longer a mosque, and in the precious Byzantine mosaics which have once again been uncovered. And the past lives on in the mosques built by Sultans Achmed I and Bagasid II after the devastating earthquake of 1509.

The events of May 27, 1960, and the political take-over by the Turkish Army under General Kemal Gürsel, were of purely domestic political significance, and nothing has happened to shake the loyalty of the Turks to their treaty obligations. For example, at no time during the troubled period in May and June, 1960, was contact lost between Headquarters AFSOUTH in Naples and the NATO bases in Turkey.

And nothing has changed in the more friendly relationships between Greece and Turkey. The chivalrous enemies of the past, the descendants of the Byzantines and the Ottomans, have become the good friends of the present, brought together by the menace of a common foe.

24

The Front in Italy

A glance at the map shows the strategic importance of Italy for the defense of the West. If the country had fallen into Communist hands in the early postwar period when the Communists played a dominant role in Parliament and pro-Communist ministers were in the Cabinet, there would be no effective defense front in Southern Europe. France would border on the Iron Curtain, and a Soviet Italy could close the Mediterranean to the free world.

Apart from such strategic considerations, it would be intolerable for the West to see Italy, to which civilization and humanity owe so much, under the heel of a Soviet dictatorship. To defend Italy is to defend the heritage that the free nations have come together to protect. The Soviets therefore will try any means to take Italy from within and prize her out of the NATO Alliance. Western self-interest demands that this ally be given all possible assistance. The NATO principle applies with redoubled force here: help for one is help for all.

The commander of Allied Land Forces Southern Europe (AFSOUTH) is the Italian General S. Bernabo, who has his headquarters in Verona. In peacetime he prepares the defense of Italy against outside attack, maintains the organization and supply of his troops, perfects their training by joint maneuvers, and keeps them ready for action at all times. As a NATO commander, General Bernabo has both Italians and Americans under him. The Italian troops consist of infantry, armored divisions, and a brigade of Alpini, together with the usual auxiliary units. The U.S. contingent is the Southern European Task Force (SETAF), a body of 6,200 men grouped around the First Missile Command. The supply organization behind SETAF is national, with its base in the United States, but it is coordinated with the Italian supply system known as Intendenza Nord S.

Headquarters LANDSOUTH is in the Palazzo Carli, which was built by the Marchese Giuseppe della Torre in the second half of the eighteenth century. Military activities are nothing new to those aristocratic halls, because the palace served the famous Austrian Field Marshal Radetzky as headquarters when he was Governor of the Lombardo-Venetian Kingdom. In 1839, it was purchased by the Imperial Austrian administration to become the seat of the Lombardo-Venetian Senate, the supreme court of the kingdom. In 1857, Emperor Francis Joseph and Empress Elizabeth lived there, and in 1866, it became Italian Crown property.

In Verona we saw General Bernabo's predecessor as commander of LANDSOUTH, General Alessandro Albert, who assured us that Italy was not merely defending her own territory. "We have no interests outside NATO," he explained. "If NATO were defeated, we too could not survive."

After our discussion with General Albert, we made a tour through the palace, walking through handsome rooms decorated with frescoes from the days of the Empire, including the study used by Radetzky, and the great hall, with its vast marble fireplaces and stucco work. There was the Imperial Seal with the double-headed eagle, the initials F. I., Fernandus Imperator, and the mottoes "*Iustitia fundamentum regnorum*" (Justice is the foundation of states) and "*Recta tueri*" (Defend Right)—both so appropriate to the NATO spirit.

The Chief of Staff, Major-General Antonio Scaramuzza, a stocky, broad-shouldered man of abounding energy with an acute and lively mind (he speaks several languages fluently), has since been replaced by the Bersaglieri Major-General Pietro Testa, but he was still at his post when we were there. From 1945 to 1950, Major-General Scaramuzza was Chief of Military Counter-Intelligence. He spoke of Italy's role in NATO:

"Italy is like a gigantic aircraft carrier anchored in the Mediterranean. It is no more than 1,200 miles from the Po Valley to Moscow, and not much farther from Puglia to the Caucasus and Stalingrad. The NATO strategic air force therefore could strike the enemy effectively wherever he decided to concentrate his forces, be it in Central Russia or the satellite countries. If the Soviets were to attack Greece or Turkey, Italy would be the most convenient supply base for NATO. And if an attack were launched in the north, Italy's ports and harbors would be less endangered than those of France, Belgium, Holland, and Germany on the North Sea and the Atlantic, which would be much nearer the front."

"But isn't Italy herself vulnerable to enemy attack?"

"Our most vulnerable spot is undoubtedly the thirty-mile-wide Gorizia gap leading into the Po Valley. Austria's neutrality has created a dangerous vacuum there. To some extent, the German Army will make up for that, since it would threaten the flank of any attacker who tried to advance along the Danube and the Inn."

Yugoslavia, he thought, could hardly be regarded even as a buffer state; even supposing that Tito did decide to resist a Soviet attack, given his limited war potential and the strong pro-Kremlin forces in his own camp, he could do little more than sound the alarm and then retreat to the hills to carry on a guerrilla struggle. The main weight of NATO defense therefore would have to be based in Italy, particularly as the upper Italian plains and the Gorizia gap would be a good springboard for a counter-attack into the Danubian area and the Balkans.

"There is one further serious threat to my country," the General went on, "and that is Communist Albania, which from its position on the Balkan side of the Adriatic can threaten the straits of Otranto and access to the Adriatic. Albania is a thorn in the long and vulnerable eastern coast of Italy."

That small country, completely cut off from Western influence, has become a Soviet satellite, and its coast is the only place where the Iron Curtain touches the Mediterranean. Albania is the eyes and ears of Moscow—or Peking—in the Mediterranean. It is of limited interest as a land base, but crucial as an air, naval, and advance rocket base. The harbor of Valona could be an ideal base for Soviet submarines. Operating from there, the Soviets could prevent all traffic through the Adriatic, and it would also be a good base for an attack on Greece. It remains to be seen whether Albania's shift of allegiance (in 1961) from Moscow to Peking has more than temporary significance. In any case, it is a shift within the Communist camp.

"In the event of Soviet aggression," said the General in conclusion, "we might have to defend ourselves by attacking that bridgehead. It could be done quickly and successfully from Greece, and from Italian bases along the Apulian coast, which is only about sixty miles from Albania."

Italy has about 375,000 men under arms, 280,000 in the army and 40,000 in the navy and air force. In addition, there are certain specialized formations. Supreme command is in the hands of General Aldo Rossi, Chief of the General Staff for National Defense.

The Italian Army consists of ten infantry divisions, of which eight are intended for use in the North Italian plains and the other two in the mountains. There are also two armored divisions and five Alpini brigades. Five divisions and four of the mountain brigades are already at the disposal of NATO, and others will join them later.

Before the Second World War, the Italian Navy was the fifth in order of size in the world, but its losses have been made good only in part. Today it consists of 1 rocket cruiser, 1 light cruiser, 6 destroyers, 9 frigates, 33 submarine chasers, 7 submarines, 61 minesweepers, 26 speed- and gunboats, 47 landing crafts and transports, and a large number of auxiliary vessels. The United States has handed over certain naval units, and the Italians themselves are carrying out a large building program. The so-called first program was completed between 1955 and 1958, when two destroyer flotilla leaders, two destroyers, four corvettes, a submarine, and certain other ships, including four frigates of the internationally recognized new Cigno class type, were added to the Navy. A second program provided for two new cruisers of over 6,000 tons each, and certain other units.

Morale in the Italian Air Force is high. Fifteen squadrons of eighteen to twenty-five machines each have already been placed under NATO. Among the planes in service today are the F-84 fighter-bomber and the F-86 fighter-interceptor. Flying training is on a very high level, chiefly because the Italian Air Force has adopted the policy of alternating its leading officers between active service and training duties. For example, Lieutenant-General Sergio Lalatta, former commander of the Fifth ATAF, was for a long time in charge of the Accademia Aeronautica, until he was relieved in the spring of 1960 by Major-General Raymo Magistrelli.

The job of closing the gap created when Austria was neutralized in the autumn of 1955, has been entrusted to the American ballistic and guided missile unit of SETAF, which is stationed at Vicenza, with headquarters in Verona and a center for supplies from the United States in Livorno. SETAF had its modest start with the U.S. Army of Occupation in Austria. When it pulled out and moved back into Italy, it found nothing but bare walls to greet it, but since that dull September morning when a convoy of fifty military trucks moved back across the Brenner Pass, SETAF has become a power without which one could hardly imagine an effective defense of Northern Italy.

With SETAF something quite new has grown up. Strictly speaking, it is a purely artillery unit, with new type artillery, a ballistic and guided missile outfit; and infantry is attached only as far as the rockets have to be defended. If it ever comes to this point, the infantry will be provided by the Italian Army, which does so already on maneuvers. German Chancellor Adenauer was the first to use the apt expression "atomic artillery." For example, both the Honest John rocket and the Corporal missile can be fitted with either conventional or atomic warheads.

SETAF consists of two Honest John and two Corporal battalions, which together form the so-called missile command, the real striking force of the unit. There is also a tank-support battalion equipped with light tanks, and a so-called sky cavalry battalion, which consists of thirty-six reconnaissance planes, of which seven are L-19s, twelve L-23s, and the rest H-13 and H-34 helicopters. There are also signals, engineer, and other auxiliary groups attached to the unit. Each Honest John battalion consists of eight transport and four firing units, and each Corporal battalion consists of four transport and two firing units.

The Honest John is a ballistic missile with a range of between fifteen to twenty miles. It is twenty-seven feet long, and with its four rear fins it looks something like a heavy dart. The ramp from which the 2.72-ton Honest John is launched is an imposing piece of engineering which is mounted on a three-axle truck, the whole weighing no more than twenty-one tons, so that the truck can use ordinary roads and bridges to reach any suitable launching site.

"How long does it take to get the rocket in position and ready for firing?" we inquired.

"The scheduled time is forty-five minutes, but we can do it much faster than that. In fact, we've just set a new record of twenty-seven minutes."

We watched a rocket team of fourteen men. Hardly had their truck stopped when each man was at his post, and within a very short time the rocket was assembled. As it swung over from the transporter to the launching ramp, it looked almost light and airy. It consists of a spin-rocket unit which gives the missile a spinning motion to keep it on course, a fuel tank, a motor compartment, and the fins. In addition there is a thirty-inch warhead weighing about 1,500 pounds.

While the rocket was being assembled, its launching and course were calculated. The Honest John is a true ballistic missile, whose flight cannot be guided. Accurate plotting is therefore essential, because the slightest deviation at the beginning of its trajectory can mean a great deal at the other end. Temperature, humidity, and, above all, winds have to be taken into account. The force and direction of the wind is ascertained with the aid of a wind-wheel mounted atop a high telescopic mast.

Unlike conventional artillery, the rocket weapon has no chance to shoot itself in by bracketing its target. As one member of the team put it, "When we've pooped off our rocket we move pronto. The enemy can easily follow the smoke trail of the rocket, so we mustn't be here when he hits back."

By now, all the necessary calculations had been made, and the Honest John was ready to go. An officer gave an order, and the powerful lever arm which raises the rocket set to work to bring it to the required elevation.

"Once Honest John is launched, its first-stage boost burns for 4.5 seconds and is exhausted at about 1,100 feet," an officer explained. "But that gives it sufficient thrust to reach a ceiling of 28,000 feet and attain a maximum range of thirty miles at an angle of 45 degrees. The rocket has an automatic priming device which is set in motion just before it reaches its target—in order to avoid disaster should it hit the ground before reaching enemy territory. It can also be exploded in flight at any altitude, or on impact."

It isn't easy to see an Honest John in action. In Italy it can be fired only in the Alps, and then only in the autumn and winter, when the herdsmen have brought the cattle down from pasture. But on one occasion we did see an Honest John fired, and saw it hit its target—during the maneuvers of the Seventh U.S. Army in Germany, not far from the zonal frontier. The missile let off a shattering roar, a continuous explosion that lasted for several seconds, and zoomed off on its course at several times the speed of sound, leaving a long trail of smoke and fire behind it.

There is no suitable place in Europe for firing the Corporal guided missile, the larger of SETAF's two weapons. The Corporal is forty-six feet long and weighs over five tons. Unlike the Honest John, which has solid fuel, the Corporal gets its thrust from compressed aniline acid. Its accuracy of fire is greater, and so is its range—up to seventy-five miles. The warheads are the same in both missiles.

As a guided missile, the flight profile of the Corporal is quite different from that of the Honest John. The Corporal rises vertically, and when it has reached the calculated altitude, it is brought on course by radio impulses and guided to its target. The Corporal has movable fins adjusted by compressed air and controlled electronically. Once the missile's course has been plotted, an electronic device sets the fins in the correct position, and the subsequent course is controlled automatically. But even in flight it is possible to change the missile's course by means of radio ground control.

A series of instruments and devices is necessary to bring the Corporal to its target: the electronic brain determines its course and works out the other necessary data; a radar device follows the missile in flight and reports back; finally, there is the so-called doppler, which collects flight data, processes it, and transmits any necessary orders to the missile's electronic brain. A Corporal unit needs fourteen trucks to carry its equipment, while an Honest John can get by with three. The Corporal will gradually be replaced by the solid-fuelled Sergeant ballistic missile, which also needs no more than three vehicles. It is much more easily transported by air and can be fired in the field by a crew without special training.

"If things ever got serious," observed Colonel Leroy C. Land, "we should first have to find out whether there were any suitable enemy targets ahead and which of them seemed likely to prove most profitable, particularly for the use of atomic warheads. Let's assume there's an ammunition dump, a divisional headquarters, an airfield, and a battery of artillery in a given area ahead of us. Provided we can establish their exact location, we ought to be able to drop our missile at a spot that would dislocate the whole show."

"And how do you get the necessary information?"

"Well, there are many ways of doing it. For example, there's the radar screen. In Korea, we soon got to know that a concentration of enemy trucks was a valuable guide to his intentions." One can see such trucks on the radar screen clearly enough to count them. With the equipment available today, one can survey an area of forty-five square miles; and even better equipment is planned.

"Another possibility is the use of parachute troops. We should have to drop them in a safe place, let them reconnoiter, and then bring them back again."

The training of parachute troops for close cooperation with these missile units is very important. We were able to observe it at Fort Bragg in the United States, which is the training center for the Third Missile Command, which provides SETAF with replacements.

"The important thing is to determine the targets ahead of you," we were told by Colonel Vincent A. Carignola, who was in command of the sky cavalry battalion previously referred to. The parachutists were his men, and he had his own headquarters, a reconnaissance unit, a transport unit, and forty-six aircraft, including helicopters— but no jets. "Should we need jets, we would request them from the Italians or NATO."

SETAF has its own lines of communication that connect it with various headquarters and other units; it makes use of mountains and hilltops to ensure an uninterrupted wireless telephonic service.

"SETAF's firepower is more or less the same as that of one of our modern divisions stationed in Germany," Major-General Harvey H. Fisher informed us when we visited him at his headquarters in Verona. "But SETAF is much more flexible, and, if necessary, could give artillery support to a number of divisions. By the way, the Honest Johns you saw during the Greek maneuvers in Macedonia were ours; we took them there and back by air—which gives you some idea of how mobile we are."

"Italy is glad to give hospitality to SETAF, on account of both its military strength and its boost to our political morale." The speaker was General Giuseppe Mancinelli, whom we were interviewing in the Defense Ministry building in Rome. "You mustn't forget that Germany mans her front in Central Europe with the assistance of a number of allies. We in Italy are alone, apart from the support given us by SETAF."

General Mancinelli shared the skepticism of General Scaramuzza with regard to Tito's role in the event of war with the Soviets. "After all, Tito's only one man, and if he refused to come to an accommodation with Moscow at a critical juncture, they might well find the means of getting rid of him."

Turning his attention to the Italian Army, the General declared, "We are doing everything possible to modernize our forces rapidly. Finance is, of course, our big problem. Defense expenditure already amounts to 18 per cent of our budget. As you know, we are making really big efforts in aircraft construction; the Fiat G-91 is evidence." This model has been accepted by NATO as the standard jet for operational reconnaissance and front-line support.

"As for rockets, we have our own five-year program. Of course, the decisions are often difficult. You order a type because you think it's the best and most modern; but who is to guarantee that it won't be obsolete when you take delivery on it in three years? And still you must place your orders. Even the most modern weapons are no good if they're only designs on our drawing boards."

The home front also cannot be neglected, because if the Soviets ever did attack, they would do their best to open up a second front with the aid of a fifth column behind the front lines.

"We've got something like seven million Communists in Italy, you know," said the General. "Of course, they're not all convinced Communists by any means, but the trained agitators of the Party would do their utmost to whip them up into revolt at the critical moment, especially if we let the Soviets advance into our country. We must prevent that. We must fight, so to speak, with our backs to the wall."

There are 40 per cent Communist and Left-Wing Socialist voters in Italy, but this does not mean that two-fifths of Italy's fighting men are Communists—not even in the Army, which is based on compulsory military service, and certainly not in the Navy or Air Force, where the men are volunteers. Italian *esprit de corps* is high; there is a pride in the uniform which soon affects the new recruits, and through them their families. It would be wrong to interpret the high radical electoral figures to mean a lack of patriotism—they are largely the reflection of great social privations coupled with the illusions of simple men who have never come into contact with Soviet reality and have been led to believe that Communism would better the lot of the poor.

Because of this, politics and strategy run in double harness in face of the Bolshevist threat. This applies to all NATO countries, of course, but it operates with particular force in Italy.

"Militarily we shall hold the front," the General assured us in conclusion, "if we remain alert and willing to make the necessary economic sacrifices to modernize our arms and equipment. But it is all-important that in the moment of danger, NATO should act with political determination—and in the very first hours."

Italy was one of the first countries to provide NATO bases; and on Easter, 1959, an agreement with the U.S. Government added Jupiter rockets, which are one-stage missiles, fifty-eight feet long and nearly nine feet in diameter, propelled by liquid fuel and capable of carrying an atomic warhead. They are fired vertically into the air and then led to their targets by inertial guidance. The Jupiter was developed by the U.S. Army under the direction of Wernher von Braun.

Thus Italy was the first country on the European continent to come into possession of strategic missiles with a range of 1,500 miles. This gives her a special place in NATO. That this is recognized by the United States was shown, for instance, by the decision of the U.S. Navy to establish the NATO center for the study of anti-submarine defense methods at La Spezia on the Tyrrhenian Sea, where this new institute, which is under SACLANT, is making use of the important research facilities and arsenals of the Italian Navy.

Italy has provided bases for the strategic missiles as willingly as it had formerly agreed to accept tactical rockets and atomic weapons. Italian public opinion accepted this necessity with sober realism, because everyone knows that troops with conventional arms would have no more chance against Soviet divisions armed with nuclear weapons than the Polish cavalry had against Hitler's tanks. As the Social-Democratic leader Saragat said, if the Italians allowed themselves to be guided by their Communists in this question, Italy would suffer the same fate as Tibet. And the Republican Deputy Pacciardi, who was Defense Minister in de Gasperi's administration, called it a matter of course that Italy's forces should have nuclear arms. "Are we Italians to provide cannon fodder while the rest of our NATO allies are equipped with nuclear weapons?"

The Italians aren't much impressed by the Rapacki plan either. Italian Defense Minister Paoli Emilio Taviani once said that it was only a short step from atomic disarmament to neutralization. The step from neutralization to Sovietization would be even shorter.

25

Malta, Bastion of the Mediterranean

Great Britain's continuing importance is perceived most readily outside the continent of Europe. It is not only for historical reasons that Malta was chosen as headquarters for the Allied Naval Forces in the Mediterranean. The strategic importance of this small island was demonstrated once again in the Second World War. Whereas the German General Staff urged Hitler to take Malta, like Crete, by parachute invasion, he obstinately confined the attack to air bombings until it was too late. Because the supply lines of the Afrika Korps were interrupted from Malta, Rommel's drive to Cairo inevitably failed, and the whole North African campaign was lost. The Allied invasion, first of Sicily and then of the Italian mainland, also would have been much more difficult if Malta had been in German hands.

Today, British, French, Italian, Greek, and Turkish forces belong to NATO Headquarters in Malta. Originally they were under Europe South in Naples, with the exception of the British Mediterranean Fleet, which always has had its base at Malta. However, on March 15, 1953, the command was taken from Naples and joined together with this British Fleet to form a fourth major European command subordinate to SACEUR. Command over the Allied Naval Forces in the Mediterranean (AFMED) was then given to Admiral Earl Mountbatten of Burma, who already commanded the British Mediterranean Fleet.

The flight from Rome to Malta takes hardly two and a half

hours. Suddenly the yellow sandy islands show up against the deep blue of the Mediterranean—Gozo, Commino, and Malta—scattered towns with large churches and white houses, towers and vineyards, stone walls edging the fields and casting deep shadows in the bright sunshine. Valletta, capital of Malta, with its imposing harbor, is armed with magnificently beautiful fortifications. Malta is a strange spot in the ocean; even in prehistoric times it was a sacred place, the Heligoland of the Mediterranean; and in both ancient and modern times, an apple of discord between the powers. In ancient days, Malta served the Phoenicians as a base. Hannibal, the great Carthaginian leader, was born there, and the language of the inhabitants is still of Punic and Phoenician origin. Saint Paul suffered shipwreck here as a prisoner on his way to Rome, and the people of Malta have been Christian and Catholic since that day.

Malta is so old that when the Phoenicians took possession, about 2000 B.C., the gods of those temples were already unknown. Later the island became Carthaginian, and after the Second Punic War, Roman. The centuries of Roman dominion brought prosperity and a high civilization, to which the remains of splendid temples, villas, and baths bear witness. Subsequently Malta knew many masters: the Arabs from 872 to 1090; after them, the Normans; then the House of Hohenstaufen, Charles of Anjou, the Aragonese, the Habsburgs. In the year 1530, the Emperor Charles V gave Malta with full sovereign rights to the Knights of Saint John, who subsequently defended it heroically against the superior armies of Sultan Soleiman the Magnificent. Their victory was the turning point in the defense of the West against the Osmanite Empire.

What Malta is today it owes largely to the Knights, who impressed their stamp on the island for 268 years. They gave the island its capital, named after the Grand Master of the Order of St. John, Jean de la Valette, who defeated the Turks. But in 1798, the Knights surrendered Malta to Napoleon Bonaparte. Two years later, the populace appealed to Nelson to come to its aid, and ever since, Malta has been British.

We were met at the airfield by Commander L. C. Lings. Valletta makes a strong impact. Here is a Renaissance city where wealth and the esthetic combine, perpetuated by a chivalrous community, the flower of Europe's aristocracy, ennobled by the ideal of Christendom's defense. To establish NATO's Mediterranean Fleet Headquarters in Floriana, on the outskirts of Valletta, seems like a continuation of history.

"NATO's lifeline, the Atlantic," declared Admiral Sir Charles Lambe, "is defended in the Mediterranean."

After the official dinner, he had asked us to come to his office. He was Commander-in-Chief at Malta until February, 1959; after that, until his untimely death in the summer of 1960, he was First Sea Lord.

"We must ensure," he said, "that in a war, Soviet submarines don't get out of the Black Sea into the Mediterranean, just as they must not get out of the Baltic into the North Sea. To do that, we need more naval flyers and more planes for anti-submarine patrols."

Sir Charles was succeeded in February, 1959, by Admiral Sir Alexander Bingley, who, in turn, was succeeded by Admiral Sir Deric Holland-Martin, on June 1, 1961.

Headquarters is an ancient building with the façade of a palace. Commander Lings, leading us to the Admiral's office, observed that the lift in the place was obviously quite modern—not earlier than the Bronze Age—but that he regarded the Stone Age steps as safer.

Sir St. John Tyrwhitt received us in the white summer uniform of the British Navy, a short-sleeved shirt and shorts. He is the only high British staff officer here who has an exclusively NATO command.

"Malta is an integrated command," he told us. "Its simple structure was given it by Lord Mountbatten. The Mediterranean and the Black Sea were divided into operational zones and put under the fleet commanders who were there as national commanders. Thus a British admiral is at Gibraltar, a French admiral in the western Mediterranean, a Greek admiral in the central Mediterranean, a Turkish admiral in the northeastern Mediterranean, and the area around Malta under the Commander-in-Chief of AFMED himself, who delegated this function to a British admiral.

"The U.S. Navy has no operational zone; its strategic interest is in the Mediterranean as a whole. The Americans contribute to our naval strength here as the sixth nation, and they are therefore represented by the Commander-in-Chief of the U.S. Naval Forces in Europe."

The Commander-in-Chief of the Central Mediterranean and the Tyrrhenian Sea at the time of our visit was Vice-Admiral Francesco Ruta, whom we had previously visited at his headquarters in Naples.

These naval commanders meet in Malta about once every ten months, under the chairmanship of the Commander-in-Chief of AFMED. In the meantime they are represented by officers of flag rank, each of whom is at the head of a department as Deputy Chief of Staff.

The chief task of Mediterranean Command in peacetime is to keep its plans up to date and maintain the Allied fleets on a war footing.

"Has Malta an operational command in peacetime?" we asked.

"Only during the annual maneuvers, which usually take place in the spring," replied Sir St. John. "In practice, a collective command has emerged through collaboration among the various national commanders and their representatives. In the event of war, Malta would immediately take over direct command. But our staff officers are not just national representatives; they are subordinate to NATO and under the orders of the Commander-in-Chief."

"Is there any direct contact between Malta and the U.S. Sixth Fleet, Sir St. John?"

"The Sixth Fleet is under AFSOUTH—our command channels meet in the hands of General Norstad—but of course our tasks overlap, and the annual fleet exercises in the Mediterranean are always planned and carried out jointly."

Some units in the Black Sea are under the orders of Allied Mediterranean Command, but coastal defense and harbor fairways are a national responsibility. Thus not the whole naval forces of these countries are under the Mediterranean Command. It is unfortunate that in March, 1959, de Gaulle should have withdrawn the French naval forces. This action disrupted the unity of the Mediterranean Command, and the hope that it would be a temporary measure has so far been disappointed.

"What is the power relationship between the NATO Mediterranean Fleet and the Soviet Black Sea Fleet?"

"If you mean without counting the U.S. Sixth Fleet, the superiority is undoubtedly on the Soviet side. But to exert any influence in the Mediterranean, the Soviet Fleet would first have to force the Straits; and even then, its effectiveness would diminish with its distance from its bases."

With a smile, Sir St. John added: "Of course, did you ever hear of an Admiral who thought he didn't need any more ships? Although it isn't battleships we need nowadays; they're out of date. In Britain we're sending our old battleships and heavy cruisers to the breakers' yards and building smaller and more useful vessels."

"So you count on the U.S. Sixth Fleet to reinforce your strength?"

"Yes, and together we shall certainly be strong enough to hold the Mediterranean. It wouldn't be easy to destroy the Sixth Fleet. Even if the aircraft carriers were lost, what remained would still be strong enough to keep its end up."

"Some people seem to think that Mediterranean Command should be put under SACLANT."

"In my opinion, that would be a great mistake. Naval problems are so important that they must be represented at the highest levels, particularly with SACEUR, which is primarily a land and air command. It is essential that a naval commander with authority should be there to say, if necessary: 'Look, what you're planning may be all right for the Army and the Air Force, but it won't do for the Navy.'" In the event of war, the Mediterranean might well become very important: for example, if the Atlantic ports and harbors of Europe were put out of action and supplies had to be sent in through Gibraltar.

When we talked to Rear-Admiral des Roziers, the Chief of the Planning Department, he declared: "What we need is less nationalism and more NATO spirit." In 1940, the Admiral, a young lieutenant then, was one of the first to leave his ship, the cruiser *Tourville* anchored in Alexandria, to join the Free French. He spent the war doing naval escort duty in the Atlantic, the Indian Ocean, and the Mediterranean, and for a time was in command of the destroyer *Le Tunisien.*

"The Soviet Black Sea Fleet serves the ancient Russian design to penetrate into the Mediterranean." Czar Paul tried to get himself elected Grand Master of the Order of St. John with the thought of turning the Mediterranean into a Russian lake. Today, the Soviets try to achieve this end by means of Arab revolts. If North Africa were to fall into Soviet hands, it would be a terrible threat to Europe. "*C'est une guerre révolutionnaire,*" he concluded.

Rear-Admiral Bruno de Moratti, who was present, took up the theme: "If North Africa ever went Communist," he said, "the Pyrenees would be our last line of defense." Admiral Moratti, who was born in Trieste, is a man of opinions of his own. "In order to wage war you need men," he declared. "You can't do it with atom bombs alone. You probably couldn't even take Malta with them."

He is a good judge, because as an Italian naval officer he saw this island stand up to over 2,000 heavy bombing attacks, and at the end be no nearer to surrender.

The Deputy Commander-in-Chief, Air Marshal Charles Eliot Chilton, was commander at Malta at the time of our visit—a break with tradition, because all previous commanders have been army men. Today, Marshal Chilton is NATO Commander-in-Chief Allied Forces Channel and Eastern Atlantic, and he is particularly well qualified for the job. He is not only an experienced flyer himself—he was a test pilot—but also a specialist in anti-submarine warfare, with which he had much experience in the Second World War.

"Even if we redouble our efforts, the Soviet submarines would still be very dangerous if they ever got through the Straits," he declared. "Our main job therefore is to stop them from doing just that."

The defense of the Mediterranean is essentially a combined operation, employing both naval and air forces. Like General Lindsay, Air Marshal Chilton thinks that, in the event of war, the NATO air forces would need to win the air battle within the first few days. That would be all the more important because Soviet planes would swarm out in all directions, in an effort to strike everywhere at once.

The Grand Harbor of Valletta, which we toured in the Admiral's boat, is one of the biggest and safest in the Mediterranean. It is about two miles long, with an endless quay on one side and dock after dock on the other. The powerful fortifications are still of value. They show traces of World War II bombardments, but have come through it astonishingly well. They rear up almost perpendicularly out of the water. Perched in the air between sea and sky, they are architectural wonders, decorated with a great eye or a huge ear—an indication of their function. During our visit, a part of the British Mediterranean Fleet was lying at anchor in the harbor, including the 40,000-ton aircraft carrier *Eagle*—well built, and an embodiment of British sea power.

The nerve system of a command that must send orders and receive reports over long distances is the so-called long-lines communications. This was the responsibility of Captain J. R. C. Trechman, a British naval officer who is an expert on the subject and co-author of a series of publications about NATO long-distance communications. He was in Washington during the discussions of standardization.

"For the moment almost every country is more or less on its own in such matters," he informed us. "Only in sea-land communications are there certain wave lengths which are used in common. Suppose, for example, a ship at sea is trying to get in touch with Algiers but can't make contact; Athens, say, may pick up the message and will then put it through to Algiers."

There is a direct telephone line from Malta to SHAPE in Paris and Europe South in Naples. "NATO laid the lines," the Captain said, "and still has to pay about $15 a day for using them." That is one of the comic anomalies of infrastructure: the line is under national administration; therefore NATO must pay. If Malta were put out of action in wartime, then some other station, perhaps Naples, would take its place.

"Can the enemy pick up our messages?"

"Yes, he can, of course; but we take our precautions. We can scramble our messages, and we can check authenticity by question and answer. However, it can always happen, as we proved for example during maneuvers, that the enemy cuts in and gives false orders. He can also attempt to jam our wave length."

Normal wireless communications over long distances go on long waves; over shorter distances on medium and short wave lengths. Medium waves, which have a range of about 150 miles, have peculiar qualities: under some circumstances, they may suddenly travel 600 or 1,000 miles. This is disconcerting, when one is trying to keep secrets from the enemy.

In the event of war, the allies would have to hand over half their long-distance wave lengths to the military authorities, and this half would have to suffice. This puts a big burden on NATO in the less developed countries, which are inclined to feel that, since NATO asks so much in the way of means of communication, it ought to build the corresponding share of infrastructure for them.

NATO has established procedures for the integration of long-lines communications. Unfortunately, some countries use the NATO code only for NATO communications. At first it was assumed that the NATO system would rapidly become general, but this met with obstacles: the apparatus varied, and it will take time before it can be standardized. How difficult such things are can be seen from the fact that the Americans have not to this day adopted the international keyboard system.

"NATO is an expensive business," declared Rear-Admiral Phillips, head of Counter-Intelligence. "But the heavy defense burdens are worthwhile; they must be regarded as a sort of insurance. You pay in for years, and even if you never have to claim, you don't let the premiums lapse. One can be sure that any such lapse would be followed by a disaster."

The Admiral thought that, on the whole, taking the navy and air force into account, the West was as strong as the Soviets; of course this was not true of the land forces, at least not if one took only the conventional forces into account.

"Not all the Soviet divisions are equipped with modern weapons," Turkish Rear-Admiral Uran pointed out. In his opinion, there is only one sensible strategy if the Soviets should attack, and that is to launch an immediate counter-attack. In particular, the strategic forces of the West must be ready at any time to strike at the enemy's vital nerve centers. That is the best form of defense. Otherwise the Soviets might succeed in what has been called their salami tactic—a slice at a time in the Mediterranean, in Iraq, in Syria.

"Would the Mediterranean Fleet go into action if the Russians succeeded in getting through the Dardanelles?"

"Let them try it first," the Admiral replied. "If they come to see us, they'd be likely to see something."

The Palace of the Grand Master in the center of the town is today the seat of the British Governor. Completed in 1574, it has a simple exterior, almost militarily severe, while its interior is of princely magnificence. But even here you are never allowed to forget that the building was originally the stronghold of a militant Order. The great armory once held equipment for 25,000 men, and the pieces which have remained there still make a priceless collection. The Parliament of Malta has always met in the Council Chamber, which is hung with splendid tapestries. These meetings ceased, however, on April 21, 1958, when Premier Dom Mintoff, the leader of the Labour Party, resigned, and the Opposition, Dr. Borg-Olivier's National Party, refused to take over the government.

"Since then," Major-General Sir Robert Edward Laycock said, "I have been forced to govern by decree, and must continue until the Maltese are willing to exercise their rights." The Governor was no dictator, and eager to abdicate his emergency powers.

The Honorable Mabel Strickland, daughter of Lord Strickland, Count della Catena, a former Governor of Malta, is a vigorous opponent of Mintoff. The island saw happier days when her father was Prime Minister. He was a statesman, a scholar, and an explorer, who added to the historical and archeological knowledge of Malta. The Constitutional Party which he founded and which his daughter now leads may have lost a great deal of its following, but the name of Strickland still means much in Malta. The Strickland house is a beautiful building in the Romanesque-Arabic style. A portico leads into a large, walled garden with high trees, flower beds, and a fountain in the center, like the Roman villas in Pompeii.

"Malta is of strategic importance for the defense of the free world," said Miss Strickland. "It is a base that must be held. The three islands, with an area of about 100 square miles and a population of 330,000, must be assisted. There is agriculture, a certain amount of trade, and, of course, tourism. But Malta is poor and cannot feed her population. Up to now, the greater part of her revenue has come from the British Navy and its dockyards. But the fleet is smaller and the dockyards are to be managed privately. This has caused a good deal of excitement among the people; and a drift to the Left would create a serious problem."

Mintoff, an astute politician, proposed only a few years ago that Malta become an integral part of the United Kingdom and be represented in Parliament on equal footing with other British citizens. In these days of colonial emancipation, this was a remarkable proposal. In April, 1955, it was accepted by the House of Commons, but in the end broke against Mintoff's excessive financial demands. Since then he has been demanding full independence. At the same time, he has let it be known with disarming bluntness that there might be still other possibilities. Malta's political leaders, he suggested, have always leaned toward the strongest power in the Mediterranean.

"If we played the game according to the old rules, we would turn to either the United States or the Soviet Union." Then he added quickly that "of course" no one in Malta was considering any such alternative. But the threat decidedly went too far. On January 5, 1959, the British Government suspended the Constitution, and Malta temporarily was again a colony. The Soviets in Malta—that would be a frightening prospect indeed! For the ancient axiom still holds good today: Whoever is lord of Malta is lord of the Mediterranean.

How the political problems of that island will ultimately be adjusted is still an open question. Dr. Borg-Olivier, Prime Minister since March, 1962, envisages independence within the Commonwealth and hopes for a solution of the economic problem through association with the Common Market.

26

Talks in the Pentagon

When the United States of America joined the North Atlantic Alliance, it established political ties of heretofore unknown strength with the Old World. But the groundwork had been laid in the preceding decades, in the course of which Americans had rediscovered their European origins; and the alliance of the Second World War deepened their awareness of a common fate. The rapid inclusion of Germans and Italians, only recently enemies, was facilitated by the many refugees who had found asylum in the United States. Even when they acclimated readily to their new environment, they retained enough of their European heritage to contribute to the sense of unity.

To this was added a growing awareness that Bolshevism aims at conquest and world revolution, and threatens all nations. Thereafter, isolationism, once a powerful political current, lost its sway.

Had the New World not come to the protection of the Old, the Soviets would long ago have reached the Mediterranean, the North Sea, and the Atlantic; and there would no longer be a free Europe. But today the frontiers of the United States are in Europe, and Europe is being defended on America's Atlantic and Pacific coasts.

The U.S. Seventh Army in Germany; the American Air Forces from Scotland to Pakistan under the command of USAFE Headquarters in Wiesbaden and NATO in Paris, Fontainebleau, and Naples; the Fourth, Fifth, and Sixth Allied Tactical Air Forces with headquarters in Ramstein, Verona, and Ismir; the missile units; the U.S. Sixth and Atlantic Fleets—all are essential to the defense of Europe's freedom, the Atlantic, and the North American continent.

The same is true of the armies, navies and air forces of all the other NATO allies.

"If the Soviets attack, we shall strike back," declared General Nathan F. Twining. "They must be left in no doubt whatever on that point. An attack on any member of NATO, regardless which, means war."

Until the middle of August, 1960, General Twining was Chairman of the Joint Chiefs of Staff; since August, 1957, he had been the top-ranking U.S. officer, in charge of strategic planning. His military career has been impressive: a graduate of the U.S. Military Academy, he was commissioned as an infantry officer in 1918. After serving five years with the infantry, he transferred to the air force. During the Second World War, he commanded the Thirteenth, Fifteenth, and Twentieth U.S. Air Forces, and saw more service in Europe and Asia than any other American Air Force General. In 1953, he became Chief of Staff of the U.S. Air Force.

His large, airy room in the Pentagon, the central point of U.S. defense planning, looks out over the Potomac; a steady stream of military and civilian planes pass in view. We continued the discussion.

"Does that include Berlin, General?"

"Of course it does." The answer was given without hesitation. "Berlin is a new Soviet test to see how far they can go—as were Quemoy and Matsu, Korea, and Vietnam. We must not give way an inch. If they attack, we must defend ourselves vigorously and at once. Only then will there be no war."

General Twining does not hold this attitude lightly. As chief of strategic planning for the United States, he was well aware of the forces arrayed against the free world. It is not only a matter of the armies of the Soviet bloc, millions strong; of the tens of thousands of tanks and planes; of the fleets of submarines and the Soviet arsenal of nuclear and long-range weapons. Military strength today rests in large part on technology—on the development of increasingly effective weapons. This requires engineers, and the Soviet Union mobilizes its resources to educate them. There are only thirty-three universities in the Soviet Union, but 700 technical colleges and more than 3,000 technical schools; these train two to three times as many engineers as the United States does.

"The necessity to remain ahead of the Soviets in natural science and technology is a matter for the whole free world," the General declared. "The Battle of Waterloo is said to have been won on the playing fields of Eton; we must take care that no one will ever be able to say that the free world lost the decisive battle in the classrooms of its schools and universities."

In the last thirty years, Soviet industrial production has increased eight-fold; in the same period in the United States, it has increased only three-fold. At present, the annual rate of industrial growth in the Soviet Union is between 7 and 8 per cent; in the United States, it is only 3 per cent.

"However," General Twining pointed out, "statistics can mislead. Our total production is two and a half times that of the Soviet Union, and our productivity is four times as great. Only 30 per cent of total Soviet annual production goes to consumer goods; in the United States, it's the other way around. In other words, the Soviets purchase their armaments by depriving the consumer."

"And in the military sphere?"

"There, the Soviets are superior to us in number of divisions and submarines. They are ahead in the development of high-yield fuel for long-range missiles. But our anti-submarine defenses are rapidly becoming more efficient. Our Strategic Air Command is by far the strongest nuclear-equipped striking force in the world. In addition, there are our strong fleet of aircraft carriers, our elastic and highly mobile tactical striking forces, and our general economic superiority. Taking all these factors into account, I can say with full conviction that we are militarily superior to the Soviet Union; and I see no reason why, with determination and efficient planning, we should not remain so throughout the 1960s. We shall never start a war; we have already demonstrated that more than once by our restraint. If it should ever come to war, it will be because the Soviets started it. Preparedness is therefore the best deterrent: so long as the Soviets realize that we are strong enough to deliver a devastating counterblow, they will never take the fatal step to war. That is what we mean when we say that our miiltary power is a factor for peace."

General Twining made it quite clear that such defensive preparedness demands sacrifices and raises economic problems not only for Europe, but also for the United States.

"We realize, General, that Europe could not defend herself today without the assistance of the United States; and we are thinking in particular of the U.S. Seventh Army. Fears have been expressed that the United States intends to reduce the size of this force."

"Under no circumstances. The Seventh Army will not be reduced

in strength," declared General Twining. "We know that without
Europe, America herself would be endangered. No one still believes
that we could retreat behind the barrier of our two oceans. They
offer no protection. The idea of 'Fortress America' is dead and buried;
it belongs to history."

The Pentagon, headquarters of America's Defense Department, is
the biggest government building in the world. Today, its name is as
evocative of military matters as the Quai d'Orsay or Ten Downing
Street long have been of foreign affairs. The building was taken into
use in January, 1943; it had been built in record time (sixteen
months) at a cost of $83 million. Its circumference is almost two
miles, and it occupies almost thirty acres of land. There are approximately seventeen miles of corridors, 7,748 windows, and 65,000
electric light switches; 1,000 new bulbs are needed daily. The telephone exchange carries 200,000 calls a day, 9,000 of them long distance. It took over 3,000 miles of electrical wiring to install the
system.

The Pentagon employs 32,000 people. Meals are provided in two
restaurants, six cafeterias, and ten bars, one of them outdoors. Some
are always open, around the clock and seven days a week. There are
also post offices, first-aid stations, and a dental clinic; banks, drug
stores, laundries and cleaners, photographers, jewelers, and pastry
shops—in sum, all the facilities of a town.

Yet the Pentagon does not seem gigantic. Its façade is harmoni-
ous; the building is only five stories high, with clean lines, and surrounded by well-kept lawns. Inside, the space has been planned carefully, and no department is more than six minutes' walk from any
other.

To enter the Pentagon is a simple matter—so simple as to astonish
the European, accustomed to bureaucratic formalities. There are no
uniformed sentries, not even secret police disguised as stern-looking
porters. No one takes notice unless a visitor needs help; then two
kindly ladies at a reception desk help one to find his way. One can
move freely through the corridors; only a few departments, such as
the Joint Chiefs of Staff and the Standing Group, are guarded
against unauthorized entry.

"We always knew that the Pentagon was impressive," we said to
Major-General Arno H. Luehman, who is in charge of the Information Division of the U.S. Air Force. "But today, coming in from
the river, we discovered that it is also beautiful."

General Luehman was born in Milwaukee in 1911. He received

his basic training in the Military Academy, the Naval War College, and the Air War College, and only a few years ago he went through the National Air College as well, graduating in 1951. As the U.S. military representative in the United Nations, he is now gathering political experience as well.

"We must not only arm, but fulfill two jobs at once," he said. "We must build up a strong force ready for immediate action, to serve as a deterrent. Second, we must keep a few steps ahead of the future. And that is expensive. Think of our missiles program—types we're working on now won't become operational for some years. It explains why our defense budget takes up such a big share of our national budget."

"Do you have to be prepared simultaneously for a big war, and a little, or limited or brushfire war, or whatever you like to call it?"

"As a matter of fact we don't much care for the expression 'limited war.' It's misleading and therefore dangerous. It tempts to the formulation that only a war that embraces the whole world is to be regarded as a general war; and that a limited war is one confined to a particular area. But that isn't the decisive criterion. Aggression is limited or total according to its objective and according to the amount of risk the aggressor is prepared to take.

"From this, it follows that we must calculate the means to employ against a threat or an attack, in accordance with the degree of risk we are prepared to take. We must have the ability to exert differentiated counter-pressure or carry through whatever counter-attack we, or NATO, consider appropriate.

"For instance, consider Lebanon. In 1958, we sent out a small expeditionary corps equipped with a variety of arms. The same could be done on a larger scale. The point was to show the Soviets that any aggression in that area would mean the danger of a big war. The same idea governs the policy with regard to Quemoy and Matsu. We would not be fighting for the possession of those two small islands, but for a more important goal: to force the lesson home to the Soviets that an attack on National China means war. And how much more important that is where Berlin is concerned!"

"Do you think the Soviets are likely to attack?"

"In any case, they're always probing. They exert pressure until they either find a weak spot or realize from our resistance that the risk is becoming too great. The United States itself will never attack." Unfortunately, the General went on, the Soviets know that, and it emboldens them and makes them more insolent. It is therefore all the more necessary to make clear to them where the risk begins.

"General White is expecting you," said he in conclusion. "General Norstad told him you would be coming. May I take you to his office now?"

Like General Norstad, who is a personal friend, Thomas D. White, from 1957 to 1961 Chief of the Staff of the Air Force, comes from Minnesota. The men resemble each other physically as well as in temperament. General White is a quiet, polite man, with sufficient moral courage to say disagreeable things if the interests of NATO require it. From 1927 to 1946, he served as military attaché in China, the Soviet Union, Italy, Greece, and Brazil. He speaks fluent Italian, Spanish, Portuguese, Russian, and Chinese. During the Second World War, he commanded the Seventh Air Force at Okinawa, and in 1943 he was appointed Deputy Chief of Staff of the U.S. Air Force. His successor is General Curtis E. Le May.

"I have a great respect for the men who are building up the new German Air Force," General White said when he greeted us. "I had the pleasure of meeting General Steinhoff personally. A great fighter pilot and a first-class man."

Steinhoff has been Germany's permanent representative in the Military Committee since October, 1960.

"Our young pilots feel a close comradeship with their American colleagues," we replied. "In fact, most of them were trained here. They swear by your way of doing things, and they were impressed by the friendliness and hospitality with which they were received."

An orderly brought in coffee. General White showed us the model of a B-58 Hustler on his desk. "This is our first supersonic bomber," he explained. "But it's only a beginning. We are already working on an atomic plane that can stay in the air for practically unlimited periods; on long-range fighter-interceptors; on X-20, or Project Dyna-Soar; and on manned rockets."

The X-20, a piloted rocket plane, is taken up by jet plane and launched in the air. On July 17, 1962, it climbed 58.7 miles, which made the pilot, Major Robert White, the third American to qualify for the astronaut wings. It has also achieved six times the speed of sound.

General White and his collaborators are already thinking beyond the air space of our earth. "Air and space are indivisible," he said. In hypersonic flight, pilots will circle the earth several times at five times the speed of sound and more, before they return into the atmosphere. Dyna-Soar is a manned air-space defense system which will operate with a device representing something between a plane and a satellite. The basic conception goes back to the calculations of the German rocket inventor Eugen Sänger. This project will help to solve many of the problems that arise in connection with putting a man into space or manning a satellite. General White thought that the speed of technical development would make space flight feasible within a few years.

"That seems to suggest that some form of manned flight is likely to remain necessary even from the military point of view?"

"Yes. As important as the development of the long-range ballistic missile undoubtedly is, it will never entirely replace the human being."

Piloted planes, long-range guided missiles, and manned spaceships all have their places in the U.S. Air Force development program; from the operational standpoint, they represent a homogeneous system. For example, after a period of indecision, it has now been decided to continue the development of America's most modern strategic intercontinental bomber, the North American B-70 Valkyrie, which will fly at three times the speed of sound and have a ceiling of over 80,000 feet; and it will probably be operational in 1963.

The B-70 will be supplemented by ICBMs. Of these, the Atlas and Titan are already operational, and before long the Minuteman, which is propelled by solid fuel, will join the American armory of strategic weapons. It is not intended that the ICBM should completely replace the manned plane. For the foreseeable future, the United States proposes to maintain a combined deterrent force. Fleets of nuclear-armed B-52 and B-58 bombers will serve to compensate for the Soviet's present advantage in the development of the ICBM.

The development of a two-engined fighter, the F-108, which would also fly at three times the speed of sound, has been abandoned. Its job will now be taken over by guided anti-aircraft missiles, particularly of the Nike type. But even in anti-aircraft defense, there will still be enough tasks for manned planes.

"We must always be a jump ahead of the enemy. The Soviets know that we will never attack. We did not attack when we enjoyed a monopoly of atomic weapons. But now that they have them too, they are exploiting them for a nuclear blackmail; politically ready for aggression, and prepared to strike the moment the situation appears favorable. Korea and Hungary are the best proofs. We therefore cannot afford to have the Kremlin get the idea that they are militarily superior to us; that is why we must continue to plan weapons for the future. To fight and win a global war is not the best way of defending our country and preserving its freedom. It is much better to be so clearly superior to the enemy that he will never dare to run the risk of war."

Among the thousands of rooms in the Pentagon, the one in which we felt most at home had the number 4C 931, which meant fourth floor, ring C, corridor 9, room 31. We soon found our way back there easily from the remotest office. It was the office of Air Force Major James F. Sunderman of Major-General Luehman's department, who looked after us with great efficiency and consideration.

The same friendly welcome awaited us in the corresponding department of the U.S. Army, in the person of Colonel Robert Shinn, whom we already knew from Bonn and Paris, and his assistant, Colonel Sidney Williams. And the U.S. Navy was no less friendly and helpful.

"Hello there," Major Sunderman greeted us. "I hope you've found your various interviews satisfactory."

While Mrs. Martin brought the coffee, and Mrs. Burnard ably supported her with the doughnuts, the Major leant back in his armchair with his hands behind his head and asked us cheerfully whether we had "anything on" for the evening of the eighteenth.

"Nothing in particular," we replied.

"In that case, you ought to be in Cape Canaveral that evening. The Air Force is going to poop off another of their firecrackers."

"But that's at least 750 miles away! A bit far for a little jaunt, don't you think? Anyway, how could we possibly get there in time?"

"Oh, I've got it all worked out. Here's the schedule. Get the orderly to wake you up at seven o'clock, breakfast at eight at the Officers' Club, and be on the airfield at nine. Nothing impossible about that. As it happens, Major Halm is flying to the naval airfield in Norfolk, Virginia in a Cessna 310. You can go with him. You'll have an hour or two to spare there, and you can use it to visit SACLANT Headquarters. And as it happens, Colonel Robert B. Good will be leaving there at three o'clock that afternoon in a C-47 to Patrick Airfield on Cape Canaveral, and you can fly with him. Get in touch with Lieutenant-Colonel Sid Spear when you get there. I've already telephoned him, and he's reserved rooms for you in the Starlight Motel at Cocoa Beach right on the sea. He's in the Information Department and he'll do everything for you. On the way back, you can visit TAC, STRAC, and USCONARC: that is to say, our

Tactical Air Force, Strategic Army Corps, and General Bruce B. Clarke, Commander-in-Chief of all the land forces in the United States. That's all been arranged. But first you must see Admiral Russell. And then Colonel Williams has made a number of appointments for you to interview various army generals."

Major Sunderman is one of those officers who sit and do their duty at a desk when they would much sooner be at the controls of a jet plane, or aboard ship, or in command of a tank brigade—the unsung heroes of administration. We often met these modest, uncomplaining men on our travels, and not only in the United States. Thanks to their personal interest and assistance, the recommendations of General Norstad and the orders of the Generals in the Pentagon were translated efficiently and pleasantly into fruitful encounters.

"If we hadn't command of the sea, we should be helpless," said Vice-Admiral George Russell. "Without a strong fleet, the United States would be cut off from Europe." The Admiral, who was born in 1901, has grown up in the tradition of the Navy and is committed to the importance of sea power. He has progressive ideas, and that is all to the good, if the Navy is to retain its significance.

"Our battleships are being sent to the breakers' yard or put into mothballs, but preferably in places where the water is fresh, or merely brackish, such as San Diego and St. John's River, to keep them from deteriorating too quickly; after all, you never know. The heavy cruiser is being replaced increasingly by the rocket-firing destroyer. But the latest development in the sphere of deterrence is the atomic submarine, armed with missiles of the Polaris type which can be fired from beneath the surface."

Today the U.S. Navy has 26 nuclear-powered submarines (nine of them fitted with Polaris missiles) and eventually it will have 182. It has 101 aircraft carriers (26 of them attack-carriers on active duty), 125 submarines, sixty-eight cruisers, 421 destroyers, and 930 escort, auxiliary, and other vessels, not counting a host of smaller vessels, making a total tonnage of 4 million, compared with 1.6 million for the Red Fleet, and 750,000 for the British Navy.

Admiral Russell spent many of his service years on board battleships and heavy cruisers, but in the Second World War he commanded the Tenth Submarine Fleet in the Pacific. He was present at Midway and Okinawa, two glorious names in the story of the U.S. Navy in the Pacific. It was there the Japanese drive was finally halted, and the way prepared for the attack on Japan itself. But the wider view has not prevented the Admiral from appreciating the strategic importance of a small inland sea like the Baltic.

"We therefore welcome the rebuilding of the German Navy. It represents another factor in the NATO defense system."

Germany's biggest ships at the moment are six former U.S. destroyers. "I've seen the Z1 myself," said the Admiral. "She had already been put into mothballs, but they restored her wonderfully. I've no doubt she's giving good service again."

"What is the relationship between SACLANT in Norfolk and the Commander-in-Chief of the U.S. Navy?" we asked.

"In his capacity as NATO Commander he isn't, of course, subordinate to us," the Admiral replied, "and he negotiates with us as he would with the admiralty of any other nation. However, as you know, he wears another hat as Commander-in-Chief of our Atlantic Fleet. In that capacity, he is subordinate to our Joint Chiefs of Staff, in which Admiral Burke represents the Navy."

"There are 175 Red divisions on a war footing; but that isn't all that counts," declared General Lyman M. Lemnitzer, Army Chief of Staff at the Pentagon from October, 1960, to October, 1962. "You mustn't be overwhelmed by mere figures."

General Lemnitzer, the son of a Pennsylvania shoemaker, is a broad-shouldered man with energetic features and compelling eyes that do not leave his interlocutor's face while he is talking. He was originally an artilleryman and during the Second World War he served chiefly with the anti-aircraft artillery. He was in command of the Thirty-fourth Anti-aircraft Brigade in England in 1942, in Tunis in 1943, and later during the landing in Sicily. In addition to front-line experience, he also served on the General Staff at Allied Headquarters, and with the Fifth U.S. Army. In 1943, he was appointed Commanding General of the American contingent of the Fifth Army; and in 1945, he became Chief of the General Staff of the Allied Supreme Command in the Mediterranean. He has also had diplomatic experience: on the Armistice Commission which negotiated the surrender of Italy with Marshal Badoglio, and again in the surrender negotiations with the Supreme Command of the German *Wehrmacht* in March, 1945, in Switzerland. In 1949, he was spokesman for the American Government during the NATO ratification debate in the Senate. When General Norstad retires on November 1, 1962, General Lemnitzer will succeed him as Supreme Allied Commander in Paris.

"We are in a very different position today, compared with 1949," said General Lemnitzer. "In NATO we have succeeded in creating a unified supreme command, and that is really a remarkable achievement."

The General considers land forces of great importance. "A country without a strong army lays itself wide open. Neither the navy nor the air force can do much if the home country is overrun by the enemy in the meantime. Only an army can defend territory without turning it into an atomic waste. And only an army can conquer and occupy without at the same time destroying the enemy country and its people. An infantryman on the spot can be more effective than a megaton threat which will perhaps never be carried out."

But, of course, it must be a powerful, highly mobile army with the latest equipment and tactical atomic weapons. As General Lemnitzer put it, "The best weapons today are the second best tomorrow. And the day after that they may be obsolete."

An army such as General Lemnitzer envisages is something more than a shield to ward off enemy blows until the strategic sword can strike; it must be strong enough to repulse the aggressor and deal a decisive counter-blow. In peacetime, such an army would be an effective part of the deterrent, because it would force the enemy to think twice before he decided to attack.

"In other words, an army should be a weapon capable of halting a Soviet attack and rolling it back even within the framework of a limited war?"

"The variety of aggressive possibilities an enemy may try is always unlimited." Even a local action could, if the countries concerned started to outbid each other, quickly develop into a general war. "We must therefore be adequately prepared for every possibility."

The question is, how much time remains for the West? It must be prepared for anything every day.

An army must be strong enough to win a land war against a powerful enemy even without the use of strategic weapons. And it should be strong enough to stop the enemy advance in the first place. It is, of course, quite clear that, given the Soviets' numerical superiority, we could not match them man for man. Therefore the balance must be restored by superior equipment, tactical atomic weapons, and first-class training.

Such an army demands a good deal in the way of modern equipment. "Security is not to be had cheaply," declared General Maxwell D. Taylor, Chairman of the Joint Chiefs of Staff since October 1,

1962. In 1960, the U.S. defense budget totalled $42.7 billion; of that $9.9 billion went to the Army alone. During 1961–62, it climbed to a new record high of $46.6 billion.

To set up a single armored division costs approximately $120 million, and an infantry division costs $59 million. These estimates were given to us by Brigadier-General T. R. Stoughton in the Pentagon. An airborne division costs "only" $40 million, because it can carry much less equipment.

The U.S. defense budget is larger than that of any other NATO country, not only absolutely, but in proportion to gross national product. The United States allots 10.4 per cent for defense; the corresponding figures for Britain, France, and Germany are 7.5, 6.8, and 5.3 per cent, respectively.

Apart from arms, equipment, and maintenance, actions which have to be carried out from time to time are not cheap, either. For example, the landing in Lebanon cost the American Army between $25 and $30 millions—$30 millions were asked for, and $20 millions were granted. Fortunately, as Lieutenant-General William Stevens Lawton explained to us, the emergency arose in July, just after the beginning of the new fiscal year, so that it was possible to meet the deficit from the normal budget. General Lawton is, so to speak, budget director of the U.S. Army, responsible for ensuring that the sums granted by Congress to implement the strategic policy of the National Security Council are properly expended.

Brigadier-General Hugo van Bond insisted that it would be a grave error to suppose that the new weapon technology had made the ordinary infantryman superfluous. Even in a nuclear war, a good deal would depend on the individual—perhaps even more than before. The decision would be obtained by human beings on the spot, and not by long-range weapons alone. There is still a great deal of scope for personal leadership. Nuclear weapons have not, as was first assumed, made generalship superfluous. Such problems were of great interest to General van Bond, since his field is Army ordnance. In conclusion, he assured us that the requirements of the NATO Alliance have the highest priority.

The most important weapon of the infantryman is still the rifle. But it has been greatly improved in recent years: the newest model is practically a light machine gun.

The people of the United States appreciate keenly the political significance of the Army. The right of the citizen to bear arms is part of the American idea of liberty, embodied in Article 2 of the Constitution. By far the greater part of America's young men still do their national service in the Army.

Today the Army is of political significance in an even wider sense. As Major-General G. Farrand, then Deputy Chief of Staff of the Army, put it, "If all you've got to set against the conventional weapons of the Soviet Union is nuclear weapons, then you've lost a great deal of political flexibility. We should always be in a position to counter aggression with corresponding means, graduated to the magnitude of the attack. But for this, you must have sufficient troops."

One must avoid the illusion of a nuclear Maginot Line acting as a barrier. If a Soviet attack should come, we must be able to meet it in a war of movement and launch our counter-attack. If we are, then it won't come to war.

All these men, accustomed to weighing facts carefully, are convinced that one must not allow oneself to be deceived by Soviet "peace offensives"—they might strike while talking peace. "To suppose that the Soviets might have given up their aim of world revolution is folly," declared Major-General J. C. Oakes of the Army Operational Staff. "Every soldier withdrawn from Europe is a victory for Soviet propaganda."

Today the United States keeps part of its troops permanently overseas. That in itself is proof that the Army is an essential part of the defensive system, including the deterrent, and that its role in war is by no means played out. There is the U.S. Seventh Army in Central Europe, a very important expeditionary force. Then there are the two groups entrusted with the defense of West Berlin; SETAF in upper Italy; two divisions and a light missile unit in Korea; a division in Hawaii, two groups in Alaska, and another in Panama to defend the Canal. In addition, there are seven Strategic Army Force (STRAF) divisions held in reserve but ready for action at any moment.

The U.S. Army, taking all military, political, and psychological factors into consideration, believes that if it should come to a big war, its course probably would be as follows: considered as a multicolored band, the "spectrum of war," the green of the cold war would merge imperceptibly, without any declaration of war, into the light red of the first phase of fighting; then the red would grow darker and darker, as the armed conflict grew more violent, with the use of both conventional and tactical nuclear weapons. This phase takes the greater part of the spectrum. In the critical end phase, when victory tips to one side or the other, might come the short violet band of total nuclear war.

The Army is essential for the entire width of the spectrum, from cold war to nuclear conflict, and beyond that, for the occupation of enemy territory and pacification. The task of the land forces is not merely to stop the enemy advance and repulse him, but also to function beforehand as part of the deterrent, and thus help to preserve peace—a task that is often ascribed to strategic nuclear weapons alone.

To remain battle-ready, an army must keep pace with the development of modern weapons. Today's infantry is a far cry from the doughboys of the First World War, with their bayonets and puttees. It is now highly motorized and equipped with tactical nuclear weapons and rockets.

Lieutenant-General Arthur Trudeau, Chief of Research and Development for the Army, discussed this subject with us in some detail. "What we need," he declared, "is small nuclear weapons—atomic hand grenades, so to speak, that you can give to every officer in the field."

There also have been great improvements and new ideas in the sphere of conventional arms—for example, the so-called flying jeep, which was developed under the General's guidance. This is a lightly armored plane which can hedgehop at about seventy-five miles an hour and reconnoiter enemy positions, while offering a poor target. It is armed for attack, and can also be used to carry troops.

General Trudeau said that the present tendency is towards the light, fast tank. The M-60, now in production, with diesel engines and the British 105 mm. gun, weighs fifty tons, but it will be the last of the heavyweights. In the course of the 1960s, there will be lighter tanks, weighing between thirty and thirty-five tons and driven by diesel engines or gas turbines. These tanks will be equipped with the so-called homing rocket target-seekers, and weigh less because they will not need a base for a heavy gun.

Light-armored cars for infantrymen are also in production, including one of duraluminum that weighs less than ten tons and could be carried by air for use in amphibious operations. The U.S. Seventh Army is already being equipped with this model.

Flying jeeps, tanks, and armored cars would protect their occupants against nine-tenths of the effect of nuclear weapons, including heat, blast, and radioactive fallout.

Trudeau regards the development of the vertical starter plane as essential, and he had a model in his office. It is, he declared, the only way to make sure that the plane can remain operational in battle areas; a highly mobile army cannot be burdened with airfield construction, which demands a tremendous expenditure of material, transport, men, labor, and time.

Further important developments include an apparatus which, by the use of infra-red rays, would permit a clear view of an entire battlefield in pitch darkness. It is likely, Trudeau said, that infra-red rays will soon replace radar in many respects. Then there is the so-called sun furnace, which is so powerful that on a dull October day, within a few seconds, it melted a hole in a piece of armor plate several inches thick. Finally, we were told of an electronic aggregate for guiding rockets; about 100 cubic inches in 1956, it is now a tiny cube.

"The Soviets are preparing chemical warfare on a big scale," the General said. "We know they train their people very thoroughly in this respect, and that today 15 per cent of all weapons stored in the Soviet Zone and Poland are of a chemical nature. The West must learn its lesson from this, and very quickly." It is not out of the question that chemical warfare may, to some extent, take the place of nuclear warfare.

The General regards the concept of peaceful coexistence as a contradiction in terms in the mouths of people committed to the destruction of the Western world; and he quoted Khrushchev's words to his comrades in 1958: "Of course we must realize quite clearly that we cannot coexist forever. One of us will have to go under. Well, we don't feel inclined to let anyone bury us. And the West doesn't care much for being buried either, so what must be done? Clearly, we must push the West into its grave."

When he chooses to talk about peaceful coexistence, Khrushchev naturally doesn't care to be reminded of such remarks, but it is well for the West to remember them, particularly when Khrushchev thinks the moment is favorable for a breathing space. He keeps his hands on the hot and cold taps of the shower, but whichever he favors at any given moment, his fundamental aim is always the same, to push the West into its grave.

In all negotiations with the Soviets, one should ask them to explain what they understand by "peace." If their representatives answer frankly, their reply can only be: "Peace is possible only when the classless society has been established; that is to say, after the victory of the world revolution." The West would know just how much hope of arriving at any real agreement such negotiations offer.

General Trudeau informed us that at the beginning of the Berlin blockade in 1948, he was instructed by General Lucius D. Clay to set up a "Task Force Trudeau" consisting of an armored division, motorized infantry, and a battalion of engineers capable not only of forcing a way through to Berlin, but of carrying out any necessary repairs and maintenance on the *Autobahn* and the Elbe bridges. He was, he told us, very sorry that this task force had never been allowed to go into action. The air lift had been a great achievement, but a breakthrough along the *Autobahn* from Helmstedt to Berlin would have had an even better effect. "The Soviets knew they were in the wrong," said General Trudeau. "We should have done it."

Perhaps such an emphatic proof of Western determination to resist Soviet aggression might have made the Soviets reconsider their plans for seizure of Korea.

27

America Defends World Peace

An urgent voice, its suppressed excitement unmistakable, came over the loudspeaker at Cape Canaveral. It was shortly after six o'clock on a December afternoon; we were standing on the wooden observation platform at the missile launching grounds. On its pad, about 2,000 yards away, stood the great Atlas rocket with which the U.S. Air Force was about to send a packet of scientific instruments and a wireless transmitter into orbit as a satellite of the earth.

The gleaming white rocket, illuminated by many searchlights, sparkled with frost. Only its nose, containing the pay load, was black. A small silver spurt of steam indicated that the liquid oxygen had already been fed. The scaffolding was withdrawn, and "Score," as the rocket was called, stood there, ready to go.

Newspapermen and photographers from many countries crowded the observation platform, all eyes turned anxiously on the distant rocket. Would things go according to plan? There is always a risk; the system has no less than 12,000 main components, which means that approximately 37,000 individual parts must all function correctly, if the firing and flight are to be successful. This demands utmost precision under conditions that few materials can withstand. Extremes of temperature develop side by side, from the minus 200° C. of the liquid oxygen, not too far from absolute zero, to the enormous heat generated by flames, which even the hardest metals cannot withstand.

The telecameras focused on the Atlas. Radio men in eighteen telephone booths steadily passed back their reports. In the armor-plated blockhouse about 150 yards from the starting pad, the final switch was thrown to set the giant into motion.

"T minus fifteen seconds, plus counting."

The gush of water cooling the base increased to maximum pressure—over 200,000 gallons a minute.

"T minus ten seconds, plus counting."

The telecameras began to whirr.

"Six, five, four, plus counting."

Cameras were poised in readiness.

"Three, two, one—zero!"

A tremendous roar sounded from the firing pad; red and yellow flames shot from the jet openings of the rocket and spread out. The loudspeaker was silent now, and you could hear the reporters counting under their breaths; ten seconds to go, and then the steel arms holding the rocket would fold back. The U.S. Air Force engineer on the platform clenched his hands and then banged wildly on the balustrade, shouting, "Go, baby, go!"

Majestically, the rocket soared from the ground, slowly at first, then at increasing speed. After a few seconds, it disappeared through the cloud cover and was lost to sight. Then it became visible once more as a glowing patch of light, when the boosters started up. A few minutes later—seemingly endless to the waiting observers and rocket team—a man hurried out of a telephone booth shouting: "Start O.K. That baby's on its way around the earth!"

"That baby," a 100-ton weight at the start and as big as the locomotive of an express train, weighed 3.9 tons when, after reaching a top speed of 16,000 miles an hour, it turned into the elliptical course which took it between 120 and 600 miles from the earth. A thrust of 3.9 million horsepower was necessary to get it into orbit. Score was now the biggest artificial satellite, almost three times as heavy as the previously biggest, Sputnik III. Although the pay load of this Atlas rocket was only about 150 pounds, compared with nearly 3,000 pounds for Sputnik III, the real success lay in the fact that here, for the first time, a satellite had been put into orbit not by guiding rockets but by electronic control. The Score sent performance data to an electronic brain capable of 10,000 calculations per second; and during the four and a half minutes that the motors were running and the rocket was still under remote control, it corrected the slightest deviation from the calculated course. Twenty hours later, Score broadcast a Christmas message of peace and good will from the U.S. President. Later it picked up wireless messages from the earth and returned them when requested.

America's space and missile program has made great progress since then, and the Soviet lead that has existed since the first sputnik went up on October 4, 1957 and has continued with the flight of their first cosmonaut Yuri A. Gagarin on April 12, 1961, and the cosmonaut "twins" Nikolaiev and Popovich in August, 1962, has been appreciably reduced. The first U.S. satellite, Explorer, went up on February 1, 1958, and the first astronaut John H. Glenn circled the earth and returned safely on February 20, 1962. Both countries have scored direct hits on the moon. But the United States was first —after two Soviet failures—to explore the close vicinity of Venus on August 27, 1962.

While being ahead of the Soviet Union in many scientific areas connected with space exploration, especially electronics, the United States started late with the development of powerful boosters. The Russian space capsule Vostok weighs over 10,000 pounds, compared to only 3,000 pounds of the Mercury which launched America's astronauts. Much bigger rockets are needed to lift up the Gemini spacecraft (for two men) or the Apollo (for a crew), and for this the Centaur and Saturn are being developed. The Advanced Saturn will be powerful enough to carry 100 tons into orbit. It will be operational in 1967 or 1968, and will be able to take an Apollo around the moon. With a nuclear rocket engine added as an upper stage, it might even supply enough energy to effect a manned landing. Of course, as soon as rendezvous technique in space is mastered, the capsule and any number of booster stages could be sent up into orbit one by one and assembled there, thus making it possible to build up whatever power may be required for a specific space flight.

For direct trips to the moon and return, however, a giant vehicle called Nova will be developed, capable of lifting 200 tons into orbit.

All these are projects of NASA, the U.S. National Aeronautics and Space Administration for civilian space exploration. Its annual budget amounts to 3.8 billion dollars in 1962–63. The military, however, must be interested in all aspects that have a direct relation to defense.

"I am a soldier," declared Major-General D. N. Yates at the time of our visit to Cape Canaveral, "and I'm not letting space experiments interfere unnecessarily with my military development plans."

Today, military defense can no longer ignore possible future threats by manned orbital weapons systems, which the Soviet Union is no doubt trying hard to develop. The U.S. military budget for space projects, most of them under General Howell M. Estes, Jr., of the Air Force, will be $1.5 billion in 1963. Existing military satellites like the Samos, for photo reconnaissance over Russia; the Midas, for detecting mass launchings of enemy missiles; the Discoverer, for classified missions, are still mainly intended to aid defense against missile threats from the ground or the air. But there are other, more advanced projects on the drawing boards or in the research stage, such as an unmanned satellite inspector to go after unidentified objects in orbit; a manned satellite interceptor to destroy hostile spacecraft; a death-ray satellite using beams of high energy against enemy targets; a twelve-man military test space station; or even an orbital weapons system. On August 20, 1962, the U.S. Defense Department ordered the Titan III into development, a solid fuel rocket capable of lifting twelve and a half tons into orbit. This is the first military rocket designed primarily for space assignments.

As for the operational missiles, the Atlas, when used as an ICBM, has a range of 6,300 miles carrying a nuclear warhead. So has the Titan I, traveling at a speed of 15,000 miles per hour. The Titan II, even more powerful, will be the first among the large ballistic missiles to use liquid fuels that are storable, permitting to keep it in ready-firing condition for a fast in-silo launch. The complicated and time-consuming task of pumping the fuel into the boosters is eliminated. More perfect still is the Minuteman, which uses solid fuels. It can be kept indefinitely, in "hardened" underground locations and directed at a predetermined target, ready for instant firing—perhaps from a central control station—in the event of a Soviet attack.

Eighty such intercontinental missiles are operational in the United States, compared to about 75 in the Soviet Union. The so-called missile gap has been closed. And in 1965, when some 1,200 ICBMs are expected to be in place, the majority of them underground, the U.S. will most probably be far ahead of the U.S.S.R.

Then there are the IRBMs, the intermediate-range ballistic missiles Jupiter and Redstone, under Army control; the Thor, of the Air Force; the Polaris, a Navy project, and others. The Polaris, propelled by solid fuel, can be fired from submerged submarines, even under ice cover. The six nuclear-powered submarines of the U.S. Navy are armed with sixteen Polaris each, and they serve as a practically invulnerable deterrent against a Soviet attack, particularly in Central Europe.

Owing to their great range, speed, and guidance system, rockets are much superior to conventional artillery. Only rockets can seek out an attacking plane at sufficient height and distance to prevent damage. However, they are still in the early stages of development—not easy to handle, and still far from accurate. In sum, rockets are not yet the "ultimate weapon."

Perfect or not, rockets are part of every modern army's equipment. In the United States and Great Britain, anti-aircraft defense is a matter for the army and not, as in continental Europe, the air force. The U.S. Army commands the Nike-Hercules, the Nike-Ajax, and the Hawk, and will command the Nike-Zeus—the advanced electronic long-range defense against ICBMs. Practical testing started with a spectacular success when such an anti-missile missile, fired from Kwajalein Island on July 19, 1962, intercepted an Atlas coming from Vandenberg Air Force Base in California. While not achieving physical impact, this Nike-Zeus came within range for a "kill" with a nuclear blast.

The Nike-Ajax, developed by the U.S. Army, was under test from 1946, and became operational in 1953. It is a complicated weapon—including the necessary ground radio apparatus, it consists of 1.5 million separate components. A Nike battery has 12 firing units and a 100-man team. These rockets would open fire on an approaching enemy long before he got close enough to drop his bombs. Accuracy is already considerable, but the Nike-Ajax cannot carry an atomic warhead, and its maximum speed of about 1,500 miles an hour is not fast enough to deal with ultra-modern bombers and fighters.

The Nike-Ajax is therefore being replaced with the Nike-Hercules, a nuclear weapon with a range of seventy-five miles and a speed of 2,000 miles an hour plus. Over sixty of these batteries are already operational in the United States, and along the Atlantic coast alone there are over 400 Nike emplacements equipped with both types of anti-aircraft rockets.

The U.S. anti-aircraft missile defense is completely decentralized. Even if headquarters were destroyed and channels of command disrupted, the units would continue to operate.

These Nike batteries, which are absolutely essential for any effective air defense, require much space. In Europe, they can operate only within the framework of the all-Europe air defense system.

Tactical Air Command, the smaller but no less efficient brother of SAC, has its headquarters at Langley Airfield in Virginia.

"When you're with TAC, no matter in what part of the world, you're at the front," said Lieutenant-General William D. Eckert, then Deputy Commander-in-Chief. He was in uniform since his fifteenth year, first in the National Guard of Indiana, and then in the U.S. Army. In 1930, he transferred to the Air Force.

TAC has thirty-five of the 105 wings of the U.S. Air Force. Of the remainder, forty-three belong to SAC and twenty-seven to Air Defense Command, which operates on the American continent. Of the TAC wings, seventeen are fighter wings equipped with B-66 Destroyers and B-57 Canberras; there are three light bomber wings and eleven troop transport wings, including four C-124 Globemasters, five C-130 Hercules, and two C-123 Providers; finally, there is a tactical rocket wing. The older types of fighter are gradually being replaced by the F-100 Voodoo and F-105 Thunderbolt, which fly at twice the speed of sound.

These squadrons are divided into two air forces, the Ninth and the Twelfth. The latter has had some experience with the watch on the Iron Curtain: up to 1957, it was stationed in Ramstein in the Palatinate. As the historiographer of the Twelfth Air Force, John W. Larsen said to us: "Together with other NATO planes, it formed a protective wall behind which the citizens were able to go about their business freely and peacefully. In Germany the Twelfth Air Force prepared itself for the task to which it may be called at any time— to erect a similar wall in any part of the world against any threat."

TAC also has the Nineteenth U.S. Air Force, which plays a very special part. It is a staff without effectives, a small and highly mobile command organization, a kind of flying headquarters. It is now under the command of Major-General Maurice A. Preston, with its base at Seymour Johnson Airfield in North Carolina. Its job, when called upon, is to set up a Composite Air Strike Force (CASF) which can get to any part of the world in the shortest possible time and be ready for action the moment it arrives. The units would be provided by the Ninth and Twelfth Air Forces, according to need. Major-General Viccellio trained them for their special tasks.

The idea of such a composite task force, for use in limited wars, originated with General O. P. Weyland, who brought it back with him from Korea, where he commanded the air forces of the U.N. What he had in mind was a self-contained, independent striking force, sufficiently powerful and mobile to fill up any dangerous military vacuum instantly, even in remote areas. Its size would vary with its assignments, which might range from suppressing local Commu-

316 NATO and the Defense of the West

nist disturbances in some neutral country to swift intervention in a war comparable to that in Korea.

"Should the Soviets ever attack, the tactical air forces in the countries bordering on the Iron Curtain and in the Far East would probably be the first to launch the nuclear counter-blow," declared Lieutenant-General Eckert. "In a big war, TAC would therefore operate side by side with SAC. But in a clash not important enough to warrant the use of SAC—i.e., a limited war—the United States would in the first place rely on her tactical air force, which would, so to speak, act as the fire brigade to put out a sudden brushfire."

"How would it go about that job?"

"Assume an appeal from the government of some small country —top secret, of course—for help against imminent Soviet attack. America decides to act. Orders would come from the White House via the Pentagon to the Commander-in-Chief of TAC."

First, various practical questions would have to be answered: How serious is the threat? How strong a force will be needed to stop enemy aggression? On the basis of such analysis, the Commander of TAC would give his instructions to the Commander of the Nineteenth Air Force.

Plans to meet any foreseeable situation are held in readiness, so that it can be decided quickly what types and units are needed from the Ninth and Twelfth Air Forces. The CASF can therefore be put together and on its way very rapidly. When it arrives in the threatened country, the enemy knows at once that it is only the advance guard of the U.S. forces, and this in itself may be sufficient to dissuade him from attack.

TAC has proved its mobility in repeated maneuvers stretching from Pole to Pole, and in action—for example, Operation Myrtle Beach at the time of the Lebanon crisis. U.S. Air Force units stationed at Myrtle Beach Airfield, South Carolina, were given the preliminary alert at 10:15 A.M., June 16, 1958. They took off and flew via the Bahamas, Lajes, Chaumont, and Wheelus in North Africa, and landed at Adana Airfield in Turkey at 4:17 A.M., exactly eighteen hours and two minutes later.

At the same time, the Soviets were deliberately fanning the Formosa crisis. There too, a CASF was sent out; in this instance, it did not go as one unit, but instead was gradually built up.

Simultaneously, TAC carried out a non-stop flight exercise over Scandinavia, refuelling in the air, first over the Bahamas, then over the Azores.

Withal, TAC still had sufficient reserves to send a strong force wherever it might be required.

This high state of preparedness is not maintained purely for the defense of the American continent. In one form or another, we have undertaken to support about forty nations against the danger of Soviet aggression, and all of them must be included in the planning.

Thanks to the development of air refueling with the KB 50-J, the TAC now has a practically unlimited range. Where, then, is the line between the tactical and the strategic now? A story, ascribed to an anonymous general, is told in TAC to explain the distinction. "Gentlemen," he began, "on a small farm there was once a cow. Every day, the farmer left his farmhouse, crossed a small bridge, milked the cow, and carried the pail back to the farmhouse. Now, if we shot his pail full of holes, that would count as close air support. If we blew up the bridge so that he couldn't get to his cow, we would cut him off from his supplies, and that would be tactical warfare. But if we shot his cow, that would be strategic warfare, because we should have destroyed the source of his supply."

Korea, Malaya, Vietnam, Jordan, Lebanon—these were all actions outside the NATO sphere, but they were nevertheless of direct concern to all NATO countries. No matter where aggression takes place in the world, it is always the same enemy; and whenever an attack is warded off, Europe and NATO feel the relief.

TAC also acts as home base for the tactical air forces under NATO. Their men are trained and supplied by TAC. Pilots and planes are rotated, so that experience is shared.

The big TAC tanker plane KB 50-J with us on board landed on Pope Field in North Carolina after it had refuelled two F-101 Voodoos and a tactical B-66 Destroyer bomber in the air. Fort Bragg is here, a vast U.S. Army Camp with training grounds and extensive terrain: fields, meadows, woods, and lakes, fifteen miles square. It is the headquarters of the Eighteenth Airborne Corps and of the Eighty-second Airborne Division.

The troops stationed at Fort Bragg are that part of the U.S. Strategic Army Force (STRAF) which would, if necessary, be sent overseas as the Strategic Army Corps. It consists of the Eighty-second and Hundred First Airborne Divisions, and the First and Fourth Infantry Divisions. The troops are ready to go anywhere at any time as an expeditionary force. The Hundred First Airborne, with headquarters at Fort Campbell, Kentucky, can be alerted within two hours and sent by air to any war arena in the world. Its first units would reach the front in no more than twenty-eight hours; its last, within six days. The Eighty-second Airborne Division can also be sent overseas by air, or, if time permits, by sea, like the First and Fourth Infantry Divisions.

We were assured that prompt and efficient as the arrangements were, STRAC was constantly striving to improve sea transport. Their newest ocean-going vessels of 10,000 tons are able to operate without normal port facilities. They can take on and put down troops and supplies anywhere along a coast, using their own ramps and equipment. These new ships have a speed of eighteen knots an hour, compared with nine to eleven knots of the Liberty and Victory ships of the last war.

STRAC plays the same role for the Army as SAC and TAC do for the Air Force. The four divisions are pentomically organized and fitted out with the latest weapons and equipment; they possess great firepower, and are highly mobile. Their motto is: "For the defense of the free world." At any threat to peace and freedom, STRAC can be sent into action—and with what speed! Whole fleets of transport planes stand by, consisting of such types as the Douglas C-124 Globemaster, which can carry a load of thirty-five tons or 200 fully equipped men, and touch down some 4,000 miles away; and the Lockheed C-134 Hercules, which can carry a load of seventeen tons or ninety fully equipped men, a distance of some 2,000 miles.

"It doesn't take long to transfer parachutists from transport planes to the front-line machines," Major-General R. F. Sink, then Commander of the Eighteenth Airborne Corps, assured us. "Then they can be dropped behind the enemy lines at once." He also commanded the Third U.S. Missile Command, a highly mobile unit grouped with ballistic missiles of the Honest John type, which can be transported by helicopter. During the last war, he was with the parachute troops as commander of a regiment of the Hundred First Airborne Division, which took part in the Normandy landings.

"STRAC is a U.S. force which is available not only in NATO territory but wherever in the world its services are required. In Europe, it would work in conjunction with SHAPE."

There are two airborne groups attached to the U.S. Seventh Army in Germany, and they too were trained at Fort Bragg.

"We could at any time send two or three groups in rotation to Europe for further training," declared General Sink. "Then our men could train side by side with the Germans, and gain much greater understanding of our joint problems. Such a group could be in Germany within twenty-four hours."

"Would that be possible with other NATO countries, too?" we wanted to know. "Greece, for example?"

"Why not? We should be very glad to coordinate our firepower with that of the Greek Army," the General replied. "And the same holds true anywhere. Radio techniques should be coordinated so that, in a war, we would not disturb each other's signals. I would advocate concern with the smallest details. We even ought to know what rations our allies get; and they, too, ought to be better informed about our affairs."

Many of the men stationed at Fort Bragg and with other STRAC units served in Korea. "That gave them some idea of what Soviet aggression means; and it makes them more ready to accept tough training willingly—just because they feel themselves citizens in uniform. Those boys know that Korea must not be repeated, either in Europe or in Asia."

Major-General William A. Harris, artillery commander of the Eighty-second Airborne Division, showed us through the headquarters of the Third Missile Command. We were familiar with the composition and tasks of such a missile unit, because it is organized on the model of SETAF, which we had already visited in upper Italy. The United States now has four such groups in operation.

"At the moment we're working to make the command more mobile," General Harris informed us. He was speaking about the project to adapt the Honest Johns and their firing ramps to transportation by helicopter. This has meanwhile been achieved. The air-transportable version is called Choppie John. "With these," General Harris said, "we shall have flying rocket artillery with maximum firepower at our disposal anywhere. That is important for NATO, because we all must maximize the effectiveness of our available forces. We could act, so to speak, as artillery sharpshooters, who destroy vital enemy targets."

The versatility and complexity of such a unit is shown by its composition: it has mobile headquarters; a special signals company with full equipment, including teleprinters with a range of about 1,200 miles; wireless communications on various frequencies; walkie-talkies; the actual missile unit itself; and, in addition, an infantry, an engineering, and a supply company; a meteorological unit; four observation helicopters and eight planes; television and infra-red equipment; radar equipment capable of being air-lifted for spotting purposes; and an intelligence group with interpreters and aerial photography equipment. Since the supply company can carry out the spot repairs, this missile command has a high degree of independence in the field. The rate of fire, three missiles per hour, is constantly increasing.

"We should take care not to underestimate the value of land forces," declared General Bruce C. Clarke. "The Soviets have far more divisions than we, but nevertheless they are modernizing them and increasing their firepower."

Before he became Commander-in-Chief of U.S. Land Forces in Europe, at the beginning of September, 1960, succeeding General Eddleman, Clarke was Commander-in-Chief of all land forces in the United States. That embraced six armies and the Washington military district, including the strategic land forces, army schools, army aviation, women's auxiliary corps, and all military installations. Until August 1, 1958, he had been Commander of the Seventh U.S. Army, with headquarters in Heidelberg. The town of Stuttgart recognized his services to German-American friendship and to the defense of Europe by presenting him with a medal, and the President of the German Federal Republic decorated him with the Federal Order of Merit. A model of an M-48 tank, carved for him by a German soldier in Grafenwöhr, always has a place of honor on his desk.

General Clarke's headquarters at Fort Monroe, Virginia, is on the site of the oldest harbor fortification in the United States, erected by a British military expedition in the year 1609, to defend the estuary of the James River. The new fort, an irregular hexagon surrounded by a moat, was planned by Napoleon's chief military engineer, Simon Bernard.

"I am particularly interested in NATO," General Clarke said, "because it is our job here to train the men who will be sent to Europe."

The U.S. Army swore in 216,500 new recruits in the last army fiscal year, and a further 70,000 went into the National Guard and the Reserve. The total strength of the U.S. Army is 870,000 men; the training of new recruits is therefore a major task. Almost a quarter of a million young men at colleges and universities are in the Reserve Officers Training Corps and every year 14,000 officers graduate from its ranks. The ROTC also comes under USCONARC.

"If war is forced upon us," said General Clarke, 'we shall need men to win it."

"You would certainly need them in Europe, General. I hope the Army cuts don't mean that the Seventh Army is to be reduced in strength."

"I know what you mean," the General replied. "When I was stationed in Stuttgart, I would gladly have had another division or two as reinforcements."

The Army represents the people to an even greater extent than the Navy and Air Force. And when the Army goes abroad, it becomes known to its hosts. The people see chiefly the soldier work together with him, and judge the whole nation by him.

"That is how it was in Germany, and how it would be in any future war. The improvement in the relationship between the United States and Germany lay largely in the hands the ordinary soldier. It was our job to get on good terms with the Germans. If we hadn't succeeded, we should have been forced to pull out. But we did succeed, and today the sight of the GI is as familiar in Stuttgart and Berlin as in Virginia."

"And they're just as welcome," we put in. "They a real earnest of German-American friendship, and a warning the Soviets that any attack on Europe is an attack on the United States."

While he was in Germany previously, General Clarke had had the Second and Third German Corps under him, and told us that he thought highly of General von Lüttwitz and General Mansel.

"I am one of those who would like to see the German Army grow more rapidly," the General declared, "but I appreciate difficulties. An army relies a great deal on uninterrupted experience, and in Germany the eleven years without training have left a gap. And the tremendous efforts being made in the background don't always get into the newspapers."

General Clarke's commitment is to the ordinary soldier, and his last words to us were about him: "The simple soldier clings to the soil—to that bit of it which is given to him to defend. Just as the peasant does when he tills his plot. And that is why people understand him best."

28

General Staff of the
Free World

"Soldi·e rarely militarists," declared General B. R. P. F. Hasselman, w· we visited in the Pentagon. "We here all have the same edu·n and background, and we understand each other. In the Milit·Committee, everyone seeks objective solutions, and therefore ·arely come up against a problem that we can't resolve in the en·

For a· time, General Hasselman was Chief of Staff of the Dutch A·nd up to June 1, 1960, he was Chairman of the Military Co·e in Permanent Session in Washington. Just as the North A·Council in Paris is the highest NATO political body, so the ·y Committee is its highest military body. It consists of the ·of the General Staff of all the allies (Iceland, which has no a· represented by a civilian), and it meets at least twice a year. ·st as the NATO Council Ministers are permanently represen· Paris by their deputies, so the Military Committee has per· military representatives in Washington. The chairmanshi·e Military Committee is changed annually in alphabetic o· the summer of 1961, it was taken over by General Adolf ·er, who succeeded the British representative. The chairm·he Military Committee in Permanent Session is appointe· committee itself.

"W·d be the Supreme Commander of NATO in the event of war·ked General Hasselman.

322

"That is something which looks like a problem only from the outside," he replied. "In principle, the Standing Group would have this function."

The Standing Group is a triumvirate of the American, British, and French representatives in the Military Committee, and its executive body.

In accordance with the NATO principle that the political power has primacy over the military, the Military Committee receives instructions from the Atlantic Council, on the basis of which it works out defense plans. The Military Committee and Standing Group control the major NATO commands: SACEUR, SACLANT, the Canadian-American Regional Planning Group, and Channel Command.

Since, of the two highest NATO organs, the political has headquarters in Paris and the military in Washington, a representative of the Standing Group is second to the NATO Council in Paris. At the moment, this representative is Major-General R. H. Barry, and he has officers of the three services from all the allied powers on his staff.

"Is the Military Committee integrated, as SHAPE is?" we asked.

"We are multi-national here, and not international," was the reply. "For example, in our Planning Group, which deals with specific problems, usually four officers of different nationalities work together. But whereas General Norstad as SACEUR has command over all the officers of his staff, regardless of nationality, and is himself only one-fifteenth American, the members of the Military Committee here represent only their own nations. But it is their job to produce a joint NATO decision, and I think I may say that they do just that."

General Hasselman is committed to NATO as a single community. He told us that the command structure of NATO is a living organism which developed well during the ten years of its existence, particularly during the past two years.

The fact that the Military Committee sits in permanence is in itself a step forward—an integration on a personal level. Formerly, the opinions of the General Staffs in the various countries had to be canvassed before anything could be done; this time-consuming procedure has been obviated by the presence of their representatives in Washington. It is of course easier to give instructions from above than to develop agreement on every question among fifteen nations. But it can and is being done.

"NATO reminds me of the bumblebee," said one of the staff officers. "A clumsy creature, theoretically unable to fly. But in fact, it does."

One must allow time for things to mature, and not force innovations too quickly. And one must be realistic. The United States has the arms, the men, and the money—it is, so to speak, the spring that makes the wheels go round. It therefore must have a special position in NATO. Anyway, the Americans make this easy for their allies, because they are the first to stress that it takes more than the mainspring to make a watch go.

The first German representative on the Military Committee was Brigadier-General H. G. von Tempelhoff. In his view, the particular value of the Committee lies in the fact that all nations are drawn into the process at the planning stage, with their various strategic desires and capabilities, just as they are in political consultations. Conclusions, political in the one case, military in the other, thus incorporate the ideas of all the allies, and represent joint endeavor. Thus every ally, large or small, can express its views before any decision is taken. This may seem a complicated process, but it has been demonstrated that clear and definite decisions can be reached rapidly.

General von Templehoff, who was born in 1907, very quickly won the regard of his colleagues by both personality and ability; he rapidly gained for Germany the stature envisaged in the Treaty. We asked him the same important question we had already put to General Hasselman:

"In case of Soviet attack, who would give orders to the major commands?"

"That's a fair question, especially since, in such an event which would probably happen very suddenly, the Chiefs of the thirteen General Staffs couldn't possibly all assemble in person at once in the Military Committee. But you must remember that the whole aim of this Committee and its executive, the Standing Group, is to give to the three main commands, SACEUR, SACLANT, and the Channel Command, already now in peacetime, everything they will need to repulse such an attack. As a result, they would be in a position to act at once."

"And what, in your view, would happen in the further course of the conflict?"

"The directives would come, as in peacetime, from the Military Committee and the Standing Group. The latter would be our supreme operational command. It is headed by the representatives of the United States, Great Britain, and France, and they can draw upon the best and most experienced officers in every conceivable military sphere, from all NATO countries. They also have safe lines of communication to all major headquarters."

The close connection with the military leadership of the United States in the Pentagon itself is an advantage at all times, and would be even more so in case of war, since the NATO sword has its main bases in the United States.

"Do you think the present form of organization could be improved?"

"It is being improved all the time, though gradually, in order to ensure its capacity for action at any given moment. One of our main aims is to get the best brains from all NATO countries in the most suitable jobs. We have also been discussing whether to keep the multi-national structure of the Military Committee or to integrate it. Each has advantages. So far, the general feeling is in favor of the multi-national organization, because it provides a forum for the military thinking of every nation."

What is the power of the Standing Group, the General Staff of the free world? Who are these men in whose hands rests part of mankind's fate, and who—albeit under strict political control—wield a power rarely equalled in human history?

The general atmosphere is simple and unassuming; there is no great display of uniforms and medals. The British representative, Air Marshal Sir George Mills, was commander of the Second ATAF before he took over his present post from Admiral Sir Michael Denny, who was in Washington when we were there. The American representative, General Clark L. Ruffner, like his predecessor Admiral Walter F. Boone, and the French representative, Admiral Max Dougout, are all men of long and varied experience.

"If the Soviet High Command were convinced that the West would not defend itself with nuclear weapons," Admiral Denny assured us, "they would lose no time in giving the order: Proceed west, full speed ahead!"

He did not mean merely that the Red Army would march at once against a NATO deprived of nuclear weapons, but that it was not enough to have them—the Soviets must also be convinced beyond doubt that NATO would use them at once in case of attack. "Without our nuclear arms, the strategic situation would be so simple for them," the Admiral went on, "that they would already be on the Atlantic coast."

If the Soviets had any doubts, they would try probing our defenses by infiltration or small acts of aggression. "That is why our shield forces are so important. They must be strong enough to resist any such attack. Should the attacker throw in reserves, the NATO shield would have to be reinforced, too. Once the Russians are convinced of this, that NATO would trump every move, they would have to make a decision: pull out their troops, or risk an all-out war."

The shield in Central Europe has its continuation in the North. It is therefore, in Sir Michael's view, essential that there be the closest possible cooperation between the center and the north, in order that no amphibious enemy breakthrough at the joint and drive deep into Central Europe. The shield needs modern land forces, equipped with atomic arms.

"Norway should be strengthened," Sir Michael said. "There, we have a small nation in a big country, vulnerable from the sea owing to the numerous sparsely settled fjords. For NATO defense, and for the protection of the Norwegians themselves, we need modern and highly mobile forces on the spot."

The American representative on the Standing Group was also a naval man, Admiral Walter F. Boone. He is a flyer as well, having served in the Naval air arm since 1926. He has commanded aircraft carriers in action, and during the Second World War he was Chief of Staff of a task force supported by carriers. For a period after the war, he was national U.S. Naval Commander of the East Atlantic and Mediterranean, and, like his colleague Sir Michael Denny, he is firmly convinced of the continued importance of naval power.

Admiral Boone sketched the general strategic situation for us: "The United States has obligations all over the world, many of them outside NATO. Through bilateral and multilateral defense pacts, we are allied with over forty nations. However, it is only right to say that our membership in NATO is the keystone of our foreign policy. The main purpose of NATO is to prevent war and to protect the territory of its members, and this it has done. There have been tension and difficulties, and much remains to be done, but on the whole the achievements have been greater than anyone would have thought possible ten years ago."

The military structure of NATO has stood the test of time. "Today it is fundamentally the same as it was in the beginning. The foundation is sound."

The conversation turned to the situation in the Baltic and the Mediterranean.

"Just take a look at the maps: from Moscow, Europe becomes a peninsula flanked by two inland seas. Strictly speaking, the whole of it is one defense territory."

From this angle, one can also see that aggression need not necessarily start in the center. The Near East, a junction of East and West, is at the same time a land bridge over which an attack could be carried into North Africa. The Soviets might well consider this one way of bringing Europe down without a frontal attack.

"In such an event, NATO would need considerable land forces," pointed out Admiral Boone. For example, in Korea the U.N. forces had undisputed command of the air, and yet they were unable to hold up the Communist advance. Admiral Boone was of the opinion that if the men in the Kremlin ever launch a war, the West must fight it through, until the objective of the NATO Alliance is achieved and the Soviet threat to the West is ended. Even after an exchange of nuclear blows, the West must have sufficient strength to force that decision.

"I am a naval flyer, as you know," he went on, "but for me there is no question about it: we shall need large land forces for the job. I have never believed that we could force the Soviets to capitulate by air power alone."

General Gelée was of the same opinion as his American colleague. "If it came to war, the advantage would lie with NATO," he declared firmly. "We are strong enough to repulse any attack and then move to the offensive." As Marshal Joffre once said, "*La guerre est une lutte de deux volontés.*" Once the will of the enemy is broken and he is ready for peace, the war is over.

Here again, as during our discussion in the Planning Department of SHAPE, we put the decisive question: "To what extent can the pseudo-religious will of this enemy to bolshevize the world ever be broken?" Just as Christianity can never abandon its aim to bring the whole world to the Cross for its own salvation, so the men in the Kremlin, blasphemously equating their world revolution with the salvation of mankind, could never abandon their aim, which to them is the fulfillment of an historic mission. Therefore an ultimate struggle started by such a regime would end only when that regime had lost the physical power to continue the war.

General Gelée declared that if we hoped to prevent such a war, we must remain strong; for his part, he did not believe that the Soviets would attack so long as they could see other possibilities of seizing power in the West. They did not desire war as such because it would be dangerous for their regime as well. They would prefer to use the Red Army to encourage revolution, just as they had done so successfully in the ring of satellite countries.

But one way or the other, land forces would still be necessary: for use against limited attacks, and for the great decision if it ever came. Whatever form war would take, it is an illusion to suppose that it would be short.

Brigadier-General Joseph R. Loiret, formerly Staff Director, gave us some supplementary details: "The Standing Group is, so to speak, NATO's strategic headquarters. The over-all strategic plans are worked out in the Military Committee. The policies of the individual allies are taken into consideration at a very early stage, and a joint NATO policy develops which the Standing Group then passes on to the main commands, who align themselves accordingly."

"And what is the position of SHAPE in all this, General Loiret?"

"Seen from a world perspective, astonishing as it may sound to a European, SHAPE is no longer strategic but operational; that is to say, its job is not to work out plans for a possible general collision between East and West, but to make preparations to deal with only one sector of that conflict. The operational plans of SHAPE and those of the other main commands are therefore brought before the Military Committee and coordinated there, before they are approved."

"Do you think that NATO ought to have one single Commander-in-Chief?"

"Not in peacetime. That would be too difficult to put through. In wartime, yes."

We put the same question to a Pentagon official from a very different office—Major-General Gerald C. Donnelly, then chief of that department of the Air Force which concerns itself with long-term planning. When you enter his office, you step, so to speak, into the future. The concern here is not only with technological advance, but with the development of military science. This department also gives thought to economic and political developments, because these provide the reality context for military planning.

What General Donnelly said does not necessarily refer to the here and now; he let his mind wander ahead to what might one day be a possibility or an objective. He therefore felt no reluctance about answering our question, which is usually regarded as politically delicate.

"Most certainly it would be an excellent idea to give NATO one personal Supreme Commander even in peacetime. But the political decision involved is not a matter for soldiers."

Couldn't one go even a little farther than that? Both in the United States and in Europe, influential people believe that the command structure should be tightened and simplified. Discussions on the point are continuous. For example, it is suggested that Channel Command could carry out its task just as well as a sub-command under SACEUR; some people even suggest that SACLANT also be subordinate to SACEUR. The question here is whether this simplification would be real or merely apparent; and if apparent, whether it might not, in view of the given situation, even complicate matters. But if NATO did decide to do this, it would become apparent that SACEUR is the most important of the major commands. By such organization, it would become what in fact it should be according to its assignment: a clear-cut and effective Supreme Command with adequate authority at the critical point.

Of course, a reorganization of this kind would in no way touch the Military Committee and Standing Group in Washington, which would remain the superior command for SHAPE; and it would certainly not affect the primacy of political over military power; that is to say, the supremacy of the North Atlantic Council.

"Our job here," said General Donnelly, "is to think about the future and strategic planning on general lines: big wars, air lifts, combined operations, and so on."

Before he came to the Pentagon, Donnelly was in the corresponding SHAPE department in Paris, from 1954 to 1957, and he knows the Continent well. He assured us that, although his department was under the Air Force, this did not mean that he believed that the big stick of Strategic Air Command could settle all problems. Both the Army and the Navy were necessary, too.

"General Norstad is quite right when he says that the shield must be strengthened. The enemy must know that wherever he attacks, he will meet with effective resistance."

General Donnelly was vigorously opposed to the theory popular for some time, and being put forward again today, though in a somewhat different form, that all NATO needs is a thin defense line along the Iron Curtain—a trip-wire, as it has been called—which would not be expected to offer any effective resistance, but merely give the alarm as soon as the first Soviet divisions should start the invasion, after which the rest would be left to the big counter-blow delivered by Strategic Air Command.

To adopt such an idea would, indeed, be fatal. The most dangerous aspect would perhaps be psychological; the Soviets might be
misled into supposing that a minor drive, such as would be necessary
to clear away the trip-wire, would never trigger off the counter-blow.
It must not be forgotten that a similar miscalculation on the part of
the Kremlin led to the war in Korea—and before that, to the bitter
civil war in Greece. If the same thing were allowed to happen on the
main Western front in Europe, there would be a terrible danger that
a probing Soviet thrust would swiftly develop into a large-scale action,
and finally into world war. This trip-wire theory also played a role in
the proposal to establish militarily thinned-out areas, and it involves
the same dangers.

General Donnelly pointed out that from the air, the countries of
Europe had become very small, and their joint air defense had been
urgently needed.

"But don't you think that even more is necessary, General? For
example, a joint European air force?"

"From the purely military point of view, it would have great
advantages. One large air force would be more powerful than the
sum of several smaller ones working together, even if the number of
planes and pilots were exactly the same. It would also be much more
economical to run, which means that, with the same means, you
could have a bigger and more powerful air force."

At the same time, it would do a great deal to increase general
confidence in European defense—not only among the big allies, but
also among the small, for whom the possession of modern planes
presents a heavy economic burden.

"Don't you think that a step in the right direction would be to
standardize plane types?"

"It would be an excellent idea. NATO would then use the same
planes everywhere. Each country would not necessarily have to possess all the types, provided the NATO forces as a whole were well
balanced. It would also be a tremendous advantage in maintenance,
repairs, supplies, and, of course, striking force."

It has often been said that modern wars have brought about such
progress as would not otherwise have been seen in decades. Military
requirements released the necessary finance, and gathered teams of
experts to work on particular projects, with remarkable results. But
the same influence has been brought to bear in other spheres, too,
and encourages development towards that greater spiritual, economic,
and political unity to achieve what is the mandate of civilized man-

kind today. During our various visits to the European headquarters of NATO, we could witness for ourselves how the soldiers of so many nations are beginning to consider themselves members of a supranational society—and we found just the same in the United States.

"We should grow closer together in NATO," said the General. "We've made good military progress, but politically we're still lagging behind."

Together with the director of the NATO Department in the Pentagon, Major-General John I. Guthrie, Donnelly believes that the military integration should be carried out on a firm basis of political union. Otherwise, there might be a danger that if the NATO fighting forces moved further toward integration, they would find themselves suspended in mid-air. "It therefore seems likely that the integration of national air forces, navies, and armies will not be realized until the nations have come together in a United States of Europe."

Our conversation turned once again to the problem of the deterrent. NATO wants peace, and will never unleash war. But because of this, NATO needs modern armaments and full preparedness. That is not its own choice; the situation has been forced on it by the constant expansionist urge of the Soviets. Ordinarily, the West is much more inclined to believe in the example of good will. Therefore it disarmed while Hitler was consolidating power, and again after the Second World War. But this conciliatory attitude is useless with totalitarian regimes; both times, it encouraged their aggressive urges, and not a readiness to maintain peace.

However, we must never forget that in the last resort, we want to win over the peoples; and that isn't merely a question of stronger battalions or a higher standard of living, or, indeed, of material values at all. As General Donnelly put it, "You can't win the souls of men without a faith—faith in a power that transcends this world."

29

Freedom—The Mission
of the West

Now that this report is coming to an end, it is perhaps time to ask whether the North Atlantic Alliance has fulfilled the expectations which accompanied its founding on April 4, 1949.

No one will deny that some of the criticism directed against it, by not only its enemies but also its friends, is justified. NATO today could be stronger. The Lisbon Conference in 1952 agreed that from ninety to 100 divisions would be necessary to defend Europe against Soviet military might, but this target has not been achieved. The new plan, adopted in December, 1957, put the minimum strength necessary for the protection of Central Europe at thirty divisions, equipped with tactical nuclear weapons. Even this has not yet been realized. Today, the keystone of the land defense of the West consists of only twenty-five divisions.

The problem of providing Europe with a joint air defense system was not solved until the autumn of 1960. Tactical NATO squadrons have had to be withdrawn from French territory because de Gaulle refuses to permit the storing of atomic warheads on French territory unless the French authorities are given a say in their use. The French Mediterranean Fleet is not to come under NATO command in the event of war. Allied troops may not be stationed on Danish and Norwegian soil in peacetime. A number of the NATO allies have not fulfilled the objectives they themselves agreed to; many of them have reduced the period of compulsory military service below the minimum level recommended by the military experts; still others are in process of abolishing compulsory military service altogether.

Speaking in London in November, 1959, the then Secretary-General of NATO, Paul-Henri Spaak, declared: "We have still not managed to obtain any worthwhile standardization of our equipment in NATO. With one or two minor exceptions, we have not succeeded in properly apportioning armament production tasks among the allies. We repeat experiments in one country which have already been concluded in another; we insist on re-inventing what has already been invented; and we refuse to trust our friends with secrets which have been known to the enemy for a long time."

Almost all these defects in NATO stem from political causes—the soldiers, within the limits set them, have in most areas done all they could. It is particularly regrettable that the principle of joint consultation, which was making such good progress, should have received some setback. It is no use trying to ignore the fact that in recent years the big powers made a number of grave decisions without previously consulting their allies.

None of these facts, which run counter to the spirit of NATO, should be glossed over. On the contrary, it is in NATO's best interests that they be clearly underlined—not as a criticism of the alliance itself, but of those members who failed in their duty towards it.

Still, after the consideration of NATO's faults and failings, one decisive fact remains: the North Atlantic Alliance did what it set out to do. Whereas before its formation, the Soviet advance seemed irresistible, since its existence no territory under NATO protection has been infringed upon. And still more important, this was attained without the use of force. The mere existence of NATO and the power behind it proved sufficient to deter the Soviet Union from attacking in Europe. And it must also be put to the influence of NATO that the Kremlin did not risk any major conflagration elsewhere in the world.

Does this mean that the threat to the West has diminished? Not in the least. The armaments budget of the Soviet Union in 1960 again showed an increase over the previous year. It far exceeds the actual Soviet military budget, and totals approximately $25 billion. To this should be added the $8 billion spent on scientific and technical training, which is geared to war production.

In his speech to the Supreme Soviet on January 14, 1960, Khrushchev gave the numerical strength of the Red Army as 3,623,000 men. But that is not a reliable figure, so long as the Soviet refuses to countenance any control on its armaments. According to Western information, the real figure is nearer four million. Insofar as numbers have decreased at all in recent years, the reduction has applied mainly to base and headquarters personnel, supply, training, and administrative units. There are 175 Soviet divisions on a war footing, and three-quarters of them are along the Western frontiers. Within thirty days, the number could be increased to 300. Within a very short time, the Soviets could throw seven million men into the struggle, not counting the sixty divisions of the satellite powers, which may be of a lower military value and unreliable.

According to a study by the Institute for Strategic Studies in London, the Soviets have 2,000 tanks immediately available for action, and a further 15,000 in reserve. They have nine airborne divisions consisting of a total of 100,000 men, and at any time, up to one-tenth of them could be dropped or landed from the air.

We have already spoken of the strength of the Red Fleet. It must be added that the Soviets have begun a great building program for the construction of 3,000-ton atomic submarines. The Red Air Force has also been completely reorganized. Formerly, its main role was seen as giving close support to the Army—as a sort of flying artillery— but today it is divided into a strategic and a tactical group. In addition, there are naval flyers operating from land bases, and the transport branch, making a total of 20,000 operational planes, 700,000 men, and over 1,000 airfields. In Eastern Europe alone, the number of airfields usable for jet planes has been trebled.

In its January, 1960, session, the Supreme Soviet decided that 1.2 million men should be "demobilized" during the next few years; the "lean years" caused by the fall of the birth rate during the war are making themselves felt, and the economy is desperately short of labor power. But Khrushchev made it clear that this reduction in numbers would not mean any reduction in Soviet military strength. Nuclear rearmament had so greatly increased the firepower that it is now possible to cut the number of effectives. He also mentioned plans to continue training the demobilized officers and men in territorial units after demobilization. This would of course mean the creation of tremendous reserves whose military value, because they could be called up at any moment, would not be far below that of men on the active list.

In particular, Khrushchev threatened with the nuclear and rocket weapons of the Soviet Union, which he said were more terrible than those of any other country; what he meant was obviously the 55-60 megaton bomb—a terror weapon in the cold war, but unimpressive as a technological feat, and too big to have real military value.

Today these Soviet strategic weapons are grouped together as an arm of their own. The commanding general, who is at the same time a rocket expert, is in charge not only of the 200,000 men who belong to this fourth service, but also of all the factories producing nuclear armaments, rockets, and guided missiles, and all research and experimental stations.

The T-3, which is the main Soviet intercontinental ballistic missile so far, is propelled by liquid fuel and is said to attain a speed of 15,000 to 18,000 miles an hour and have a ceiling of over 300 miles and range of 6,000. And there is little doubt that the two trial shots fired in January, 1960, from the mainland into the Pacific Ocean between Hawaii and the Fiji Isles were intended to show the world that the Soviet Union has rockets of even greater range, perhaps over 7,000 miles. Their accuracy was demonstrated by the twin shots of August, 1962, carrying the cosmonauts Nikolaiev and Popovich into orbit, one day apart yet in close formation.

The T-4 is an intermediate rocket which can carry a warhead weighing over three-quarters of a ton 1,000 miles. The T-2 is an intermediate rocket with a range of about 1,500 miles. In addition, the Soviet Union has a whole series of tactical rocket weapons—the T-1, which is propelled by liquid fuel and has a range of 300 miles and can be fired from mobile ramps, and the T-5, which is a similar weapon with a range of about 100 miles. There are also various smaller rockets which can be fired from motorized ramps. The main types of tactical guided missiles are the J-1, driven by two solid-fuel motors, and the T-7a, for ranges varying from 100 to 300 miles.

The radar-controlled T-6 is an anti-aircraft rocket which is already operational and said to be very effective. It has a speed of some 1,300 miles an hour and a ceiling of eleven miles, being about the equivalent of the Nike. The T-7 is a guided missile for greater heights, with gravity guidance. The T-8 rocket is effective up to a ceiling of over fifteen miles; it is a guided infra-red missile which homes on the warm exhaust of the target plane. The M-100 is an air-to-air missile for use against other planes, with an effective range of almost five miles.

The Soviet Union also has a number of guided missiles in use in the Red Navy. The Comet is a solid-fuel rocket with a range of about 100 miles, and can be fired from under water. It is said to be relatively cheap to produce, and is being provided to the Red Navy on a mass scale. Mass production of the Golem, which has a range of about 300 miles, has also begun. It is a liquid-fuel rocket fired from surfaced submarines. Both these weapons are intended primarily for use against land targets.

This is a short summary of the harsh military truth, and it represents the background of Khrushchev's constant threats. That he is prepared to negotiate at all must be attributed to the existence of NATO, and the West also owes its ability to negotiate to the Alliance. If the power of NATO did not exist, Khrushchev would not negotiate, but just issue ultimatums, and enforce them. For this reason also, the military power of NATO must be maintained and increased.

With almost gratifying frankness, the men in the Kremlin do not leave any doubt that they have never abandoned their aim to establish a Soviet world empire, and that they never will abandon it. They declare that, as part of Marxist-Leninist dogma, it is unshakable. Only the tactical means vary according to circumstances; and the rhythmic alternation between cold-war hostility and a pretended readiness to negotiate—without, however, any concessions—is itself a weapon in the psychological war.

Stalin's death on March 5, 1953, altered little. At first, the so-called collective leadership, uncertain as to the succession, adopted a more cautious foreign policy; but when the peoples dared to reach for greater freedom Red tanks at once rolled through the Soviet Zone and East Berlin on June 17, 1953. And in February, 1954, Molotov torpedoed the Berlin conference by presenting Stalin's old uncompromising plan for Germany, coupled with even more exacting demands.

In 1955, at the Geneva summit conference, Bulganin switched to an "offensive of smiles." He put his signature to joint instructions of the heads of government to their Foreign Ministers to bring about German unity by free elections. But already in November, the cold war was on again. When the Foreign Ministers met in Geneva to carry out their instructions, Molotov declared coldly that the time was not ripe for free elections in Germany, and he demanded the setting up of an "All-German Council" on a basis of parity—i.e., the formal recognition of the Pankow puppet regime, without any guarantee as to future German unification.

If the indictment of the dead Stalin at the Twentieth Congress of the Communist Party in Moscow on February 25, 1956, looked like the dawn of another liberalization, the illusion was shattered in the following November when Khrushchev bloodily suppressed the uprising of the Hungarian people. Then, in 1957, Bulganin dispatched a new series of letters to the statesmen of the West which seemed to suggest an approaching new "thaw," but on October 4 of the same year, the Soviets put their first satellite into orbit, and the thaw froze in again, in the cold war of Sputnik diplomacy. And finally Khrushchev, having in the meantime become undisputed leader in the Kremlin, felt himself strong enough to deliver an ultimatum to the West—his Berlin note of November 27, 1958.

But if Khrushchev had hoped to disrupt NATO by his policy of strength, by parading the military might of the Soviets and indulging in nuclear blackmail, he was certainly disappointed; and it was seen once again that the Alliance is strongest when danger seems greatest. What the Mayor of Berlin, Willy Brandt, said about his fellow Berliners was true of the whole Western world: "We have gradually got out of the habit of being afraid."

That may well have been the reason why Khrushchev drew back in 1959 and allowed the tension to relax. On May 27, he extended the time limit on Berlin; and in his discussions with President Eisenhower at Camp David on September 26, 1959, he dropped his ultimatum altogether—at least for the time being.

The "thaw" policy of the Soviet Government undoubtedly paid dividends, because it led to a temporary reduction of Western willingness to make sacrifices for defense. But when Khrushchev realized that the Camp David discussions were not going to give him what he had hoped for, and when his visit to Paris in March, 1960, brought home to him that his anti-German card wasn't a trump, and that there was no hope of disrupting the West, he abruptly switched back to the cold war. The U-2 incident on May 1, 1960, was nothing but a useful and welcome pretext to torpedo the summit conference and to mobilize the world-wide front of Bolshevism for a new attack on the West. The Foreign Ministers' Conference in Geneva in the spring of 1962 has hardly changed the existing situation.

The open support given to Fidel Castro's anti-American regime in Cuba was intended as a direct threat to the United States mainland; and the Congo crisis was exploited by Khrushchev for an even wider aim—to wreck the U.N. unless it makes itself an accomplice to Soviet penetration of Africa. How far this drive will go and what countries will be dragged into it will be decided from time to time as the Soviet offensive proceeds. Whether it goes beyond the limits of the cold war will depend on the unity and determination of the

NATO Alliance—which, despite its periodic problems, consolidated when the illusions regarding the "thaw" were dissipated. By his thrust into Africa, Khrushchev obviously is also trying to turn NATO's flank.

Up to the time of the abortive summit conference, the immediate aim of Soviet policy was to isolate the German Federal Republic and persuade the United States, France, and Great Britain to sacrifice it. But that policy failed, and now the Soviets are trying to isolate the United States from its European allies. The success of either of these variants would mean the end of Western defense and the victory of Bolshevism. The fact that for a while the main weight of the Soviet offensive was directed against the United States did not mean any real relaxation of pressure on Berlin and the German Federal Republic. With the erection of the Berlin Wall on August 13, 1961, the pressure has been increased and people are being brutally killed when they try to escape to the West. The situation was not changed by the Geneva Disarmament Conference, which has been dragging on monotonously since March 14, 1962, due to the Soviet refusal to submit to any international control. The withdrawal of the Soviet Commander from Berlin on August 23, 1962, followed by the appointment of Helmut Poppe, a Major-General in the army of Ulbricht's puppet regime; the Soviet threat to sign a separate peace treaty and turn the Berlin access routes over to that regime; the installation of anti-aircraft missiles along the air corridors: all these are measures to increase tension until it reaches a new climax.

It is, of course, inevitable that once the Soviets realize the futility of rocket rattling and war threats, they will again switch to a policy of apparent *détente*. What do the Soviets understand by peaceful coexistence? Do these two plain words have the same meaning for them as they do for the West—namely, peaceable and fruitful relationships among various governmental and economic systems, republics, monarchies, capitalist and socialist countries, parliamentary democracies and authoritarian states living side by side, each recognizing the right and existence of the others?

There is no need to speculate, because Khrushchev himself has explained it very clearly. In a speech delivered at the beginning of October, 1959, in Novosibirsk, after his return from the United States, he declared: "What peaceful coexistence means must be properly understood. Coexistence means the continuation of the struggle between two social systems, but a struggle with peaceable means and without war, and without the interference of one state in the internal affairs of another. It is a struggle, and that is our conviction, which must be fought out economically, politically, and ideologically."

In other words, peaceful coexistence means that the struggle is carried on with all possible means, short only of war—and even that will hold good only as long as NATO remains strong enough to deprive the Soviets of any reasonable hope of success by military means. There is the economic war, coupled with the political war of nerves —always with the same unchanging objective—the final victory of Communism all over the world. And this is not merely Khrushchev's personal policy, which might therefore change when he is eliminated —it is basic to Soviet dogma.

The political methods of the struggle are familiar: there are the Communist Parties centrally directed from Moscow—in all countries all over the world; there is the infiltration into democratic parties; the setting up of camouflage organizations (600 of them in the German Federal Republic alone); Communist influence on the press, broadcasting, the schools; and Communist boring-from-within tactics in the trade unions, factories, civil service, local administration, police, armies, and even the government itself, where possible. Is not all this interference in internal affairs of other states? By no means, the Soviets reply blandly, because all this work is being carried out by "national" Communist Parties!

Then there are the psychological methods: propaganda from Soviet broadcasting centers, while at the same time 2,000 Soviet jamming stations do their best to drown the broadcasts of the West; the flood of Communist leaflets—five million go through the mail every month in Germany alone, and another five million are distributed illegally; the activities of Communist agents—17,000 at work in the German Federal Republic (during the past eight years, no less than 16,000 Communist agents were caught, of whom 1,566 were brought to trial and sentenced); and finally, espionage, the stirring up of resentments, the steady attempts at demoralization—to mention only a few of the means by which the Soviets operate their version of "peaceful coexistence."

The third front on which Khrushchev has declared war against the West is the economic one, and this raises a very serious problem. He does not mean peaceful industrial and commercial competition. The battlefield is in the underdeveloped countries, where the Soviets plan to gain political influence by economic means. What the Soviets are aiming at was envisaged by Oswald Spengler in his book *The*

Years of Decision, published in 1932: to stir up the "colored world revolution" and, in alliance with it, spread the power of Communism until the final world-wide triumph is achieved. Three-fifths of the world population live in underdeveloped countries, the majority of them colored. Their annual per capita income is below $100, compared with average incomes ranging from $500 to $1,800 in Western Europe and the United States, where one-fifth of mankind lives. Between these two extremes we find the Soviet Union, Japan, and one or two Latin American countries which can be regarded as semi-developed, with average incomes between $100 and $500.

The offensive in this sphere started long ago, and it has already brought the Soviet Union considerable success at relatively low cost. "Between 1950 and 1960," NATO Secretary-General Dirk U. Stikker stated in June, 1962, "the West devoted $57 billion to economic advancement in underdeveloped countries. In the same period, aid from the Soviet bloc amounted to a total of $3.6 billion, only one billion of which has so far reached its destination." The goods delivered by the Soviet bloc over the years are worth only one half of what the United States spends yearly to assist the developing countries (apart from military assistance); and they are only a fraction of the $4.1 billion which even the Federal Republic of Germany alone raised from 1957 to 1961. An additional $1.25 billion has been earmarked for foreign aid by the German Federal Government until the end of the 1962 fiscal year.

Western aid was in large part in the form of free investments distributed over a great many countries and peoples, whereas the Soviets concentrated assistance at certain points carefully chosen for political effect. All in all, the West granted twenty to thirty times as much aid as the Soviet bloc. However, the political dividends drawn by the Soviets from their small share were incomparably greater than those obtained by the West.

In the Soviet sphere, all economic activities without exception are under political control, and this is a powerful weapon in Soviet hands. It is perhaps time for the West to ask itself whether free economic competition, which has worked so well in the West, is equally effective in the struggle against the Soviet economic and political offensive in the underdeveloped countries, and whether it would not be advisable for the West to plan and coordinate its economic policy and organize its economic resources, as it already does with its military resources.

A tremendous step was taken when France, Italy, and the three

Benelux countries decided to integrate their national economies in a European Economic Community and concluded the Treaty of Rome on March 25, 1957. About 170 million people on a territory of 450 square miles joined in a Common Market of free trade. They abolished internal tariff barriers, quotas, and other restrictions to the flow of goods, capital, and labor, and established mutually adjusted policies on fiscal matters, transportation, wages, and social welfare. The results of this momentous decision have already exceeded all expectations. Trade among the six countries has increased by 72 per cent, and trade between the Six and the rest of the world by 59 per cent. Industrial productivity increased 29 per cent between 1959 and 1961—as against 13 per cent for Great Britain and 8 per cent for the United States.

It seems certain that Great Britain will join the Common Market and then other states—for instance Denmark, Norway, and Eire—will follow. Greece is associated with the Common Market, and negotiations are in progress with Turkey, Spain, Austria, and Switzerland. Eighteen newly independent African nations—former territories of the Six, have also decided to continue their economic association.

Economic integration is only the beginning. Closer political association is bound to follow. A nucleus has been formed around which Europe may finally achieve its long sought unity. At the same time, the Common Market and the United States ought to move toward what President Kennedy—in his "Interdependence Day" speech on July 4, 1962—has called an Atlantic Partnership that would create a wide area of, at first, reduced tariffs and finally free trade. Such a partnership would promote prosperity in the entire free world and would present a powerful check to Soviet economic aggression.

If the economic power of the NATO peoples is strengthened by cooperation, it will be easier to increase Western aid to the underdeveloped countries. Great Britain, France, Germany, and the other European nations all have contributed to this endeavor, partly by immediate assistance to the Asian and African countries, partly via the World Bank, the International Finance Corporation, and other agencies. All this has been done in manifold ways, using the most various means and channels, as is usual in the Free Western world.

However, in order to avoid duplication, waste, and frustration, an over-all plan for rational and controlled aid is necessary. As the fifth conference of NATO parliamentarians in Washington recommended as early as 1959, a group of prominent, independent experts should assess the total requirements of all underdeveloped countries and draft a program to start them on the road to industrial and general economic development. Such a program need not be confined to the NATO countries; in fact, it should be supported by all the nations of the free world.

In other words, what is needed is a Marshall Plan for the under-developed countries. Both moral and political principles argue in favor of such a policy: a feeling of responsibility toward the less favored nations, and the hope that these peoples, when they attain economic standards more worthy of human beings, will also embrace a political order that defends and upholds the dignity of man. This calls for confidence and faith. No one can predict in which direction these peoples will turn. We must not harbor hopes of quick economic or political reward; indeed, we must not expect gratitude. However, in the long run such a policy will bear fruit. The free world will never have anything to fear from free peoples, and will be able to look forward with a clear conscience to the decisions of those whose freedom it helps to develop and improve.

Under no circumstances could the West afford to leave the field to the Soviet Union and look on while the underdeveloped countries drift into Communist hands. The obligation to act rests on all of us. As Paul-Henri Spaak succinctly put it: "The Communist challenge is not a challenge of the Soviet Union to the United States, it is a challenge of the whole Communist world to the whole free world. But in my opinion, we have nothing to fear provided that the peoples of the free world all join together to meet this challenge. If they remain united they will be victorious."

At the same time, it should not be forgotten that economically weak and underdeveloped countries in Europe itself, such as Greece, Turkey, Iceland, and Italy—and also Eire and Spain, though they do not belong to NATO—must receive aid, on the solid principle that charity begins at home, to help them bring their economies up to the general level.

However, all economic, political, and cultural plans would be in vain if freedom itself were not adequately defended by a militarily strong NATO. We must never forget that as far as the Soviets are concerned, a *détente* merely means—to paraphrase a word of Clause-witz—the continuation of the same struggle by adoption of other means. Much as a *détente* and a real understanding based on the free will of the people were to be denied, we must never forget that this is not what Khrushchev means by peaceful coexistence. Therefore it would be folly, a frivolous game with existence, if the free world ever allowed itself to be inveigled into lowering its guard.

Experience suggests that a regime which rose by violence, is based on violence, and has raised violence to a principle, can survive only by violence. It may well be that this is the fundamental weakness of a regime which is desperately anxious to create an impression of strength and unity.

Variety, controversy, and a flexible quest for solutions are the foundations of human freedom. Bolshevism, which ruthlessly suppresses the impulses of human nature, regards such behavior as a sign of weakness. Hitler, to the misfortune of Germany and many other countries, was certain that the "degenerate" democracies would never summon enough strength to form an effective front against him. Every concession merely served to reinforce this erroneous judgment. Today once again, the chief danger to world peace might be that the totalitarian aggressor will mistake the profound desire of the free peoples for peace, and their willingness to negotiate, as a sign of weakness. From this point of view, the shock produced in the West by Soviet war threats, by subversive orders to all Communist Parties and fifth columns, by Khrushchev's support of Castro in Cuba, by his efforts to wreck the U.N. in order to gain a free hand in the Congo—the shock was of a salutary nature. This warning, necessary despite all that had gone before, will be effective for a while. But there is a danger that a reaction against this shock will pave the way again for a new "offensive of smiles" whenever the men in the Kremlin conclude that this would better suit their purposes.

As long as the United States had a monopoly of nuclear power, or, together with Great Britain, enjoyed a great superiority, world peace was secure. Today the nuclear armaments piled up by the Soviets have created a balance of terror. But it is a precarious balance. Because the use of strategic weapons by either side would mean the loss of millions of lives and intolerable devastation, the danger of conventional war has once again increased. The men in the Kremlin might be persuaded to believe that the Western powers would hesitate to employ nuclear weapons to repel an act of aggression that did not actually threaten their existence. Even if they recognized their error at once after the attack, it would be too late.

Thus it is all the more urgent for the countries joined in NATO to increase the strength of their shield forces. These must be strong enough to halt a conventional attack and to force the Soviets to make

344   NATO and the Defense of the West

a second decision: either to break off the attack and withdraw, or to unleash an all-out war which—whatever happened to the West—would bring about the collapse of the Soviet regime. For this purpose, thirty divisions are needed in Central Europe, and another sixty in reserve, readily available to the NATO commanders.

The shield forces will thereby become an effective part of the deterrent. These divisions must be uniformly equipped with tactical nuclear weapons and thoroughly trained in their use, like the Soviet divisions they would face. At the same time, they must be in a position to fight with conventional weapons, in order that the policy of the NATO powers may remain flexible enough to choose the kind of defense appropriate at any given moment.

On the Western side, the President of the United States and the British Cabinet will decide if and when nuclear weapons are to be used by the West. France is also a member of the atomic club now, and she will undoubtedly press on as rapidly as possible to the production of nuclear weapons and their carriers. In consequence, the Western nuclear powers will have to agree on a joint policy. But one thing is clear: the preservation of peace must remain our chief anxiety, and the United States, as by far the strongest nuclear power of the West, must never allow the Soviets to doubt for one moment not only the ability but also the determination of the West to deliver an immediate counter-blow.

The vigorous efforts of the United States after the "Sputnik shock" of October, 1956, have practically closed the so-called missile gap. Now that the Polaris is operational, the ancient expression "command of the sea" has taken on a new meaning; and the Soviets have been very largely deprived of the advantage of a surprise attack with ICBMs. The U.S. solid-fuel rocket Minuteman has also become operational during 1962, safely hidden in underground emplacements. The establishment, in the autumn of 1960, of a central planning department under General Thomas S. Power, Commander of SAC, to determine the most suitable enemy targets was of political importance, apart from its obvious military implications; because the effectiveness of the deterrent must be known to the Soviets and to America's own allies if public opinion is to be strengthened to resist attempts at intimidation and to reject Soviet "neutralist" propaganda.

The welcome realism of the Soviets has so far restrained them from making direct attack on any part of NATO territory, but they have never ceased their efforts to split NATO and separate the United States from her European allies. Such efforts, if successful, would fundamentally change the entire situation, and therefore the Soviets stop at nothing short of war: threats, promises, subversion. They fail repeatedly, but as often as they fail they try again, and they will continue to try. All their attacks on the free status of Berlin are part and parcel of the general plan to undermine, demoralize, and finally destroy NATO. Their most daring thrust so far was the erection of the wall on August 13, 1961—in open defiance of the existing agreements and treaties. It was a hard blow for the city of Berlin; but the psychological aspects are even more fraught with danger. The fact that this wall was permitted to go up without immediate counter-action may encourage the Soviet leadership's tendency toward miscalculation. If the Soviets should once come to believe that they could commit "limited" acts of aggression with impunity (which would, in fact, shatter the whole concept of Western defense because the West would not dare to answer with effective retaliation), then the danger of the Third World War would be very real indeed.

The indispensable basis for effective military preparedness is political unity; and in this matter the West must allow neither fear nor the enemy to counsel them. The North Atlantic Alliance arose at a critical time in the history of Europe, whose peoples had once more come to a realization of their essential community. By their side was the great American nuclear advantage. Today, any people foolish enough to abandon the alliance of the free world would soon find itself friendless and alone, exposed to the nuclear blackmail of the Soviets. And if NATO should cease to exist, there would be no second chance to create another, because there would hardly ever again be so powerful a deterrent to Soviet interference as once existed in America's atomic monopoly.

The aggressive policy of the Soviets keeps the world in a constant political fever, but at the same time it encourages a feeling of solidarity in the free world, thus strengthening NATO. To make any prophecies is not the task of this book, though one can say without fear of exaggeration that the coming years will be dominated by the same struggle between Bolshevism and the free world, by the same struggle for freedom against oppression, that has run like a red thread through the history of the world. Our generation will never be in a position to contract out of it, nor should it ever wish to.

We know that it would be too easy to see the world in categories of good and evil, black and white. We must not forget that the people behind the Iron Curtain, and the people in Russia in particular, are faced with the same struggle. Unfortunately, today they are crushed by a regime which stops at nothing in its attempts to establish the rule of Godlessness throughout the world.

At the same time, there can be no doubt whatever that humanity stands on the side of the free world and buttresses the political order which the free peoples have developed. Of course it is a humanity with weaknesses and failings. Even in the hands of the West, the hydrogen bomb remains a terrible weapon, threatening death to millions of people. Long-range missiles and strategic weapons of a destructive power greater than the world has ever known do not become sacramental objects because they are in the hands of NATO. But what does give them a moral justification is NATO's determined commitment to ensure that they shall not be used.

But the defense of the West cannot rest solely on military strength. From time immemorial, as long as there has been a struggle for freedom, it was carried as well by moral force—by the power of the spirit. The West will have that power when it recognizes freedom not only as a national or economic value, to be protected against the external enemy, but as a moral obligation—a God-given human birthright to be realized among all mankind.

It is not only a matter of freedom from external domination, but also of a people's spiritual freedom. The fateful names of Marathon and Salamis stand beside those of Harmodios and Aristogeiton, who freed Athens from tyranny. Their statue, the work of Anthenor, was captured and carried off by Xerxes, but Xerxes himself was vanquished by the power of liberty, which those two men had served, and thus their deed, too, stands at the beginning of Europe's freedom. And there is one certainty on which we can rely: the allies of freedom are not confined to the peoples of the North Atlantic Community. They are to be found wherever men live, no matter what their tongue or race. Their humanity itself makes them, whether they know it or not, allies of the free world.

If in this decade, introduced by the tocsin of freedom sounding defiantly in Berlin and heard far behind the Iron Curtain, NATO can succeed in preserving world peace, then perhaps in the time gained, human nature itself will come to our aid in the great moral and spiritual struggle.

Once that happens, NATO will no longer need its military strength; the victory through peace and for peace will have been won—not for this people or that, but for the freedom of all mankind.

Appendix I

NORTH ATLANTIC TREATY
Washington, D.C., 4 April, 1949*

The Parties to this Treaty reaffirm their faith in the purposes and principles of the Charter of the United Nations and their desire to live in peace with all peoples and all Governments.

They are determined to safeguard the freedom, common heritage and civilization of their peoples, founded on the principles of democracy, individual liberty and the rule of law.

They seek to promote stability and well-being in the North Atlantic area.

They are resolved to unite their efforts for collective defence and for the preservation of peace and security.

They therefore agree to this North Atlantic Treaty:

ARTICLE 1

The Parties undertake, as set forth in the Charter of the United Nations, to settle any international dispute in which they may be involved by peaceful means in such a manner that international peace and security and justice are not endangered, and to refrain in their international relations from the threat or use of force in any manner inconsistent with the purposes of the United Nations.

ARTICLE 2

The Parties will contribute toward the further development of peaceful and friendly international relations by strengthening their free institutions, by bringing about a better understanding of the principles upon which these institutions are founded, and by promoting conditions of stability and well-being. They will seek to eliminate conflict in their

* The Treaty came into force on 24 August, 1949, after the deposition of the ratifications of all signatory states.

international economic policies and will encourage economic collaboration between any or all of them.

ARTICLE 3

In order more effectively to achieve the objectives of this Treaty, the Parties, separately and jointly, by means of continuous and effective self-help and mutual aid, will maintain and develop their individual and collective capacity to resist armed attack.

ARTICLE 4

The Parties will consult together whenever, in the opinion of any of them, the territorial integrity, political independence or security of any of the Parties is threatened.

ARTICLE 5

The Parties agree that an armed attack against one or more of them in Europe or North America shall be considered an attack against them all, and consequently they agree that, if such an armed attack occurs, each of them, in exercise of the right of individual or collective self-defence recognized by Article 51 of the Charter of the United Nations, will assist the Party or Parties so attacked by taking forthwith, individually and in concert with the other Parties, such action as it deems necessary, including the use of armed force, to restore and maintain the security of the North Atlantic area.

Any such armed attack and all measures taken as a result thereof shall immediately be reported to the Security Council. Such measures shall be terminated when the Security Council has taken the measures necessary to restore and maintain international peace and security.

ARTICLE 6*

For the purpose of Article 5 an armed attack on one or more of the Parties is deemed to include an armed attack on the territory of any of the Parties in Europe or North America, on the Algerian Departments of France, on the occupation forces of any Party in Europe, on the islands under the jurisdiction of any Party in the North Atlantic area north of the Tropic of Cancer or on the vessels or aircraft in this area of any of the Parties.

ARTICLE 7

This Treaty does not affect, and shall not be interpreted as affecting, in any way the rights and obligations under the Charter of the Parties

* The definition of the territories to which Article 5 applies was revised by Article 11 of the Protocol to the North Atlantic Treaty on the accession of Greece and Turkey.

which are members of the United Nations, or the primary responsibility of the Security Council for the maintenance of international peace and security.

ARTICLE 8

Each Party declares that none of the international engagements now in force between it and any other of the Parties or any third State is in conflict with the provisions of this Treaty, and undertakes not to enter into any international engagement in conflict with this Treaty.

ARTICLE 9

The Parties hereby establish a council, on which each of them shall be represented to consider matters concerning the implementation of this Treaty. The Council shall be so organized as to be able to meet promptly at any time. The Council shall set up such subsidiary bodies as may be necessary; in particular it shall establish immediately a defence committee which shall recommend measures for the implementation of Articles 3 and 5.

ARTICLE 10

The Parties may, by unanimous agreement, invite any other European State in a position to further the principles of this Treaty and to contribute to the security of the North Atlantic area to accede to this Treaty. Any State so invited may become a party to the Treaty by depositing its instrument of accession with the Government of the United States of America. The Government of the United States of America will inform each of the Parties of the deposit of each such instrument of accession.

ARTICLE 11

This Treaty shall be ratified and its provisions carried out by the Parties in accordance with their respective constitutional processes. The instruments of ratification shall be deposited as soon as possible with the Government of the United States of America, which will notify all the other signatories of each deposit. The Treaty shall enter into force between the States which have ratified it as soon as the ratifications of the majority of the signatories, including the ratifications of Belgium, Canada, France, Luxembourg, the Netherlands, the United Kingdom and the United States, have been deposited and shall come into effect with respect to other States on the date of the deposit of their ratifications.

ARTICLE 12

After the Treaty has been in force for ten years, or at any time thereafter, the Parties shall, if any of them so requests, consult together for the purpose of reviewing the Treaty, having regard for the factors then affecting peace and security in the North Atlantic area, including the development of universal as well as regional arrangements under the Charter of the United Nations for the maintenance of international peace and security.

ARTICLE 13

After the Treaty has been in force for twenty years, any Party may cease to be a party one year after its notice of denunciation has been given to the Government of the United States of America, which will inform the Governments of the other Parties of the deposit of each notice of denunciation.

ARTICLE 14

This Treaty, of which the English and French texts are equally authentic, shall be deposited in the archives of the Government of the United States of America. Duly certified copies will be transmitted by that Government to the Governments of the other signatories.

Appendix II

PROTOCOL TO THE NORTH ATLANTIC TREATY ON THE ACCESSION OF GREECE AND TURKEY
London, 22 October, 1951*

The Parties to the North Atlantic Treaty, signed at Washington on 4 April, 1949,

Being satisfied that the security of the North Atlantic area will be enhanced by the accession of the Kingdom of Greece and the Republic of Turkey to that Treaty,

Agree as follows:

ARTICLE 1

Upon the entry into force of this Protocol, the Government of the United States of America shall, on behalf of all the Parties, communicate to the Government of the Kingdom of Greece and the Government of the Republic of Turkey an invitation to accede to the North Atlantic Treaty, as it may be modified by Article II of the present Protocol. Thereafter the Kingdom of Greece and the Republic of Turkey shall each become a Party on the date when it deposits its instrument of accession with the Government of the United States of America in accordance with Article 10 of the Treaty.

ARTICLE 2

If the Republic of Turkey becomes a Party to the North Atlantic Treaty, Article 6 of the Treaty shall, as from the date of the deposit by the Government of the Republic of Turkey of its instrument of accession with the Government of the United States of America, be modified to read as follows:

"For the purpose of Article 5, an armed attack on one or more of the Parties is deemed to include an armed attack—

* After final ratification of this Protocol, Greece and Turkey acceded to the Treaty on 18 February, 1952.

(1) on the territory of any of the Parties in Europe or North America, on the Algerian Departments of France, on the territory of Turkey or on the islands under the jurisdiction of any of the Parties in the North Atlantic area north of the Tropic of Cancer;

(2) on the forces, vessels, or aircraft of any of the Parties, when in or over these territories or any other area in Europe in which occupation forces of any of the Parties were stationed on the date when the Treaty entered into force or the Mediterranean Sea or the North Atlantic area north of the Tropic of Cancer."

ARTICLE 3

The present Protocol shall enter into force when each of the Parties to the North Atlantic Treaty has notified the Government of the United States of America of its acceptance thereof. The Government of the United States of America shall inform all the Parties of the North Atlantic Treaty of the date of the receipt of each such notification and of the date of the entry into force of the present Protocol.

ARTICLE 4

The present Protocol, of which the English and French texts are equally authentic, shall be deposited in the Archives of the Government of the United States of America. Duly certified copies thereof shall be transmitted by the Government to the Governments of all the Parties to the North Atlantic Treaty.

Appendix III

PROTOCOL TO THE NORTH ATLANTIC TREATY
ON THE ACCESSION
OF THE FEDERAL REPUBLIC OF GERMANY
Paris, 23 October, 1954*

The Parties to the North Atlantic Treaty signed at Washington on 4 April, 1949,

Being satisfied that the security of the North Atlantic area will be enhanced by the accession of the Federal Republic of Germany to that Treaty, and

Having noted that the Federal Republic of Germany has, by a declaration dated 3 October, 1954, accepted the obligations set forth in Article 3 of the Charter of the United Nations and has undertaken upon its accession to the North Atlantic Treaty to refrain from any action inconsistent with the strictly defensive character of that Treaty, and

Having further noted that all member governments have associated themselves with the declaration also made on 3 October, 1954, by the Governments of the United States of America, the United Kingdom of Great Britain and Northern Ireland and the French Republic in connection with the aforesaid declaration of the Federal Republic of Germany.

Agree as follows:

ARTICLE 1

Upon the entry into force of the present Protocol, the Government of the United States of America shall on behalf of all the Parties communicate to the Government of the Federal Republic of Germany an invitation to accede to the North Atlantic Treaty. Thereafter the Federal Republic of Germany shall become a Party to that Treaty on the date when it deposits its instrument of accession with the Government of the United States of America in accordance with Article 10 of the Treaty.

* After final ratification of this Protocol, the Federal Republic of Germany acceded to the Treaty on 5 May, 1955.

ARTICLE 2

The present Protocol shall enter into force, when (a) each of the Parties to the North Atlantic Treaty has notified to the Government of the United States of America its acceptance thereof, (b) all instruments of ratification of the Protocol modifying and completing the Brussels Treaty have been deposited with the Belgian Government, and (c) all instruments of ratification or approval of the Convention on the Presence of Foreign Forces in the Federal Republic of Germany have been deposited with the Government of the Federal Republic of Germany. The Government of the United States of America shall inform the other Parties to the North Atlantic Treaty of the date of the receipt of each notification of acceptance of the present Protocol and of the date of the entry into force of the present Protocol.

ARTICLE 3

The present Protocol, of which the English and French texts are equally authentic, shall be deposited in the Archives of the Government of the United States of America. Duly certified copies thereof shall be transmitted by that Government to the Governments of the other Parties to the North Atlantic Treaty.

Appendix IV

EXCERPTS FROM THE BRUSSELS TREATY
Signed in Brussels on March 17, 1948

His Royal Highness the Prince Regent of Belgium, the President of the French Republic, President of the French Union, Her Royal Highness the Grand Duchess of Luxembourg, Her Majesty the Queen of the Netherlands and His Majesty the King of Great Britain, Ireland and the British Dominions beyond the Seas,

Resolved

To reaffirm their faith in fundamental human rights, in the dignity and worth of the human person and in the other ideals proclaimed in the Charter of the United Nations;

To fortify and preserve the principles of democracy, personal freedom and political liberty, the constitutional traditions and the rule of law, which are their common heritage;

To strengthen, with these aims in view, the economic, social and cultural ties by which they are already united;

To co-operate loyally and to co-ordinate their efforts to create in Western Europe a firm basis for European economic recovery;

To afford assistance to each other, in accordance with the Charter of the United Nations, in maintaining international peace and security and in resisting any policy of aggression;

To take such steps as may be held to be necessary in the event of a renewal by Germany of a policy of aggression;

To associate progressively in the pursuance of these aims other States inspired by the same ideals and animated by the like determination;

Desiring for these purposes to conclude a treaty for collaboration in economic, social and cultural matters and for collective self-defence;

Have appointed as their Plenipotentiaries: [The text then names them] who, having exhibited their full powers found in good and due form,

have agreed as follows:

ARTICLE 1

Convinced of the close community of their interests and of the necessity of uniting in order to promote the economic recovery of Europe, the High Contracting Parties will so organise and co-ordinate their economic activities as to produce the best possible results, by the elimination of conflict in their economic policies, the co-ordination of production and the development of commercial exchanges.

The co-operation provided for in the preceding paragraph, which will be effected through the Consultative Council referred to in Article 7 as well as through other bodies, shall not involve any duplication of, or prejudice to, the work of other economic organisations in which the High Contracting Parties are or may be represented but shall on the contrary assist the work of those organisations.

ARTICLE 2

The High Contracting Parties will make every effort in common, both by direct consultation and in specialised agencies, to promote the attainment of a higher standard of living by their peoples and to develop on corresponding lines the social and other related services of their countries.

The High Contracting Parties will consult with the object of achieving the earliest possible application of recommendations of immediate practical interest, relating to social matters, adopted with their approval in the specialised agencies.

They will endeavour to conclude as soon as possible conventions with each other in the sphere of social security.

ARTICLE 3

The High Contracting Parties will make every effort in common to lead their peoples towards a better understanding of the principles which form the basis of their common civilisation and to promote cultural exchanges by conventions between themselves or by other means.

ARTICLE 4

If any of the High Contracting Parties should be the object of an armed attack in Europe, the other High Contracting Parties will, in accordance with the provisions of Article 51 of the Charter of the United Nations, afford the Party so attacked all the military and other aid and assistance in their power.

ARTICLE 5

All measures taken as a result of the preceding Article shall be immediately reported to the Security Council. They shall be terminated as soon as the Security Council has taken the measures necessary to maintain or restore international peace and security.

The present Treaty does not prejudice in any way the obligations of the High Contracting Parties under the provisions of the Charter of the United Nations. It shall not be interpreted as affecting in any way the authority and responsibility of the Security Council under the Charter to take at any time such action as it deems necessary in order to maintain or restore international peace and security.

ARTICLE 6

The High Contracting Parties declare, each so far as he is concerned, that none of the international engagements now in force between him and any other of the High Contracting Parties or any third State is in conflict with the provisions of the present Treaty.

None of the High Contracting Parties will conclude any alliance or participate in any coalition directed against any other of the High Contracting Parties.

ARTICLE 7

For the purpose of consulting together on all the questions dealt with in the present Treaty, the High Contracting Parties will create a Consultative Council, which shall be so organised as to be able to exercise its functions continuously. The Council shall meet at such times as it shall deem fit.

At the request of any of the High Contracting Parties, the Council shall be immediately convened in order to permit the High Contracting Parties to consult with regard to any situation which may constitute a threat to peace, in whatever area this threat should arise; with regard to the attitude to be adopted and the steps to be taken in case of a renewal by Germany of an aggressive policy; or with regard to any situation constituting a danger to economic stability.

ARTICLE 8

In pursuance of their determination to settle disputes only by peaceful means, the High Contracting Parties will apply to disputes beween themselves the following provisions:

The High Contracting Parties will, while the present Treaty remains in force, settle all disputes falling within the scope of Article 36, paragraph 2, of the Statute of the International Court of Justice by referring them to the Court. . . .

ARTICLE 9

The High Contracting Parties may, by agreement, invite any other State to accede to the present Treaty on conditions to be agreed between them and the State so invited. . . .

ARTICLE 10

The present Treaty . . . shall enter into force on the date of the deposit of the last instrument of ratification and shall thereafter remain in force for fifty years. . . .

Appendix V

ANALYSIS OF THE TERMS OF THE PARIS AGREEMENTS

The Paris Agreements comprise:

1. *Documents signed by two Parties* (France and the Federal Republic of Germany). Subject: Franco-German disputes (the resolution of cultural, economic and other difficulties) and the Saar.

2. *Documents signed by four Parties:* France, the United States, the United Kingdom and the Federal Republic of Germany relating to German sovereignty:

a. Protocol on the termination of the Occupation régime in the Federal Republic;

b. Amendments to the Convention on Relations between the Occupying Powers and the Federal Republic (Revocation of the Occupation Statute, Retention of Rights, stationing of Allied forces, state of emergency, hypothesis of reunification);

c. Amendments to the Convention on the Rights and Obligations of Foreign Forces in Germany;

d. Amendments to the Convention on the Settlement of Matters arising out of the War and the Occupation;

e. Amendments to the Finance Convention;

f. Convention on the Presence of Foreign Forces in the Federal Republic of Germany.

(The Conventions cited at a, b, c, d and e above are those signed in Bonn on 26 May, 1952, and designed to end the Occupation régime.)

3. *Documents signed by five Parties:* Belgium, the Netherlands, Luxembourg, France and the United Kingdom. Subject: Declaration inviting the Federal Republic of Germany and Italy to accede to the Brussels Treaty.

4. *Documents signed by seven Parties:* Belgium, the Netherlands, Luxembourg, France, the United Kingdom, the Federal Republic of Germany and Italy.

Subject:

a. Protocol revising and completing the Brussels Treaty;

b. Protocol on the forces of Western European Union;

c. Protocol on the control of armaments;

d. Protocol on the Agency of Western European Union for the Control of Armaments;

e. Exchange of letters relating to the jurisdiction of the International Court of Justice;

f. Resolution on the Production and Standardization of Armaments.

5. *Documents signed by the 14 North Atlantic Treaty countries:*

a. Protocol to the North Atlantic Treaty on the Accession of the Federal Republic of Germany;

b. Resolution by the North Atlantic Council to implement Section IV of the Final Act of the London Conference (authority of SACEUR);

c. Resolution of Association taking note of the obligations accepted by the Federal Republic on the signature of the London Agreements and of the declaration relating to such obligations.

Appendix VI

Chairmen of the North Atlantic Council

1949–1950	Mr. Dean G. Acheson	(United States)
1950–1951	M. Paul van Zeeland	(Belgium)
1951–1952	Mr. Lester B. Pearson	(Canada)
1952–1953	Mr. Ole Bjørn Kraft	(Denmark)
1953–1954	M. Georges Bidault M. Pierre Mendès-France	} (France)
1954–1955	Mr. Kristinn Gudmunsson Mr. Gudmundur I. Gudmundsson	} (Iceland)
1956	M. Gaetano Martino	(Italy)

Presidents of the North Atlantic Council*

1957	M. Gaetano Martino M. Giuseppe Pella	} (Italy)
1957–1958	M. Joseph Bech	(Luxembourg)
1958–1959	Mr. Joseph M. A. H. Luns	(Netherlands)
1959–1960	Mr. Halvard M. Lange	(Norway)
1960–1961	M. Marcello Mathias M. Franco Nogueira	} (Portugal)
1961–1962	M. Selim Sarper	(Turkey)

* In accordance with the recommendations of the Committee of Three, it was decided that each year a Foreign Minister of one of the member countries would become President of the North Atlantic Council, and that the Secretary General would be Chairman at all working sessions of the Council.

Appendix VII

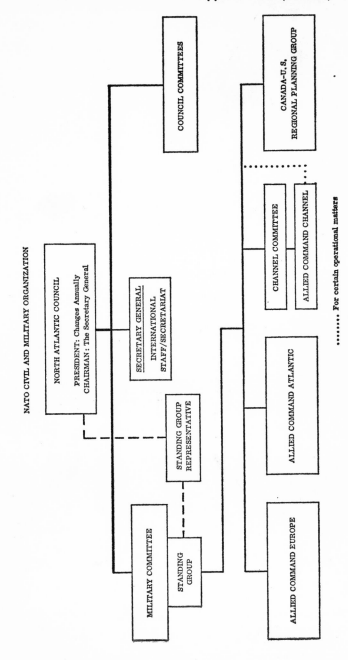

NATO CIVIL AND MILITARY ORGANIZATION

NORTH ATLANTIC COUNCIL

PRESIDENT: Changes Annually
CHAIRMAN : The Secretary General

COUNCIL COMMITTEES

SECRETARY GENERAL
INTERNATIONAL
STAFF/SECRETARIAT

MILITARY COMMITTEE

STANDING
GROUP

STANDING GROUP
REPRESENTATIVE

CANADA–U.S.
REGIONAL PLANNING GROUP

CHANNEL COMMITTEE

ALLIED COMMAND CHANNEL

ALLIED COMMAND ATLANTIC

ALLIED COMMAND EUROPE

········· For certain operational matters

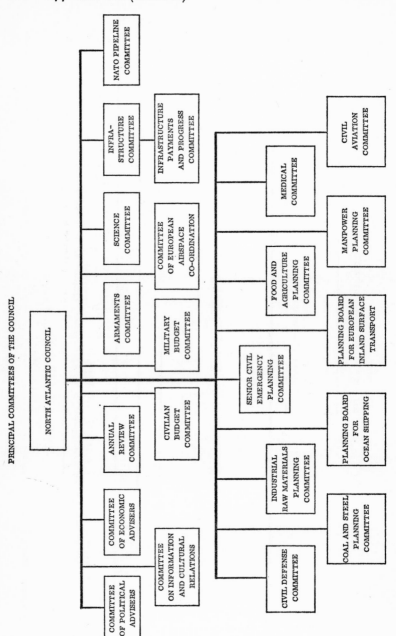

PRINCIPAL COMMITTEES OF THE COUNCIL

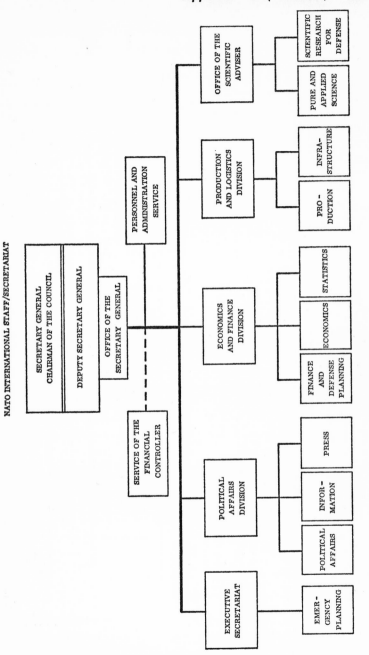

NATO INTERNATIONAL STAFF/SECRETARIAT

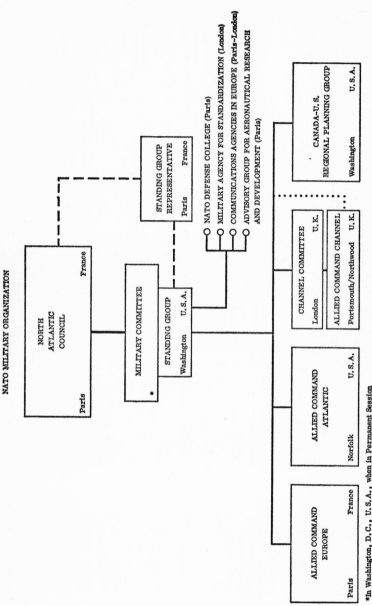

NATO MILITARY ORGANIZATION

NORTH ATLANTIC COUNCIL
Paris   France

STANDING GROUP REPRESENTATIVE
Paris   France

MILITARY COMMITTEE
*

STANDING GROUP
Washington   U.S.A.

○ NATO DEFENSE COLLEGE (Paris)
○ MILITARY AGENCY FOR STANDARDIZATION (London)
○ COMMUNICATIONS AGENCIES IN EUROPE (Paris–London)
○ ADVISORY GROUP FOR AERONAUTICAL RESEARCH AND DEVELOPMENT (Paris)

ALLIED COMMAND EUROPE
Paris   France

ALLIED COMMAND ATLANTIC
Norfolk   U.S.A.

CHANNEL COMMITTEE
London   U.K.

ALLIED COMMAND CHANNEL
Portsmouth/Northwood   U.K.

CANADA–U.S. REGIONAL PLANNING GROUP
Washington   U.S.A.

*In Washington, D.C., U.S.A., when in Permanent Session

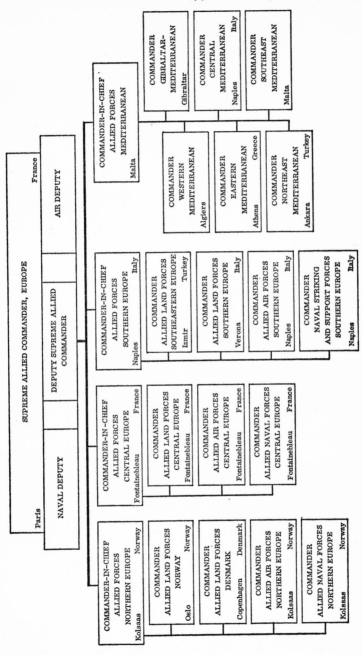

ALLIED COMMAND EUROPE

SUPREME ALLIED COMMANDER, EUROPE
Paris

DEPUTY SUPREME ALLIED COMMANDER

NAVAL DEPUTY

AIR DEPUTY
France

COMMANDER-IN-CHIEF ALLIED FORCES NORTHERN EUROPE
Kolsaas   Norway

- COMMANDER ALLIED LAND FORCES NORWAY
  Oslo   Norway
- COMMANDER ALLIED LAND FORCES DENMARK
  Copenhagen   Denmark
- COMMANDER ALLIED AIR FORCES NORTHERN EUROPE
  Kolsaas   Norway
- COMMANDER ALLIED NAVAL FORCES NORTHERN EUROPE
  Kolsaas   Norway

COMMANDER-IN-CHIEF ALLIED FORCES CENTRAL EUROPE
Fontainebleau   France

- COMMANDER ALLIED LAND FORCES CENTRAL EUROPE
  Fontainebleau   France
- COMMANDER ALLIED AIR FORCES CENTRAL EUROPE
  Fontainebleau   France
- COMMANDER ALLIED NAVAL FORCES CENTRAL EUROPE
  Fontainebleau   France

COMMANDER-IN-CHIEF ALLIED FORCES SOUTHERN EUROPE
Naples   Italy

- COMMANDER ALLIED LAND FORCES SOUTHEASTERN EUROPE
  Izmir   Turkey
- COMMANDER ALLIED LAND FORCES SOUTHERN EUROPE
  Verona   Italy
- COMMANDER ALLIED AIR FORCES SOUTHERN EUROPE
  Naples   Italy
- COMMANDER NAVAL STRIKING AND SUPPORT FORCES SOUTHERN EUROPE
  Naples   Italy

COMMANDER-IN-CHIEF ALLIED FORCES MEDITERRANEAN
Malta

- COMMANDER GIBRALTAR-MEDITERRANEAN
  Gibraltar
- COMMANDER CENTRAL MEDITERRANEAN
  Naples   Italy
- COMMANDER SOUTHEAST MEDITERRANEAN
  Malta
- COMMANDER WESTERN MEDITERRANEAN
  Algiers
- COMMANDER EASTERN MEDITERRANEAN
  Athens   Greece
- COMMANDER NORTHEAST MEDITERRANEAN
  Ankara   Turkey

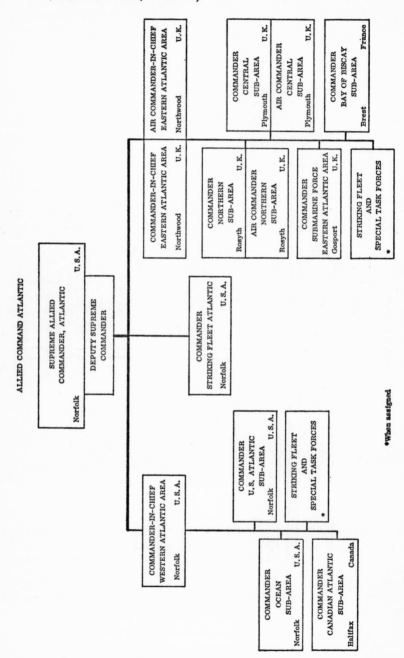

ALLIED COMMAND ATLANTIC

SUPREME ALLIED COMMANDER, ATLANTIC — Norfolk — U.S.A.

DEPUTY SUPREME COMMANDER

COMMANDER-IN-CHIEF WESTERN ATLANTIC AREA — Norfolk — U.S.A.

COMMANDER STRIKING FLEET ATLANTIC — Norfolk — U.S.A.

COMMANDER-IN-CHIEF EASTERN ATLANTIC AREA — Northwood — U.K.

AIR COMMANDER-IN-CHIEF EASTERN ATLANTIC AREA — Northwood — U.K.

COMMANDER U.S. ATLANTIC SUB-AREA — Norfolk — U.S.A.

STRIKING FLEET AND SPECIAL TASK FORCES *

COMMANDER OCEAN SUB-AREA — Norfolk — U.S.A.

COMMANDER CANADIAN ATLANTIC SUB-AREA — Halifax — Canada

COMMANDER NORTHERN SUB-AREA — Rosyth — U.K.

AIR COMMANDER NORTHERN SUB-AREA — Rosyth — U.K.

COMMANDER SUBMARINE FORCE EASTERN ATLANTIC AREA — Gosport — U.K.

STRIKING FLEET AND SPECIAL TASK FORCES *

COMMANDER CENTRAL SUB-AREA — Plymouth — U.K.

AIR COMMANDER CENTRAL SUB-AREA — Plymouth — U.K.

COMMANDER BAY OF BISCAY SUB-AREA — Brest — France

*When assigned

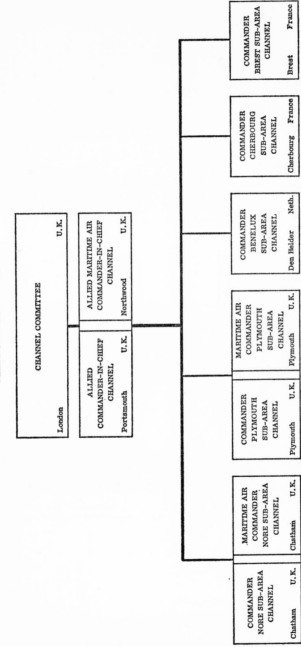

ALLIED COMMAND CHANNEL

Appendix VIII

ABBREVIATIONS

ACCHAN	Allied Command Channel
ACE	Allied Command Europe
ACLANT	Allied Command Atlantic
AFCENT	Allied Forces Central Europe
AFMED	Allied Forces Mediterranean
AFNORTH	Allied Forces Northern Europe
AFSOUTH	Allied Forces Southern Europe
AGARD	Advisory Group for Aeronautical Research and Development
BALTAP	Allied Command Baltic Approaches
CHANCOMTEE	Channel Committee
CINCAFMED	Commander-in-Chief Allied Forces Mediterranean
CINCAIREASTLANT	Air Commander-in-Chief Eastern Atlantic Area
CINCEASTLANT	Commander-in-Chief Eastern Atlantic Area
CINCENT	Commander-in-Chief Allied Forces Central Europe
CINCHAN	Commander-in-Chief Channel and Southern North Sea
CINCNORTH	Commander-in-Chief Allied Forces Northern Europe
CINCSOUTH	Commander-in-Chief Allied Forces Southern Europe
CINCWESTLANT	Commander-in-Chief Western Atlantic Area
COMAIRCENTLANT	Air Commander Central Atlantic Sub-Area
COMAIRNORLANT	Air Commander Northern Atlantic Sub-Area
COMBISCLANT	Commander Bay of Biscay Atlantic Sub-Area
COMCANLANT	Commander Canadian Atlantic Sub-Area

COMCENTLANT	Commander Central Atlantic Sub-Area
COMNORLANT	Commander Northern Atlantic Sub-Area
COMOCEANLANT	Commander Ocean Atlantic Sub-Area
COMSTRIKEFLTLANT	Commander Striking Fleet Atlantic
COMSUBBEASTLANT	Commander Submarine Force Eastern Atlantic
COMUSLANT	Commander US Atlantic Sub-Area
CUSRPG	Canada-United States Regional Planning Group
ELLA	Europe Long Lines Agency
EMCCC	European Military Communications Coordinating Committee
ENCA	European Naval Communications Agency
ERFA	European Radio Frequency Agency
MAS	Military Agency for Standardization
MC	Military Committee
NATO	North Atlantic Treaty Organization
NMR	National Military Representatives with SHAPE
SACEUR	Supreme Allied Commander Europe
SACLANT	Supreme Allied Commander Atlantic
SGN	Standing Group NATO
SGREP	Standing Group Representative
SHAPE	Supreme Headquarters Allied Powers Europe
TCC	Temporary Council Committee

Index